Orlando Williams Wight, Blaise Pascal, Orlando Williams Wight

The Provincial Letters of Blaise Pascal

Orlando Williams Wight, Blaise Pascal, Orlando Williams Wight

The Provincial Letters of Blaise Pascal

ISBN/EAN: 9783337145958

Printed in Europe, USA, Canada, Australia, Japan

Cover: Foto ©Thomas Meinert / pixelio.de

More available books at **www.hansebooks.com**

THE

PROVINCIAL LETTERS

OF

BLAISE PASCAL.

A NEW TRANSLATION;

WITH

HISTORICAL INTRODUCTION AND NOTES,

BY REV. THOMAS M'CRIE.

PRECEDED BY

A LIFE OF PASCAL, A CRITICAL ESSAY, AND A
BIBLIOGRAPHICAL NOTICE.

"Ad tuum, Domine Jesu, tribunal appello."—PASCAL.
"That miracle of universal genius."—SIR WILLIAM HAMILTON.

EDITED BY

O. W. WIGHT, A. M.

NEW YORK:
DERBY & JACKSON, 498 BROADWAY.
1860.

EDITOR'S PREFACE.

THIS volume—the first of Pascal's works—is composed of five parts : 1st, " Life, Genius, and Discoveries of Pascal," from the North British Review ; 2d, " Pascal considered as a Writer and a Moralist," by M. Villemain ; 3d, " Historical Introduction to the Provincial Letters," by the translator ; 4th, Bibliographical Notice ; and, 5th, " The Provincial Letters," translated by the Rev. Thomas M'Crie.

The leading article in the second number of the North British Review, there entitled " Pascal's Life, Writings, and Discoveries," which we entitle Life, Genius, and Discoveries of Pascal, in order to designate its contents with more precision, contains the best general summary of Pascal's career that we have been able to find. It gives especially a full and reliable account of Pascal's labors in the field of scientific discovery. Information upon this point we have regarded as the more necessary, inasmuch as the purely scientific writings of Pascal, having become obsolete after the lapse of two centuries, are not deemed worthy of translation and reproduction in our series of French Classics.

The Essay of M. Villemain on " Pascal considered as a Writer and a Moralist," written as an introduction to his edition of the Provincial Letters, and subsequently published among his *Mélanges*, is one of the finest pieces of literary criticism in the French language. In translating it for present use, we have aimed to be faithful to the original; but that delicate eloquence, which no foreign words can adequately reproduce, which is a characteristic of M. Villemain's style, we have felt and admired; but when we have thought to compass it with some form of expression, we have always found it eluding our grasp, as the sunlight escapes when an attempt is made to shut it into a room.

The "Historical Introduction," by the translator, Rev. Mr. M'Crie, is an able review of the times in which Pascal wrote his celebrated Provincial Letters. It contains an honest, judicious statement of the questions that arose during the controversy in which Pascal and the Port-Royalists were engaged. It exhibits adequate theological scholarship, becoming moderation, and an integrity that is proof against the zeal of party and sect.

The Bibliographical Notice indicates the various sources of information in regard to Pascal and his works.

We have adopted, without alteration, except in the correction of typographical errors, M'Crie's translation of the Provincial Letters. He has fully comprehended Pascal's meaning, has thoroughly understood the points discussed, and has rendered his author with remarkable fidelity into English. His notes are sufficiently copious, and give just the kind of information needed by any reader who has not made an especial study of Port-Royal and its famous controversy with the Jesuits. Mr. M'Crie's translation is not faultless, however; it does not adequately represent the inimitable style of Pascal. Inimitable! We use the word advisedly, and it conveys an ample apology for our translator. That style so vivacious, so piquant, so graceful, so delicate, so easy, so natural, is at once the admiration and despair of

great French writers. Who can translate it, if great artists
in language cannot successfully imitate it in Pascal's own
tongue? Our readers, then, must accept this translation, and
comfort themselves with the very important fact that they
have Pascal's meaning faithfully rendered into English. ·

We add the whole of Mr. M'Crie's modest Preface, not
only in justice to him, but for the information it contains :

" The following translation of the Provincial Letters was
undertaken several years ago, in compliance with the suggestion of a revered parent, chiefly as a literary recreation
in a retired country charge, and, after being finished, was
laid aside. It is now published at the request of friends,
who considered such a work as peculiarly seasonable, and
more likely to be acceptable at the present crisis, when general attention has been again directed to the popish controversy, and when such strenuous exertions are being made by
the Jesuits to regain influence in our country.

" None are strangers to the fame of the Provincials, and
few literary persons would choose to confess themselves altogether ignorant of a work which has acquired a world-wide
reputation. Yet there is reason to suspect that few books
of the same acknowledged merit have had a more limited
circle of *bona fide* English readers. This may be ascribed,
in a great measure, to the want of a good English translation. Two translations of the Provincials have already appeared in our language. The first was contemporary with
the Letters themselves, and was printed at London in 1657,
under the title of ' *Les Provinciales ;* or, The Mysterie of
Jesuitism, discovered in certain Letters, written upon occasion of the present differences at Sorbonne, between the Jan-

suists and the Molinists, from January 1656 to March 1657, S. N. Displaying the corrupt Maximes and Politicks of that Society. Faithfully rendered into English. *Sicut Serpentes.*' Of the translation under this unpromising title, it may only be remarked, that it is probably one of the worst specimens of 'rendering into English' to be met with, even during that age when little attention was paid to the art of translation. Under its uncouth phraseology, not only are the wit and spirit of the original completely shrouded, but the meaning is so disguised that the work is almost as unintelligible as it is uninteresting.

" Another translation of the Letters—of which I was not aware till I had completed mine—was published in London in 1816. On discovering that a new attempt had been made to put the English public in possession of the Provincials, and that it had failed to excite any general interest, I was induced to lay aside all thoughts of publishing my version; but, after examining the modern translation, I became convinced that its failure might be ascribed to other causes than want of taste among us for the beauties and excellences of Pascal. This translation, though written in good English, bears evident marks of haste, and of want of acquaintance with the religious controversies of the time ; in consequence of which, the sense and spirit of the original have been either entirely lost, or so imperfectly developed, as to render its perusal exceedingly tantalizing and unsatisfactory.

" It remains for the public to judge how far the present version may have succeeded in giving a more readable and faithful transcript of the Provincial Letters. No pains, at least, have been spared to enhance its interest and insure its fidelity. Among the numerous French editions of the Letters, the basis of the following translation is that of Amsterdam, published in four volumes, 12mo., 1767; with the notes of Nicole, and his prefatory History of the Provincials, which were translated from the Latin into French by Mademoiselle de Joncourt. With this and other French editions I have compared Nicole's Latin translation, which appeared in 1658, and received the sanction of Pascal.

"The voluminous notes of Nicole, however interesting they may have been at the time, and to the parties involved in the Jansenist controversy, are not, in general, of such a kind as to invite attention now; nor would a full translation even of his historical details, turning as they do chiefly on local and temporary disputes, be likely to reward the patience of the reader. So far as they were fitted to throw light on the original text, I have availed myself of these, along with other sources of information, in the marginal notes. Some of these annotations, as might be expected from a Protestant editor, are intended to correct error, or to guard against misconception.

"To the full understanding of the Provincials, however, some idea of the controversies which occasioned their publication seems almost indispensable. This I have attempted to furnish in the Historical Introduction; which will also be found to contain some interesting facts, hitherto uncollected, and borrowed from a variety of authorities not generally accessible, illustrating the history of the Letters and the parties concerned in them, with a vindication of Pascal from the charges which this work has provoked from so many quarters against him."

Another translation exists, made by George Pearce, Esq

and published by Longmans in 1849. It is in every way inferior to the translation of Mr. M'Crie.

The three different introductions to this volume, which afford a survey of Pascal from a scientific, from a literary, and from a theological point of view, give the amplest means of forming a correct and adequate judgment of that wonderful man, whom the great Sir William Hamilton called "a miracle of universal genius."

We hope soon to add another volume from Pascal, containing the Thoughts; and now send forth the Provincial Letters, devoutly praying Heaven that they may continue to spread the "plague of ridicule" through ranks hostile to spiritual freedom and eternal truth.

O. W. WIGHT.

FEBRUARY, 1859.

CONTENTS.

LETTER I.

LETTER II.

LETTER III.

LETTER IV.

LETTER V.

LIFE, GENIUS, AND SCIENTIFIC DISCOVERIES OF PASCAL.

In looking back on the great events by which civilization and knowledge have been advanced, and in estimating the intellectual and moral energies by which their present position has been attained, we cannot fail to perceive that the master-steps in our social condition have been the achievement of a few gifted spirits, some of whose names neither history nor tradition has preserved. We do not here allude to the progress of individual States, struggling for supremacy in trade or in commerce, in arts or in arms, but to those colossal strides in civilization which command the sympathy and mould the destinies of mankind.

Every nation has its peculiar field of glory—its band of heroes—its intellectual chivalry—its cloud of witnesses; but heroes however brave, and sages however wise, have often no reputation beyond the shore or the mountain range which confines them; and men who rank as demigods in legislation or in war, are often but the oppressors and the corrupters of their more peaceful and pious neighbors. Traced in the blood of their victims, and emblazoned in acts of strangled liberty, their titles of renown have not been registered in the imperishable records of humanity. Without the stamp of that philanthropy and wisdom which the family of mankind can cherish, their patents of nobility are not passports to immortality. The men who bear them have no place in the world's affections, and their name and their honors must perish with the community that gave them.

But while there are deeds of glory which benefit directly only the people among whom they are done, or the nation whom they exalt, they may nevertheless have the higher character of exercising over our species a general and an inestimable influence. When Regulus sacrificed his life by denouncing to the Roman senate the overtures of Carthage, he was as much a martyr for truth as for Rome, and every country and every age will continue to admire the moral grandeur of the sacrifice. When Luther planted the standard of the Reformation in Germany, and confronted the Pope, wielding the sceptre of sovereign power, he became the champion of civil and religious liberty in every land; the assertor of the rights of universal conscience—the apostle of truth, who taught the world to distinguish the religion of priestcraft from the faith once delivered to the saints. Hence may the Roman patriot become the guide and the instructor of civilized as well as of barbarous nations; and the hero of the Reformation, the benefactor of the Catholic as well as of the Protestant Church.

It is not easy to estimate the relative value of those noble bequests which man thus makes to his species. Deeds of Roman virtue and of martyr zeal are frequently achieved in humble life, without exciting sympathy or challenging applause; but when they throw their radiance from high places, and cast their halos round elevated rank or intellectual eminence, they light up the whole moral hemisphere, arresting the affections of living witnesses, and, through the page of history, commanding the homage and drawing forth the aspirations of every future age.

It has not been permitted to individuals to effect with their single arm those great revolutions which urge forward the destinies of the moral, the intellectual, and the political world. The benefactors of mankind labor in groups, and shine in constellations; and though their leading star may often be the chief object of admiration, yet his satellites must move along with him, and share his glory. Surrounded with Kepler, and Galileo, and Hook, and Halley, and Flamsteed, and Laplace, Newton completes the seven pleiads by whom the system of the universe was developed. Luther, and Calvin, and Zwingle, and Knox form the group which rescued Christendom from Papal oppression. Watt, and Arkwright, and Brindley, and Bell have made water and iron the connecting links of nations, and have armed mechanism with superhuman strength, and almost human skill. By the triple power of perseverance, wisdom, and eloquence, Clarkson, and Wilberforce, and Fox have wrenched from the slave his manacles and fetters; and we look forward with earnest anticipation to the advent and array of other sages who shall unshackle conscience and reason—unlock the world's granaries for her starving children—carry the torchlight of education and knowledge into the dens of ignorance and vice—and, with the amulet of civil and religious liberty, emancipate immortal man from the iron-grasp of superstition and misrule.

Although we have glanced at some of the principal groups of public benefactors, yet there are others which, though less prominent in the world's eye, are, nevertheless, interesting objects both for our study and imitation. In one of these stands pre-eminent the name of Pascal, possessing peculiar claims on the love and admiration of his species. As a geometer and natural philosopher, his inventive genius has placed him on the same level with Newton, and Leibnitz, and Huygens, and Descartes. As a metaphysician and divine, he baffled the subtlety and learning of the Sorbonne; as a writer, at once powerful and playful, eloquent and profound, he shattered the strongholds of Jesuitism; and as a private Christian, he adorned the doctrine of his Master with lofty piety, inflexible virtue, and all those divine graces which are indigenous in the heart which suffering and self-denial have abased.

The celebrated Bayle has affirmed that the life of Pascal is worth a hundred sermons, and that his acts of humility and devotion will be more effective against the libertinism of the age than a dozen of missionaries. The observation is as instructive as it is just. During the brief interval which we weekly consecrate to eternity, the impressions of Divine truth scarcely survive the breath which utters them. The preacher's homily, however eloquent, is soon forgotten; and the missionary's expostulation, however earnest, passes away with the heart-throb which it excites; and if a tear falls, or a sigh escapes amid the pathos of severed friendship, or the terrors of coming judgment, the evaporation of the one and the echo of the other are the only results on which the preacher can rely. It is otherwise, however, with the lessons which we ourselves learn from illustrious examples of departed piety and wisdom.

The martyr's enduring faith appeals to the heart with the combined energy of precept and example. The sage's gigantic intellect, purified and chastened with the meek and lowly spirit of the Gospel, becomes a beacon-light to the young and an anchor to the wavering. And when faith is thus ennobled by reason, reason is hallowed in return; and under this union of principles, too often at variance, hope brightens in their commingled radiance, and the unsettled or distracted spirit rests with unflinching confidence on the double basis of secular and celestial truth. Even in a heathen age, the doubts and fears of Diocles were instantly dissipated, when he saw Epicurus on his bended knees doing homage to the Father of gods and men.

There is, perhaps, no period in the history of our faith when the life and labors of Pascal—his premature genius and his brilliant talents—his discoveries and his opinions—his sorrows and his sufferings—his piety and his benevolence—his humility and his meekness—could be appealed to with more effect than that in which our own lot is cast. When a political religion is everywhere shooting up in rank luxuriance, as the basis of political institutions; when the temple of God has become the haunt of the money-changers, and the sacred offices of the ministry are bought and sold like the produce of the earth;[1] when the wealth which God himself conferred, and the intellectual gifts which he gave, are marshalled in fierce hostility against the evangelism of his word;—in such an age, it may be useful to hold up the mirror to a Roman Catholic layman—to the sainted and immortal Pascal—to reflect to all classes, to priest and people, a photogenic picture of a life of bright example, pencilled by celestial light; and, as time obliterates its shaded groundwork, developing new features for our love and admiration.

Blaise Pascal was born at Clermont, on the 19th June, 1623. His family, who had been ennobled by Louis XI. about 1478, held from that time important offices in Auvergne; and his father, Stephen Pascal, was the first President of the Court of Aides at Clermont-Ferrand. His mother, Antoinette Begon, died in 1626, leaving behind her one son, Blaise, and two daughters, Gilberte, born in 1620, and Jacqueline, born in

---

[1] This is more applicable to England than to America.—ED.

1625.   But though thus deprived of those inestimable instructions which maternal fondness can alone supply, the loss was, to a great extent, compensated by the piety and affection of their remaining parent.   Abandoning to his brother his professional duties in Auvergne, that he might devote all his time to the education of his family, Stephen Pascal took up his residence in Paris in 1631.   Here he became the sole instructor of his son in literature and science, and of his two daughters in Latin and in belles-lettres; and with the lessons of secular wisdom he blended that higher learning which formed so conspicuous a feature in the future history of his family.

It was now the spring-tide of science throughout Europe, and Stephen Pascal was one of its most active promoters.   His knowledge of geometry and physics had gained him the friendship of Descartes, Gassendi, Roberval, Mersenne, Carcavi, Pailleur, and other philosophers in Paris, who assembled at each other's houses to impart and receive instruction.   This little band of sages maintained an active correspondence with the congenial spirits of other lands, and in this interchange of discovery, the achievements and the domain of science were simultaneously extended.   Men of rank and influence offered their homage to the rising genius of the age; and such was the progress of this infant association, that, under the enlightened administration of Colbert, it became the nucleus of the celebrated Academy of Sciences, which Louis XIV. established by "royal ordonnance" in 1666.

At the meetings of this society, Blaise Pascal was occasionally present.   Though imperfectly apprehended, the truths of science inflamed his youthful curiosity, and such was his ardor for knowledge, that, at the age of eleven, he was ambitious of teaching as well as of learning; and he composed a little treatise on the cessation of the sounds of vibrating bodies when touched by the finger.   Perceiving his passion for mathematical studies, and dreading their interference with the more appropriate pursuits in which he was engaged, his father prohibited the study of geometry, but, at the same time, gave him a general idea of its nature and objects, and promised him the full gratification of his wishes when the proper time should arrive. The aspirations, however, of heaven-born genius were not thus to be repressed.   The very prohibition to study geometry served but to enhance the love of it. In his leisure hours he was found alone in his chamber, tracing, in lines of coal, geometrical figures on the wall; and on one occasion he was surprised by his father, just when he had succeeded in obtaining a demonstration of the thirty-second proposition of the First Book of Euclid, that the three angles of a triangle are equal to two right angles. Astonished and overjoyed, his father rushed to his friend M. Pailleur to announce the extraordinary fact; and the young geometer was instantly permitted to study, unrestrained, the Elements of Euclid, of which he soon made himself master, without any extrinsic aid. From the geometry of planes and solids, he passed to the higher branches of the science; and before he was sixteen years of age, he composed a treatise on the Conic Sections, which evinced the most extraordinary sagacity.

Stephen Pascal was now in the zenith of his happiness, that fatal point in the horoscope of man which the world covets and the Christian dreads. In the city of the sciences, which Paris was and still is, his son was deemed a prodigy of genius, and his daughters, with the exterior graces of their sex and the highest mental endowments, had attracted the admiration of the distinguished circles which they had just begun to adorn. An event, however, occurred, which threw this joyous family into despair. Impoverished by wars and financial embezzlements, the government found it necessary to reduce the dividends on the Hotel de Ville in Paris. The annuitants grumbled at their loss, and meetings for discussion and expostulation were treated by the State as seditions. Stephen Pascal, who had invested much of his property in the Hotel de Ville, was accused of being one of the ringleaders in the movement; and the tyrant minister, Cardinal Richelieu, who could not brook even the constitutional expression of dissent, ordered him to be arrested and thrown into the Bastile. Aware, however, of the designs of the Government through the kindness of a friend, he at first concealed himself in Paris, and subsequently took refuge in the solitudes of Auvergne. Thus driven from his home at a time when his youthful family required his most anxious and watchful care, we may conceive the indignation of the citizen when made the victim of calumny and oppression; but who can estimate the agonies of a parent thus severed from his children? The thunder-cloud, however, which so blackly and suddenly lowered upon him, as suddenly cleared away. The God of the storm so directed it; and marvellous was the play of the elements by which its lightnings were chained and its growling hushed. Tyrants are sometimes gay, and in their gayety accessible. When their consciences cannot be reached by the appeals of justice and truth, nor their hearts softened by tears and cries, they may be soothed by a timely jest, or an insinuating smile, or even turned from their firmest purpose by a bold and unexpected solicitation. If, by her graceful movements, Herodias's daughter could command from a heathen tyrant a deed of cruelty which he himself abhorred, another damsel might in like circumstances count upon an act of mercy from a Christian cardinal. Though it is doubtful to whom we owe it, the experiment was tried, and succeeded.

The Abbé Bossut informs us that Cardinal Richelieu had taken a fancy to have Scudery's tragi-comedy of *L'Amour Tyrannique* performed in his presence by young girls. The Duchess d'Aiguillon, who was charged with the management of the piece, was anxious that little Jacqueline Pascal, then about thirteen years of age, should be one of the actresses. Gilberte, her eldest sister, and in her father's absence the head of the family, replied with indignation, that "the cardinal had not been sufficiently kind to them to induce them to do him this favor." The duchess persisted in her request, and made it understood that the recall of Stephen Pascal might be the reward of the favor which she solicited. The friends of the family were consulted, and it was determined that Jacqueline should play the part which was assigned her. The tragi-comedy was performed on the 3d April, 1639. The part by Jacqueline was played with a grace and spirit which enchanted the spectators, and particularly the cardinal. The enthusiasm of Richelieu must have been anticipated, for Jacqueline was prepared to take advantage of it. When the play was finished, she approached the cardinal, and recited the following verses, with the design of obtaining the recall of her father:

> " Ne vous étonnez pas, incomparable Armand,
> Si j'ai mal contenté vos yeux et vos oreilles :
> Mon esprit agité de frayeurs sans pareilles,
> Interdit à mon corps et voix et mouvement :

Mais pour me rendre ici capable de vous plaire,
Rappelez de l'exil mon misérable Père."

Which may be thus rendered:

" O marvel not, Armand, the great, the wise,
If I have slightly pleased thine ear—thine eyes;
My sorrowing spirit, torn by countless fears,
Each sound forbiddeth save the voice of tears:
With power to please thee, wouldst thou me inspire—
Recall from exile now my hapless sire."

The cardinal, taking her in his arms and kissing her while
she was repeating the verses, replied, "Yes, my dear child, I
grant you what you ask; write to your father that he may return with safety." The Duchess d'Aiguillon took advantage
of the incident, and thus spoke in praise of Stephen Pascal:
"He is a thoroughly honest man; he is very learned, and it is
a great pity that he should remain unemployed. There is his
son," added she, pointing to Blaise Pascal, "who, though he is
scarcely fifteen years of age, is already a great mathematician."
Encouraged by her success, Jacqueline again addressed the cardinal: "I have still, my lord, another favor to ask." "What
is it, my child? Ask whatever you please; you are too charming to be refused any thing." "Allow my father to come himself to thank your eminence for your kindness." "Certainly,"
said the cardinal; "I wish to see him, and let him bring his
family along with him." On the following day Jacqueline sent
an account of this interesting episode to her father, and the
moment he received the grateful intelligence he set off for Paris.
Immediately on his arrival he hastened with his three children
to Ruel, the residence of the cardinal, who gave him the most
flattering reception. "I know all your merit," says Richelieu.
"I restore you to your children; and I recommend them to
your care. I am anxious to do something considerable for you."
In fulfilment of this promise, Stephen Pascal was appointed
Intendant of Rouen, in Normandy, in 1641. His family accompanied him to that city, and in the same year his eldest
daughter Gilberte, then twenty-one, was married to M. Perier,
who had distinguished himself in the service of the Government, and who was afterwards counsellor to the Court of Aides
in Clermont.

Released by the return of his father from the only affliction which had hitherto tried him, and free to pursue the sciences without the interruption of professional cares, Blaise Pascal conceived the idea of constructing a machine for performing arithmetical operations. He was now scarcely nineteen years of age, and he himself informs us that he contrived this machine in order to assist his father in making the numerical calculations which his official duties in Upper Normandy required. The construction of such a machine, however, was a much more troublesome task than its contrivance, and Pascal not only injured his constitution, but wasted the most valuable portion of his life in his attempts to bring it to perfection.

A clockmaker in Rouen, to whom he had described his earliest model, made one of his own accord, which, though beautiful in its external aspect, was utterly unfit for its purpose. This "little abortion," as Pascal calls it, was placed in the cabinet of curiosities at Rouen, and annoyed him so much that he dismissed all the workmen in his service, under the apprehension that other imperfect models might be made of the new machine which they were employed to construct. Some time afterwards the Chancellor Seguier, having seen the first model, encouraged him to proceed, and obtained for him in May, 1649, the exclusive privilege of constructing it. Thus freed from the risk of piracy, he made more vigorous efforts to improve it. He abandoned, as he assures us, all other duties, and thought of nothing but the construction of his machine.

The first model which he executed proved unsatisfactory, both in its form and its materials. After successive improvements he made a second; and this again was succeeded by a third, which went by springs, and was very simple in its construction. This machine he actually used several times in the presence of many of his friends; but defects gradually presented themselves, and he executed more than fifty models, all of them different—some of wood, others of ivory and ebony, and others of copper—before he completed the machine, to which he invited the attention of the public.

From the general description which Pascal has published of this remarkable invention, and particularly from the dedication of it to Chancellor Seguier, it is evident that he expected much more reputation from it than posterity has awarded. This over-

estimate of its merits, founded, no doubt, on the length of time
and the mental energy which it had exhausted, is still more
strongly exhibited in a letter which he wrote to Christina,
Queen of Sweden, in 1650, accompanying one of the machines.[1]
It was in this year that Christina was crowned, with unusual
pomp and splendor. She had announced herself as the patron
of letters and the arts throughout Europe, and had invited Pascal, along with Descartes, Grotius, Gassendi, Saumaise, and
others, to invest her throne with the lustre of their genius and
learning. The state of his health prevented Pascal from thus
paying homage to the young and admired queen; but, in the
letter to which we have referred, he has made ample compen-
sation for his absence. He addresses her Majesty in a tone
frank and manly—in a strain of compliment chaste and elegant
—in language rich and beautiful—ennobling, by the happiest
antithesis, bold and touching sentiments worthy of a sage to
utter and of a queen to receive. Though only in his twenty-
seventh year, Pascal had witnessed, and even experienced, the
truth, that nations who vaunt most loudly their superiority in
science and learning have been the most guilty in neglecting
and even starving their cultivators. The French monarch had
indeed given him the exclusive privilege of his invention—the
right of expending his time, his money, and his health, in per-
fecting a machine for the benefit of France and the world; but
like a British patent, bearing the great seal of England, it was
not worth the wax which the royal insignia so needlessly
adorned. The minister, it must be owned, had recalled his
father from an unjust exile, and balanced the injustice by a
laborious office in the provinces; but no honor—no official station—no acknowledgment of services was ever given to his
illustrious son, the pride of his country and the glory of his

---

[1] Pascal appears, from a passage in this letter, to have sent to Christina, through
M. de Bourdelot, a fuller history and description of the machine than the one
which he published. This singular character, who is described as a sprightly buffoon, and who engrossed more of the queen's notice than the most eminent of her
savans, was an Abbé, whose real name was Pierre Michon, whom, though a priest,
the Pope permitted to practice medicine. Saumaise took him to Stockholm, where
he seems to have been the Beau Brummel, the wit and the butt of the royal table,
and necessarily a more important personage there than the gravest philosopher
Christina, however, was obliged, by popular clamor, to dismiss him, and he after
wards became physician to the great Condé.

age. At the very moment, too, when Pascal was composing his letter to Christina, Descartes, one of the most immortal names in the scientific annals of France, and several of his distinguished countrymen, were adorning the court of the Scandinavian queen; and it was, doubtless, under the pressure of feelings which these facts inspired that he penned the following beautiful passage, which we have extracted from a letter which has not even been noticed by his most eminent biographers.

After mentioning the various motives which had influenced him in submitting his invention to her Majesty, he thus proceeds:

"What has really determined me to this is the union that I find in your sacred person of two things that equally inspire me with admiration and respect—which are, sovereign authority and solid science; for I have an especial veneration for those who are elevated to the supreme degree either of power or of knowledge. The latter may, if I am not mistaken, as well as the former, pass for sovereigns. The same degrees are met in genius as in condition; and the power of kings over their subjects is, it seems to me, but an image of the power of minds over inferior minds, on whom they exercise the right of persuasion, which is among them what the right of command is in political government. This second empire appears to me even of an order so much the more elevated, as minds are of an order more elevated than bodies; and so much the more just, as it can be shared and preserved only by merit, while the other can be shared and preserved by birth or fortune. It must be acknowledged, then, that each of these empires is great in itself; but, madame, your Majesty, without being offended, will allow me to say, one without the other appears to me defective. However powerful a monarch may be, something is wanting to his glory, if he has not mental pre-eminence; and however enlightened a subject may be, his condition is always lowered by dependence. Men who naturally desire what is most perfect, have hitherto sought in vain this sovereign *par excellence*. All kings and learned men have fallen so far short of this excellence, that they have only half fulfilled their aim; and scarcely have our predecessors, since the beginning of the world, seen a king even moderately learned: this master-piece has been reserved for the age of your Majesty. And that this

great marvel might appear accompanied with all possible subjects of wonder, the degree that men could not attain has been
reached by a young queen, in whom are met the advantage of
experience with the tenderness of youth, the leisure of study
with the occupation of royal birth, and the eminence of science
with the feebleness of sex. It is your Majesty, madame, that
furnishes to the world this unique example that was wanting to
it. In you it is that power is dispensed by the light of science,
and science distinguished with the splendor of authority. On
account of this marvellous union, your Majesty sees nothing
beneath your power, as you see nothing above your mind; and
therefore you will be the admiration of all ages that are to
come, as you are the work of all the ages that are passed.
Reign, then, incomparable princess, in a manner wholly new;
let your genius conquer every thing that is not subjected to
your arms: reign by right of birth, during a long course of
years, over so many triumphant provinces; but reign continually by the force of your merit over the whole extent of the
earth. As for me, having been born under the former of your
empires, I wish all the world to know that I glory in living
under the latter; and it is to bear witness to this that I dare to
lift my eyes even to my queen, in giving her this first proof of
my dependence. This, madame, is what determines me to make
to your Majesty this present, although unworthy of you."[1]

Such are the noble yet loyal sentiments which men of the
highest genius have ever cherished, though they may not have
had the courage, even when they had the opportunity, to avow
them. Those who have been the most forward to counsel submission to the "empire of power," have been the first to forget what is due to the "empire of knowledge." Though the
friend of social order, and almost of passive obedience, Pascal,
even before a queen, has placed the dignity of Science on the
same level with the dignity of Power; and it would have been
well for our social interests had the friends and advisers of
other sovereigns been equally true to their convictions. When
the great rights of intelligence are trampled under foot, they
will rise again, like the mangled polypus, from new centres of

---

[1] We have translated this letter from the amended text of M. Cousin. See his
Jacqueline Pascal, p. 401.—ED.

---

life and motion. New rights will again spring up from the trodden germ, and discontents, which have their hot-bed in the feelings more than in the wants of the people, will propagate themselves with a vital energy, to which resistance will be vain. In the history of modern revolutions, let European nations read, "if they can read," the lessons which they teach. Let them be pondered by the unstable governments of France and England, where the vessel of the State is ever on a tempestuous ocean—now braving the storm, now yielding to it—now among bristling rocks, now in the open sea; but whether she rides in distress or in triumph, Faction is ever at the helm, and personal and family ambition in the hold. Poetry, with her lyrics, may charm the adventurers on their cruise—Science may guide them through quicksands, and storms, and darkness—and Mechanism, with her brawny arm, may push them across every obstacle of wind and wave; but when genius, and skill, and enterprise have filled the treasury and exalted the nation, the Poet, the Philosopher, and the Inventor are neither permitted to labor in its service nor share in its bounty. Her offices and her honors have been already pledged to the minions of corruption; and whether genius appears in the meek posture of a suppliant, or in the proud attitude of a benefactor, her cries are stifled and her claims overborne. It is pre-eminently in France and in England where the accidents of birth and fortune repress the heaven-born rights of moral and intellectual worth. It is pre-eminently in the Russian empire where a paternal, though an absolute monarch, dispenses to every servant of the State a just share of its wealth and its honors.[1]

[1] By an imperial ukase, issued in 1835, the science and literature of Russia, as embodied in her Imperial Academy of Sciences, was endowed upon a most liberal scale—involving an expenditure more than ten times larger than that which Peter the Great had devoted to it. By this ukase, each of the ordinary members of the Academy was provided with a salary of 5000 roubles, with an addition of 1000 roubles after twenty years' service. A provision was also made for their widows and children under twenty-one. After twenty-five years' service, the widow and children are entitled, on the death of the Academician, to a full year's salary, and to one-half of that salary as a pension for life. For shorter terms of service, the pension is reduced to one-third or one-fourth of the annual allowance.

As an honorary member of an institution so wisely and generously endowed, the writer of this article has felt it his duty to make his countrymen acquainted with the great liberality of the Emperor Nicholas, the only sovereign in the world who has made a permanent and suitable provision for the cultivators of science and literature, and their families

The arithmetical machine of Pascal, which has led us into this digression, excited a considerable sensation throughout Europe, and many attempts were made to improve its construction and extend its power. De L'Epine, Boitissendeau, and Grillet, in France, P. Morland and Gersten, in England, and Poleni in Italy, applied to this task all their mathematical and mechanical skill; but none of them seems to have devised or constructed a machine superior to that of Pascal. The celebrated Leibnitz, however, directed his capacious mind to this difficult problem, and there is reason to believe that the two models of a calculating machine, which he actually made, surpassed Pascal's both in ingenuity and power; but its complicated structure, and the great expense and labor which the actual execution of it required, discouraged its inventor, and his friends could not prevail upon him to publish any detailed account of its mechanism.

The construction of a calculating machine, which truly deserves the name, was reserved for our distinguished countryman, Mr. Babbage. While all previous contrivances performed only particular arithmetical operations under a sort of copartnery between the man and the machine, in which the latter played a very humble part, the extraordinary invention of Mr. Babbage actually substitutes mechanism in the place of man. A problem is given to the machine, and it solves it by computing a long series of numbers following some given law. In this manner, it calculates astronomical, logarithmic, and navigation tables, as well as tables of the powers and the products of numbers. It can integrate, too, innumerable equations of finite differences, and, in addition to these functions, it does its work cheaply and quickly, it *corrects whatever errors are accidentally committed, and it prints all its calculations.*

This grand invention of the age was, after much negotiation, patronized by the British government, and Mr. Babbage gratuitously devoted all the energies of his mind to its completion; but the liberality of the State was not commensurate with the genius of the inventor. The government had contracted for the machine originally submitted to its notice. During its progress, Mr. Babbage invented one more perfect and useful, the construction of which required a fresh appeal to the treasury. The purse-bearer of the State was perplexed with a question of differences, which the machine could not, and which the House of Commons would not solve. The Shylock of the Exchequer was inexorable, and he not only insisted on his pound of flesh, but upon the very nerves, arteries, and veins with which it was penetrated! It would puzzle the engine, as it does us, to estimate the loss of national honor which this transaction may involve. Some Eastern monarch, intent upon glory, or perhaps some democratic community in the Far West, intent upon gain, may welcome and naturalize this exile of mechanism, and cheaply supply the navies of England with astronomical and nautical tables to guide them through the ocean.

Although Descartes could not be brought to believe that Pascal, at the age of twelve, wrote the treatise on Conics which went by his name, he was, nevertheless, universally esteemed as a geometer of the highest order; and we have now to view him as an original discoverer in physics. When the engineers of Cosmo de Medicis wished to raise water higher than thirty-two feet by means of a sucking-pump, they found it impossible to take it higher than thirty-one feet. Galileo, the Italian sage, was applied to in vain for a solution of the difficulty. It had been the belief of all ages that the water followed the piston, from the horror which nature had of a vacuum, and Galileo improved the dogma by telling the engineers that this horror was not felt, or at least not shown, beyond heights of thirty-one feet! At his desire, however, his disciple Torricelli investigated the subject. He found that when the fluid raised was mercury, the horror of a vacuum did not extend beyond thirty inches, because the mercury would not rise to a greater height; and hence he concluded that a column of water thirty-one feet high, and one of mercury thirty inches, exerted the same pressure upon the same base, and that the antagonist force which counterbalanced them must in both cases be the same; and having learned from Galileo that the air was a heavy fluid, he concluded, and he published the conclusion in 1645, that the weight of the air was the cause of the rise of water to thirty-one feet and of mercury to thirty inches. Pascal repeated these experiments in 1646, at Rouen, before more than five hundred persons, among whom were five or six Jesuits of the college, and he obtained precisely the same results as Torricelli. The explanation of them, however, given by the Italian philosopher, and with which he was unacquainted, did not occur to him; and though he made many new experiments on a large scale with tubes of glass fifty feet long, they did not conduct him to any very satisfactory results. He concluded that the vacuum above the water and the mercury contained no portion of either of these fluids, or any other matter appreciable by the senses; that all bodies have a repugnance to separate from a state of continuity, and admit a vacuum between them; that this repugnance is not greater for a large vacuum than a small one; that its measure is a column of water thirty-one feet high; and that beyond this limit a great or a small vacuum is formed above the water with the same facility, provided no foreign obstacle prevents it. These experiments and results were published by our author in 1647, under the title of *Nouvelles Expériences touchant le Vuide;* but no sooner had they appeared than they experienced from the Jesuits and the followers of Aristotle the most violent opposition. Stephen Noel, a Jesuit, and rector of the College de Paris, assailed the new doctrines in a letter addressed to Pascal himself, and afterwards in a work, entitled *Le Plein du Vuide,* which was printed in 1648. To these objections Pascal replied in two letters, addressed to Noel; but though he had no difficulty in overturning the contemptible reasoning of his antagonist, he found it necessary to appeal to new and more direct experiments.

The explanation of Torricelli had been communicated to him a short time after the publication of his work; and assuming that the mercury in the Torricellian tube was suspended by the weight or pressure of the air, he drew the conclusion that the mercury would stand at different heights in the tube if the column of air was more or less high. These differences, however, were too small to be observed under ordinary circumstances; and he therefore conceived the idea of observing the mercury at Clermont, a town in Auvergne, situated about 400 toises above Paris, and on the top of the Puy de Dôme, a mountain 500 toises above Clermont. The state of his own health did not permit him to undertake a journey to Auvergne; but in a letter, dated the 15th November, 1647, he requested his brother-in-law, M. Perier, to go immediately to Clermont to make the observations which he required. M. Perier was then at Monlins, but was prevented by his professional occupations, as well as by the state of the weather, from fulfilling the anxious desire of Pascal till the 19th September, 1648; and on the 22d September he sent to his friend a full account of the experiment, with an explanation of the delay which had taken place.

On the morning of Saturday, the 19th September, the day fixed for the interesting observation, the weather was unsettled; but about five o'clock the summit of the Puy de Dôme began to appear through the clouds, and Perier resolved to proceed with the experiment. The leading characters in Clermont, whether ecclesiastics or laymen, had taken a deep interest in the subject, and had requested Perier to give them notice of his plans. He accordingly summoned his friends, and at eight in the morning there assembled in the garden of the Pères Minimes, about a league below the town, M. Bannier, one of the Pères Minimes, M. Mosnier, canon of the cathedral church, along with Messrs. La Ville and Begon, counsellors in the Court of Aides, and M. La Porte, doctor and professor of medicine in Clermont. These five individuals were not only distinguished in their respective professions, but also by their scientific acquirements; and M. Perier expresses his delight at having been on this occasion associated with them.

M. Perier began the experiment by pouring into a vessel sixteen pounds of quicksilver, which he had rectified during the preceding days. He then took two glass tubes, four feet long, of the same bore, and hermetically sealed at one end, and open at the other; and making the ordinary experiment of a vacuum with both, he found that the mercury stood in each of them at the same level, and at the height of twenty-six inches, three lines and a half. This experiment was repeated twice, with the same result. One of these glass tubes, with the mercury standing in it, was left under the care of M. Chastin, one of the religious of the house, who undertook to observe and mark any changes in it that might take place during the day; and the party already named set out, with the other tube, for the summit of the Puy de Dôme, about 500 toises above their first station. Upon arriving there they found that the mercury stood at the height of twenty-three inches and two lines—no less than three inches and one and a half lines lower than it stood at the Minimes. The party was "struck with admira-

tion and astonishment at this result;" and "so great was their
surprise, that they resolved to repeat the experiment under
various forms." The glass tube, or the barometer, as we may
call it, was placed in various positions on the summit of the
mountain;—sometimes in the small chapel which is there;
sometimes in an exposed, and sometimes in a sheltered position;
sometimes when the wind blew, and sometimes when it was
calm; sometimes in rain, and sometimes in a fog; and under
all these various influences, which fortunately took place during
the same day, the quicksilver stood at the same height of
twenty-three inches, two lines. During their descent of the
mountain they repeated the experiment at *Lafond de l'Arbre*, an
intermediate station, nearer the Minimes than the summit of
the Puy, and they found the mercury to stand at the height of
twenty-five inches, a result with which the party was greatly
pleased, as indicating the relation between the height of the
mercury and the height of the station. Upon reaching the
Minimes they found that the mercury had not changed its
height, notwithstanding the inconstancy of the weather, which
had been alternately clear, windy, rainy, and foggy. M. Perrier repeated the experiments with both the glass tubes, and
found the height of the mercury to be still twenty-six inches,
three and a half lines.

On the following morning M. de la Marc, priest of the oratory, to whom M. Perier had mentioned the preceding results,
proposed to have the experiment repeated at the top and bottom
of the towers of Nôtre Dame, in Clermont. He accordingly
yielded to his request, and found the difference to be two lines.
Upon comparing these observations, M. Perier obtained the following results, showing the changes in the altitude of the mercu-
rial column, corresponding to certain differences of altitude:

Difference of Altitude. TOISES.	Changes in the height of the Mercury. LINES.
500	$87\frac{1}{2}$
150	$15\frac{1}{3}$
27	$2\frac{1}{3}$
7	$\frac{1}{2}$

When Pascal received these results all his difficulties were removed; and perceiving, from the two last observations in the

preceding table, that twenty toises, or about 120 feet, produced
a change of two lines, and seven toises, or forty-two feet, a
change of half a line, he made the observation at the top and
bottom of the steeple of St. Jacques de la Boucherie, which was
about twenty-four or twenty-five toises, or about 150 feet high ;
and he found a difference of more than two lines in the mer-
curial column; and in a private house, ninety steps high, he
found a difference of half a line.

After this important experiment was made, Pascal intimated
to M. Perier that different states of the weather would occasion
differences in the barometer, according as it was cold, hot, dry,
or moist; and in order to put this opinion to the test of experiment, M. Perier, who was then living at Clermont, instituted a
series of observations, which he continued from the beginning
of 1649, till March, 1651. Corresponding observations were
made at the same time at Paris, and at Stockholm, by the
French ambassador, M. Chanut, and Descartes ; and from these
it appeared that the mercury rises in weather which is cold,
cloudy, and damp, and falls when the weather is hot and dry,
and during rain and snow ; but still with such irregularities
that no general rule could be established. At Clermont, the
difference between the highest and the lowest state of the mercury was one inch, three and a half lines; at Paris the same;
and at Stockholm two inches, two and a quarter lines.

This grand experiment, and the results which it established,
produced a great sensation throughout the scientific world.
The Jesuits were silenced, but not soothed; and when they
durst not again impugn the great truth which had been so
triumphantly established, they strove to deprive Pascal of the
merit of the discovery. In the Preface to the Theses on Philosophy, which had been supported in the College of Jesuits,
the author charged Pascal with appropriating to himself the
discovery of Torricelli, and maintained that the experiments
which he had made in Normandy had been previously performed in Poland, by a Capuchin of the name of Valerien
Magni. These Theses were dedicated to M. de Ribeyre, a
friend of Pascal's, and first president of the Court of Aides at
Clermont; and in order to remove the unfavorable impression
which the charges might have made, Pascal gave a minute
account of his proceedings in a beautiful letter, adorned with

2*

that gracefulness of style and honesty of sentiment which he
so singularly combined.

To this letter M. Ribeyre replied in a manner every way
satisfactory, and concluding in terms so touching and beautifully expressed, that we cannot withhold the passage from our
readers:

"Sir, if you have believed yourself in need of justification
with respect to me,—I have known your candor and sincerity
too well to suppose that you could ever be convicted of having
done aught against the virtue which you profess, which appears
in all your actions, and in your manners. *I honor and revere
it in you more than your science;* and as you equal the most
famous of the age in both, do not think it strange, if, adding
to the common esteem of other men the obligation of a friendship contracted long years ago with your father, I subscribed
myself more than any other, sir, your, &c.   RIBEYRE."

The serenity of Pascal's mind was again disturbed by another
attempt to deprive him of his discovery. The illustrious Descartes, to whose transcendent genius we have already done
homage, was the individual who preferred this claim. It was
made in June, 1647, in a letter to M. Carcavi, who immediately
communicated it to Pascal; but such were his feelings on the
occasion, that he never condescended to notice the reclama-
tion. Baillet, in his life of the French philosopher, informs us
that in 1647 Descartes met young Pascal in the Place Royale,
in Paris, where they conversed respecting his experiments at
Rouen. Descartes stated that they were conformable to the
principles of his philosophy, and is said to have advised Pascal
to repeat the experiment on a mass of air, and also to have
suggested the great experiment on the Puy de Dôme. On the
authority of this statement, Baillet accuses Pascal of plagiarism:
but Descartes himself has made no such charge; and even if
we admit the correctness of all that he wrote to Carcavi, the
admission will neither add to his own fame nor detract from
that of Pascal.[1]

---

[1] As this portion of scientific history has not been examined, the following
abstract of it may be interesting. On the 11th of June, 1649, Descartes wrote thus
to Carcavi: " Hoc tamen persuasum habeo tibi non displiciturum quod te rogare
audeam ut me doceas successum experimenti cujusdam quod D. Pascal fecisse aut

In pursuing his experiments on the weight of the air, Pascal was led to inquire into the general laws of the equilibrium of fluids, and in the year 1653 he composed two treatises[1] on that subject, which were not published till 1663, the year after his death. In order to determine the general conditions of the equilibrium of fluids, Pascal supposes two unequal apertures to be made in a vessel filled with a fluid and closed on all sides. If two pistons are applied to these apertures, and pressed by forces proportional to the area of the apertures, the fluid will remain *in equilibrio*. Having established this truth by two methods equally ingenious and satisfactory, he deduces from it the different cases of the equilibrium of fluids,—and particularly with solid bodies, compressible and incompressible, when either partly or wholly immersed in them. But the most remarkable part of this treatise, and one which, of itself, would have immortalized him, is his application of the general principle to the construction of what he calls the *Mechanical Machine for multiplying forces*, an effect which, he says, may be produced to any extent we choose, as one man may, by means of this machine, raise a weight of any magnitude. This new machine is the *Hydrostatic Press*, first introduced by our celebrated countryman, M. Bramah; and to whatever extent it has been used, we have no hesitation in saying that it will yet perform more important functions than have hitherto been assigned to it.

Pascal's treatise on the weight of the whole mass of air forms the basis of the modern science of Pneumatics. In order to prove that the mass of air presses by its weight on all the

facere dicitur in montibus Arverniæ, ad sciendum utrum argentum vivum adscendat ulterius in tubulo ad radices montis, et quantum altius ascendat, quam in ejus cacumine. *Jus mihi esset hoc ipsum ab ipso potius quam a te expectare, ideo quod ego ipse jam biennium effluxit, auctor fuit ejus experimenti faciendi, cumque certum reddiderim, me de successu non dubitare, quanquam id experimentum nunquam fecerim."*—Ren. Descartes Epistolæ, Pars iii., Epis. i., 67, p. 279. Amstael, 1683. Carcavi gave him the desired information on the 9th of July, 1649, but took no notice of the charge against his friend. In his reply of the 7th of August, Descartes thanks him for the account of Pascal's experiment, and adds, "Intererat mea id rescire, ipse enim petii ab illo, jam exacto biennio, *ut id faceret, eumque pulchri successus certum reddidi quod esset omnino conforme meis principiis, utinque quo nunquam de eo cogitasset, eo quod contrariâ tenabatur sententiâ."*—Id. Ib., Epist. 69, p. 283. There is an obvious contradiction in these passages. If Descartes' principles suggested the experiment, his personal suggestion of it must be a mistake.

[1] *De l'Equilibre des Liqueurs* and *De la Pesanteur de la Masse de l'Air.*

bodies which it surrounds, and also that it is elastic and compressible, he carried a balloon half filled with air to the top of the Puy de Dôme. It gradually inflated itself as it ascended, and when it reached the summit it was quite full, and swollen, as if fresh air had been blown into it; or, what is the same thing, it swelled in proportion as the weight of the column of air which pressed upon it was diminished. When again brought down, it became more and more flaccid, and when it reached the bottom, it resumed its original condition. In the nine chapters, of which the treatise consists, he shows that all the phenomena and effects hitherto ascribed to the horror of a vacuum arise from the weight of the mass of air; and after explaining the variable pressure of the atmosphere in different localities, and in its different states, and the rise of water in pumps, he calculates that the whole mass of air round our globe weighs 8,983,889,440,000,000,000 French pounds.

Having thus completed his researches respecting elastic and incompressible fluids, Pascal seems to have resumed, with a fatal enthusiasm, his mathematical studies; but, unfortunately for science, several of the works which he composed have been lost.[1] Others, however, have been preserved, which entitle him to a high rank among the greatest mathematicians of the age. Of these, his *Traité du Triangle Arithmétique*, his *Tractatus de numericis ordinibus*, and his *Problemata de Cycloide* are the chief. By means of the *Arithmetical Triangle*,[2] an invention equally ingenious and original, he succeeded in solving a number of theorems, which it would have been difficult to demonstrate in any other way, and in finding the co-efficients of different terms of a binomial raised to an even and positive power. The same principles enabled him to lay the foundation of the doctrine of probabilities, an important branch of mathematical science, which Huygens, a few years afterwards, improved, and which, in our own day, the Marquis Laplace and M. Poisson have so greatly extended. These treatises, with the

[1] These works were entitled *Promotus Apollonius Gallus*, in which he extended the theory of Conic Sections, and described several unknown properties of these curves; *Tactiones Sphericæ, Tactiones Conicæ, Loci plani et solidi; Perspectivæ methodi*, etc. The Abbé Bossut endeavored to find them, but in vain.

[2] This triangle is an isosceles right-angled triangle, divided into triangular cells, similar to the original triangle.

exception of that on the Cycloid, were composed and printed in the year 1654, but were not published till 1668, after the death of their author.

Although Pascal's health had suffered from the severity of his early studies, yet it was not till 1641, when he had reached his eighteenth year, that his constitution was seriously impaired. From that time "he never lived a day without pain." The labor which he had bestowed on his arithmetical machine, and on his physical and mathematical researches, gradually undermined his constitution, and at the close of 1647 he labored for three months under a paralytic attack, which deprived him wholly of the use of his limbs. About this time he took up his residence in Paris, along with his father and his sister Jacqueline. Here he resumed all his scientific pursuits, and devoted himself wholly to those nobler studies which at all seasons of life become an immortal nature, but which are peculiarly appropriate when the languid and shattered ark is about to surrender its undying occupant. The study of Christian truth, and the practice of Christian graces, engrossed all his thoughts; and though his father's piety was always ardent, yet, under the instruction and example of his son, it acquired new brightness, and he died in 1651, full of faith and hope. Under the same holy tuition, his sister Jacqueline was led to renounce the world and its pleasures, and to spend the rest of her days in the convent of Port-Royal, doing the will and following the example of her Master.

But even these sacred duties were found to be too much for so weak a frame; and, in order to give his mind complete relaxation, he made several journeys in Auvergne and other provinces, from which he derived considerable advantage. In 1653, however, after Jacqueline's departure for Port-Royal, Pascal found himself desolate and alone in Paris—deprived of the kind control of parental affection, and without those tender cares with which a sister's love had so assiduously watched him. His master-passion for study and for duty again seized him. He became first its servant, and then its slave, till his feeble and wasted frame reminded him of his own mortality. In order to give him even a chance of recovery, the total renunciation of study, and even of the slighter exertions of the mind, became imperative. His occupations were henceforth to be in the open air, or in the society of a few congenial friends; and though the change was a violent inroad upon all his habits, whether mental or physical, yet he yielded to the stern decree an implicit obedience. It is a strange fact in the history of our unfathomable nature that this godlike man, whom suffering had so singularly exalted, and who had seemed to all around him already embalmed for eternity, should, in almost the last extremity of his being, have acquired a taste for the very poison which had been dispensed to save him. In solitude at home, and prohibited from every mental occupation, he naturally relished the society of friends whom he esteemed and loved, and who, doubtless, offered to him all the idolatry of their affections; but habits had begun to be formed which threatened to interfere with the higher purposes of his being, and it was not improbable that a return to health, through the world's intervention, might not be a return to his Maker. Bossut informs us that he had begun to like society, and had even entertained serious thoughts of entering into the married state,—in the hope that an amiable companion might enliven his solitude and alleviate his sufferings. But Providence had otherwise decreed. In the month of October, 1654, when he went to take his usual drive to the Bridge of Neuilly, in a carriage with four horses, the two leaders became restive at a part of the road where there was no parapet, and precipitated themselves into the Seine. Fortunately, the traces which yoked them to the poles gave way, and Pascal in his carriage stood in perilous safety on the verge of the precipice. The effect of such a shock upon a frame so frail and sensitive may be easily conceived. Pascal fainted away; and though his senses returned after a considerable interval, his disturbed and shattered nerves never again recovered their original tone. During his sleepless nights and moments of depression he saw a precipice at his bedside, into which he was in danger of falling; and it is said that he believed it to be real, till a chair was placed between his bed and the visionary gulf which alarmed him.

Pascal did not fail to profit by this alarming incident. Regarding it as a message from heaven to renounce the pleasures of society, he resolved to follow where Providence so clearly led; and, under the instruction of his sister, to whom he had himself taught the same difficult lesson, he was enabled to carry his resolution into effect. The spiritual bread which he had thrown upon the waters returned to him after many days; and he must have felt, as we ought to feel, that it is only in the commerce of holy living that the exchange is always in favor of the giver, and that it is but in the mutual breathings of souls panting for immortality, that the inspirations become fuller and stronger. The green and smiling earth, which gives up its springs to cool the burning ether above, exhibits to us the gift returned in gentle dews or in refreshing showers. This interesting event in the life of Pascal, then in the thirty-first year of his age, has been mentioned in the following manner by his sister, Madame Perier:

"Jacqueline Pascal was then a religious, and led a life so eminent for sanctity, that she edified all the convent. Being in that state, she with pain beheld the man to whom, next under God, she stood indebted for all the heavenly graces she enjoyed, remain himself out of the possession of these graces; and as my brother made her frequent visits, so she made him frequent harangues on that subject: and this she did at last with so much force and energy, and yet with so much winning and persuasive sweetness at the same time, that she prevailed upon him, just as he had at first prevailed on her, absolutely to quit the world; and he accordingly went into a firm resolution of bidding a final adieu to all public company, and of retrenching all the little unprofitable superfluities of life, even with the risk of his health,—because he thought salvation preferable to all things, and the health of his soul infinitely more valuable than that of his body."

Thus freed from the embarrassments of social life, Pascal retired to the country, renouncing the pursuits of science, and devoting all his time to the study of the Scriptures, and the discharge of the duties they enjoined. His great mind was never greater than now, and though the mortal coil which enwrapped it was frail, and fast mouldering away, it still afforded scope and shelter for the mighty spirit within. It is when the material seed is exhausted in the quickening of its germ, that vegetable life bursts forth in all its strength and beauty. It was not to be expected that a mind of such energy as Pascal's would be permitted to indulge in an inglorious repose, when the interests of truth, secular and divine, required its aid. Its past acquisitions were but preparations for a future battle-field; and no sooner was it equipped in the full panoply of its intellectual might, than there was provided an occasion for its highest exercise. It was in the defence of Port-Royal and its immortal band of saints and sages, and of the great truths which reason and revelation combined to sanction, that Pascal was summoned from his retreat, and girt himself for the contest.

About six miles beyond Versailles, and in a secluded valley, stood the celebrated Abbey of Port-Royal des Champs, so called to distinguish it from Port-Royal de Paris, the town residence of the abbess, Angelique Arnaud. After having reformed the abuses and regulated the affairs of her own nunnery, she extended her pious cares to other institutions, where sacred vows had given way to secular pleasures, and where penitence and fasting had passed into riot and intemperance. There the scions of rank and power revelled in all the gayety of the capital. Luxurious fêtes polluted the sacred groves by day, while dancing, and gambling, and stage-plays closed the visible revels of the night. Confiding in a stronger arm than her own, the undaunted abbess succeeded in her holy enterprise. Open profligacy disappeared from the recreant nunneries, and her own institution acquired new celebrity and distinction. But, exalted as was her new position and that of her thriving community, it was destined, through suffering, to rise to still higher purity and glory. In the cycle of the seasons an unhealthy summer occurred. Heat and moisture united their deleterious powers; and dense vapors, rising from the marshy soil, scattered their gaseous poison over the valley. The nunnery became a hospital; and, in order to save its inmates, the establishment was transferred to Port-Royal de Paris, a hotel which the mother of the abbess had purchased for their reception.

At this time the Catholic Church was divided, as every other church has since been, into two parties—the one maintaining in their purity the great evangelical truths which Scripture so clearly reveals, and the other accommodating its doctrines to the weakness of human reason, and making them palatable to that large and powerful section of society who consider religion but as a generalization of moral duties, and its ministers as a

national police, whose function it is to wield the terrors of the
Divine law in support of the altar and the throne. In managing
the affairs of the Church, these two parties were equally at
variance. To maintain the purity of its discipline—to exalt
the character of its literature—to keep up a high morality in
its clergy, and to correct the flagrant abuses which had pro-
faned its altars, were unceasingly the objects of the Catholic
Evangelists. Against such innovations, genius and casuistry
plied their skill; the minions of corruption stood forth in fero-
cious array; and the petty tyrants, who directed the consciences
and the will of kings, threatened with their fiercest vengeance
the exposure of their crimes.

The parties thus placed in order of battle were the Jansenists
and the Jesuits. Cornelius Jansen, bishop of Ypres, born in
1585, and John du Verger D'Hauranne, abbot of Saint Cyran,
born in 1581, at Bayonne, were the founders of Jansenism, a
system of evangelical doctrine which they found embodied in
the almost inspired writings of Augustine, and which was given
to the world under the title of *Augustinus*, a posthumous work
of Jansen, which appeared in 1640, about two years after his
death. While he was at the College of Louvaine along with
Duverger, his health suffered from intense study. His physicians recommended a change of air; and, on the invitation of
his friend, he accompanied him to Bayonne. Here, under the
roof of Duverger, the two youthful divines spent six years in
unremitting and successful study, and acquired the highest
reputation for their piety as well as their learning. The Bishop
of Bayonne extended to them his patronage. Duverger became
a canon in the Cathedral, and Jansen head-master of the New
College; and thus did a community of feeling and of destiny
weld their young hearts into the warmest and most enduring
friendship. Duverger was soon afterwards appointed Grand
Vicar to Henry de la Rochepozay, bishop of Poitiers, who, in
1620, resigned to him the abbacy of the Monastery of Saint
Cyran.

When Cardinal Richelieu was bishop of Luçon, he was struck
with the high talent and noble mien of the abbot; and after
his ambitious views began to be developed, he sought to pro-
pitiate his alliance by the offer of the richest bishoprics and
abbacies in his gift. Saint Cyran, however, was animated with

loftier objects. Possessing the highest endowments of the
sage, he adorned them with the highest attributes of the saint,
and these he had already pledged in the service of a better
Master. The cardinal was chagrined at the rejection of his
offers; and when he found himself unable to attach Saint
Cyran to his interests as a tool, he began at first to dread him,
and at last to treat him as an enemy. There were events in
the cardinal's early life which Saint Cyran could disclose, and
there were schemes in his head which he might successfully
resist. Already had he refused to sanction the divorce of the
Duke of Orleans, to make way for his marriage to the cardinal's niece; and it became a measure of personal security to
deprive his self-created enemy of the power of injuring him.
The holy abbot was accordingly sent, in 1638 (the very year of
Jansen's death), to the castle of Vincennes, where the odor of
his sanctity and the radiance of his learning hallowed, for four
years, that gloomy prison, till, a few months before his death,
his hated oppressor was summoned to a still narrower and
darker home.

While the sisterhood of Port-Royal were residing in Paris,
the abbess became acquainted with this remarkable individual.
Pledged to the same Master, and intent on the same prize, they
resolved to re-establish Port-Royal, in order to maintain and
propagate the great evangelical principles which they had
adopted. The disciples—may we not say the worshippers?—of
Saint Cyran were equally distinguished by their learning, their
talents, and their piety; and under his orders there assembled
at Port-Royal des Champs a sacred band, who, throwing all
their wealth into its treasury, resolved to consecrate themselves to God, and, in fasting and prayer, to devote their lives
to the improvement and instruction of their species. Anthony
Arnaud and Arnaud D'Andilly, the brothers of the abbess;
Lemaitre and De Saci, her two nephews; Nicole, Tillemont,
Lancelot, Hermand, Renaud, and Fontaine, formed the noble
group who, in unequal dimensions and dissimilar attitudes,
occupied the grand pediment of that Christian temple. But
beneath its heavenward cusp one blank was left, which Pascal
was soon to fill. Having had frequent occasion to visit his
sister Jacqueline, the philosopher of Clermont became acquainted with the celebrated brotherhood of Port-Royal. To his

opinions and aspirations theirs were ardently responsive. The same throb of piety beat in each heart; the same flash of genius glanced in each eye; the same notes of eloquence fell from each tongue. Each and all of them looked to intellectual labor as their daily toil; to temperance and self-denial as their spiritual medicine; to the grave as their resting-place; and to heaven as their home.

We could have wished to give our readers some account of the holy men who occupied the farm-house of Les Granges, close to the Abbey of Port-Royal, and of the eminent persons who came to enjoy their society and benefit by their instructions; but the task, excepting in fragments, is beyond our limits. Anthony Arnaud was the undaunted hero of the Port-Royal enterprise. He had bravely striven with the Jesuits, and beaten them in many a well-contested field. He had dared even to assail the errors of Malebranche and Descartes; but though he never failed to crush, in his gigantic grasp, the more tangible and outstanding heresies of his antagonists, yet the gossamer and cobwebs of the Jesuits escaped unhurt in its interstices. It required the fine touch, the tapering fingers, and the sharp lancet of Pascal to unravel the tangled web, to extract the truth from its meshes, and to exhibit it in its native beauty, for the reception of mankind. Arnaud and his associates soon recognized the capacity of their young friend for so delicate a task; and, aided by their learning and research, he threw himself into the breach between the Jansenists and the Jesuits.

The *Augustinus* of Jansen—the text-book of Port-Royal theology—had been assailed by the Jesuits with the most rancorous hostility; and when unable to meet its doctrines in the fair field of discussion, they pretended to deduce from it *five* propositions which it did not contain, and which they clothed in language of such double meaning, that they were capable of two or three different interpretations, and misled even honest inquirers. We cannot even attempt to give a meager outline of the European controversy which these propositions—occupying, in all, about *fifteen* lines—called forth, or of the dramatic incidents to which they gave rise. At its commencement, it agitated not only France, but Italy. It disquieted kings and princes—it shook the Vatican; and before its close, it overthrew the perfidious but triumphant Jesuits who excited it, and laid prostrate the temporal power of the Popes who misjudged it. The cause of truth, indeed, which genius and learning had plead in vain, received the first shock; and the holy men, who stood faithful to the end, became exiles or dungeon slaves for its sake. But though the avenging arm was not lifted up in immediate or general retribution, it yet struck at individual victims—it executed stern retaliation on the families of ungodly princes—and sent the agonies of conscience, and the pangs of death, to wield their fiercest power over their guilty minions.

The first step in this exciting movement was taken in the Sorbonne, on the 1st of July, 1649, when M. Cornet, Syndic of the Faculty, submitted to that body *seven* propositions, containing heretical doctrines, which, he asserted, were making rapid progress among the bachelors of divinity. During the sharp discussion which ensued, several of the speakers pointed out its bearing on the doctrines of Saint Augustine, so often authorized by Popes and Councils; and M. Marcan prophetically declared, " that it was well enough discerned, that under pretext of these propositions Jansen was aimed at, and that *the design was to cause the censure to fall one day upon that author*." It was decided, however, in a meeting packed for the purpose, that the propositions should be examined; and a committee of eight doctors was accordingly appointed for the purpose.

Although the disciples of Augustine had lost no time in unmasking the designs and denouncing the malice of the Jesuits, yet the committee resolved, and allowed their resolution to transpire, to condemn the propositions, " without making any distinction of the different senses of which they were capable." At the meeting held for this purpose on the 2d of August, M. St. Amour, a distinguished Jansenist, served upon them an appeal to Parliament, signed by sixty doctors, for the purpose of preventing any decision in the Faculty. When M. Brousset had begun to report the appeal to the Great Chamber, the president, M. Mole, instantly stopped him. The affair, he said, was too important to be rashly judged; and following out this opinion, he, in a few days, proposed a truce of some months, which the Jansenists accepted, and to which he pledged himself on the part of the Jesuits. This triumph of the Jansenists, however, was of short duration. The Jesuits broke the pledge of the president. They confessed that they were bound to *do nothing* for a few months, but they were not pledged to *say nothing;* and on the strength of this defence, they had prepared their condemnation of the propositions ; and in September they circulated it through the kingdom, denouncing them as heretical, scandalous, and contrary to Scripture!

This gross breach of faith excited general indignation. The Jansenists, full of the energy which their cause inspired, again appealed to Parliament for an interdict against the proceedings of the committee. Parties were heard. Five of the Jesuits had the effrontery to declare that they had never passed any censure, while all of them asserted that they had never published it. In order to restore peace to the Church, the president proposed that the Jesuits should pledge themselves, in the presence of the Court, "to do nothing more for the future;" and addressing himself to their leader, M. Cornet, he asked his concurrence. Cornet replied, " *Sir, we pledge ourselves to make good all that we promised to President Mole.*" Indignant at the equivocation, the president replied, " *Ha ! Gentlemen, speak plain French ; these loose words and general promises are not discourses to be held in this company. The Sorbonne hath not the repute of using equivocations.*" Unwilling to issue an interdict, the president again proposed a mutual agreement. " War," he said, " was kindled both without and within the empire : we had suffered famine, and there were still other scourges that threatened us, and it was a thing of ill relish to see division among the doctors." The Jansenists, however, insisted on the interdict, and on the 5th of October the Parliament " enjoined and prohibited the parties from publishing the said draught of censure; from agitating or bringing into question the propositions contained therein, and writing and publishing any thing concerning them."

Though now under legal restraint, the Jesuits were as little restrained by law as they had been by honor. They audaciously sent to Rome the disowned and prohibited censure, as a *True Censure* of the propositions issued by the Faculty of the Sorbonne, and, as such, it was " brought before the Pope in the Assembly of the Holy Office, to be the subject of debate for his

Holiness and that tribunal." Three out of the five consulters approved of the censure, and all the cardinals would have con-- curred, had not one of them, more upright than the rest, boldly maintained, "*that the censure, and not the proposition, was heretical.*" Upon this the Pope exclaimed, "Beware of Cardinal N——, who says that our consulters are heretics;" to which the cardinal replied, "Excuse me, blessed Father; I do not say that my lords the consulters are heretics, but that their censures are heretical. But still, it is true that they would be heretics should they continue obstinately therein."

The intrigues of the Jesuits, and their repeated attempts to deceive and prejudice the Pope, rendered it necessary that a decision on the five propositions should be obtained from the highest authority. A letter, signed by eleven French bishops, was accordingly addressed to his Holiness, requesting the establishment of a solemn congregation, at which the subject should be discussed before the Pope pronounced judgment; and M. St. Amour, and other four deputies, were sent to Rome to carry out the views of the bishops. The Jesuits appointed a similar deputation, and both parties arrived at Rome. The activity of M. St. Amour annoyed the Jesuits, and they tried every means to frighten him from Italy. Even Cardinal D'Este intimated to him that his residence in Rome was one of real danger; and a French ecclesiastic informed him, in secret, that there was a plan to seize him at night and immure him in the prison of the Inquisition. Notwithstanding these threats, the heroic Jansenist stood firm at his post; and on the 10th of July, 1651, he had an audience of the Pope. After stating that the Jesuits in France had made sure of the Pope's opinion, his Holiness replied, says M. St. Amour, " by showing me a crucifix, which he said was his counsel in such affairs as these; and having heard what would be represented to him by such as argued therein, he kneeled down before that crucifix, to take at the feet thereof his resolution according to the inspiration given to him by the Holy Spirit, whose assistance was promised to him, and could not fail him."

On the 21st of June, 1652, the Jansenist deputation had their long-promised audience of Innocent X. The members addressed his Holiness in succession, and brought before him several striking facts, within his own knowledge, which placed beyond a doubt the intrigues and calumnies of his opponents; and there was reason to believe that the Pope took a favorable view of the cause. Advice, however, and even warnings, from kings and bishops, overset the papal mind, and created doubts and fears which an appeal to his crucifix seemed unable to remove. The King of Poland urged the condemnation of the five propositions, and declared that he was "*more apprehensive in his dominions of the divisions which might arise about them than the wars of the Tartars and Muscovites;*" and there is reason to believe that the French king and his tyrant minister rested their own personal safety, as well as that of their kingdom, on the condemnation of truths eternal and immutable. To such influences the Holy Father was constrained to yield; and though he honored the deputies with a grand audience on the 19th May, 1653, and listened for hours to their learned and unanswerable appeals, yet on the 31st of May the bull of condemnation was placarded in the streets, and copies sent to the French king and bishops, without any communication even of the fact of its having been passed being made to the deputation! Upon taking leave of Innocent, the Jansenist deputies were received with a degree of kindness which excited the greatest joy even in Rome. Annoyed by this expression of opinion, the Jesuits solicited an audience of the Pope, to request from him a declaration of his dissatisfaction with his subjects. The application, however, was in vain.

The feelings and conduct of the Pope are thus described, in a dispatch from the French ambassador to the Secretary of State:

"On Thursday last I told the Pope that the doctors who bear the title of St. Augustine's defenders were desirous to kiss his feet before their departure, being ready to return into France. His Holiness answered me, that whatever business he might have he would admit them to audience on Friday morning: which he did, *and caressed the doctors extremely*, and told them that he had not condemned the doctrine of St. Augustine or St. Thomas, nor the point of grace effectual by itself, leaving this part of the controversy in the same posture as Clement VIII. and Paul V. had left it; but that as they themselves had declared that the five propositions had three senses, one Calvinistic, one Pelagian, and one true and Catholic, they ought to be pronounced erroneous and temerarious, inasmuch as in a certain manner and intent they were heretical."

Although the Jansenists yielded implicit obedience to the decision of the Roman Pontiff, the Jesuits were restless and dissatisfied. Aided by the king and the government, they used every means to annoy and oppress their adversaries. They denounced the Jansenist leaders as deists; they charged the deputies with having circulated libels against the king; they ridiculed them in silly caricatures; they afterwards established an anti-Jansenist test, with suitable penalties to enforce it; and they ejected from their offices the Professor of Divinity at Caen and the Principal of the College of Montaigu. But this was not all. The writings of Jansen—the object of all their hostility—had not yet been condemned. To effect this, the Jesuits of Church and State united their strength. Cardinal Mazarin even lent his influence; and it was speedily decreed, in a muster of Parisian doctors, that the condemned propositions were actually contained in the *Augustinus* of Jansen!

In this emergency the indomitable Arnaud rushed to the combat. In a vigorous letter, written in 1655, he declared that the condemned propositions were not to be found in the writings of Jansen; and he boldly announced his own orthodox opinions on the perplexing questions of grace and free-will. The doctors of the Sorbonne were again in arms. Arnaud was charged not only with heresy, but with disrespect to the Roman See; and hence it became necessary that charges so grave in themselves, and so serious in their consequences, should be fully and fairly canvassed by the public.

Such was the state of this extraordinary controversy, when Pascal became the champion of truth and of Port-Royal. Under the signature of Louis de Montalte, he composed a series of letters,[1] addressed to a friend in the country, containing animadversions on the morals and policy of the Jesuits. The first of these letters was published on the 23d January, 1656, and they were continued at intervals till the 24th March, 1657, when the eighteenth and last letter made its appearance.[2]

[1] The Letters appeared first with the title of *Lettres écrites par Louis de Montalte, à un Provincial de ses amis, et aux RR. PP. Jésuites, sur la morale et la Politique de ces Pères.*

[2] A nineteenth letter, dated 1st June, 1657, has been added in some modern

The *first* of the *Provincial Letters*, as they are now called, is introduced with a notice of the proposed censure of Arnaud. In a series of imaginary conversations with doctors and monks, Pascal investigates, with much humor and elegance of style, the meaning of the term *proximate power* (*pouvoir prochain*), which the Molinists had invented for the purpose of drawing down a censure upon Arnaud. This letter produced a great sensation. It roused the public, who had hitherto been indifferent to the subject; but so active and zealous were the enemies of Arnaud, that a week afterwards they succeeded, by a majority of votes, in expelling him from the Faculty of Theology in the Sorbonne.[1] The second letter, dated January 29, treats of the subject of *sufficient grace*, which, according to the Jesuits, was of no avail without *efficacious grace*—an inconsistency which the author exposes in a strain of the happiest and most convincing raillery, and which leads him to address to the Dominicans an eloquent and glowing admonition. In the *third* and fourth letters, which immediately followed the decision of the Sorbonne, he ridicules with great effect the Dominicans, who seem on this occasion to have abandoned the doctrine of St. Thomas, and he shows in the clearest manner that the sentiments of Arnaud coincide with those of the Fathers; that the censure pronounced upon him was as absurd as it was unjust; and that the heresy charged against him was not in his *writings*, but in his *person*. Thus did it appear that the *proximate power* of the Jesuits was that which left man *powerless;* and their *sufficient* grace that which *sufficeth not*. In these four letters Pascal assumes the character of a person not much versed in such controversies. He consults various learned doctors, proposes doubts, and obtains solutions of them, and in this way he makes the subject so plain that the Jesuits and the Dominicans became the objects of universal ridicule. "Pascal," says an eminent French critic, "explains every question so clearly, that we are compelled out of gratitude to agree with him." In the six following letters the Jesuits are scourged with the most unmerciful severity, and yet with stripes

editions, on the subject of the proposed establishment of the Inquisition in France.
1 At this meeting, which was held on the 31st January, 1656, 206 members of the Faculty were present. For M. Arnaud, there were 71 votes of doctors; against him, 80; and 40 votes of mendicant friars,—15 members declining to vote.
VOL. I.—3

so quietly and measuredly applied that the sound of the lash, like that of the cricket or the grasshopper, scarcely affects our ears. The writhing of the unseen culprit becomes almost visible; and we think we hear him, in words not expressed, acknowledging the justice of his punishment.

Almost every religious order had its casuists, who decided cases of conscience, and affixed as it were a numerical value to human actions. Crimes became virtues when tested by the *intention* of the criminal; and thus did the casuist priests, with the privileges of the confessional, become at once the arbiters and the tyrants of conscience. The theological ethics of the Jesuits abounded in those misleading principles, in which their casuists were intrenched. Their doctrines of *probabalism*, of *mental restriction*, and of the *direction* of *intention*, were often applied with singular subtilty and talent; but, in an age of ignorance and superstition, the actual decisions of such judges as the Jesuits, administering such codes of casuistic law, must have been, as they were, scandalous and revolting. Against cases of this kind, carefully collected from their writings, Pascal directs the artillery of his sarcasm. Their new system of morality—their remiss and their rigid casuistry—their substitution of obscure authorities for that of the Fathers—their artifices for evading the authority of the Gospel, the Councils, and the Popes—the privileges of sinning, and even of killing, granted to priests and friars—their corrupt maxims respecting judges—their false worship of the Virgin Mary—their facilities for procuring salvation while living in sin, are all exposed with a severity of satire, a gayety of sentiment, an elegance of style, and an exuberance of wit, which have interested all classes of readers.

In the remaining *eight* letters the morals, the maxims, and the calumnies of the Jesuits are again discussed; but, as if the subject had become too grave for ridicule, and their crimes too flagrant for satire, Pascal assails them with the severest reproof, and in the most fervid eloquence. Abandoning his previous tactics, he attacks the whole body of the Jesuits, and addressing his two last letters to Father Annat, the very confessor of the king, who had charged the author with being a heretic and a Port-Royalist, he makes the following bold reply: "You feel yourselves smitten by an invisible hand—a hand, however, which makes your delinquencies visible to all; and in vain do you try to strike at me in the dark, through the persons of those with whom you suppose me to be associated. I fear you not, either on my own account or on that of any other, being bound by no tie either to a community or to any individual whatsoever. All the influence which your society possesses can be of no avail in my case. From this world I have nothing to hope, nothing to dread, nothing to desire. Through the goodness of God I have no need of any man's money or any man's patronage. Thus, father, I elude all your attempts to lay hold of me. You may touch Port-Royal if you choose, but you shall not touch me. You may turn people out of the Sorbonne, but that will not turn me out of my domicile. You may hatch plots against priests and doctors, but not against me, for I am neither the one nor the other. And thus, father, you never perhaps had to do, in the whole course of your experience, with a person so completely beyond your reach, and, therefore, so admirably qualified for dealing with your errors—one perfectly free—one without engagement, entanglement, relationship, or business of any kind—one, too, who is pretty well versed in your maxims, and determined, as God shall give him light, to discuss them, without permitting any earthly consideration to arrest or slacken his endeavors."

The effect produced by the Provincial Letters far exceeded the most sanguine expectations of the Port-Royalists. Read and understood by the world, to whom Jansenism and Jesuitism were subjects of indifference, they were devoured by all classes, and the Jesuits became everywhere the subject of mirth and ridicule. Even their friends at court enjoyed in secret the humiliation of their spiritual tyrants, and the gay and profligate society of the capital found the cheapest absolution, and indulgences, without price, in the moral law of the Jesuits. Thus driven from the field as casuists and as divines, they had no place of refuge in literature or science. The most distinguished writers and philosophers of the day, if not all Jansenists, were, at least, none of them Jesuits. The shaft which struck them was shot from a bow doubly strung, which genius and piety had combined to bend, and though it was not barbed with upas, nor guided to a vital part, it yet shook the seat of life, and, by a sure though lingering process, brought its victim to the tomb.

After this blow, the Jesuits were unable to recover either their station or their influence. The political power, indeed, previously intrusted to them against Port-Royal, was now put forth with new force, and wielded with unscrupulous malignity. Anne of Austria, the Regent of France, and Cardinal Mazarin, her unprincipled minister, were the guilty authors of this attack upon Port-Royal. A troop of archers, aided by the police, marched to its sacred groves. The masters and scholars were ejected from its schools; the recluses were banished from its sanctuary, and an order of council was issued to eject every scholar, postulant, and novice both from their Abbey-in-the-Fields, and their residence in the capital. An event, however, occurred as strange in its nature as it was powerful in its influence, which arrested the sécular arm, and stayed for awhile the fanatical vengeance of the Jesuits.

Among the scholars at Port-Royal, Marguerite Perier, the neice of Pascal, was an object of peculiar interest. She was eleven years of age, and had for three years been afflicted with a *fistula lachrymalis*. The most celebrated surgeons in Paris had, during six months, exhausted in vain all the resources of their art. Her nose and cheeks were deformed with the most loathsome sores. The bones had even become carious, her attendants almost shrunk from her presence, and so desperate was the case that the surgeons had decided on the application of the cautery. Her father was summoned to witness the operation, and he had set out on his journey to be present on the appointed day. Previous to this event, M. de la Potherie, a priest resident in Paris, had obtained one of the thorns said to be from our Saviour's crown, which, at the urgent request of the virgins, had been sent for adoration to the different monasteries in Paris. The inhabitants of Port-Royal were naturally anxious to show the same respect to the sacred relic; and on Friday, the 24th March, 1656, the nuns and scholars marched through the church in solemn procession, and kissed the holy thorn as they passed. Marguerite Perier had been advised to apply her eye to the thorn after she had kissed it, and no sooner had she done this than the disease disappeared. Several of the physicians and surgeons, who had been previously consulted, were called to witness the cure. They could not believe their eyes; and so complete was the cure that they could scarcely distinguish Mademoiselle Perier from her companions.[1] This extraordinary cure was at first kept secret by the ladies of Port-Royal, but it was soon made known in Paris by the medical attendants. The mind of the capital was agitated—the Jesuits trembled, and their political agents paused in their deed of persecution. The regent sent the king's surgeon to inquire into the truth of the story, and when it was reported to her to be true, she pondered over the event. All good Catholics regarded the Miracle of the Thorn as an interposition of Providence to save the monastery; and Anne of Austria, unable to resist the general feeling, which she probably did not share, recalled her archers from their work of sacrilege, and permitted the saints and sages of Port-Royal to resume their intellectual and pious labors.

The respite thus obtained for the condemned monastery disconcerted the plans of its relentless enemies. The Jesuits at first threw doubts over the story of the Holy Thorn, and called in question the testimony of those who had witnessed it; and when they found these attempts to be unavailing, they published the most scandalous libels against the Port-Royalists. In the *Rabat-joie des Jansénistes*, published anonymously, but written by Father Annat, the king's confessor, this holy slanderer, after trying to put down the story as untrue, admitted it to be a real miracle, and maintained that God had allowed it to be wrought amid a conclave of heretics, in order to prove that Christ died for all men ! Pascal, who had seen with his own eyes the disease, and had also witnessed its cure, could not but view the event as miraculous; and, as a Roman Catholic, he naturally regarded it as produced by the touch of the Holy

[1] We have abridged this account from the third note of Nicole (Willelmus Wendrockius) on the Sixteenth Provincial Letter. Nicole was then in Paris enjoying the society of Pascal, his intimate friend. He went to Port-Royal, and witnessed with his own eyes the fact of the cure, having been assured by Pascal and the surgeons of the fact of the disease. "Tum ego Parisiis versabar externus, nec mediocrem cum clarissimo vire D. Pascal omnibus Europæ mathematicis notissimo usum contraxeram, propter illorum, in quibus aliquando gravioribus fatigatus acquiesce, studiorum societatem. Is erat istius puellæ avunculus: idem et tanti miraculi testis omni exceptione major. Hujus usus ipse quoque cum ceteris Portum Regium petii, commonstrari mihi puellam curavi: *at sicut tum illi integerrimæ fidei viro, tum spectatissimis medicis et chirurgis de morbo credideram, de sanitate mihi credidi.*"—Lud. Montalt. Lett. Prov., p. 489, Ed. 4, Colon. 1665.

Thorn. He entered the lists, therefore, with Father Annat and the Jesuits, and repels, in his sixteenth letter, the base calumnies which they had circulated against his friends. The following appeal to them is at once beautiful and eloquent:

" Cruel, cowardly persecutors ! Must, then, the most retired cloisters afford no retreat from your calumnies? While these consecrated virgins are employed, night and day, according to their institution, in adoring Jesus Christ in the holy sacrament, you cease not, night or day, to publish abroad that they do not believe that he is either in the eucharist or even at the right hand of his Father; and you are publicly excommunicating them from the Church, at the very time when they are in secret praying for the whole Church, and for you! You blacken with your slanders those who have neither ears to hear nor mouths to answer you! But Jesus Christ, in whom they are now hidden, not to appear till one day together with him, hears you, and answers for them. At the moment I am now writing, that holy and terrible voice is heard which confounds nature and consoles the Church. And I fear, fathers, that those who now harden their hearts, and refuse with obstinacy to hear them, while he speaks in the character of God, will one day be compelled to hear him with terror, when he speaks to them in the character of a Judge."

We are unwilling to enter into any discussion respecting the apparently supernatural cure of Mademoiselle Perier. As Protestants, we reject the miracle—as men, we admit the fact. Unwilling to believe that the Church of Christ was either to be sustained or adorned by miraculous gifts, we cannot believe that the occurrence of events which baffle human reason is any proof of the purity of the Church with which they are associated. We may believe that meteoric stones fall from the sky, when we see them whizzing across our path and dropping warm at our feet; but we need not believe that they have fallen from the moon, or formed part of a shattered planet. Those who take away human life on circumstantial evidence, or on direct testimony, must believe that an extraordinary, if not an instantaneous cure, was performed on Mademoiselle Perier, or rather took place on the day the procession passed the fancied relic; but it would require more evidence than can be produced, and that, too, of a very peculiar kind, to prove that the cure was effected by the touch of a thorn, and that the thorn employed had ever existed in our Saviour's crown.

But, whatever be our opinion of this event, there is no doubt that the regent and her minister viewed it as divine. It paralyzed their vindictive arm; and while they were the depositaries of power, that arm was never again lifted against Port-Royal. The pious world were equally impressed with its supernatural character. Crowds of devotees thronged to the sacred scene. The Queen of Poland, the Princess Guimenée— the Dukes and Duchesses of Luynes, Liancourt, and Pont-chateau—the Marquesses of Sevigné and Sablé, annually retired to it for instruction; and the celebrated Duchess de Longueville, with the Prince and Princess de Conti, her brother and sister, became worshippers at Port-Royal. About the same time, Madame de Montpensier, the niece of Louis XIII., paid a visit to the Abbey, and carried back to the queen regent the most favorable account of its principles and its inmates.[1]

These indications of prosperity, however, were but the foreshadows of a coming storm. The Jesuits viewed them with an evil eye, and the popularity of Port-Royal spurred them on to new acts of aggression. On the death of Cardinal Mazarin, the young monarch, Louis XIV., yielded to the desires of the Jesuits. Having refused to sign the anti-Jansenist formulary of 1660, the novices and scholars were expelled from the monastery; the small schools of Port-Royal and the neighborhood were shut up; and, in consequence of a decree of the 13th of April, 1661, a troop of horse appeared at the abbey, and drove into prison or exile its higher functionaries. Arnaud was banished. Singlin, the father confessor, was thrown into the Bastille, where he died; and Angélique Arnaud, after a bold remonstrance addressed to the queen, took leave of the companions of her solitude, and closed a holy and a useful life, strong in the faith which had so long sustained her, and animated with those hopes which affliction brightens, and death embalms.

In the midst of these calamities, Pascal was engrossed with profound researches in geometry, an occupation well fitted to give serenity to a heart bleeding from the wounds of his beloved

[1] *Mémoires de Mademoiselle de Montpensier*, tom. iii., p. 810.

associates. He had long before renounced the study of the sciences; but during a violent attack of toothache, which deprived him of sleep, the subject of the cycloid forced itself upon his thoughts. Fermat, Roberval, and others, had trodden the same ground before him; but in less than eight days, and under severe suffering, he discovered a general method of solving this class of problems by the summation of certain series; and as there was only one step from this discovery to that of Fluxions, Pascal might, with more leisure and better health, have won from Newton and from Leibnitz the glory of that great invention.

The Duke de Roannes, and other friends of Pascal, conceived the idea of making this discovery subservient to the interests of religion, in so far as it showed that a profound geometer might be an humble Christian. With this view, in June, 1658, Pascal, under the assumed name of *Amos Dettonville*, the anagram of *Louis de Montalte*, offered prizes of forty and twenty pistoles for the best determination of the area and the centre of gravity of any segment of the cycloid, and the dimensions and centre of gravity of solids, half and quarter solids, &c., which the same segment would generate by revolving round an absciss or an ordinate. Huygens, Slusius, Wren, and Richi transmitted *partial* solutions. Wallis, and Lallouère, a Jesuit, were the only real competitors; but neither of them succeeded. Dettonville published his own solution in his *Traité Générale de la Roulette*, which appeared in January, 1659; and though the whole affair was arranged by his friend Carcavi, a lawyer, as well as a mathematician, yet Pascal was involved in a dispute with the two disappointed candidates, who charged him with injustice. Posterity, however, has rescued his name from this unmerited reproach, while it has stamped with its highest praise the beauty and originality of his researches.

The miraculous cure of Marguerite Perier, whom Pascal dearly loved, and who had been his "spiritual daughter in baptism," left a deep impression on his heart. He spoke of it as a special manifestation of the Almighty, at a time "when faith appeared to be extinguished in the hearts of the majority of mankind." His mind was therefore full of the subject of miracles, and he resolved to dedicate the rest of his life to the composition of a great work on the Evidences of Religion. The war, however, which he was at this time waging against the Jesuits lasted three years, and the unexpected intrusion of the geometry of the cycloid, upon the year following, interfered with the execution of this great undertaking. He had devoted to it, however, the last year in which he was permitted to labor, and the various portions of it which he had written were collected by his Port-Royal friends, and published, in 1670, under the title of *Pensées de M. Pascal sur la Religion, et sur quelques autres sujets.* This little work, which has been translated into every European language, is pregnant with great and valuable lessons, and has met with general admiration. Original and striking views of divine truth pervade its pages, and fragments of profound thought, and brilliant eloquence, and touching sentiment, everywhere remind us of its gifted author. Appealing to minds of the highest order, his opinions on the solemn questions of faith and duty cannot fail to have a transcendent influence over hearts which studies and sufferings, like his own, have enlightened and subdued.

The two last years of Pascal's life were marked with few events excepting those of suffering and of duty; but even these few have not been recorded by his biographers. We find, however, in one of his letters to Fermat, some interesting information respecting his health and movements, and also some important particulars relative to his religious and philosophical opinions. In a letter dated July 25th, 1660, Fermat, then in his 67th year, proposes to meet Pascal in September or October, at some place intermediate between Clermont and Thoulouse; and in order to secure an interview, he adds that if Pascal is unwilling to travel, he will thus expose himself to the risk of seeing him at his own house, and of having in it two invalids[1] at the same time. To this proposal Pascal replied in a beautiful letter, dated De Bienassis, 10th August, 1660, from which the following is an extract:

"I will also say to you, that although you are the only one in all Europe whom I regard as a great geometrician, no mere geometrician would have had any attraction for me; but I fancy there is so much intelligence and sincerity in your con-

---

[1] Fermat died in 1668, a few months after Pascal.

versation, that for this reason I have desired to meet you. For to speak to you frankly of geometry, I find it the highest exer-cise of the mind; but at the same time I know it to b̔e so use-less that I make little difference between a man who is only a geometrician and a skilful artisan. I call it, therefore, the most beautiful occupation in the world; but in fact it is only an oc-cupation, and I have often said that it is good to make the essay, but not the employment of our force; so that I would not go two steps for geometry, and I am confident that you are very much of my opinion. But at present there is this more-over in me, that I am engaged in studies so different from geometry, that I am scarcely conscious of its existence. I turned my attention to it a year or two since, for quite a par-ticular reason, and my object having been accomplished, I may never think of it again; besides that, my health is not yet firm enough for it, for I am so feeble that I cannot walk without a cane, nor hold myself on a horse; neither can I ride but a very short distance in a carriage, for which cause I have been twenty-two days on the road from Paris here. The physicians order me the waters of Bourbon during the month of Septem-ber, and I have been engaged, so far as I can be engaged, for two months to go thence into Poitou by water as far as Sau-mur, to remain till Christmas with the Duc de Roannes, gover-nor of Poitou, who has for me sentiments above my worth. But as I shall pass by Orleans in going to Saumur by the river, if my health does not allow me to go further, I will go hence to Paris. So you see, sir, what is the present state of my life, an account of which I am obliged to give you, in order to as-sure you of the impossibility of accepting the honor which you deign to offer me, and which I desire with all my heart to be able some day to acknowledge, either to you or your children, to whom I am quite devoted, having a particular regard for those who bear the name of a man most eminent.

"I am, etc.,   PASCAL."

The opinion which Pascal here expresses of geometry as a study—his fine allusion to his higher pursuits—his reference to the accident which turned his mind to the cycloid, and his ac-count of his own health and plans, have a peculiar interest. We cannot, however, learn that he performed the journeys, and paid the visit to the Duke de Roannes, to which he alludes ; but it is probable, from Madame Perier's silence, that he returned from Bienassis to Paris, where new calamities awaited him. Agitated with the occurrences at Port-Royal, his sister Jac-queline, who had become sub-prioress of the abbey, sunk under the conflict between expediency and conscience, and died on the 4th October, 1661, *the first victim*, as she herself expressed it, *of the Formulary*,—the anti-Jansenist test which the Jesuit king had exacted from the nunneries. She is the author of some excellent compositions in poetry, and had gained the poetical prize given at Rouen, on the day of the Conception. Upon hearing of her death, Pascal said, with a deep sigh, " *May God give us grace to die like her.*"

His own last hour, so frequently, and almost miraculously delayed, was now rapidly approaching. Madame Perier had come to Paris with her family to watch over her beloved brother, and from the nature of his habits she occupied a sepa-rate dwelling. He had taken into his own house a poor man with his wife and family, whom he generously supported, but one of the sons having been seized with the small-pox, Pascal thought it unsafe for Madame Perier to expose herself and her children to infection ; and he therefore took up his residence with her on the 19th June, 1662. He had no sooner made the change than he was seized with an alarming illness, and on the 17th August it assumed such an aspect of immediate danger, that he himself requested a consultation of the faculty. The wise men pronounced " the illness to be no more than a megrim in the head, joined with some vapors ;" but Pascal judged other-wise, and desired the Holy Communion to be dispensed to him next morning. During the night a violent convulsion ensued, and though he was given over as dead, he recovered so com-pletely, as to be able to take the Sacrament. In answer to the usual questions of the priest, respecting his belief in " the princi-pal mysteries of the faith," he replied : " *Yes, sir, I do verily be-lieve them all from the bottom of my heart and soul ;*" and his last prayer was, " *May the all-gracious God never forsake me.*" Another convulsion immediately supervened, and this great man expired at one o'clock in the morning of the 19th August, 1662, in the fortieth year of his age. Upon opening his body the stomach and liver were found diseased, and the intestines in a

state of gangrene; and when his skull was laid open, it was
found to contain " an enormous quantity of brain, the substance
of which was very solid and condensed." His remains were
interred in his parish church of St. Etienne-du-Mont, where a
marble tablet, erected by Mons. Perier and his wife, preserves
a local memory of his talents and virtues.

It would be fruitless to delineate the character of a man in
whose life and writings the most exalted virtues have shone so
brightly and conspicuously. In no age of the Church, have the
graces of Faith, Hope, and Charity, been so finely blended, as
in Pascal's life. Genius threw round them its attractive halo,
and the crown of martyrdom hallowed the combination. Though
he was never immured in a dungeon, nor tied to the stake, nor
prostrate beneath the Jesuit's axe, his life was a prolonged martyrdom, and the Church of Christ is at this moment reaping the
fruits of his labors and his sufferings. There is, however, one
point of Pascal's character—the least obtrusive, though the
most attractive—which demands our notice—his humility, and
simplicity of mind. In referring to these qualities, a distinguished friend of his own beautifully remarked, " that the grace
of God makes itself known in men of great genius by little
things, and in men of little understanding by the greatest."
The little mind has no scale, no unit of length, by which it can
measure its awful distance from the Supreme Intelligence. The
philosopher can take for his unit, his own vast distance from the
unlettered peasant; and he finds it but a grain of sand in the
sea-beach of the globe—but an infinitesimal atom in the whole
matter of the universe.

As an elegant writer, Pascal has long occupied the highest
level; and we can scarcely charge his countrymen with extravagance, when they assert that his Provincial Letters have no
model either among ancient or modern writers. Voltaire has
said that the best comedies of Molière have not more wit than
the first Provincial Letter, and that Bossuet has nothing more
sublime than the last. The remarkable simplicity and elegance
which characterize the style of Pascal, were doubtless owing to
the great labor which he bestowed on his writings. His friend
Nicole, speaking in general of them, informs us that he was
guided by rules of composition which he had himself discovered;
that he often spent twenty whole days on a single letter, and

that he wrote some of them *seven* times over, before they attained the perfection in which they finally appeared.

We have anxiously sought for some authentic information regarding the secrecy under which the Provincial Letters were published, and the time when the author became generally known. It is obvious, from the prefaces to the different editions of Nicole's translations of them, that in 1660 they were not acknowledged by Pascal; but, on the other hand, Madame Perier informs us " that his manner in writing was so peculiar, and so proper to him alone, that as soon as the Provincial Letters were seen abroad in the world, it was as plainly seen that they came from his hand, notwithstanding all the mighty precautions he took to keep them concealed, even from his most intimate friends." But whatever be the truth, it does not appear that during the five years which elapsed between the publication of the Letters and the death of Pascal, he was either annoyed or persecuted as their author.

It would be improper to conclude an account of the life and writings of Pascal, without adverting to the great lessons which they so impressively convey. During the progress of the Reformation, the attention of Roman Catholics was necessarily directed to the doctrine and discipline of their Church; and a body of learned ecclesiastics, and pious laymen, were gradually led to acknowledge the corruptions which had disfigured it as a missionary institution. The sound theology of Augustine, sanctioned by holy writ, had given way to a creed palatable to the secular mind; and the new discipline which that creed tolerated, held but a light and a loose rein over the will and actions of men. The Church's most sacred rites were freely dispensed to individuals who used them but as cloaks for sin, or as substitutes for holiness. Jansen, as we have seen, stood forth, the champion of the doctrine of grace; and Arnaud, in his able work, *De la fréquente Communion,* exposed and lashed the indiscriminate admission to the Lord's Table which characterized the reign of the Jesuits. Round the standard of primitive truth which was thus planted on the towers of Port-Royal, men of high attainments and noble lineage speedily assembled; and a party was formed within the Catholic Church, which maintained its ancient faith, and struggled, under suffering and persecution, to restore its ancient purity.

Without the support of any organized body, and opposed by the wealth, and power, and vicious policy of the State, the members of the Port-Royal band maintained the combat with a boldness and success unexampled in the history of civilization. Each individual wrought as if the result depended on his single arm; and though their weapons were various in kind, and different in temper, they struck the same plague-spot of corruption; and if they did not stop its growth, they never failed to deaden its vitality. But it was neither by their brilliant talents, nor by their unity of effort, that they thus kept in check the intrigues and menaces of power. It was their high *moral courage*, their fearless heroism, their trust in an arm stronger than their own, that enabled them to endure and to triumph. The men, indeed, who left father and mother for their Master's sake—who abandoned lucrative professions, and gave all they had to the treasury of the faithful, were not likely to flinch from suffering, or quail before mortals like themselves. When Nicole, the comrade of Arnaud in his hottest encounters, desired one day to have some rest from his toils, Arnaud exclaimed, "*You rest! will you not have the whole of eternity for rest?*" And when some of the gentler spirits of Port-Royal were desirous of yielding some secondary point, as a measure of expediency, Pascal unceasingly repeated to them words which can never lose their meaning or their value: "*You wish to save Port-Royal. You can never save it; but you may be traitors to truth.*"

Two hundred years have passed away since these noble witnesses pronounced and sealed their testimony. In that long interval of time empires have fallen, and races of kings disappeared. Revolution has swept away time-hallowed institutions, and even systems of faith have surrendered their most cherished errors; but, amid all these changes, Providence has left us a clue by which we can trace through the labyrinth of its ways the march and the workings of those great principles which the Port-Royalists labored to establish. The persecution of the Jansenists proved the destruction of the Jesuits. The Papal power, made contemptible by the exposure of its fallibility and ignorance, lost its hold even over its most bigoted votaries. The equality of man's rights, the dignity of his station, and the claims of the poor—not for deeds of charity alone,

but for acts of justice—doctrines taught and practised by Pascal
and the Port-Royalists—contributed to foster those yearnings
after civil liberty which, when unchained in an evil hour from
religion, led to the annihilation of that royal house which persecuted the Jansenists and razed Port-Royal to the ground.

Should such times again occur, if they have not already occurred, let us look to the Pascals and Arnauds of former days,
and let us be assured, as they were, that Truth will admit of
no compromise; and that over the great questions of Faith,
Expediency must have no control. Let us read that lesson to
our children; let us show them it in practice; and when the
field of conflict is about to become their inheritance, we shall
leave it with the conviction that their labors, in imitation and
in aid of ours, will advance the cause of truth and righteousness, and hasten the day when "the tabernacle of God shall be
among men, and when they who overcome shall inherit all
things."

PASCAL

CONSIDERED AS A WRITER AND A MORALIST.

BY M. VILLEMAIN.

In surveying the varieties of human knowledge, we perceive two great divisions under which all the acquirements of the intellect are comprised. In the one, mind is employed upon matter; in the other, upon itself. The one contains the whole science of external objects, from the most common mechanism to that of the heavens; the sole object of the other is the heart of man; and its instruments are Ethics, Eloquence, and Poetry.

Does the same genius possess the power to master these two opposite spheres of knowledge? Or is their separation as insurmountable as their diversity is manifest? When physical science was imperfect and new, it could not alone suffice for the complete activity of a powerful mind; besides, it needed imagination, to cover its ignorance and errors. Pythagoras, who gave the Greeks the science of numbers, taught Ethics in harmonious verses; and the divine Plato supported upon Geometry his brilliant metaphysics. But when science had gathered within her domain a multitude of observations and facts, she was bound to retire within herself, and henceforth maintain an independent existence. Thus by the progress of human knowledge began the divorce of science and letters; and our increased knowledge has been divided, as an empire too vast is separated into independent kingdoms.

There are reckoned men who would make an exception to this law of human weakness; and they, too, confirm it. If they have embraced the extremes, they have not been able to carry them to the same point. One of the two perfections is always opposed to the other; and they are, when united, mediocre and sublime. A man appeared, to give to the human mind two titles of glory at once; but his first flights exhausted the forces of nature, and he had no time to complete his work. Yet what a spectacle is presented by the labors and attempts of this man arrested in the midst of his task! What monuments are the unformed outgushings of his genius!

We here propose to bring together some reflections upon those of Pascal's works that are foreign to the mathematical sciences. Pascal wrote to one of the profoundest geometricians of his time: " I call geometry the most beautiful occupation in the world;[1] but, in fine, it is only an occupation; and I have often said that it is good for the trial, but not the employment of our force." Without joining in this hard.and perhaps capricious anathema against a science so much admired in our times, it is permitted to seek by preference the greatness of the human mind in those monuments of lofty reason and inimitable eloquence, which speak to all centuries, and transmit to the future the man of genius in his completeness. In the exact sciences, the discovery is separated, thus to speak, from the discoverer; it is corrected, extended, perfected by other hands, and becomes a simple link in the successive order of truths that must be discovered by the patience of centuries; but the writer who has stamped great thoughts or generous sentiments with eloquence, has done all at once, and remains immortal himself with his works.

In reflecting upon that premature instinct which turned, from infancy, the genius of Pascal towards geometry, and made him discover the elements of the science which, without knowing it, he desired, it would be superfluous to inquire whether the faculty that he first manifested was necessarily in him the most natural and the highest. All talents suppose innate germs; but a multitude of external circumstances and transitory impressions, a thousand hazards that we do not calculate upon, may determine the development of the faculties of the mind, in an order which does not suppose the pre-eminence of one over another. The father of Pascal wished to occupy his son with the study of letters; but he was himself a passionate geometrician, and he lived only for this science. While denying it to his son, he promised it to him in the future, as a reward of his efforts; he told him that geometry was a science for men. It is always seen, in less important cases, that children imitate instead of obeying, that they repeat actions and forget counsels, that, in fine, their curiosity especially seeks what is denied them. Is it not probable that, in a mind prodigiously active and penetrating like Pascal's, the eagerness to know a secret and prohibited thing still served to excite the mathematical talent? Once developed, this passion for the exact sciences, one of the most powerful over the minds possessed by it, retained that ardent genius by the attraction of the discoveries, the novelty of the experiments, the certainty of the truths, and consumed with excessive labors the greatest portion of that life so short, and so soon devoured.

But how could there come from the midst of these arid and withering studies, the skilful and passionate orator, the creator of French style? Our great writers have all been produced, either by the sudden gush of a first and unique inspiration, or by long patience in a single labor. Pascal is a sublime writer on first quitting his geometrical books. In the eloquent pages that occupied but a portion of the few years accorded to this extraordinary man, you perceive neither the beginning nor the progress of genius,—the limit is reached at the outset; the trace of steps does not appear.

Perhaps this singular phenomenon ought to be explained in part by the very influence of the abstract studies that occupied Pascal, at a period when such high knowledge, still destitute of the perfection and the facility of method, imposed upon the mind the effort of a continued creation. All was originality in a study incomplete and new. A sort of enthusiasm and elevated imagination was attached to all the essays of science. We can imagine how much more fruitful and inspiring must have been the habit of such contemplations than the frivolous labors to which literature had too often been confined under the protection of Richelieu. Could the French genius and language be happily developed by those writers, who sought in style only style itself, and made the study of words a distinct science? In order to find what makes men eloquent, it is necessary to seek what exalts the mind. Ancient liberty created ancient eloquence. Poetic imitation reproduced it in the verses of Corneille. But our institutions left no place for it elsewhere than upon the stage.

When the mind cannot occupy itself with the great interests of country and of liberty, when it is deprived, thus to speak, of public existence, there still remain to it noble sources of inspiration. These are the intimate emotions of the soul, lofty views of nature, and the love of speculative truth. To these sublime fountains Pascal went, and thence drew his eloquence. Good taste, contempt of false ornaments and vain rhetoric, sprang, for him, from the greatness of the objects with which he had occupied his mind. Originality followed him from geometry into letters,—he invented his language, as he had found the principles of science, under an eternal law of fitness and truth. Perhaps if he had received from nature a less vivid imagination, he would have extinguished it forever in the coldness of abstract studies. But a mind like his, far from yielding to geometry, received from it that vigor of deduction and those irresistible arguments that become the arms of his speech.

How much, too, must the mind of Pascal have been animated by intercourse with those illustrious recluses, whom he was destined to surpass and defend! I know how easy it is to refuse admiration for virtues that are no longer in use, for talents that have left only a flame. To-day the highest title of Port-Royal is, that it was the school of Racine. Nicole, Hermant, Sacy, are no longer read. The fame of Arnauld is a question,— his quarrels appear ridiculous. Nevertheless, the most enlightened minds of a polished century studied with admiration these authors so much disdained; and Louis XIV. directed his policy and power against the firmness of a few theologians. Port-Royal had, then, a real grandeur, attested by persecution as well as by enthusiasm.

At the commencement of an epoch in which religion was destined to be clothed with all the splendors of art and genius, a few men of grave manners, of free and elevated minds, most of them united by blood or the closest friendship, formed, far from the world, a society wholly occupied with labor and meditation. Studious lovers of antiquity, their writings bear its manly and strong character. With more reason than elegance, they nevertheless give the first model of good taste and sound literature. They have known affairs and life; they have admitted into their bosoms men beaten by the storms of faction. These pious recluses are the innocent but faithful friends of the

ambitious coadjutor of Paris.[1] Port-Royal received more than
one noble relic of the Fronde; and that independence at once
violent and frivolous, which had agitated the State without the
wisdom to reform it, came to seek an asylum in religion. There
was found nearly all united, like one of the tribes of antiquity,
the family of Arnaulds, astonishing by variety of talents and
uniform elevation of characters. If difference of manners admitted of such a singular parallel, we should call them the Appii
of Port-Royal,—all ardent, skilful, obstinate. They, too, like the
Romans, had to sustain one of those long enmities which in the
ancient republics made part of the heritage of families. Antoine Arnauld, a vehement antagonist of the Jesuits, in a famous
suit, had brought upon his numerous children the hatred of
that vindictive and powerful society, and had transmitted to
them the courage and the talent to brave it.

But, it may be said, of what importance are the five unintelligible propositions of Jansenius, and so many long and sterile controversies? Such ready contempt would be very unphil-
osophical. Circumstances and forms change; the occupations
of the human mind are renewed; but in all times, under different names, there exists a conflict between arbitrary authority
and independence of thought, between those who would introduce absolute submission into the domain of intelligence and
those who claim the natural and free exercise of reason: it is
the quarrel of Socrates and Anytus, of the Stoic philosophers
and the emperors, of Henri IV. and the League, of the Hol-
landers and Philip II. Speculative, religious, political, literary,
this controversy is modified, transformed, ennobled, or abased,
by a thousand chances, by a thousand accidents of civilization
or manners: but it always subsists; it pertains to the dignity
itself of our nature—to that noble privilege which makes
thought in man the first and most precious possession that another can wish to invade, that he may be called upon to defend.

In this endless struggle the recluses of Port-Royal, while appearing to discuss only scholastic subtilties, represented the
liberty of conscience, the spirit of examination, the love of justice and truth. Their adversaries plead the opposite cause—
that of blind domination over minds and souls. Pascal was in-

<hr />

[1] Cardinal de Retz.

dignant at the yoke which such doctrines imposed on reason.
His lofty genius refused to bend beneath this insolent usurpa-
tion of the noblest faculties of man vainly taking refuge in the
sanctuary of conscience and faith. He saw his virtuous friends
devoting themselves with obstinate zeal to profound studies
upon the origin and monuments of religion; he saw them resigned, solitary, humble with a true humility, afraid of finding
ambition in the priestly office, and preferring persecution, as in
the first days of Christianity. The society of the Jesuits, on
the contrary, was menacing, accredited,—distributed favor or
disgrace, and eagerly pursued with calumny and decrees of
exile a body of learned, religious, irreproachable men, whose
only crime was that of maintaining their own opinions and following their own conscience. Could the noble and pure soul
of Pascal remain indifferent at the sight of such a combat?

He had at first approached Port-Royal, preoccupied with
the philosophy of Epictetus and the uncertainties of Montaigne.
The candor of the virtuous Sacy struck him with a new light.
The vast erudition, the indefatigable spirit of Arnauld; the insinuating reason, the judicious elegance, and the gentleness of
Nicole, who seemed the Melancthon of that orthodox and moderate reform; the natural eloquence and imagination of Le-
maistre, agitated in every way that soul passionately in love with
truth. In his fruitful conversations with minds worthy of him,
Pascal showed the superiority of his intellect, whatever might
be the subject; and these men, whose memory was fed with
vast reading, seemed to find again in their most precious recol-
lections the thoughts that Pascal produced at the instant from
himself, as if he had been destined to carry everywhere that
species of divination which, in childhood, he had exercised
upon geometry. The recluses were especially great theologians,
but every thing that can interest the human mind—philosophy,
history, antiquity—became the subject of their conversations.
Arnauld was a profound geometrician, and that clearness, that
vigor of logic, that inflexibility of deduction which Pascal had
loved in geometry, seemed the common character of the language, books, doctrines, and, if you will, of the errors of Port-
Royal. What ties must have united that society, natural
among lofty intellects, brought together by love of meditation
and study! What fidelity, not of party, but of conviction and

virtue, must have been cemented by that noble intercourse!
We can imagine how, from that time, the theological labors of
the recluses became the exclusive study of Pascal, and how the
countless charms of his satirical genius—satirical by force of
reason—lent themselves so readily to reinvest with naturalness
and elegance the learned demonstrations with which the experience of his friends furnished him.

Thus the *Provincial Letters* were produced by the necessity
of appealing from the Sorbonne to the public, and of explaining
those subtile questions of grace that served as a pretext for the
persecution of Arnauld, the most illustrious supporter of Port-
Royal. Those letters appeared under a false name, almost
furtively; they defended an illustrious man oppressed; they
attacked an abuse of theological power in an age when religion
was the primary object of attention; they were not aimless,
but responded to one of the most real interests of the time.
Brevity, clearness, an unknown elegance, a biting and natural
pleasantry, words that stuck to the memory, made them successful and popular. Pascal so clearly explains the question,
that out of gratitude one is obliged to judge as he judges.
I should admire the *Provincial Letters* less if they had not
been written before Molière. Pascal has anticipated good
comedy. He introduces upon the stage several actors,—an indifferent person who receives all the confidences of anger and
passion, sincere party men, false party men more zealous than
others, sincere conciliators everywhere repelled, hypocrites
everywhere welcomed. It is a true comedy of manners, with
change of costume. But the scene becomes still more comic
when, reduced to two characters, it exhibits to us the *naïve*
interpreter of casuists with an apparent disciple, who, sometimes by ingenious contradictions, sometimes by an ironical
docility, excites and favors the indiscreet vivacity of a *bon père*.
Animated by such a listener, the Jesuit develops with a proud
confidence the maxims of his authors, measures the degree
of his admiration by that of their stupidity, and renders
probable by his praises what seems an improbable reproach.
The dialogue of the two interlocutors is greatly prolonged; but
the form assumed is so happy, so varied in the details, and
produces an illusion so natural, that it is impossible to grow
weary of it. Plato, combating the subtilties of the rhetori-

72

72

cians, gives the model of this excellent species of satire. His *Euthydemus*, who boasts of teaching virtue by an abridged method, resembles a father Jesuit explaining *devotion made easy*. But it must be confessed that, for the purposes of ridicule, the casuists of Pascal are still better than the sophists of Plato.

The subject of the *Provincial Letters* is therefore not—very far from it—sterile and unfavorable, as some would willingly suppose, out of admiration for the author's genius: not only did Pascal know how to create, but he chose well. Certainly, of all the aberrations of the mind, one of the most singular is that of wishing to justify vice by virtue, of doing bad acts with good motives, of continually falsifying ethics while protesting respect for them, and, by force of distinctions, of even coming to find in the laws of God the privilege of meritoriously injuring men. Besides, nothing is more amusing than the contrast between the severity of persons and the laxity of principles. Such are the resources that presented themselves to Pascal, and he made use of them with wonderful effect. In attributing to his adversaries the formal and premeditated design of corrupting morals, he doubtless makes an exaggerated supposition; but he gives to all his attacks a point of unity from which they derive vivacity and support. Moreover, can we affirm with Voltaire[1] that the whole book is false, inasmuch as no society ever thought of establishing itself by destroying morals? Is the moral instinct so invincible and determined that it could not be reduced and perverted by an imposing authority? What man has never hesitated in regard to his duties, and has not sometimes desired the privilege of being remiss without blame and without remorse? This feebleness of our hearts sufficiently explains the favor that a complaisant system of ethics may obtain. Has not more than one celebrated writer propagated his philosophy by his ethics, and corrupted in order to succeed?

We can conceive, while deploring such a scandal, that in a religious, but unequally enlightened century, a society which aspired to the domination of consciences, and carried its empire into countries differing in manners, customs, national and domestic prejudices, may, through ambition, have softened the

[1] *Siècle de Louis XIV.*, t. ii.

moral rule that it wished to make adopted by so many opposite
minds. You are tempted to doubt Pascal's veracity, while
reading in his letters that strange citation in which priests,
ministers of mildness and peace, sanctify duelling and authorize
homicide; but the author of those maxims is not only a Jesuit,
but a Spaniard, a Sicilian, of some country where revenge remains hereditarily consecrated—where devotion, innate in the
manners of the inhabitants, could obtain every thing except
the sacrifice of passions like it indigenous and national.

Doubtless, the culpable casuists who flattered these different
prejudices of peoples, had altered the most beautiful character
of the Christian law—the sublime uniformity of its ethics, independent of places, times, and men. It was, therefore, a just
and salutary work undertaken by Pascal, that of sternly combating the lax complaisance which degraded religion, and of
bringing into disrepute that strange jurisprudence which had,
thus to speak, introduced into the sublime truths of morals and
conscience subtilties of chicanery and crafty forms of procedure. With what natural fire—with what pitiless irony—
with what humor worthy of the ancient comedy—did Pascal
fulfil this generous mission! Have not the doctrines of *probability* and the *regulation of motive* become immortal by the
ridicule with which he clothed them? That art of pleasantry,
which the ancients called a part of eloquence—that mockery
and *naïve* atticism which Socrates made use of—that instructive and comic piquancy which Rabelais soiled with the cyni-
cism of his words—that inner and profound humor that animates
Molière and is often found in Lesage—in fine, that perfection of
esprit, which is nothing else than a superior and lively reason,—
such is the imperishable merit of the first *Provincial Letters*.

When we regard the life of Pascal, so limited in its course,
so afflicted by suffering and the sadness inseparable from profound studies—when we read those detached thoughts which
seem the product of the restlessness of a sublime spirit, we can
at first scarcely conceive of that superabundance of humor
with which this man floods the arid fields of scholasticism. Is
laughter, then, so near to sadness in those rare intellects which
regard human nature from a lofty point? We should be
tempted to believe it in reading Pascal, Shakspeare, and Molière. It has been said, in order to explain such an alliance,

that the habit of observing inspires sadness. This sentiment
pertains rather to the elevation itself of the intellectual faculties, because such minds feel more sensibly the limits and the
impotence of thought, and are saddened by their very force,
even while they laugh or are indignant at the common weakness.   .

Pascal had completed his first ten letters—Arnauld was defended, avenged. His apologist had carried the war into the
camp of his enemies; and the rapid, humorous, familiar exposition of the erroneous principles of their doctors on moral
questions had amused the public, and struck the powerful
society with the plague of ridicule. Then it was that the discussion took a more serious turn—that Pascal changed, thus to
speak, his genius. The Jesuits, especially occupied with caus-
ing the writings of this dangerous opponent to be interdicted
and suppressed, nevertheless attempted to refute them; but,
with little art, little logic, like men disconcerted by the surprise of an attack so bold. It must be avowed, moreover, that
the society had not then in its bosom the celebrated men who
have made it illustrious. Bourdaloue was unknown, and had
not yet learned his potent dialectics in Pascal himself. The
defenders of the society, feeble, unskilful, contumelious, and
unreadable, only served to rouse the genius of its terrible adversary. It was in answering them, that, under this form of
simple letters, Pascal reached without effort the highest eloquence of logic and wrath. You have read a hundred times
the passage in which Pascal, after having described with marvellous energy the long and strange war between violence and
truth—two powers, he says, which have no ascendency over
each other—nevertheless predicts the triumph of truth, because
it is eternal and powerful like God himself. Has Demosthenes,
Chrysostom, or Bossuet, inspired by the tribune, uttered any
thing stronger or more sublime than those words thrown in at
the end of a polemical letter?

This grand eloquence is the natural tone of the last *Provincial Letters*. Every thing in them is bitter, vehement, passionate. Those same questions with which Pascal had at first
played, which he had as it were exhausted by pleasantry, he
resumes and renews with seriousness and anger, so as to make
his enemies look back with regret upon that railing style of

which they had at first complained. Now he ulcerates and tears open the first wounds of humiliated self-love. Those odious doctrines concerning homicide, which he had almost indulgently handled in only covering them with contempt, he attacks *corps à corps*, with all the power of inexorable dialectics, as a crime against State and Church, nature and piety. His vehemence seems to increase in pursuing another offence, too common in times of division and party—calumny, that moral assassination of which his adversaries had made both frequent use and *naïvely* apologized for; two things that correct but do not redeem each other. In this controversy, Pascal seems sometimes to approach a vehemence more injurious than Christian. In repelling calumny, he is prodigal of invective. His generous soul, profoundly indignant at the misfortune of his friends, is no longer able to moderate his words. Strong in his genius, in his resentment, in the mystery that still shielded his name, he cries out, addressing himself to all his adversaries: " You feel yourselves struck by an invisible hand ; you attempt in vain to attack me in the person of those with whom you believe me to be united. I fear you neither for myself nor for any other. All the credit you may have is useless so far as I am concerned. I hope nothing from the world; I apprehend nothing from it; I wish nothing from it. I need, by the grace of God, neither the wealth nor the authority of any one. Thus, my fathers, I escape all your snares.''

Need we be astonished that, in a position so elevated, and the only one that was worthy of him, Pascal was carried away, even to the emotions and the violent liberty of the ancient tribune ? The circumstances, the times, were greatly changed, but the eloquence was the same.

Is the question concerning some great interest of patriotism or glory ? No ; the question is concerning the defence of a few humble nuns accused of heresy. But what imports the subject ? Listen to the tone of the orator and the indignation of the good man: " Cruel and base persecutors, must it be then that the most retired cloisters are not asylums against your calumnies ? etc. You publicly cut off from the Church those holy virgins, while they are praying in secret for you and the whole Church. You calumniate those who have no ears to hear you, no mouth to reply to you."

If Pascal, in his letters, has united all the secrets of the most
energetic and most passionate eloquence, some of his Thoughts
inform us that this talent was supported by meditation upon all
the resources of art, and by a very profound theory which he
invented for his own use.   It is futile enough to read principles
upon taste written by men without genius.   But when a great
writer explains some general ideas on the art of speech, he
necessarily adapts them to his own character, to the habits of
his own mind; he puts in them something of himself; and this
revelation is more instructive than the very principles of art.
Pascal, so profound a geometrician, had conceived, by the superiority of his reason, the use and limits of the scientific spirit
carried into the arts.   What he wrote on the spirit of geometry
and the spirit of taste is the completest refutation of the literary
paradoxes which Fontenelle, D'Alembert, and Condillac published in the following century.   Pascal, whose genius had no
prejudices, because it had no limits,[1] fixes the character of positive sciences and that of letters, without being arrested through
fear of taking something from himself, in limiting the dominion
of such or such a faculty, and as it were sure of finding his
place in all the departments of human intelligence.   Pascal, in
fact, combined in the highest degree the two extreme powers
of thought—reasoning and imagination.   His life, his character,
his works, show this alliance ; and it is found in a marked degree in the greatest work to which his genius was directed.
No one, in the same century, received perhaps, with a more
ardent and sincere enthusiasm, the truths of Christianity ; but
the habit of reasoning, breaking through his enthusiasm, still
agitated him with the torments of doubt.   Can we otherwise
explain that forecast which revealed to him so many objections
little known to his age, and inspired him with the thought of
fortifying and defending what no one had yet attacked?   The
illustrious contemporaries of Pascal, filled with a conviction not
less pure, but more peaceable, limited themselves to developing
the consequences of a religion whose principles encountered no
adversaries,—they raised the roof of the temple without fearing
that any hand might be bold enough to undermine its columns.

---

[1] Villemain may here seem somewhat extravagant in his praise, but even Sir
W. Hamilton has called Pascal a "miracle of universal genius."

Pascal alone, warned of peril by his own experience, meditated a work in which he hoped to leave unanswered none of the doubts of skepticism which this great genius had, thus to speak, tried in every sense upon himself. The hand of the architect is still entirely visible in the ruins of that monument commenced. But who would dare to reconstruct it in idea, and calculate the combination of its scattered and formless parts?

In the sands of Egypt we discover superb porticos that no longer lead to a temple which the ages have destroyed, vast *débris*, remains of an immense city, and, upon the fallen capitals, antique paintings, whose dazzling colors will never pass away, which preserve their frail immortality in the midst of these ancient ruins : such appear the Thoughts of Pascal— mutilated relics of his great work.

It is known that he began it, already mortally infected with that mournful languor which was so soon to consume his life. Having upon the earth no other action than that of the intellect, he continued it until he drew his last breath. Such, however, was the intensity of his ills, that some other preoccupation than that of ethical truths became necessary to him. More than once, we are told by the historians of his life, he resumed with ardor the most laborious meditations of geometry, and gave himself wholly up to them, in order to distract physical pains. Was it not rather against other pains that he sought such a remedy? Did he not find in them repose from the disturbed activity of his soul too much assailed by thoughts?

In fact, consider this sublime intellect, captive in a miserable body, fatigued by so many prodigious efforts, and continually finding before it all those great problems of human destiny, that cannot be resolved, like those of science :

" I know not who has put me into the world, nor what the world is, nor what I am myself. I am in terrible ignorance of all things. I know not what is my body, what my senses, what my soul,—and that very part of me, which thinks what I am saying, which reflects upon every thing, and upon itself, no more knows itself than the rest."

This terrible ignorance, which Pascal retraces with too much energy not to have suffered from it, was the enemy whose yoke, more overwhelming than faith, he labored to shake off. The same uncertainties had agitated the ancient philosophers, had sometimes troubled them even to despair. This torment of the loftiest intellects had returned with increased energy in all the great renewals of civilization, at the moment when men, after having journeyed a long time supported by the old beliefs, feel them escaping, equally impotent to dispense with them, or to make use of them. Thus, towards the last centuries of the Empire, when polytheism was falling on every hand, and the last disciples of Plato were in vain endeavoring to create a faith, and to re-establish a worship by the force of reason, the most eloquent of these philosophers, Porphyry, is represented to us in a melancholy that reaches delirium, ready to commit suicide, in order to escape from the torture of doubt. Thus, with some of those speculative Germans who have worked upon the ruins accumulated by a century of skepticism, madness seems sometimes born from the too habitual and too ardent contemplation of the great mysteries of human existence. Doubt turned in every direction, and, everywhere sterile, pushes on these eager minds towards a sort of mystic theurgy; as if to believe were a repose necessary to the soul, as if the illusions of enthusiasm were the first good for it after truth.

Pascal, whose superiority of genius had made him traverse in advance the whole field of disquietudes that the human mind can experience, in a civilization of several centuries,— Pascal, instructed in all by the conflict to which he had abandoned the powers of his soul, threw himself into the arms of Christian faith. It alone explained to him the origin of human life, the greatness and the misery of man. But what restless efforts in order to arrive at this repose! "In regarding," he says, "the whole mute world, and man without light abandoned to himself, and as it were strayed into this corner of the universe, without knowing who has placed him here, what he has come to do here, and what he will become in dying, I am frightened, like a man who should be borne sleeping into a desert island, and should awake without knowing where he is. I see other persons about me, of a nature similar to my own. I ask them whether they are better instructed than I, and they tell me no,—and thereupon these unhappy wanderers (*égarés*), having looked about them, and having seen some pleasing objects, give themselves up to them, and become attached to them. As for me, I have not been able to stop there, nor to

be at rest in the society of these beings similar to myself, unhappy and powerless like myself."

Do we not feel, in these words, all the suffering, all the labor
of this great genius, to find the truth? Can we now be surprised at the depth of sadness and eloquence that animates
under his pen a few metaphysical Thoughts thrown out at
hazard? What are all the interests of earth, what are all
passions, in comparison with that great interest of the spiritual
being searching after itself? In an intellect that sees every
thing, the combat against doubt is the greatest effort of human
thought. Pascal himself sometimes succumbs to it,—he seeks
strange aids against so great a peril. You are astonished that
he once tosses up (*mette à croix ou pile*) to determine the existence of God and the immortality of the soul, and settles his
conviction by a calculus of probability. You remember how
Rousseau, more feeble and more capricious, made his hope of
eternal salvation depend upon the throwing of a stone. Herein
must be recognized the impotence, and, thus to speak, the despair of thought, after long efforts to penetrate the incompre-
hensible. It was the torment of Pascal, a torment so much
the greater, as it was proportioned to his genius. A positive
religion could alone emancipate and comfort him. It gave him
some security, in subjecting him to the power of belief. When
we read that Pascal carried under his garments a symbol formed
of mystic words, a species of amulet, we feel that his powerful intellect had recoiled even to such superstitious practices, in
order to flee farther from a terrific uncertainty. Herein was
his terror. The imaginary precipice which, after a sad accident, the enfeebled senses of Pascal believed they saw opening
beneath his steps, was a faint image of this abyss of doubt that
internally terrified his soul.

Thus passed away the too-brief life of this great man. At
first he sought to emancipate human reason,—he reclaimed the
independence of thought and the authority of conscience; then
he consumed himself with efforts to construct dykes and barriers against the limitless invasion of skepticism. This powerful
and inflexible mind embraces with a profound conviction, as a
safeguard, the dogmas of Christianity, and gives them, by his
submission, perhaps the greatest of human testimonies. But if
the conviction is entire, the demonstration is imperfect, the

proofs are not united, the reasoning is not conclusive: there remain some indications of the struggle through which Pascal had
passed, and extraordinary marks of his force, rather than a perfect monument of his victory. Be they what they may, these
remains exist to astonish frivolous Pyrrhonism, to put it in
doubt of itself, and to afford the learned and wise a subject of
long meditation.

It has been said that Pascal did not speak to the heart, that
his religion had the appearance of a yoke imposed, rather than
of a consolation promised. Vincent de Paul and Fénelon would
doubtless have obtained more conversions than Pascal. We do
not feel in him that tenderness of soul, that affection for men
which the Gospel breathes, which constitutes the power of the
New Law. He always profoundly interests,—he is so far from
being a declaimer and so true! His bitter words against human
nature are not invectives; they are cries of grief concerning
himself. We are struck with a sort of sad respect, when we
see the internal ill of this sublime intellect. His misanthropy
seems an expiation of his genius,—he is himself more humiliated
than exalted by it. He is not like the Stoic of antiquity, an
impassive contemplater of our miseries,—he bears them all in
himself: "But," he says, "in spite of all these miseries that
touch us, that hold us by the throat, we have an irrepressible
instinct that supports us." This instinct of spiritualism opposed
to our mortal weakness, this contrast of greatness and nothingness, alone fills Pascal's sublimest chapters on the nature of
man. It inspires him with emotions of an incomparable eloquence, and thoughts of fearful depth. We are astonished to
see him descend from such high metaphysics to truths of observation, to seize the minutest secrets of the heart, and penetrate
the whole nature of man with a vast and sad regard.

Pascal does not, like la Bruyère, describe and portray,—but
he seizes and expresses the principle of human actions. He
writes the history of the race, not that of the individual. Judging the things of earth with a liberty and a disinterestedness
wholly philosophic, he often arrives by a very different route to
the same end at which the boldest innovators arrive,—but he
does not stop there; he sees beyond. Sometimes he seems to
disturb the fundamental principles of society, of property, of
justice; but soon he strengthens them by a higher thought.

He is sublime by good sense as well as by genius. His style bears in itself the impress of these two characters. Nowhere will you find more boldness and simplicity, more grandeur and naturalness, more enthusiasm and familiarity. A celebrated writer has remarked that he is perhaps the only original genius that taste has almost never the right to blame, and this is true; but we do not think of it while reading him.[1]

[1] We here add Pascal's "Profession of Faith," which was found in his handwriting after his death.—ED.

"I love poverty, because Jesus Christ loved it. I love property, because it affords the means of assisting the wretched. I keep faith with all. I do not render evil to those who injure me; but I wish them a condition like mine, in which neither evil nor good is received on the part of man. I try to be just, true, sincere and faithful to all men; and I have a tenderness of heart for those with whom God has closely united me; and whether I am alone, or in the sight of man, I perform all my actions as in the sight of God who is to judge them, and to whom I· have devoted them all.

"These are my convictions; and I bless every day of my life my Redeemer who has inspired me with them, and who, of a man full of weakness, wretchedness, concupiscence, pride, and ambition, has made a man exempt from all these evils by the force of his grace, to which all the glory is due, for in myself are only wretchedness and error."

4⁰

HISTORICAL INTRODUCTION

TO

THE PROVINCIAL LETTERS.,

BY THE TRANSLATOR.

THE Church of Rome, notwithstanding her pretensions to infallibility, has been fully as prolific in theological contro- versy and intestine discord as any of the Reformed Churches. She has contrived, indeed, with singular policy, to preserve, amidst all her variations, the semblance of unity. Protest- anism, like the primitive Church, suffered its dissentients to fly off into hostile or independent communions. The Papacy, on the contrary, has managed to retain hers within the out- ward pale of her fellowship, by the institution of various religious orders, which have served as safety-valves for exu- berant zeal, and which, though often hostile to each other, have remained attached to the mother Church, and even proved her most efficient supporters. Still, at different times, storms have arisen within the Romish Church, which could be quelled neither by the infallibility of popes nor the author- ity of councils. It is doubtful if religious controversy ever raged with so much violence in the Reformed Church, as it did between the Thomists and the Scotists, the Dominicans and Franciscans, the Jesuits and the Jansenists, of the Church of Rome.

Uninviting as they may now appear, the disputes about grace, in which the last mentioned parties were involved, gave occasion to the Provincial Letters. The origin of these dis putes must be traced as far back as the days of Augustine and the Pelagian controversy of the fifth century. The motto of Pelagius was free-will ; that of Augustine was efficacious grace. The former held that, notwithstanding the fall, the human will was perfectly free to choose at any time between good and evil ; the latter, that in consequence of the fall, the will is in a state of moral bondage, from which it can only be freed by divine grace. With the British monk, election is suspended on the decision of man's will; human nature is still as pure as it came originally from the hands of the Creator : Christ died equally for all men ; and, as the result of his death, a general grace is granted to all mankind, which any may comply with, but which all may finally forfeit. With the African bishop, election is absolute—we are predestinated, not from foreseen holiness, but that we might be holy ;[1] all men are lying under the guilt or penal obligation of the first sin, and in a state of spiritual helplessness and corruption ; the sacrifice of Christ was, in point of destination, offered for the elect, though, in point of exhibition, it is offered to all ; and the saints obtain the gift of perseverance in holiness to the end.[2]

Pelagius, whose real name was Morgan, and who is supposed to have been a Welshman, belonged to that numerous class of thinkers, who, from their peculiar idiosyncrasy, are apt to start at the sovereignty of divine grace, developed in the plan of redemption, as if it struck at once at the equity of God and the responsibility of man. He is said to have betrayed his heretical leanings, for the first time, by publicly expressing his disapprobation of a sentiment of Augustine, which he heard quoted by a bishop: "*Da quod jubes, et jube quod vis*—Give, Lord, what thou biddest, and bid what thou wilt." It would be easy to show that, in recoiling from the odious picture of the orthodox doctrine, drawn by his own fancy, he fell into the very consequences which he was so eager to avoid. The deity of Pelagius being subjected

[1] Non quia per nos sancti et immaculati futuri essemus, sed elegit prædestinavitque ut essemus. (De Prædest., Aug. Op., tom. x. 815.)
[2] De dono Persever. (Ib., 822.)

to the changeable will of the creature, all things were left to
the direction of blind chance or unthinking destiny ; while
man, being represented as created with concupiscence, to
account for his aberrations from rectitude—in other words,
with a constitution in which the seeds of evil were implanted
—the authorship of sin was ascribed, directly and primarily,
to the Creator.[1]

Augustine was a powerful but unsteady writer, and has
expressed himself so inconsistently as to have divided the
opinions of the Latin Church, where he was recognized as a
standard, canonized as a saint, and revered under the title
of "The Doctor of Grace." On the great doctrine of salvation by grace, he is scriptural and evangelical ; and hence he
has been frequently quoted with admiration by our Reformed
divines, partly to evince the declension of Rome from the
faith of the earlier fathers, partly from that veneration for
antiquity, which induces us to bestow more notice on the
ivy-mantled ruin, than on the more graceful and commodious
modern edifice in its vicinity. When arguing against Pelagianism, Augustine is strong in the panoply of Scripture ; when
developing his own system, he fails to do justice either to
Scripture or to himself. Loud, and even fierce, for the entire
corruption of human nature, he spoils all by admitting the
absurd dogma of baptismal regeneration. Chivalrous in the
defence of grace, as opposed to free-will, he virtually abandons the field to the enemy, by teaching that we are justified .
by our works of evangelical obedience, and that the faith
which justifies includes in its nature all the offices of Christian
charity.

During the dark ages, the Church of Rome, professing the
highest veneration for St. Augustine, had ceased to hold the
Augustinian theology. The Dominicans, indeed, yielded a
vague allegiance to it, by adhering to the views of Thomas
Aquinas, "the angelic doctor" of the schools; from whom
they were termed Thomists ; while the Franciscans, who opposed them, under the auspices of Duns Scotus, from whom

[1] Neander, Bibl. Repos., iii. 94 ; Leydecker, de Jansen. Dogm., 413

they were termed Scotists, leaned to the views of Pelagius.
The Scotists, like the modern advocates of free-will, inveighed
against their opponents as fatalists, and charged them with
making God the author of sin ; the Thomists, again, retorted
on the Scotists, by accusing them of annihilating the grace
of God. But the doctrines of grace had sunk out of view,
under a mass of penances, oblations, and intercessions, founded
on the assumption of human merit, and on that very confusion of the forensic change in justification with the moral
change in sanctification, in which Augustine had unhappily
led the way. At length the Reformation appeared ; and as
both Luther and Calvin appealed to the authority of Augustine, when treating of grace and free-will, the Romish divines,
in their zeal against the Reformers, became still more decidedly Pelagian. In the Council of Trent, the admirers of
Augustine durst hardly show themselves ; the Jesuits carried
everything before them ; and the anathemas of that synod,
which were aimed at Calvin fully as much as Luther, though
they professed to condemn only the less guarded statements
of the German reformer, were all in favor of Pelagius.

The controversy was revived in the Latin Church, about
the close of the sixteenth century, both in the Low Countries
and in Spain. In 1588, Lewis Molina, a Spanish Jesuit,
published lectures on " The Concord of Grace and Free-
Will ;" and this work, filled with the jargon of the schools,
gave rise to disputes which continued to agitate the Church
during the whole of the succeeding century. Molina conceived that he had discovered a method of reconciling the
divine purposes with the freedom of the human will, which
would settle the question forever. According to his theory,
God not only foresaw from eternity all things possible, by a
foresight of intelligence, and all things future by a foresight
of vision ; but by another kind of foresight, intermediate between these two, which he termed *scientia media*, or middle
knowledge, he foresaw what *might* have happened under
certain circumstances or conditions, though it never may take
place. All men, according to Molina, are favored with a

general grace, sufficient to work out their salvation, if they choose to improve it; but when God designs to convert a sinner, he vouchsafes that measure of grace which he foresees, according to the middle knowledge, or in all the circumstances of the case, the person will comply with. The honor of this discovery was disputed by another Jesuit, Peter Fonseca, who declared that the very same thing had burst upon his mind with all the force of inspiration, when lecturing on the subject some years before.[1]

Abstruse as these questions may appear, they threatened a serious rupture in the Romish Church. The Molinists were summoned to Rome in 1598, to answer the charges of the Dominicans; and after some years of deliberation, Pope Clement VIII. decided against Molina. The Jesuits, however, alarmed for the credit of their order, never rested till they prevailed on the old pontiff to re-examine the matter; and in 1602, he appointed a grand council of cardinals, bishops, and divines, who convened for discussion no less than seventy-eight times. This council was called *Congregatio de Auxiliis*, or council on the aids of grace. Its records being kept secret, the result of their collective wisdom was not known with certainty, and has been lost to the world.[2] The probability is, that like Milton's "grand infernal peers," who reasoned high on similar points,

"They found no end, in wandering mazes lost."

Those who appealed to them for the settlement of the question, had too much reason to say, as the man in Terence does to his lawyers—"*Fecistis probe ; incertior sum multo quam dudum.*"[3]

But this interminable dispute was destined to assume a more popular form, and lead to more practical results. In

[1] The question of the middle knowledge is learnedly handled by Voetius (Disp. Theol., i. 264). by Hoornbeck (Socin. Confut.), and other Protestant divines. who have shown it to be untenable, useless, and fraught with absurdity.
[2] Dupin, Eccl. Hist., 17th cent. 1–14.
[3] "Well done, gentlemen ; you have left me more in the dark than ever."

1604, two young men entered, as fellow-students, the university of Louvain, which had been distinguished for its hostility to Molinism. Widely differing in natural temperament as well as outward rank, Cornelius Jansen, who was afterwards bishop of Ypres, and John Duverger de Hauranne, afterwards known as the Abbé de St. Cyran, formed an acquaintance which soon ripened into friendship. They began to study together the works of Augustine, and to compare them with the Scriptures. The immediate result was, an agreement in opinion that the ancient father was in the right, and that the Jesuits, and other followers of Molina, were in the wrong. This was followed by an ardent desire to revive the doctrines of their favorite doctor—a task which each of them prosecuted in the way most suited to his respective character.

Jansen, or Jansenius, as he is often called,[1] was descended of humble parentage, and born October 28, 1585, in a village near Leerdam, in Holland. By his friends he is extolled for his penetrating genius, tenacious memory, magnanimity, and piety. Taciturn and contemplative in his habits, he was frequently overheard, when taking his solitary walks in the garden of the monastery, to exclaim: "*O veritas! veritas!* —O truth! truth!" Keen in controversy, ascetic in devotion, and rigid in his Catholicism, his antipathies were about equally divided between heretics and Jesuits. Towards the Protestants, his acrimony was probably augmented by the consciousness of having embraced views which might expose himself to the suspicion of heresy; or, still more probably, by that uneasy feeling with which we cannot help regarding those who, holding the same doctrinal views with ourselves, may have made a more decided and consistent profession of them. The first supposition derives countenance from the private correspondence between him and his friend St. Cyran, which shows some dread of persecution ;[2] the second is con-

---

[1] He was the son of a poor artisan, whose name was Jan, or John Ottho; hence Jansen, corresponding to our Johnson, which was Latinized into Jansenius.

[2] Petitot, Collect. des Mémoires, Notice sur Port-Royal, tom. xxxiii.

firmed by his acknowledged writings. He speaks of Protestants as no better than Turks, and gives it as his opinion that "they had much more reason to congratulate themselves on the mercy of princes, than to complain of their severities, which, as the vilest of heretics, they richly deserved."[1] His controversy with the learned Gilbert Voet led the latter to publish his *Desperata Causa Papatus*, one of the best exposures of the weaknesses of Popery. When to this we add that the Calvinistic synod of Dort, in 1618, had condemned Arminius and the Dutch Remonstrants as having fallen into the errors of Pelagius and Molina, the position of Jansen became still more complicated. Of Arminius he could not approve, without condemning Augustine; with the Protestant synod he could not agree, unless he chose to be denounced as a Calvinist.

But the natural enemies of Jansen were, without doubt, the Jesuits. To the history of this Society we can only now advert in a very cursory manner. It may appear surprising that an order so powerful and·politic should have owed its origin to such a person as Ignatius Loyola, a Spanish soldier: and that a wound in the leg,·which this hidalgo received at the battle of Pampeluna, should have issued in his becoming the founder of a Society which has embroiled the world and the Church. But in fact, Loyola, though the originator of the sect, is not entitled to the honor, or rather the disgrace, of organizing its constitution. This must be assigned to Laynez and Aquaviva, the two generals who succeeded him— men as superior to the founder of the Society in talents as he excelled them in enthusiasm. Ignatius owed his success to circumstances. While he was watching his arms as the knight-errant of the Virgin, in her chapel at Montserrat, or

p. 19. This author's attempt to fix the charge of a conspiracy between Jansen and St. Cyran to overturn the Church, is a piece of special pleading, bearing on its face its own refutation.

[1] The followers of Jansen were not more charitable than he in their judgments of the Reformed, and showed an equal zeal with the Jesuit to persecute them, when they had it in their power. (Benoit, Hist. d l' Edit de Nantes, iii. 200.)

squatting within his cell in a state of body too noisome for human contact, and of mind verging on insanity, Luther was making Germany ring with the first trumpet-notes of the Reformation. The monasteries, in which ignorance had so long slumbered in the lap of superstition, were awakened; but their inmates were totally unfit for doing battle on the new field of strife that had opened around them. Unwittingly, in the heat of his fanaticism, the illiterate Loyola suggested a line of policy which, matured by wiser heads, proved more adapted to the times. Bred in the court and the camp, he contrived to combine the finesse of the one, and the discipline of the other, with the sanctity of a religious community; and proposed that, instead of the lazy routine of monastic life, his followers should actively devote themselves to the education of youth, the conversion of the heathen, and the suppression of heresy. Such a proposal, backed by a vow of devotion to the Holy See, commended itself to the pope so highly that, in 1540, he confirmed the institution by a bull, granted it ample privileges, and appointed Loyola to be its first general. In less than a century, this sect, which assumed to itself, with singular arrogance, the name of "The Society of Jesus," rose to be the most enterprising and formidable order in the Romish communion.

Never was the name of the blessed Jesus more grossly prostituted than when applied to a Society which is certainly the very opposite, in spirit and character, to Him who was "meek and lowly," "holy, harmless, undefiled, and separate from sinners." The Jesuits may be said to have invented, for their own peculiar use, an entirely new system of ethics. In place of the divine law, they prescribed, as the rule of their conduct, a "blind obedience" to the will of their superiors, whom they are bound to recognize as "standing in the place of God," and in fulfilling whose orders they are to have no more will of their own "than a corpse, or an old man's staff." The glory of God they identify with the aggrandizement of their Society; and holding that "the end sanctifies the means," they scruple at no means, foul or fair, which they conci ive may advance such an end.[1] The supreme power is vested in the general, who is not responsible to any other authority, civil or ecclesiastical. A system of mutual espionage, and a secret correspondence with head-quarters at Rome, in which everything that can, in the remotest degree, affect the interests of the Society is made known, and by means of which the whole machinery of Jesuitism can be set in motion at once, or its minutest feelers directed to any object at pleasure, presents the most complete system of organization in the world. Every member is sworn, by secret oath, to obey the orders, and all are confederated in a solemn league to advance the cause of the Society. It has been defined to be "a naked sword, the hilt of which is at Rome." Such a monstrous combination could not fail to render itself obnoxious. Constantly aiming at ascendency in the Church, in which it is an *imperium in imperio,* the Society has not only been embroiled in perpetual feuds with the other orders, but has repeatedly provoked the thunders of the Vatican. Ever intermeddling with the affairs of civil-governments, with allegiance to which, under any form, its principles are utterly at variance, it has been expelled in turn from almost every European State, as a political nuisance. But Jesuitism is the very soul of Popery; both have revived or declined together; and accordingly, though the order was abolished by Clement XIV. in 1775, it was found necessary to resuscitate it under Pius VII. in 1814; and the Society was never in greater power, nor more active operation, than it is at the present moment. It boasts of immortality, and, in all probability, it will last as long as the Church of Rome. It has been termed "a militia called out to combat the Reformation," and exhibiting, as it does to this day, the same features of ambition, treachery, and intolerance, it seems destined to fall only in

---

[1] *Cæca quadam obedientia.—Ut Christum Dominum in superiore quolibet agnoscere studeatis.—Perinde ac si cadaver essent, vel similiter atque senis baculus.—Ad majorem Dei gloriam.* (Constit. Jesuit. pars vi. cap. 1; Ignat. Epist., &c.)

the ruins of that Church of whose unchanging spirit it is the genuine type and representative.[1] In prosecuting the ends of their institution, the Jesuits have adhered with singular fidelity to its distinguishing spirit. As the instructors of youth, their solicitude has ever been less to enlarge the sphere of human knowledge than to bar out what might prove dangerous to clerical domination; they have confined their pupils to mere literary studies, which might amuse without awakening their minds, and make them subtle dialecticians without disturbing a single prejudice of the dark ages. As missionaries, they have been much more industrious and successful in the manual labor of baptizing all nations than in teaching them the Gospel.[2] As theologians, they have uniformly preferred the views of Molina; regarding these, if not as more agreeable to Scripture and right reason, at least (to use the language of a late writer) as "more consonant with the common sense and natural feelings of mankind."[3] As controversialists, they were the decided foes of all reform and all reformers, from within or without the Church. As moralists, they cultivated, as might be expected, the loosest system of casuistry, to qualify themselves for directing the consciences of high and low, and becoming, through the confessional, the virtual governors of mankind. In all these departments they have, doubtless, produced men of abilities; but the very means which they employed to ag-

[1] Balde, whom the Jesuits honor in their schools as a modern Horace, thus celebrates the longevity of the Society, in his *Carmen Seculare de Societate Jesu*, 1640:—

"Profuit quisquis voluit nocere.
Cuncta subsident sociis; ubique
Exules vivunt, et ubique cives!
Sternimus victi, supreamus imi,
    Surgimus plures toties cadendo."

[2] Their famous missionary, Francis Xavier, whom they canonized, was ignorant of a single word in the languages of the Indians whom he professed to evangelize. He employed a hand-bell to summon the natives around him; and the poor savages, mistaking him for one of their learned Brahmans, he baptized them until his arm was exhausted with the task, and boasted of every one he baptized as a regenerated convert!

[3] Macintosh, Hist. of England, ii. 353.

grandize the Society have tended to dwarf the intellectual growth of its individual members: and hence, while it is true that "the Jesuits had to boast of the most vigorous controversialists, the most polite scholars, the most refined courtiers, and the most flexible casuists of their age,"[1] it has been commonly remarked, that they have never produced a single great man.

Casuistry, the art in which the Jesuits so much excelled, is, strictly speaking, that branch of theology which treats of cases of conscience, and originally consisted in nothing more than an application of the general precepts of Scripture to particular cases. The ancient casuists, so long as they confined themselves to the simple rules of the Gospel, were at least harmless, and their ingenious writings are still found useful in cases of ecclesiastical discipline; but they gradually introduced into the science of morals the metaphysical jargon of the schools, and instead of aiming at making men moral, contented themselves with disputing about morality.[2] The main source of the aberrations of casuistry lay in the unscriptural dogma of priestly absolution—in the right claimed by man to forgive *sin*, as a transgression of the law of God; and the arbitrary distinction between sins as venial and mortal—a distinction which assigns to the priest the prerogative, and imposes on him the obligation, of drawing the critical line, or fixing a kind of tariff on human actions, and apportioning penance or pardon, as the case may seem to require. In their desperate attempt to define the endless forms of depravity on which they were called to adjudicate, or which the pruriency of the cloister suggested to the imagination, the casuists sank deeper into the mire at every step; and their productions, at length, resembled the common sewers of a city, which, when exposed, become more pestiferous

---

[1] Macintosh, Hist. of England, ii. 357.
[2] Augustine himself is chargeable with having been the first to introduce the scholastic mode of treating morality in the form of trifling questions, more fitted to gratify curiosity, and display acumen, than to edify or enlighten. His example was followed. and miserably abused, by the moralists of succeeding ages. (Buddei Isagoge, vol. i. p. 565.)

than the filth which they were meant to remove. Even under the best management, such a system was radically bad;
in the hands of the Jesuits it became unspeakably worse.
To their "modern casuists," as they were termed, must we
ascribe the invention of *probabilism, mental reservation,* and
the *direction of the intention,* which have been sufficiently explained and rebuked in the Provincial Letters. We shall
only remark here, that the actions to which these principles
were applied were not only such as have been termed indifferent, and the criminality of which may be doubtful, or dependent on the intention of the actor : the probabilism of the
Jesuits was, in fact, a systematic attempt to legalize crime,
under the sanction of some grave doctor, who had found out
some excuse for it ; and their theory of mental reservations,
and direction of the intention, was equally employed to sanctify the plainest violations of the divine law. Casuistry, it is
true, has generally vibrated betwixt the extremes of impracticable severity and contemptible indulgence ; but the charge
against the Jesuits was, not that they softened the rigors of
ascetic virtue, but that they propagated principles which
sapped the foundation of all moral obligation. "They are a
people," said Boileau, "who lengthen the creed and shorten
the decalogue."

Such was the community with which the Bishop of Ypres
ventured to enter the lists. Already had he incurred their
resentment by opposing their interests in some political nego-
tiations ; and by publishing his "Mars Gallicus," he had
mortally offended their patron, Cardinal Richelieu ; but,
strange to say, his deadly sin against the Society was a posthumous work. Jansen was cut off by the plague, May 8,
1638. Shortly after his decease, his celebrated work, entitled "Augustinus," was published by his friends Fromond
and Calen, to whom he had committed it on his death-bed.
To the preparation of this work he may be said to have devoted his life. It occupied him twenty-two years, during
which, we are told, he had ten times read through the works
of Augustine (ten volumes, folio!) and thirty times collated

those passages which related to Pelagianism.[1]   The book itself, as the title imports, was little more than a digest of the
writings of Augustine on the subject of grace.[2]   It was divided into three parts; the first being a refutation of Pelagianism, the second demonstrating the spiritual disease of man,
and the third exhibiting the remedy provided.   The sincerity
of Jansen's love to truth is beyond question, though we may
be permitted to question the form in which it was evinced.
The radical defect of the work is, that instead of resorting to
the living fountain of inspiration, he confined himself to the
cistern of tradition.   Enamored with the excellences of Augustine, he adopted even his inconsistencies.   With the former he challenged the Jesuits; with the latter he warded off
the charge of heresy.   As a controvertist, he is chargeable
with prejudice, rather than dishonesty.   As a reformer, he
wanted the independence of mind necessary to success.   Instead of standing boldly forward on the ground of Scripture,
he attempted, with more prudence than wisdom, to shelter
himself behind the venerable name of Augustine.

If by thus preferring the shield of tradition to the sword
of the Spirit, Jansen expected to out-manœuvre the Jesuits,
he had mistaken his policy.   "Augustinus," though profess-
edly written to revive the doctrine of Augustine, was felt by
the Society as, in reality, an attack upon them, under the
name of Pelagians.   To conscious delinquency, the language
of implied censure is ever more galling than formal impeach-
ment.   Jansen's portrait of Augustine was but too faithfully
executed; and the disciples of Loyola could not fail to see
how far they had departed from the faith of the ancient
Church; but the discovery only served to incense them at
the man who had exhibited their defection before the world.
The approbation which the book received from forty learned
doctors, and the rapture with which it was welcomed by the

[1] Lancelot, Tour to Alet, p. 173; Leydecker, p. 122.
[2] The whole title was: "Augustinus Cornelii Jansenii episcopi, seu
doctrina sancti Augustini de humanæ naturæ sanctitate ægritudinæ
medica, adversus Pelagianos et Massilienses." Louvain, 1640.

friends of the author, only added to their exasperation. The
whole efforts of the Society were summoned to defeat its
influence. Balked by the hand of death of their revenge on
the person of the author, they vented it even on his remains.
By a decree of the pope, procured through their instigation,
a splendid monument, which had been erected over the grave
of the learned and much-loved bishop, was completely demolished, that, in the words of his Holiness, "the memory
of Jansen might perish from the earth." It is even said that
his body was torn from its resting-place, and thrown into
some unknown receptacle.[1]   His literary remains were no less
severely handled.   Nicholas Cornet, a member of the Society,
after incredible pains, extracted the heretical poison of "Augustinus," in the form of seven propositions, which were afterwards reduced to five. These having been submitted to the
judgment of Innocent X., were condemned by that pontiff in
a bull dated 31st May, 1653. This decision, so far from restoring peace, awakened a new controversy. The Jansenists,
as the admirers of Jansen now began to be named by their
opponents, while they professed acquiescence in the judgment
of the pope, denied that these propositions were to be found
in "Augustinus." The succeeding pope, Alexander VII.,
who was still more favorable to the Jesuits, declared formally,
in a bull dated 1657, "that the five propositions were certainly taken from the book of Jansenius, and had been condemned in the sense of that author." But the Jansenists
were ready to meet him on this point; they replied, that a
decision of this kind overstepped the limits of papal authority, and that the pope's infallibility did not extend to a judgment of facts.[2]

The reader may be curious to know something more about
these famous five propositions, condemned by the pope, which,
in fact, may be said to have given occasion to the Provincial
Letters. They were as follows :—

[1] Leydecker, p. 132; Lancelot, p. 180.
[2] Ranke, Hist. of the Popes, vol. iii. 143; Abbé Du Mas, Hist. des
Cinq Propositions, p. 48.

1. There are divine precepts which good men, though willing, are absolutely unable to obey.

2. No person, in this corrupt state of nature, can resist the influence of divine grace.

3. In order to render human actions meritorious, or otherwise, it is not requisite that they be exempt from necessity, but only free from constraint.

4. The semi-Pelagian heresy consisted in allowing the human will to be endued with a power of resisting grace, or of complying with its influence.

5. Whoever says that Christ died or shed his blood for all mankind, is a semi-Pelagian.

The Jansenists, in their subsequent disputes on these propositions, contended that they were ambiguously expressed, and that they might be understood in three different senses—a Calvinistic, a Pelagian, and a Catholic or Augustinian sense. In the first two senses they disclaimed them, in the last they approved and defended them. Owing to the extreme aversion of the party to Calvinism, while they substantially held the same system under the name of Augustinianism, it becomes extremely difficult to convey an intelligible idea of their theological views. On the first proposition, for example, while they disclaimed what they term the Calvinistic sense, namely, that the best of men are liable to sin in all that they do, they equally disclaim the Pelagian sentiment, that all men have a general sufficient grace, at all times, for the discharge of duty, subject to free will ; and they strenuously maintained that, without efficacious grace, constantly vouchsafed, we can do nothing spiritually good. In regard to the resistibility of grace, they seem to have held that the will of man might always resist the influence of grace, if it chose to do so; but that grace would effectually prevent it from so choosing And with respect to redemption, they appear to have compromised the matter, by holding that Christ died for all, so as that all might be partakers of the grace of justification by the merits of his death; but they denied that

Christ died for each man in particular, so as to secure his final salvation ; in this sense, he died for the elect only.

Were this the proper place, it would be easy to show that, in the leading points of his theology, Jansen did not differ from Calvin, so much as he misunderstood Calvinism. The Calvinists, for example, never held, as they are represented in the Provincial Letters,[1] "that we have not the power of resisting grace." So far from this, they held that fallen man could not but resist the grace of God. They preferred, there-fore, the term "invincible," as applied to grace. In short, they held exactly the *victrix delectatio* of Augustine, by which the will of man is sweetly but effectually inclined to comply with the will of God.[2] On the subject of necessity and con-straint their views are precisely similar. Nor can they be considered as differing essentially in their views of the death of Christ, as these, at least, were given by Jansen, who ac-knowledges in his "Augustinus," that, "according to St. Augustine, Jesus Christ did not die for all mankind." It is certain that neither Augustine nor Jansen would have sub-scribed to the views of grace and redemption held by many who, in our day, profess evangelical views. Making allow-ance for the different position of the parties, it is very plain that the dispute between Augustine and Pelagius, Jansen and Molina, Calvin and Arminius, was substantially one and the same. At the same time, it must be granted that on the great point of justification by faith, Jansen went widely astray from the truth ; and in the subsequent controversial writings of the party, especially when arguing against the Protestants, this departure became still more strongly marked, and more deplorably manifested.[3]

[1] Letter xviii. pp. 310–313.

[2] Witsii Œconom. Fœd., lib. iii. ; Turret. Theol., Elenct. xv. quest. 4; De Moor Comment. iv. 496; Mestrezat, Serm. sur Rom., viii. 274.

[3] I refer here particularly to Arnauld's treatise. entitled "Renverse-ment de la Morale de Jesus Christ par les Calvinistes," which was an-swered by Jurieu in his "Justification de la Morale des Reformez," 1685, by M. Merlat, and others. Jurieu has shown at great length, and with a severity for which he had too much provocation, that Arnauld and his friends, in their violent tirades against the Reformed, neither acted in

The revenge of the Jesuits did not stop at procuring the condemnation of Jansen's book; it aimed at his living followers. Among these none was more conspicuous for virtue and influence than the Abbé de St. Cyran, who was known to have shared his counsels, and even aided in the preparation of his obnoxious work. While Jansen labored to restore the theoretical doctrines of Augustine, St. Cyran was ambitious to reduce them to practice. In pursuance of the moral system of that father, he taught the renunciation of the world, and the total absorption of the soul in the love of God. His religious fervor led him into some extravagances. He is said to have laid some claim to a species of inspiration, and to have anticipated for the Saviour some kind of temporal dominion, in which the saints alone would be entitled to the wealth and dignities of the world.[1] But his piety appears to have been sincere, and, what is more surprising, his love to the Scriptures was such that he not only lived in the daily study of them himself, but earnestly enforced it on all his disciples. He recommended them to study the Scriptures on their knees. "No means of conversion," he would say, "can be more apostolic than the Word of God. Every word in Scripture deserves to be weighed more attentively than gold. The Scriptures were penned by a direct ray of the Holy Spirit; the fathers only by a reflex ray emanating therefrom." His whole character and appearance corresponded with his doctrine. "His simple mortified air, and his humble garb formed a striking contrast with the awful sanctity of his countenance, and his native lofty dignity of manner."[2] Possessing that force of character by which men of strong minds silently but surely govern others, his proselytes soon increased, and he became the nucleus of a new class of reformers.

St. Cyran was soon called to preside over the renowned

good faith, nor in consistency with the sentiments of their much admired leaders, Augustine and Jansen.

[1] Fontaine, Mémoires, i. 200; Mosheim, Eccl. Hist., cent. xvii. 2.
[2] Lancelot, p. 123.

monastery of Port-Royal. Two houses went under this name, though forming one abbey. One of these was called Port-Royal des Champs, and was situated in a gloomy forest, about six leagues from Paris; but this having been found an unhealthy situation, the nuns were removed for some time to another house in Paris, which went under the name of Port-Royal de Paris. The Abbey of Port-Royal was one of the most ancient belonging to the order of Citeaux, having been founded by Eudes de Sully, bishop of Paris, in 1204. It was placed originally under the rigorous discipline of St. Bene-dict, but in course of time fell, like most other monasteries, into a state of the greatest relaxation. In 1602, a new ab-bess was appointed in the person of Maria Angelica Arnauld, sister of the famous Arnauld, then a mere child, scarcely eleven years old! The nuns, promising themselves a long period of unbounded liberty, rejoiced at this appointment. But their joy was not of long duration. The young abbess, at first, indeed, thought of nothing but amusement; but at the age of seventeen a change came over her spirit. A cer-tain Capuchin, wearied, it is said, or more probably disgust-ed, with the monastic life, had been requested by the nuns, who were not aware of his character, to preach before them. The preacher, equally ignorant of his audience, and supposing them to be eminently pious ladies, delivered an affecting dis-course, pitched on the loftiest key of devotion, which left an impression on the mind of Angelica never to be effaced. She set herself to reform her establishment, and carried it into effect with a determination and self-denial quite beyond her years. This "reformation," so highly lauded by her pane-gyrists, consisted chiefly in restoring the austere discipline of St. Benedict, and other severities practised in the earlier ages, the details of which would be neither edifying nor agreeable. The substitution of coarse serge in place of linen as underclothing, and dropping melted wax on the bare arms, may be taken as specimens of the reformation introduced by Mère Angelique. In these mortifying exercises the abbess showed an example to all the rest. She chose as her dormitory the filthiest cell in the convent, a place infested with toads and vermin, in which she found the highest delight, declaring that she "seemed transported to the grotto of Bethlehem." The same rigid denial of pleasure was extended to her food, her dress, her whole occupations. Clothed herself in the rudest dress she could procure, nothing gave her greater offence than to see in her nuns any approach to the fashions of the world, even in the adjustment of the coarse black serge, with the scarlet cross, which formed their humble apparel.[1] Yet, in the midst of all this "voluntary humility," her heart seems to have been turned mainly to the Saviour. It was Jesus Christ whom she aimed at adoring in the worship she paid to "the sacrament of the altar." And in a book of devotion, composed by her for private use, she gave expression to sentiments too much savoring of undivided affection to Christ to escape the censure of the Church. It was dragged to light and condemned at Rome.[2] There is reason to believe that, under the direction of M. de St. Cyran, her religious sentiments, as well as those of her community, became much more enlightened. Her firmness in resisting subscription to the formulary and condemning Jansen, in spite of the most cruel and unmanly persecution, and the piety and faith she manifested on her death-bed, when, in the midst of exquisite suffering, and in the absence of the rites which her persecutors denied her, she expired in the full assurance of salvation through the merits of the only Saviour, form one of the most interesting chapters in the martyrology of the Church.

But St. Cyran aimed at higher objects than the management of a nunnery. His energetic mind planned a system of education, in which, along with the elements of learning, the youth might be imbued with early piety. Attracted by his fame, several learned men, some of them of rank and for-

[1] Mémoires pour servir a l'Histoire de Port-Royal, vol. i. pp. 35, 57, 142.
[2] Ib., p. 456. The title of this work was, "The Secret Chaplet of the Holy Sacrament."

tune, fled to enjoy at Port-Royal des Champs a sacred retreat
from the world. This community, which differed from a
monastery in not being bound by any vows, settled in a farm
adjoining the convent, called Les Granges. The names of
Arnauld, D'Andilly, Nicole, Le Maitre, Sacy,[1] Fontaine,
Pascal, and others, have conferred immortality·on the spot.
The system pursued in this literary hermitage was, in many
respects, deserving of praise. The time of the recluses was
divided between devotional and literary pursuits, relieved by
agricultural and mechanical labors. The Scriptures, and
other books of devotion, were translated into the vernacular
language; and the result was, the singular anomaly of a
Roman Catholic community distinguished for the devout and
diligent study of the Bible. Protestants they certainly were
not, either in spirit or in practice. Firm believers in the infallibility of their Church, and fond devotees in the observance of her rites, they held it a point of merit to yield a blind
obedience, in matters of faith, to the dogmas of Rome. None
were more hostile to Protestantism. St. Cyran, it is said,
would never open a Protestant book, even for the purpose of
refuting it, without first making the sign of the cross on it,
to exorcise the evil spirit which he believed to lurk within
its pages.[2] From no community did there emanate more
learned apologies for Rome than from Port-Royal. Still, it
must be owned, that in attachment to the doctrines of grace,
so far as they went, and in the exhibition of the Christian
virtues, attested by their sufferings, lives, and writings, the
Port-Royalists, including under this name both the nuns and
recluses, greatly surpassed many Protestant communities.
Their piety, indeed, partook of the failings which have always characterized the religion of the cloister. It seems to
have hovered between superstition and mysticism. Afraid
to fight against the world, they fled from it; and, forgetting
that our Saviour was driven into the wilderness to be tempt-

[1] Sacy, or Saci, was the inverted name of Isaac Le Maitre, celebrated
for his translation of the Bible.
[2] Mosheim, Eccl. Hist., cent. xvii. §2.

ed of the devil, they retired to a wilderness to avoid temptation. Half conscious of the hollowness of the ceremonial they practised, they sought to graft on its dead stock the vitalities of the Christian faith. In their hands, penance was sublimated into the symbol c: penitential sorrow, and the mass into a spiritual service, the benefit of which depended on the preparation of the heart of the worshipper. In their eyes, the priest was but a suggestive emblem of the Saviour ; and to them the altar, with its crucifix and bleeding image, served only as a platform on which they might obtain a more advantageous view of Calvary. Transferring to the Church of Rome the attributes of the Church of God, and regarding her still, in spite of her eclipse and disfigurement, as of one spirit, and even of one body, with Christ, infallible and immortal, they worshipped the fond creation of their own fancy. At the same time, they attempted to revive the doctrine of religious abstraction, or the absorption of the soul in Deity, and the total renouncement of everything in the shape of sensual enjoyment, which afterwards distinguished the mystics of the Continent. Even in their literary recreations, while they acquired an elegance of style which marked a new era in the literature of France, they betrayed their ascetic spirit. Poetry was only admissible when clothed in a devotional garb. It was by stealth that Racine, who studied at Port-Royal, indulged his poetic vein in the profane pieces which afterwards gave him celebrity. And yet it is candid to admit, that the mortifications in which this amiable fraternity engaged, consisted rather in the exclusion of pleasure than the infliction of pain, and that the object aimed at in these austerities was not so much to merit heaven as to attain an ideal perfection on earth. Port-Royalism, in short, was Popery in its mildest type, as Jesuitism is Popery in its perfection ; and had it been possible to present that system in a form calculated to disarm prejudice and to cover its native deformities, the task might have been achieved by the pious devotees of Les Granges. But the same merciful Providence which, for the preservation of the human species, has furnished the snake with his rattle, and taught the lion to "roar for his prey," has so ordered it that the Romish Church should betray her real character, in order that his people might "come out of her, and not be partakers of her sins, that they receive not of her plagues." The whole system adopted at Port-Royal was regarded, from the commencement, with extreme jealousy by the authorities of that Church; the schools were soon dispersed, and the Jesuits never rested till they had destroyed every vestige of the obnoxious establishment.

The enemies of Port-Royal have attempted to show that St. Cyran and his associates had formed a deep-laid plot for overturning the Roman Catholic faith. From time to time, down to the present day, works have appeared, under the auspices of the Jesuits, in which this charge is reiterated; and the old calumnies against the sect are revived—a periodical trampling on the ashes of the poor Jansenists (after having accomplished their ruin two hundred years ago), which reminds one of nothing so much as the significant grinning and yelling with which the modern Jews celebrate to this day the downfal of Haman the Agagite.[1] In one point only could their assailants find room to question their orthodoxy—the supremacy of the pope. Here, certainly, they were led, more from circumstances than from inclination, to lean to the side of the Gallican liberties. But even Jansen himself, after spending a lifetime on his "Augustinus," and leaving it behind him as a sacred legacy, abandoned himself and his treatise to the judgment of the pope. The following are his words, dictated by him half an hour before his death: "I feel that it will be difficult to alter anything. Yet if the Romish see should wish anything to be altered, I am her obedient son; and to that Church in which I have always lived, even to this bed of death, I will prove obedient. This is my last will." The same sentiment is expressed by Pascal, in one

[1] We may refer particularly to Petitot, in his Collection des Mémoires, tom. xxxiii., Paris, 1824; and to a History of the Company of Jesus. by J. Cretineau-Joly, Paris, 1845. With high pretensions to impartiality, these works abound with the most glaring specimens of special pleading

of his letters. Alas! how sad is the predicament in which the Church of Rome places her conscientious votaries! Both of these excellent men were as firmly persuaded, no doubt, of the faith which they taught, as of the facts which came under their observation; and yet they held themselves bound to cast their religious convictions at the feet of a fellow-mortal, notoriously under the influence of the Jesuits, and professed themselves ready, at a signal from Rome, to renounce what they held as divine truth, and to embrace what they regarded as damnable error! A spectacle more painful and piteous can hardly be imagined than that of such men struggling between the dictates of conscience, and the night-mare of that "strong delusion," which led them to " believe a lie."

In every feature that distinguished the Port-Royalists, they stood opposed to the Jesuits. In theology they were antipodes—in learning they were rivals. The schools of Port-Royal already eclipsed those of the Jesuits, whose policy it has always been to monopolize education, under the pretext of charity. But the Jansenists might have been allowed to retain their peculiar tenets, had they not touched the idol of every Jesuit, " the glory of the Society," by supplanting them in the confessional. The priests connected with Port-Royal, from their primitive simplicity of manners and severity of morals, and, above all, from their spiritual Christianity, acquired a popularity which could not fail to give mortal offence to the Society, who then ruled the councils both of the Church and the nation. Nothing less than the annihilation of the whole party would satisfy their vengeful purpose. In this nefarious design they were powerfully aided by Cardinal Richelieu, and by Louis XIV., a prince who, though yet a mere youth, was entirely under Jesuitical influence in matters of religion; and who, having resolved to extirpate Protestantism, could not well endure the existence of a sect within the Church, which seemed to favor the Reformation by exposing the corruptions of the clergy.[1]

---

[1] Voltaire, Siècle de Louis XIV., t. ii.

To effect their object, St. Cyran, the leader and ornament of the party, required to be disposed of. He was accused of various articles of heresy; and Cardinal Richelieu at once gratified his party resentment and saved himself the trouble of controversy, by immuring him in the dungeon of Vincennes. In this prison St. Cyran languished for five years, and survived his release only a few months, having died in October, 1643. His place, however, as leader of the Jansenist party, was supplied by one destined to annoy the Jesuits by his controversial talents fully more than his predecessor had done by his apostolic sanctity. Anthony Arnauld may be said to have been born an enemy to the Jesuits. His father, a celebrated lawyer, had distinguished himself for his opposition to the Society, and having engaged in an important law-suit against them, in which he warmly pleaded, in the name of the university, that they should be interdicted from the education of youth, and even expelled from the kingdom. Anthony, who inherited his spirit, was the youngest in a family of twenty children, and was born February 6, 1612.[1] Several of them were connected with Port-Royal. His sister, as we have seen, became its abbess; and five other sisters were nuns in that establishment. He is said to have given precocious proof of his polemic turn. Busying himself, when a mere boy, with some papers in his uncle's library, and being asked what he was about, he replied, "Don't you see that I am helping you to refute the Hugonots?" This prognostication he certainly verified in after life. He wrote, with almost equal vehemence, against Rome, against the Jesuits, and against the Protestants. He was, for many years, the *facile princeps* of the party termed Jansenists; and was one of those characters who present to the public an aspect nearly the reverse of the estimate formed of them by their private friends. By the latter he is represented as the best of men, totally free from pride and passion. Judging from his physiognomy,

---

[1] Mémoires de P. Royal, i. 13. Bayle insists that his father had twenty-two children. Dict., art. *Arnauld.*

his writings and his life, we would say the natural temper of
Arnauld was austere and indomitable. Expelled from the
Sarbonne, driven out of France, and hunted from place to
place, he continued to fight to the last. On one occasion,
wishing his friend Nicole to assist him in a new work, the latter observed, "We are now old, is it not time to rest?"
"Rest!" exclaimed Arnauld, "have we not all eternity to
rest in?"

Such was the character of the man who now entered the
lists against the redoubtable Society. His first offence was
the publication, in 1643, of a book on "Frequent Communion;" in which, while he inculcates the necessity of a spiritual preparation for the eucharist, he insinuated that the
Church of Rome had a two-fold head, in the persons of Peter
and Paul.[1]   His next was in the shape of two letters, published in 1656, occasioned by a dispute referred to in the first
Provincial Letter, in which he declared that he had not been
able to find the condemned propositions in Jansen, and added some opinions on grace. The first of these assertions was
deemed derogatory to the holy see ; the second was charged
with heresy. The Jesuits, who sighed for an opportunity of
humbling the obnoxious doctor, strained every nerve to procure
his expulsion from the Sarbonne, or college of divinity in the
university. This object they had just accomplished, and everything promised fair to secure their triumph, when another
combatant unexpectedly appeared, like one of those closely-
visored knights of whom we read in romance, who so oppor-
tunely enter the field at the critical moment, and with their
single arm turn the tide of battle. Need we say that we
allude to the author of the PROVINCIAL LETTERS ?

Bayle commences his Life of Pascal by declaring him to be
"one of the sublimest geniuses that the world ever produced." Seldom, at least, has the world ever seen such a
combination of excellences in one man. In him we are called
to admire the loftiest attributes of mind with the loveliest

---

[1] Weisman, Hist. Eccl., ii. 204.

simplicity of moral character. He is a rare example of one
born with a natural genius for the exact sciences, who applied the subtlety of his mind to religious subjects, combining
with the closest logic the utmost elegance of style, and
crowning all with a simple and profound piety. Blaise Pascal was born at Clermont, 19th June, 1623. His family had
been ennobled by Louis XI., and his father, Stephen Pascal,
occupied a high post in the civil government. Blaise manifested from an early age a strong liking for the study of
mathematics, and, while yet a child, made some astonishing
discoveries in natural philosophy. To these studies he devoted the greater part of his life. An incident, however, which
occurred in his thirty-first year—a narrow escape from sudden death—had the effect of giving an entire change to the
current of his thoughts. He regarded it as a message from
heaven, calling him to renounce all secular occupations, and
devote himself exclusively to God. His sister and niece being nuns in Port-Royal, he was naturally led to associate with
those who then began to be called Jansenists. But though
he had several of the writings of the party, there can be no
doubt that it was the devotion rather than the theology of
Port-Royal that constituted its charm in the eyes of Pascal.
His sister informs us, in her memoirs of him, that " he had
never applied himself to abstruse questions in divinity." Nor,
beyond a temporary retreat to Port-Royal des Champs, and
an intimacy with its leading solitaries, can he be said to have
had any connection with that establishment. His fragile
frame, which was the victim of complicated disease, and his
feminine delicacy of spirit, unfitting him for the rough col-
lisions of ordinary life, he found a congenial retreat amidst
these literary solitudes ; while, with his clear and compre-
hensive mind, and his genuine piety of heart, he must have
sympathized with those who sought to remove from the
Church corruptions which he could not fail to deplore, and to
renovate the spirit of that Christianity which he loved fa
above any of its organized forms. His life, not unlike a per
petual miracle, is ever exciting our admiration, not unmingled

however, with pity. We see great talents enlisted in the support, not indeed of the errors of a system, but of a system of errors—we see a noble mind debilitated by superstition—we see a useful life prematurely terminating in, if not shortened by, the petty austerities and solicitudes of monasticism. Truth requires us to state, that he not only denied himself, at last, the most common comforts of life, but wore beneath his clothes a girdle of iron, with sharp points, which, as soon as he felt any pleasurable sensation, he would strike with his elbow, so as to force the points of iron more deeply into his sides. Let the Church, which taught him such folly, be responsible for it ; and let us ascribe to the grace of God the patience, the meekness, the charity, and the faith, which hovered, seraph-wise, over the death-bed of expiring genius. The curate who attended him, struck with the triumph of religion over the pride of an intellect which continued to burn after it had ceased to blaze, would frequently exclaim : " He is an infant—humble and submissive as an infant !" He died on the 19th of August, 1662, aged thirty-nine years and two months.

While Arnauld's process before the Sarbonne was in dependence, a few of his friends, among whom were Pascal and Nicole, were in the habit of meeting privately at Port-Royal, to consult on the measures they should adopt. During these conferences one of their number said to Arnauld : " Will you really suffer yourself to be condemned like a child, without saying a word, or telling the public the real state of the question ?" The rest concurred, and in compliance with their solicitations, Arnauld, after some days, produced and read before them a long and serious vindication of himself. His audience listened in coolness and silence, upon which he remarked : "I see you don't think highly of my production, and I believe you are right; but," added he, turning himself round and addressing Pascal, " you who are young, why cannot you produce something ?" The appeal was not lost upon our author ; he had hitherto written almost nothing, but he engaged to try a sketch or rough draft, which they might fill up; and retiring to his room, he produced, in a few hours, instead of a sketch, the first letter to a provincial. On reading this to his assembled friends, Arnauld exclaimed, "That is excellent! that will go down; we must have it printed immediately."

Pascal had, in fact, with the native superiority of genius, pitched on the very tone which, in a controversy of this kind, was calculated to arrest the public mind. Treating theology in a style entirely new, he brought down the subject to the comprehension of all, and translated into the pleasantries of comedy, and familiarities of dialogue, discussions which had till then been confined to the grave utterances of the school. The framework which he adopted in his first letter was exceedingly happy. A Parisian is supposed to transmit to one of his friends in the provinces an account of the disputes of the day. It is said that the provincial with whom he affected to correspond was Perrier, who had married one of his sisters. Hence arose the name of the *Provincials*, which was given to the rest of the letters.

This title they owe, it would appear, to a mistake of the printer; for in an advertisement prefixed to one of the early editions, it is stated that "they have been called 'Provincials,' because the first having been addressed without any name to a person in the country, the printer published it under the title 'Letter written to a Provincial by one of his Friends.'" This may he regarded as an apology for the use of a term which, critically speaking, was rather unhappy. The word *provincial* in French, when used to signify a person residing in the provinces, was generally understood in a bad sense, as denoting an unpolished clown.[1] But the title,

---

[1] The title under which the Letters appeared when first collected into a volume was, " *Lettres écrites par Louis de Montalte, a un Provincial de ses amis, et aux RR. PP. Jesuites, sur la morale et la politique de ces Peres.*"

Father Bouhours, a Jesuit ridicules the title of the Letters, and says he is surprised they were not rather entitled " Letters from a Country Bumpkin to his Friends," and instead of " The Provincials" called " The Bumpkins"—" *Campagnardes.*" (Remarques sur la langue Fran., p. ii. 306 Dict. Univ., art. *Provincial.*)

uncouth as it is, has been canonized and made classical forever ; and " The Provincials" is a phrase which it would now
be fully as ridiculous to attempt to change as it could be at
first to apply it to the Letters.

The most trifling particulars connected with such a publication possess an interest. The Letters, we learn, were published at first in separate stitched sheets of a quarto size;
and, on account of their brevity, none of them extending to
more than one sheet of eight pages, except the last three,
which were somewhat longer, they were at first known by
the name of the " LITTLE LETTERS." No stated time was
observed in their publication. The first letter appeared January 13, 1656, being on a Wednesday ; the second on January 29, being Saturday ; and the rest were issued at intervals varying from a week to a month, till March 24, 1657,
which is the date of the last letter in the series ; the whole
thus extending over the space of a year and three months.

All accounts agree in stating that the impression produced
by the Provincials, on their first appearance, was quite unexampled. They were circulated in thousands in Paris and
throughout France. Speaking of the first letter, Father
Daniel says : " It created a fracas which filled the fathers of
the Society with consternation. Never did the post-office
reap greater profits ; copies were despatched over the whole
kingdom ; and I myself, though very little known to the
gentlemen of Port-Royal, received a large packet of them,
post-paid, in a town of Brittany where I was then residing."
The same method was followed with the rest of the letters.
The seventh found its way to Cardinal Mazarin, who laughed
over it very heartily. The eighth did not appear till a month
after its predecessor, apparently to keep up expectation.[1]
In short, everybody read the " Little Letters," and, whatever might be their opinions of the points in dispute, all
agreed in admiring the genius which they displayed. They
were found lying on the merchant's counter, the lawyer's

[1] Daniel, Entretiens, p. 19.

desk, the doctor's table, the lady's toilet; and everywhere they were sought for and perused with the same avidity.[1] The success of the Letters in gaining their object was not less extraordinary. The Jesuits were fairly checkmated; and though they succeeded in carrying through the censure of Arnauld, the public sympathy was enlisted in his favor. The confessionals and churches of the Jesuits were deserted, while those of their opponents were crowded with admiring thousands.[2] " That book alone," says one of its bitterest enemies, " has done more for the Jansenists than the ' Augustinus' of Jansen, and all the works of Arnauld put together."[3] This is the more surprising when we consider that, at that time, the influence of the Jesuits was so high in the ascendant, that Arnauld had to contend with the pope, the king, the chancellor, the clergy, the Sorbonne, the universities, and the great body of the populace; and that never was Jansenism at a lower ebb, or more generally anathematized than when the first Provincial Letter appeared.

This, however, was not all. Besides having the tide of public favor turned against them, the Jesuits found themselves the objects of universal derision. The names of their favorite casuists were converted into proverbs: *Escobarder* came to signify the same thing with " paltering in a double sense ;" Father Bauny's grotesque maxims furnished topics for perpetual badinage ; and the Jesuits, wherever they went, were assailed with inextinguishable laughter. By no other method could Pascal have so severely stung this proud and self-conceited Society. The rage into which they were thrown was extreme, and was variously expressed. At one time it found vent in calumnies and threats of vengeance. At other times they indulged in puerile lamentations. It was amusing to hear these stalwart divines, after breathing fire and slaughter against their enemies, assume the querulous tones of injured and oppressed innocence. " The perse-

---

[1] Petitot, Notices, p. 121.
[2] Benoit, Hist. de l'Edit. de Nantes, iii. 198.
[3] Daniel, Entretiens, p. 11.

cution which the Jesuits suffer from the buffooneries of Port-Royal," they said, "is perfectly intolerable : the wheel and the gibbet are nothing to it; it can only be compared to the torture inflicted on the ancient martyrs, who were first rubbed over with honey and then left to be stung to death by wasps and wild bees. Their tyrants have subjected them to empoisoned raillery, and the world leaves them unpitied to suffer a sweet death, more cruel in its sweetness than the bitterest punishment."[1]

The Letters were published anonymously, under the fictious signature of Louis de Montalte, and the greatest care was taken to preserve the secret of their authorship. As on all such occasions, many were the guesses made, and the false reports circulated ; but beyond the circle of Pascal's personal friends, none knew him to be the author, nor was the fact certainly or publicly known till after his death. The following anecdote shows, however, that he was suspected, and was once very nearly discovered : After publishing the third letter, Pascal left Port-Royal des Champs, to avoid being disturbed, and took up his residence in Paris, under the name of M. de Mons, in a *hotel garni*, at the sign of the King of Denmark, Rue des Poiriers, exactly opposite the college of the Jesuits. Here he was joined by his brother-in-law, Perrier, who passed as the master of the house. One day Perrier received· a visit from his relative, Father Frétat, a Jesuit, accompanied by a brother monk. Frétat told him that the Society suspected M. Pascal to be the author of the "Little Letters," which were making such a noise, and advised him as a friend to prevail on his brother-in-law to desist from writing any more of them, as he might otherwise involve himself in much trouble, and even danger. Perrier thanked him for his advice, but said he was afraid it would be altogether useless, as Pascal would just reply that he could not hinder people from suspecting him, and that though he should deny it they would not believe him. The monks took their departure, much to the relief of Perrier, for

[1] ·Nicole, Notes sur la xi. Lettre iii. 332.

at that very time several sheets of the seventh or eighth letter, newly come from the printer, were lying on the bed,
where they had been placed for the purpose of drying, but,
fortunately, though the curtains were only partially drawn,
and one of the monks sat very close to the bed, they were
not observed. Perrier ran immediately to communicate the
incident to his brother-in-law, who was in an adjoining apart-
ment; and he had reason to congratulate him on the narrow
escape which he had made.[1]

As Pascal proceeded, he transmitted his manuscripts to
Port-Royal des Champs, where they were carefully revised
and corrected by Arnauld and Nicole. Occasionally, these
expert divines suggested the plans of the letters; and by
them he was, beyond all doubt, furnished with most of his
quotations from the voluminous writings of the casuists,
which, with the exception of Escobar, he appears never to
have read. We must not suppose, however, that he took
these on trust, or gave himself no trouble to verify them.
We shall afterwards have proof of the contrary. The first
letters he composed with the rapidity of new-born enthusiasm; but the pains and mental exertion which he bestowed
on the rest are almost incredible. Nicole says "he was often
twenty whole days on a single letter: and some of them
he recommenced seven or eight times before bringing them
to their present state of perfection."[2] We are assured that
he wrote over the eighteenth letter no less than thirteen
times.[3] Having been obliged to hasten the publication of
the sixteenth, on account of a search made after it in the
printing office, he apologizes for its length on the ground
that "he had found no time to make it shorter."[4]

[1] Recueil de Port-Royal, 278, 279; Petitot, pp. 122, 123.
[2] Histoire des Provinciales, p. 12.
[3] Petitot, p. 124. The eighteenth letter embraces the delicate topic
of papal authority, as well as the distinction between *faith* and *fact*,
in stating which we can easily conceive how severely the ingenuous
mind of Pascal must have labored to find some plausible ground for
vindicating his consistency as a Roman Catholic. To the Protestant
reader, it must appear the most unsatisfactory of all the Letters.
[4] Prov. Let., p. 418.

The fruits of this extraordinary elaboration appear in every letter; but what is equally remarkable, is the art with which so many detached letters, written at distant intervals, and prompted by passing events, have been so arranged as to form an harmonious whole. The first three letters refer to Arnauld's affair; the questions of grace are but slightly touched, the main object being to interest the reader in favor of the Jansenists, and excite his contempt and indignation against their opponents. After this prelude, the fourth letter serves as a transition to the following six, in which he takes up maxims of the casuists. In the eight concluding letters he resumes the grand objects of the work—the morals of the Jesuits and the question of grace. These three parts have each their peculiar style. The first is distinguished for lively dialogue and repartee. Jacobins, Molinists, and Jansenists are brought on the stage, and speak in character, while Pascal does little more than act as reporter. In the second part, he comes into personal contact with a casuistical doctor, and extracts from him, under the pretext of desiring information, some of the weakest and worst of his maxims. At the eleventh letter, Pascal throws off his disguise, and addressing himself directly to the whole order of the Jesuits, and to their Provincial by name, he pours out his whole soul in an impetuous and impassioned torrent of declamation. From beginning to end it is a well-sustained battle, in which the weapons are only changed in order to strike the harder.

The literary merits of the Provincials have been universally acknowledged and applauded. On this point, where Pascal's countrymen must be considered the most competent judges, we have the testimonies of the leading spirits of France. Boileau pronounced it a work that has "surpassed at once the ancients and the moderns." Perrault has given a similar judgment: "There is more wit in these eighteen letters than in Plato's Dialogues; more delicate and artful raillery than in those of Lucian; and more strength and ingenuity of reasoning than in the orations of Cicero. We have nothing more beautiful in this species of writing."[1] "Pascal's style," says the Abbé d'Artigny, "has never been surpassed, nor perhaps equalled."[2] The high encomium of Voltaire is well known : "The Provincial Letters were models of eloquence and pleasantry. The best comedies of Molière have not more wit in them than the first letters ; Bossuet has nothing more sublime than the last ones." Again, the same writer says : "The first work of genius that appeared in prose was the collection of the Provincial Letters. Examples of every species of eloquence may there be found. There is not a single word in it which, after a hundred years, has undergone the change to which all living languages are liable. We may refer to this work the era when our language became fixed. The Bishop of Luçon told me, that having asked the Bishop of Meaux what work he would wish most to have been the author of, setting his own works aside, Bossuet instantly replied, ' The Provincial Letters.' "[3] "Pascal succeeded beyond all expression," says D'Alembert ; " several of his bon-mots have become proverbial in our language, and the Provincials will be ever regarded as a model of taste and style."[4] To this day the same high eulogiums are passed on the work by the best scholars of France.[5]

To these testimonies it would be superfluous to add any criticism of our own, were it not to prepare the English reader for the peculiar character of our author's style. Pascal's wit is essentially French. It is not the broad humor of Smollet ; it is not the cool irony of Swift ; far less is it the envenomed sarcasm of Junius. It is wit—the lively, polite, piquant wit of the early French school. Nothing can be finer than its spirit ; but from its very fineness it is apt to evaporate in the act of transfusion into another tongue. Nothing

[1] Perrault, Parallele des Anc. et Mod., Bayle, art. *Pascal.*
[2] D'Artigny, Nouveaux Mémoires, iii. p. 34.
[3] Voltaire, Siècle de Louis XIV., tom. ii. pp. 171, 274.
[4] D'Alembert, Destruct. des Jesuites, p. 54.
[5] Bordas-Demoulin, Eloge de Pascal, p. xxv. (This was the prize essay before the French Academy, in June, 1842.)

can be more ingenious than the transitions by which the author
glides insensibly from one topic to another; and in the more
serious letters, we cannot fail to be struck with the mathematical precision of his reasoning. But there is a species of
iteration, and a style of dovetailing his sentiments, which
does not quite accord with our taste; and the foreign texture
of which, in spite of every effort to the contrary, must shine
through any translation.

High as the Provincials stand in the literary world, they
were not suffered to pass without censure in the high places
of the Church. The first effect of their publication, indeed,
was to raise a storm against the casuists, whom Pascal had so
effectually exposed. The curés of Paris, and afterwards the
assembly of the clergy, shocked at the discovery of such a
sink of corruption, the existence of which, though just beneath their feet, they never appear to have suspected, determined to institute an examination into the subject. Hitherto
the tenets of the casuists, buried in huge folios, or only taught
in the colleges of the Jesuits, had escaped public observation. The clergy resolved to compare the quotations of Pascal with these writings; and the result of the investigation
was, that he was found to be perfectly correct, while a multitude of other maxims, equally scandalous, were dragged to
light. These were condemned in a general assembly of the
clergy.[1] Unfortunately for the Jesuits, they had not a single
writer at the time capable of conducting their vindication.
Several replies to the Provincials were attempted while they
were in the course of publication; but these were taken up
by the redoubtable Montalte, and fairly strangled at their
birth.[2] Shortly after the Letters were finished, there appeared "An Apology for the Casuists," the production of a

---

[1] Nicole, Hist. des Provinciales.
[2] The names of these unfortunate productions alone survive; 1.
"First Reply to Letters, &c.. by a Father of the Company of Jesus."
2. "Provincial Impostures of Sieur de Montalte, Secretary of Port-
Royal. discovered and refuted by a Father of the Company of Jesus."
3. "Reply to a Theologian," &c. 4. "Reply to the Seventeenth Letter, by Francis Annat," &c., &c.

Jesuit named Pirot, who, with a folly and frankness which proved nearly as fatal to his order as it did to himself, attempted to vindicate the worst maxims of the casuistical school.   This Apology was condemned by the Sorbonne, and subsequently at Rome; its author died of chagrin, and the Jesuits fell into temporary disgrace.[1]

But, with that tenaciousness of life and elasticity of limb which have ever distinguished the Society, it was not long before they rebounded from their fall and regained their feet. Unable to answer the Letters, they succeeded in obtaining, in February, 1657, their condemnation by the Parliament of Provence, by whose orders they were burnt on the pillory by the hands of the common executioner.   Not content with this clumsy method of refutation, they succeeded in procuring the formal condemnation of the Provincials by a censure of the pope, Alexander VII., dated 6th September, 1657. In this decree the work is "prohibited and condemned, under the pains and censures contained in the Council of Trent, and in the index of prohibited books, and other pains and censures which it may please his holiness to ordain."   It is almost needless to say, that these sentences neither enhanced nor lessened the fame of the Provincials.   It must be interesting to know what the feelings of Pascal were, on learning that this work, into which he had thrown his whole heart, and mind, and strength, and which may be said to have been at once his *chef-d'œuvre* and his confession of faith, had been condemned by the head of that Church which he had hitherto believed to be infallible.   Warped as his fine spirit was by education, his unbending rectitude forbids the supposition that he could surrender his cherished and conscientious sentiments at the mere dictum of the pope.   An incident occurred in 1661, shortly before his death, strikingly illustrative of his conscientiousness, and of the sincerity of purpose with which the Letters were written.   The persecution had begun to rage against Port-Royal; one *mandement* after another,

---

[1] Eichhorn, Geschichte der Litteratur, vol. i. pp. 420–423.

requiring subscription to the condemnation of Jansen, came
down from the court of Rome; and the poor nuns, shrink-
ing, on the one hand, from violating their consciences by sub-
scribing what they believed to be an untruth, and trembling,
on the other, at the consequences of disobeying their ecclesiastical superiors, were thrown into the most distressing em-
barrassment. Their " obstinacy," as it was termed, only provoked their persecutors to more stringent demands. In these
circumstances, even the stern Arnauld and the conscientious
Nicole were tempted to make some compromise, and drew up
a declaration to accompany the signature of the nuns, which
they thought might save at once the truth and their consistency. To this Pascal objected, as not sufficiently clear, and
as leaving it to be inferred that they condemned " efficacious
grace." He could not endure the idea of their employing an
ambiguous statement, which appeared, or might be supposed
by their opponents, to grant what they did not really mean
to concede. The consequence was a slight and temporary
dispute—not affecting principle so much as the mode of
maintaining it—in which Pascal stood alone against all the
members of Port-Royal. On one occasion, after exhausting
his eloquence upon them without success, he was so deeply
affected, that his feeble frame, laboring under headache and
other disorders, sunk under the excitement, and he fell into a
swoon. After recovering his consciousness, he explained the
cause of his sudden illness, in answer to the affectionate
inquiries of his sister: " When I saw those," he said, " whom
I regard as the persons to whom God has made known his
truth, and who ought to be its champions, all giving way, I
was so overcome with grief that I could stand it no longer."
Subsequent *mandements*, still more stringent, soon saved the
poor nuns from the temptation of ambiguous submissions, and
reconciled Pascal and his friends.[1]

[1] Recueil de Port-Royal, pp. 314-323. Some papers passed between
Pascal and his friends on this topic. Pascal committed these. on his
death-bed, to his friend M. Domat, " with a request that he would burn
them if the nuns of Port-Royal proved firm, and print them if they
should yield." (Ib., p. 322.) The nuns having stood firm, the proba-

But we are fortunately furnished with his own reflections on the subject of the Provincials, in his celebrated "Thoughts on Religion :"

"I feared," says he, "that I might have written errone-ously, when I saw myself condemned; but the example of so many pious witnesses made me think differently. It is no longer allowable to write truth. IF MY LETTERS ARE CON-DEMNED AT ROME, THAT WHICH I CONDEMN IN THEM IS CON-DEMNED IN HEAVEN."[1]

It is only necessary to add, that Pascal continued to main-tain his sentiments on this subject unchanged to the last. On his death-bed, M. Beurrier, his parish priest, administered to him the last rites of his Church, and came to learn, after hav-ing confessed him, that he was the author of the "Provincial Letters." Full of concern at having absolved the author of a book condemned by the pope, the good priest returned, and asked him if it was true, and if he had no remorse of conscience on that account. Pascal replied, that "he could assure him, as one who was now about to give an account to God of all his actions, that his conscience gave him no trou-ble on that score; and that in the composition of that work he was influenced by no mad motive, but solely by regard to the glory of God and the vindication of truth, and not in the least by any passion or personal feeling against the Jesuits." Attempts were made by Perefixe, archbishop of Paris, first to bully the priest for having absolved such an impenitent offender,[2] and afterwards to force him into a false account of his penitent's confession. It was confidently reported, on the pretended authority of the confessor, that Pascal had ex-pressed his sorrow for having written the Provincials, and

bility is that they were destroyed. Had they been preserved, they might have thrown some further light on the opinions of Pascal regarding papal authority.

[1] *Si mes Lettres sont condamnées à Rome, ce que j'y condamne, est condamné dans le ciel.* (Pensées de Blaise Pascal, tom. ii. 163. Paris, 1824.)

[2] " How came you," said the archbishop to M. Beurrier, "to admin-ister the sacraments to such a person ? Didn't you know that he was a Jansenist ?" (Recueil, 348.)

that he had condemned his friends of Port-Royal for want of due respect to papal authority. ˙ Both these allegations were afterwards distinctly refuted—the first by the written avowal of M. Beurrier, and the other by two depositions formally made by Nicole, showing that the real ground of Pascal's brief disagreement with his friends was directly the reverse of that which had been assigned.[1]

Few books have passed through more editions than the Provincials. The following, among many others, may be mentioned as French editions:—The first, in 1656, 4to; a second in 1657, 12mo; a third in 1658, 8vo; a fourth in 1659, 8vo; a fifth in 1666, 12mo; a sixth in 1667, 8vo; a seventh in 1669, 12mo; an eighth in 1689, 8vo; a ninth in 1712, 8vo; a tenth in 1767, 12mo.[2] The later editions are beyond enumeration. The Letters were translated into Latin, during the lifetime of ˙ Pascal, by his intimate friend, the learned and indefatigable Nicole, under the assumed name of "William Wendrock, a Saltzburg divine."[3] Nicole, who was a complete master of Latin, has given an elegant, though somewhat free version of his friend's work. He has frequently added to the quotations taken from the writings of the Jesuits and others; a liberty which he doubtless felt himself the more warranted to take, from the share he had in the original concoction of the Letters. Nicole's preliminary dissertation and notes were translated by Mademoiselle de Joncourt, a lady, it is said, "possessed of talents and piety, who, to the graces peculiar to her own sex, added the accomplishments which are the ornament of ours."[4] Besides this, the Provincials have been translated into nearly all

[1] Recueil de Port-Royal, pp. 327–330; Petitot, p. 165.
[2] Walchii Biblioth. Theol., ii. 295.
[3] The title of Nicole's translation, now rarely to be met with, is, *Ludovici Montaltii Litteræ Provinciales, de Morali et Politica Jesuitarum Disciplina. A Willelmo Wendrockio, Salisburgensi Theologo.* Several editions of this translation were printed. I have the first, published at Cologne in 1658, and the fifth, much enlarged, Cologne, 1679.
[4] Avertissement, Les Provinciales, ed. 1767. Mad. de Joncourt, or Joncoux, took a deep interest in the falling fortunes of Port-Royal. (See some account of her in Madame Schimmelpenninck's History of the Demolition of Port-Royal, p. 135.)

the languages of Europe. Bayle informs us that he had seen an edition of them in 8vo, with four columns, containing the French, Latin, Italian, and Spanish.[1] The Spanish translation, executed by Gratien Cordero of Burgos, was suppressed by order of the Inquisition.[2] But all the efforts made for the suppression of the Provincials only served to promote their popularity ; and their enemies found that, if they would silence, they must answer them.

Forty years elapsed after the publication of the Provincials before the Jesuits ventured on a reply. At length, in 1697, appeared an answer, entitled *Entretiens de Cleandre et d'Eudoxe, sur les Lettres au Provincial.* The author is known to have been Father Daniel, the historiographer of France. This learned Jesuit undertook the desperate task of refuting the Provincials, in a form somewhat resembling that of the Letters themselves, being a series of supposed conversations between two friends, aided by an abbe, "who is excessively frank and honest, one who never could bear all his life to see people imposed upon." The dialogue is conducted with considerable spirit, but is sadly deficient in *vraisemblance.* The author commences with high professions of impartiality. Cleander and Eudoxus are supposed to be quite neutral—somewhat like the free-will of Molina, "in a state of perfect equilibrium, until good sense and stubborn facts turn the scale." But, alas ! the equilibrium is soon lost, without the help either of facts or of sense. The friends have hardly uttered two sentences, till they begin to talk as like two Jesuits as could well be imagined. Party rage gets the better of literary discretion ; the Port-Royalists are "honest knaves," "true hypocrites," "villains animated with stubborn fury ;" Arnauld's "pen may be known by the gall that drops from it ;" Nicole "swears like a trooper," and as to Pascal he is all these characters in turn, while his book is " a repertory of slander," and is " villainous in a supreme degree !" The whole strain of Daniel's reply corresponds with this

---

[1] Bayle, Dict., art. *Pascal.*
[2] Daniel, Entretiens, p. 111..

specimen of its spirit. Avoiding the error of Pirot, and yet
without renouncing the favorite dogmas of the Society, such
as probabilism, equivocations, and mental reservations, which
he only attempts to palliate, Father Daniel has exhausted his
skill in an attack on the sincerity of Pascal. His main object is to convey the impression that the Provincials are a
libel, written in bad faith, and full of altered texts and false
citations. In selecting this plan of defence, the Jesuit champion evinces considerably more ingenuity than ingenuousness.
He was well aware that, at the time of their publication, the
Letters had been subjected to a sifting process of examination by the most clear-sighted Jesuits, who had signally failed
in proving any falsifications. But he knew also, that, during
the forty years that had elapsed, the writings of the casuists
had fallen into disuse and contempt, mainly in consequence
of the scorching which they had received from the wit and
eloquence of Pascal, and that it would be now a much easier
and safer task to call in question the fidelity of citations which
none would give themselves the trouble of verifying. In this
bold attempt to turn the tables against the Jansenists, by accusing them of chicanery and pious fraud, the very crimes
which they had succeeded in establishing against their opponents, the unscrupulous Jesuit could be at no loss to find,
among the voluminous writings of the casuists, some plausible grounds for his charges. At all events, he could calculate on the readiness with which certain minds, fonder of gen
eralizing than of investigating facts, would lay hold of the
mere circumstance of a book having been written in defence
of his order, as sufficient to show that a great deal may be
said on both sides. As to the manner in which Daniel has
executed his task, it might be sufficient to say, that it has
been acknowledged by the Jesuits themselves to be a failure.
Even at its first appearance, great efforts were made to suppress it altogether, as likely to do more harm than good to
the Society; and in their references to it afterwards, we see
the disappointment which they felt. "There was lately published," says Richelet, "an answer to the Lettres Provin-

ciales, which professes to demolish them, but which, nevertheless, will not do them much harm. Do you ask how?
The reason is, that although this answer shows the horrid
injustice, the abominable slanders, and injurious falsehoods of
the Provincials, against one of the most famous societies in
the Church, yet these Letters have so long, by their facetious
touches, got the laughers of all denominations on their side,
that they have acquired a credit and authority of which it
will be difficult to divest them. It must be confessed that
prejudice, on this occasion, is very unjust, very cruel, and
very obstinate in its verdict; since, though these Letters have
been condemned by popes, bishops, and divines, and burnt
by the hands of the hangman, yet they have taken such deep
root in people's minds as to bid defiance to all these powers."[1] " The reply," says another writer, " as may be easily
imagined, was not so well received as the Letters had been.
Father Daniel professed to have reason and truth on his side;
but his adversary had in his favor what goes much further
with men, the arms of ridicule and pleasantry."[2] This, however, is a mere begging of the question. *Ridentem dicere
verum, quid vetat?* It is quite possible that Father Daniel
may be lugubriously in the wrong, and Pascal laughingly in
the right. This was very triumphantly made out in the answer to Daniel's work, which appeared in the same year with
the *Entretiens*, under the title of " Apology for the Provincial Letters, against the last Reply of the Jesuits, entitled
Conversations of Cleander and Eudoxus." The author was
Don Mathieu Petitdidier, Benedictine of the congregation of
St. Vanne, who died bishop of Macra.[3] In this masterly performance, the accusations of Daniel are shown to be totally
groundless, his answers jesuitical and evasive, and his arguments untenable. The " Apology" was never answered, and
Daniel's work sank out of sight.

Subsequent apologists of the Jesuits have followed the

---

[1] Bayle, Dict., art. *Pascal*, note K.
[2] Abbé de Castres, Les Trois Siècles, ii. 63.
[3] Barbier, Dict. des Ouvrages Anon. et Pseudon.

line of defence adopted by Father Daniel. The continued repetition of his charges, though they have been long since disposed of, renders it necessary to advert to them. For the strict fidelity of Pascal's citations, we have not merely the testimony of contemporary witnesses, but what will be to many a sufficient guarantee, the solemn assertion of Pascal himself. In a conversation that took place within a year of his death, and which has been preserved by his sister, he thus answers the chief articles of accusation that had been brought against the Provincials:—

" I have been asked, first, if I repented of having written the Provincial Letters? I answered that, far from repenting, if I had it to do again, I would write them yet more strongly.

" I have been asked, in the second place, why I named the authors from whom I extracted these abominable passages which I have cited? I answered, If I were in a town where there were a dozen fountains, and I knew for certain that one of them was poisoned, I should be under obligation to tell the world not to draw from that fountain; and, as it might be supposed that this was a mere fancy on my part, I should be obliged to name him who had poisoned it, rather than expose a whole city to the risk of death.

" I have been asked, thirdly, why I adopted an agreeable, jocose, and entertaining style? I answered, If I had written dogmatically, none but the learned would have read my book; and they had no need of it, knowing how the matter stood, at least as well as I did. I conceived it, therefore, my duty to write, so that my Letters might be read by women, and people in general, that they might know the danger of all those maxims and propositions which were then spread abroad, and admitted with so little hesitation.

" Finally, I have been asked, if I had myself read all the books which I quoted? I answered, No. To do this, I had need have passed the greater part of my life in reading very bad books. But I have twice read Escobar throughout; and for the others, I got several of my friends to read them; but

I have never used a single passage without having read it my-self in the book quoted, without having examined the case in which it is brought forward, and without having read the preceding and subsequent context, that I might not run the risk of citing that for an answer which was in fact an objection, which would have been very unjust and blamable."[1]

If this solemn declaration, emitted by one whose heart was a stranger to deceit, and whose shrewdness placed him beyond the risk of delusion, is not accepted as sufficient, we might refer to the mass of evidence collected at the time in the *Factums* of the curés of Paris and Rouen, to the voluminous notes of Nicole, and to the Apology of Petitdidier, in which the citations made by Pascal are authenticated with a carefulness which not only sets all suspicion at rest, but leaves a large balance of credit in the author's favor, by showing that, so far from having reported the worst maxims of the Jesuitical school, or placed them in the most odious light of which they were susceptible, he has been extremely tender towards them. But, indeed, the truth was placed beyond all dispute, through the efforts of the celebrated Bossuet, in 1700, when, by a sentence of an assembly of the clergy of France, the morals of the Jesuits, as exhibited in their "monstrous maxims, which had been long the scandal of the Church and of Europe," were formally condemned, and when it may be said that the Provincial Letters met at once their full vindication and their final triumph.[2]

Another class of objectors, whom the Jesuits have had the good fortune to number among their apologists, are the sceptical philosophers, whose native antipathy to Jansenism, as a phase of serious religion, renders them willing to sacrifice truth for the sake of a sneer at his disciples. D'Alembert

---

[1] Tabaraud, *Dissertation sur la foi qui est due au Temoignage de Pascal dans ses Lettres Provinciales*, p. 12.—This work, published some years ago in France, contains a complete justification of Pascal's picture of the Jesuits in the Provincials, accompanied with a mass of authorities. The above sentiments have been introduced into Pascal's Thoughts. (See Craig's translation, p. 185.)

[2] Vie de Bossuet. t. iv. p. 19; Tabaraud, Dissert. sur la foi, &c., p. 43.

expresses his regret that Pascal did not lampoon Jesuits and Jansenists alike ;[1] and Voltaire, in the mere wantonness of his cynical humor, if not from a more worthless motive, has appended to his high panegyric on the Provincials, already quoted, the following qualifications: "It is true that the whole of Pascal's book is founded upon a false principle. He has artfully charged the whole Society with the extravagant opinions of some few Spanish and Flemish Jesuits, which he might with equal ease have detected among the casuists of the Dominican and Franciscan orders; but the Jesuits alone were the persons he wanted to attack. In these Letters he endeavored to prove that they had a settled design to corrupt the morals of mankind—a design which no sect or society ever had, or ever could have. But his business was not to be right, but to entertain the public."[2] Every clause here contains a fallacy. The charge of party-spirit, insinuated throughout, is perfectly gratuitous. Never, perhaps, was any man more free from this infirmity than Pascal. That it was pure zeal for the morality of the Gospel which engaged him to take up his pen against the Jesuits, can be doubted by none but those who make it a point to call in question the reality of all religious conviction.[3] Equally unfounded is the imputation of levity. Pascal was earnest in his raillery. A deep seriousness of purpose lurked under the smile of his irony. Voltaire describes himself, not the author of the Provincials, when he says that " his business was not to be right, but to entertain the public." As to Pascal having " endeavored to prove that the Jesuits had a settled design to corrupt the morals of mankind," we are not surprised at Father Daniel saying so ; but it is unaccountable how any but a Jesuit, who professed to have read the Letters, could advance a theory so distinctly anticipated and dis-

---

[1] " The shocking doctrine of Jansenius, and of St. Cyran, afforded at least as much room for ridicule as the pliant doctrine of Molina, Tambourin, and Vasquez." (D'Alembert, Dest. of the Jesuits, p. 55.)
[2] Voltaire, Siècle de Louis XIV., ii. 367.
[3] Eichhorn, Geschichte der Lit., i. 426.

claimed in the Letters themselves. "Know, then," it is said
in letter fifth, "that their object is not the corruption of
manners—that is *not their design.* But as little is it their
sole aim to reform them—that would be bad policy."[1]
"Alas!" says the Jesuit, in letter sixth, "our main object,
no doubt, should have been to establish no other maxims
than those of the Gospel; and it is easy to see, from our
rules, that if we tolerate some degree of relaxation in others,
it is rather out of complaisance than *design.*"[2] In truth,
nothing is more clearly marked throughout the Letters than
this distinction between the design of the Society and the
tendency of its policy—a distinction which leaves very small
scope for the sage apophthegm of the philosophical historian.
There is some reason to think that Voltaire expressed himself
in this manner, with the view of procuring the recommendation of Father Latour to enter the Academy—an object for
the accomplishment of which, it is well known, he made the
most unworthy concessions to the Jesuits.[‡]

Later critics, in speaking of the Provincials, have indulged
in a similar strain of vague depreciation; as a specimen of
which we might have referred to Schlegel, who talks of their
being "nothing more than a master-piece of sophistry,"[3]
and repeats the charge of profaneness, which Pascal has so
triumphantly refuted in his eleventh letter. It would be a
sad waste of time to answer this ridiculous objection. Nor
will it be surprising to those who know the history of Blanco
White, to find him indulging in a sceptical vein on this as on
other subjects. "Pascal and the Jansenist party," he says,
" accused them of systematic laxity in their moral doctrines ;
but the charge, I believe, though plausible in theory, was
perfectly groundless in practice. The strict, unbending maxims of the Jansenists, by urging persons of all characters and
tempers on to an imaginary goal of perfection, bring quickly
their whole system to the decision of experience. A greater

[1] Prov. Let., p. 196.   † Ib., p. 220.
[2] Tabaraud. p. 117; Bord. Demoulin, Eloge de Pascal, Append.
[3] Schlegel, Lectures on Hist. of Lit. ii. 188.

knowledge of mankind made the Jesuits more cautious in the culture of devotional feelings. They well knew that but few can prudently engage in open hostility with what, in ascetic language, is called the world."[1] The strange mixture of truth and error in this statement leaves an unfavorable impression on the mind, the fallacy of which we feel ere we have time to analyze it. It is true that nothing could be more opposite to the laxity of the Jesuits than the asceticism of Port-Royal. But it is doing injustice to Pascal to insinuate that he measured Jesuitical morality by "the strict, unbending maxims of the Jansenists;" and it is flagrantly untrue that the Jesuits merely aimed at reducing monastic enthusiasm to the standard of common sense and ordinary life. We repeat that the real charge which Pascal substantiates against them is, not that they softened the austerities of the cloister, but that they sacrificed the eternal laws of morality—not that they prudently suited their rules to men's tempers, but that they licensed the worst passions and propensities of our nature—not that they declined urging all to forsake the world (which he never expected), but that they sought, for their own politic ends, to veil its impurities, and countenance its evil customs.

Disguising their hostility to science, under the mask of friendship to literature, the Jesuits have succeeded in making to themselves friends of many who are acquainted with them only through the medium of their writings. And it is the remarkable fact of our day, that, while on the Continent, where they are practically known, the Jesuits have enlisted against themselves the pens of its most eminent novelists, historians, and philosophers, in Protestant England it is quite the reverse. The most talented of our periodical writers have exerted all their powers to white-wash them, to paint and paper them, and set them off with ornamental designs; and where they have not dared to defend, they have tried to blunt the edge of censure against them. Following in the

[1] Letters from Spain, p. 86.

same line of defence, a certain class of Protestant writers,
fond of historical paradox, and of appearing superior to vulgar prejudices, have volunteered to protect the Jesuits. " No
man is a stranger to the fame of Pascal," says Sir James
Macintosh ; " but those who may desire to form a right judgment on the contents of the *Lettres Provinciales* would do
well to cast a glance over the *Entretiens d'Ariste et d'Euge-
nie*, by Bouhours, a Jesuit, who has ably vindicated his
order."[1] Sir James had heard, perhaps, of Father Daniel's
Entretiens de Cleandre et d'Eudoxe, but it is very evident
that he had never even " cast a glance over" that book; for
the work of Bouhours, which he has confounded with it, is a
philological treatise, which has no reference whatever to the
Provincial Letters ; and yet he could say that the Jesuit
"has ably vindicated his order !" Next to the art which
the Jesuits have shown in smuggling themselves into places
of power and trust, is that by which they have succeeded in
hoodwinking the merely literary portion of society.

But, not to dwell longer on these objections, the Provincials are liable to another charge, seldomer advanced, and
not so easily answered ; which is, that the loose casuistical morality denounced by Pascal was not confined to the
Jesuits, nor to any one of the orders of the Romish Church,
much less, as Voltaire says, to "a few Spanish and Flemish
Jesuits," but was common to all the divines of that Church,
and was, in fact, the native offspring and inevitable growth
of the practices of confession and absolution. It is admitted
that the Jesuits were mainly responsible for its preservation
and propagation ; that they have been the most zealous in
reducing it to practice ; that, even after it had incurred the
anathemas of popes, bishops, and divines, and after it had
been disclaimed by all the other orders of the Church, the
Jesuits pertinaciously adhered to it ; and that, even to this
day, they have identified themselves with the worst tenets
of the casuists. But Protestants writers have generally al- .

---

[1] Macintosh, History of England, vol. ii. 359, note.

leged, not without reason, that the corruptions of casuistical divinity may be traced from the days of Thomas Aquinas and Cajetan, whom the Church of Rome owns as authorities; that the "new casuists" merely carried the maxims of their predecessors to their legitimate conclusions; and that though condemned by some popes, the censure has been only partial, and has been more than neutralized by the condemnation of other works written against the morality of the Jesuits. Thus, in a work entitled "Guimenius Amadeus," the author, who was the Jesuit Moya, boldly claimed the sanction of the most venerated names in favor of the modern casuists. This work, it is true, was condemned to the flames in 1680, by Pope Innocent XI., who was favorable to the Jansenists; but the Jesuits boast of having obtained other papal constitutions, reversing the judgment of that pontiff, whom they do not scruple to stigmatize with heresy.[1] It cannot be denied that the Jesuits have all along succeeded in obtaining for their system the sanction of the highest authorities in the Church; while those works which undertook to advocate a purer morality were printed clandestinely, without privilege or approbation, under fictitious names of authors and printers; nor can it be forgotten that the Provincial Letters, the most powerful exposure of Jesuitical morality that ever appeared, were censured at Rome, and burnt by the hands of the executioner.[2] In short, and without entering into the question so ingeniously handled by Nicole and other Jansenists, whether the modern casuists were justified in their excesses by the ancient schoolmen, it is undeniable that this is the weakest point of the Provincials, and one on which the thorough-going Jesuit occupies, on popish principles, the most advantageous ground. The disciples of Loyola constitute the very soul of the Papacy; and they must be held as the genuine exponents of that atro-

[1] Eichhorn, Geschichte der Litter., vol. i. pp. 423–425; Weisman, Hist. Eccl., vol. ii. 21; Jurieu, Prejugez Legitimes cont. le Papisme, p. 386; Claude. Defence of the Reformation, p. 29.

[2] Jurieu, Justification de la Morale des Reformez contre M. Arnauld, i. p. 30.

cious system of morals which, engendered in the privacy oi
the cloister during the dark ages, reached its maturity in the
hands of a designing priesthood, who still find it too convenient a tool for their purposes to part with it.

There are other respects in which we cannot fail to detect,
throughout these Letters, the enfeebling and embarrassing
influence of Popery over the naturally ingenuous mind of the
author. Among all the maxims peculiar to the Jesuits, none
are more pernicious than those in which they have openly
taught that disobedience to the Papal See releases subjects
from their allegiance and oaths of fidelity to their sovereigns,
and authorizes them to put heretical rulers to death, even
by assassination.[1]   On this point Pascal has failed to speak
out the whole truth. Whether it may have been from genuine
dread of heresy, or from a wish to spare the dignity of the
pope, it is easy to see the timidity, the circumspection, the
delicacy with which he touches on the point of papal authority.

The Jansenists have been called the Methodists of the
Church of Rome; but the term is applicable to them rather
in the wide sense in which it has been applied, derisively, to
those who have sought reformation or aimed at superior
sanctity within the pale of an established Church, than as
applied to the party now known under that designation.
They disclaimed the title of Jansenists, as a nickname applied

---

[1] A disingenuous attempt has been sometimes made to identify these
nefarious maxims with certain principles held by some of our reformers.
There is an essential difference between the natural right claimed, we
do not say with what justice, for subjects to proceed against their rulers
as tyrants. and the right assumed by the pope to depose rulers as heretics.   And it is equally easy to distinguish between the disallowed acts
of some fanatical individuals who have taken the law into their own
hands, and the atrocious deeds of such men as Chatel and Ravaillac,
who could plead the authority of Mariana the Jesuit, that "to put ty-
rannical princes to death is not only a lawful. but a laudable, heroic,
and glorious action." (Dalton's Jesuits; their Principles and Acts,
London, 1843.)   The Church of St. Ignatius at Rome is or was adorned, it seems, with pictures of all the assassinations mentioned in Scripture, which they have, most presumptuously, perverted in justification of
their feats in this department. (D'Alembert, Dest. of the Jesuits, p.
101.)

to them by their adversaries. They held themselves to be the true Catholics, the representatives of the Church as it existed down, at least, to the days of St. Bernard, whom they termed " the last of the fathers." They ascribed a species of semi-inspiration to the early fathers of the Church. They reverenced the Scriptures, but received them at secondhand, through the medium of tradition. To be a Catholic and a Christian were with them convertible terms. Hence the horror evinced by Pascal, in his concluding letters, at the bare thought of "heresy existing in the Church." "Embarrassed at every step," it has been well observed, " by their professed submission to the authority of the popes, galled and oppressed by their necessary acquiescence in the flagrant errors of their Church, these good men made profession of the great truths of Christianity under an incomparably heavier weight of disadvantage than has been sustained by any other class of Christians from the apostolic to the present times. Enfeebled by the enthusiasm to which they clung, the piety of these admirable men failed in the force necessary to carry them through the conflict with their atrocious enemy, 'the Society.' They were themselves in too many points vulnerable to close fearlessly with their adversary, and they grasped the sword of the Spirit in too infirm a manner to drive home a deadly thrust. . . . . . The Jansenists and the inmates of Port-Royal displayed a constancy that would doubtless have carried them through the fires of martyrdom ; but the intellectual courage necessary to bear them fearlessly through an examination of the errors of the papal superstition, could spring only from a healthy form of mind, utterly incompatible with the dotings of religious abstraction, and the petty solicitudes of sackclothed abstinence. The Jansenists had not such courage ; if they worshipped not the Beast, they cringed before him ; he placed his dragon-toot upon their necks, and their wisdom and their virtues were lost forever to France."[1]

[1] Taylor, Natural Hist. of Enthusiasm, p. 256.

It is the policy of the Jesuits at present, as of old, to deny,
point-blank, the truthfulness of Pascal's statements of their
doctrine and policy—to reiterate the exploded charge of his
having garbled his extracts—and, after affecting to join in
the laugh at his pleasantry, and to forgive, for the wit's sake,
his injustice to their innocent and much-calumniated fathers,
to declare that, of course, he could not himself believe the
half of what he said against them, nor comprehend the profound questions of casuistry on which he presumed to argue.
Under this affectation of charity, they dexterously evade Pascal's main charges, and slyly insinuate a vindication of the
heresies of which they have been convicted.   Thus, in a late
publication, one of their number actually attempts to vindicate the old Jesuitical doctrine of *probabilism!*[1]   At the
same time, they retain, with undiminished tenacity, the moral
maxims which Pascal condemns.   The discovery lately made
of the Theology of Dens, still taught by the Jesuits in Ire-
land, is a proof of this; for it is nothing more than a collection of the most wicked and obscene maxims of casuistical
morality.   Matters are no better in France.   Dr. Gilly men-
tions a publication issued at Lyons, in 1825, which is so bad
that the reviewer says, " We cannot, we dare not copy it; it
is a book to which the cases of conscience of Dr. Sanchez
were purity itself."[2]   The disclosures made still more recently by M. Michelet and M. Quinet, are equally startling,
and will, in all probability, issue in another expulsion of the
Jesuits from France.

The policy of the Society, as hitherto exhibited in the
countries where they have settled, describes a regular cycle
of changes.   Commencing with loud professions of charity,
of liberal views in politics, and of an accommodating code of
morals, they succeed in gaining popularity among the non-

[1] De l'Existence et de l'Institut des Jesuites. Par le R. P. de Ra-
vign an,de la Compagnie de Jesus. Paris, 1845, p. 83. *Probabilism* is
the doctrine, that if any opinion in morals has been held by any *grave
doctor* of the Church, it is *probably true*, and may be safely followed in
practice.
[2] Gilly, Narrative of an Excursion to Piedmont, p. 156

religious, the dissipated, and the restless portion of society. Availing themselves of this, and carefully concealing, in Protestant country, the more obnoxious parts of their creed, their next step is to plant some of the most plausible of their apostles in the principal localities, who are instructed to establish schools and seminaries on the most charitable footing, so as to ingratiate themselves with the poor, while they secure the contributions of the rich; to attack the credit of the most active and influential among the evangelical ministry; to revive old slanders against the reformers; to disseminate tracts of the most alluring description ; and, when assailed in turn, to deny everything and to grant nothing. Rising by these means to power and influence, they gradually monopolize the seats of learning and the halls of theology—they glide, with noiseless steps, into closets, cabinets, and palaces—they become the dictators of the public press, the persecutors of the good, and the oppressors of all public and private liberty. At length, their treacherous designs being discovered, they rouse against themselves the storm of natural passions, which, descending on them first as the authors of the mischief, sweeps away along with them, in its headlong career, everything that bears the aspect of that active and earnest religion, under the guise of which they had succeeded in duping mankind.

What portion of this cycle they have reached among us, it is needless to demonstrate. They have evidently got beyond the first stage; and it is highly probable that, in proof of it, the present publication may elicit a more than ordinary exhibition of their skill in the science of defamation and denial. It is far from being unlikely that, at the present point of their revolution, they may find it their interest, after all the mischief that Pascal has done them, and all the ill that they have spoken against Pascal, to claim him as a good Catholic, and take advantage of the prestige of his name to insinuate, that the Church which could boast of such a man is not to be lightly esteemed. And, in fact, it requires no small exercise of caution to guard ourselves against such an illusion. It is difficult to characterize Popery as it deserves without apparent uncharitableness to individuals, such as Fenelon and Pascal, who, though members of a corrupt Church, possessed much of the spirit of true religion. But, though it would be impossible to class such eminent and pious men with an infidel cardinal or a Spanish inquisitor, it does not follow that they are free from condemnation. It has been justly remarked, that "their example has done much harm, and been only the more pernicious from their eminence and their virtues. It is difficult to calculate how much assistance their well-merited reputation has given to prop the falling cause of Popery, and to lengthen out the continuance of a delusion the most lasting and the most dangerous that has ever led mankind astray from the truth."[1] With regard to our author, in particular, it may be well to remember, that he was virtuous without being indebted to his Church, and evangelical in spite of his creed; that his piety, for which he is so much esteemed by us, was the very quality that ex-posed him to odium and suspicion from his own communion; that the truths, for his adherence to which we would claim him as a brother in Christ, were those which were reprobated by the authorities of Rome; and that the following Letters, for which he is so justly admired, were, by the same Church, formally censured and ignominiously burnt, along with the Bible which Pascal loved, and the martyrs who have suffered for "the truth as it is in Jesus."

[1] Douglas on Errors in Religion, p. 113.

LIST OF WORKS

TO BE CONSULTED WITH REFERENCE TO PASCAL AND HIS WRITINGS.

Recueil de plusieurs pièces pour servir à l'histoire de Port-Royal. Utrecht, 1740, in–12.

Mémoires pour servir à l'histoire de Port-Royal et à la vie de la mère Angélique. Utrecht, 1742, t. iii.

Vies intéressantes des religieuses de Port-Royal, 1751, t. ii.

Lettres, opuscules et mémoires de madame Perier, de Jacqueline, sœur de Pascal, et de Marguerite Perier, sa nièce, publiés sur les manuscrits originaux, par M. P. Faugère. 1845, 1 vol. in–8.

COUSIN, *Jacqueline Pascal.* Paris, 1845, in–18.

The five works whose titles are given above, although separated by wide intervals of time, and all subsequent to the seventeenth century, may be regarded as the most direct sources for the history of Pascal and that of his family, because they are almost exclusively composed of contemporaneous documents ; for which reason we place them at the head of this bibliographical notice.

Eloge de Pascal, by Nicole (in Latin), reproduced by the Abbé Bossut, at the head of his edition.

BAILLET, *Vie de Descartes,* IIe part., p. 330.

Sentiments de M.... (Boullier) *sur la Critique des Pensées de Pascal, par M. de Voltaire,* 1741 et 1753. An excellent composition by a French Protestant, a refugee in Holland. Boullier was the only champion who defended Pascal against Voltaire ; and he did it, according to M. Sainte-Beuve, with gravity and vigor, planting himself from the outset at the centre of attack. See *Port-Royal,* vol. iii., p. 323 et sequens.

Eloge de Blaise Pascal, par Condorcet, 1776. Reprinted in the *Œuvres de Condorcet,* Paris, Didot, 1847, in–8, t. iii., p. 567 et seq.

Remarques de Voltaire sur les pensées de Pascal. Sixty-four of these remarks, under the date of 1728, are preceded by an Advertisement added by Voltaire ; eight others bear the date of May 10, 1743, and are applied to certain of the *Pensées* published by P. Desmolets, which the early editors had rejected from their collection ; finally ninety-four appeared, for the first time, in the octavo edition which Voltaire caused to be published at Geneva, in 1778.

Discours sur la vie et les ouvrages de Pascal, by the Abbé Bossut, inserted in the edition of 1779, 5 vol. in–8, and reprinted separately, with additions and corrections, in 1781.

Sur Pascal: CHATEAUBRIAND, *Génie du Christianisme,* IIIe part., liv. ii., chap. vi.

Eloge de Blaise Pascal, par Alexis Dumesnil. Paris, 1813, in–8.

Eloge de Blaise Pascal, accompagné de notes historiques et critiques, by Georges-Marie Raymond. Lyon, 1816, in-8. 2ᵉ édit.
J. H. MONNIER, *Essai sur Blaise Pascal.* Paris, 1822, in-8.
Discours préliminaire de l'édition des Pensées, par M. Frantin. Dijon, 1835, 2ᵉ édit., 1853.
Journal des Savants, 1839, p. 554.
REUCHLIN, *Pascal's Leben.* Stuttgard, 1840.
COUSIN. *Sur la nécessité d'une nouvelle édition des Pensées de Pascal.* Report to the French Academy. (*Journal des Savants,* avril-novembre, 1842.) Reprinted under the following title : *Des Pensées de Pascal,* etc. Paris, 1843, in-8. See M. Foisset's *compte-rendu* of this work, in the *Correspondant,* April, 1843. A new edition (*revue et corrigée*) appeared in 1849. In a preface to this new edition, M. Cousin discusses, at great length, the question of Pascal's philosophic skepticism. Inasmuch as a great deal of needless controversy has grown out of a misapprehension—the confounding of skepticism in philosophy with skepticism in religion, we will here give M. Cousin's very clear statement of the question. There probably will be no difference of opinion among those competent to form a judgment, when the point shall be definitely understood.

"Already, in 1828,"[1] says M. Cousin, "we had found Pascal a skeptic, even in Port-Royal and Bossut; in 1842, we found him still more skeptical in the autograph manuscript, and, in spite of the lively controversy that has been awakened on the subject, our conviction has not been for a single moment shaken—it has been even strengthened by new studies.

" ' What! Pascal a skeptic?' such is the cry raised in almost every quarter. ' What Pascal are you putting in the place of him who has hitherto been regarded as one of the greatest defenders of the Christian religion?' A truce, gentlemen ; let us understand each other, I beg you. I have not said that Pascal was a skeptic in religion : that were indeed a little too absurd : far from that, Pascal believed in Christianity with all the powers of his soul........The question must be stated with clearness and precision :—Pascal was a skeptic in philosophy and not in religion ; and because he was a skeptic in philosophy he attached himself so much the more closely to religion, as to the last resource of humanity in the impotence of reason, in the ruin of all natural truth among men. This is what I have said, what I now maintain......

" What is skepticism? It is a philosophical opinion that consists precisely in rejecting all philosophy as impossible, on the ground that man is incapable of reaching by himself any truth, still less those truths that constitute what is called, in philosophy, Ethics and Natural Religion, that is, the freedom of man, the law of duty, the distinction between just and unjust, between good and evil, the sanctity of virtue, the immateriality of the soul, and Divine Providence. All philosophers worthy of the name aspire to these truths. In order to reach them one takes one course, another another : processes differ ; hence diverse methods and schools, less opposed to each other than one at first sight would believe, whose history expresses the movement and progress of human intelligence and civilization. But the most different schools pursue the same end,—the

---

[1] *Cours de l'histoire de la philosophie moderne,* IIᵉ Série, t. ii., leç. xii., p. 388.

establishment of truth ; and they set out from a common principle, from the firm conviction that man has received from God the power of attaining truths of the moral order, as well as those of the physical order. This natural power, which they place in sensation or reflection, in sentiment or intellect, is among themselves a subject of family quarrel ; but they are all agreed upon the essential point, that man possesses the power of reaching truth ; for upon this condition, and this alone, philosophy is not a chimera.   .

"Skepticism is the adversary, not only of such or such a school of philosophy, but of all schools. We must not confound skepticism and doubt. Doubt has its legitimate use, its wisdom, its utility. It serves philosophy in its way, for it warns her of her aberrations, and reminds reason of its imperfections and limits. It may be applied to such a result, such a process, such a principle, even such an order of cognitions ; but as soon as it is applied to the faculty of knowing, if it contests with reason her power and her rights, from that moment doubt is no longer doubt, it is skepticism. Doubt does not shun truth, it seeks it, and the better to attain it, watches over and holds in check the procedures—often rash—of reason. Skepticism does not seek the truth, for it knows, or thinks it knows, that there is none and can be none for man. Doubt is to philosophy an inconvenient, often an importunate, always a useful friend : skepticism is to it a mortal enemy. Doubt occupies, in some sort, the place in the empire of philosophy of the constitutional opposition in the representative system ; it acknowledges the principle of the government, only criticises its acts, and that too, in the very interest of the government. Skepticism resembles an opposition that labors to ruin the established order, and exerts itself to destroy the principle itself in virtue of which it speaks. In days of peril, the constitutional opposition hastens to the support of the government, while the other opposition invokes dangers, and in them places its hopes of triumph. Thus, when the rights of philosophy are menaced, doubt, feeling itself also menaced, rallies to her as to its own principle ; skepticism, on the contrary, then lifts the mask and openly betrays.

"Skepticism is of two kinds : it is either its own end, and rests tranquilly in the negation of all certitude ; or it has a secret aim quite different from its apparent object. In the bosom of philosophy it has the appearance of combating for the unlimited liberty of the human mind, against the tyranny of what it calls philosophical dogmatism, while in reality it is conspiring in favor of a foreign tyranny.

"Who does not remember, for example, having seen in our times a French writer[1] preaching, in one volume of the "Essay on Indifference," the most absolute skepticism, in order to conduct us, in the other volumes, to the most absolute dogmatism that ever existed?

"It remains to ascertain whether skepticism, as we have just defined it in general, is or is not in the book of 'Thoughts.'

"According to us, it is, and manifests itself on every page, at every line. Pascal breathes skepticism ; he is full of it ; he proclaims its principle, accepts all its consequences, and pushes it at the outset to its final term, which is the avowed contempt and almost hatred of all philosophy.

"Yes, Pascal is a declared enemy of philosophy : he believes in it

---

[1] The allusion is to the Abbé de Lamennais.—ED.

140 BIBLIOGRAPHICAL NOTICE.

neither much nor little; he absolutely rejects it."—(*Blaise Pascal*, *préface de la nouvelle édition*, pp. 3-6.)

Du scepticisme de Pascal. (*Revue des Deux Mondes*, 15 décembre, 1844 —15 janvier, 1845.)

BORNAS-DEMOULIN, *Eloge de Pascal* (concours de l'Académie française, en 1842).

PROSPER FAUGÈRE, *Eloge de Pascal* (même concours).

Fait inédit de la vie de Pascal, par M. François Collet. Paris, 1848, in-8 de 44 pages.

Histoire de la Littérature française de M. Nisard, t. i.

Pensées, fragments et lettres de Blaise Pascal, published for the first time after the original manuscripts in great part inedited, by M. Prosper Faugère. Paris, 1844, 2 vols. in-8. See M. Sainte-Beuve's *Compte-rendu* of this work in the *Revue des Deux Mondes*, 1er juillet, 1844.

ALEX. THOMAS, *de Pascali; an vere scepticus fuerit.* 1844, in-8 (thesis for a doctorate).

De l'Amulette de Pascal, étude sur le rapport de la santé de ce grand homme à son génie, par le docteur Lélut. Paris, 1846, in-8.

North British Review. August, 1844 (Article on Pascal).

Edinburgh Review. January, 1847 (Article on Pascal).

L'ABBÉ FLOTTE, *Etudes sur Pascal.* 1843-1845, in-8.

VINET, *Etudes sur Pascal*, 1844-1847.

De la méthode philosophique de Pascal, par Lescœur, 1850.

L'ABBÉ MAYNARD, *Pascal, sa vie, son caractère*, etc. Paris, 1850, 2 vol. in-8. The principal object of this book is to defend Pascal against the charge of skepticism.

SAINTE-BEUVE, *Port-Royal*, t. ii., liv. iii., chap. i. ii. iii. iv. v. vi. vii. ; t. iii., liv. iii., chap. viii. ix. x. xi. xii. xiii. xvii. xviii. xix. xx. xxi.

HAVET, *Etude sur les Pensées de Pascal* (Introduction of his edition of the *Pensées*). Paris, Dezobry, 1852, in-8.

Revue de théologie et la philosophie chrétienne. Vol. 8, 1854. Several articles on Pascal, in which M. F.-L. Fréd. Chavannes aims to show the part played by the idea of authority in the life of the author of the *Pensées*.

Revue chrétienne, 1854. *Pascal et le vicaire savoyard*, par J.-F. Astié.

Pensées de Pascal, édition variorum, par Charles Louandre. Paris, Charpentier, 1858.

Pensées de Pascal, édition complète, avec des notes, un index et une préface par J.-F. Astié. Paris et Lausanne, 1857.

Select Memoirs of Port-Royal; to which are added, Tour to Alet, Visit to Port-Royal, Gift of an Abbess, Biographical Notices, &c., from original documents; by M. A. Schimmelpenninck. Fifth edition, 3 vols. 8vo. London : Longman, Brown & Co., 1859.

Whoever wishes to read the *Provinciales* in the original, will find a pure text and beautiful typography in the Lefèvre edition, among the *Chefs-d'Œuvre Littéraires du XVII. Siècle;* Didot Frères, Paris.

THE PROVINCIAL LETTERS.

∫ LETTER I.

DISPUTES IN THE SORBONNE, AND THE INVENTION OF PROXIMATE
POWER—A TERM EMPLOYED BY THE JESUITS TO PROCURE THE
CENSURE OF M. ARNAULD.

PARIS, *January* 23, 1656.

SIR,—We were entirely mistaken. It was only yesterday
that I was undeceived. Until that time I had labored under
the impression that the disputes in the Sorbonne were vastly
important, and deeply affected the interests of religion. The
frequent convocations of an assembly so illustrious as that of
the Theological Faculty of Paris, attended by so many extraordinary and unprecedented circumstances, led one to form
such high expectations, that it was impossible to help coming
to the conclusion that the subject was most extraordinary.
You will be greatly surprised, however, when you learn from
the following account, the issue of this grand demonstration,
which, having made myself perfectly master of the subject,
I shall be able to tell you in very few words.

Two questions, then, were brought under examination; the
one a question of fact, the other a question of right.

The question of fact consisted in ascertaining whether M.
Arnauld was guilty of presumption, for having asserted in
his second letter[1] that he had carefully perused the book of

---

[1] Anthony Arnauld, or Arnaud, priest and doctor of the Sorbonne,
was the son of Anthony Arnauld, a famous advocate, and born at Paris,
February 6, 1612. He early distinguished himself in philosophy and
divinity, advocating the doctrines of Augustine and Port-Royal, and op-

Jansenius, and that he had not discovered the propositions condemned by the late pope; but that, nevertheless, as he condemned these propositions wherever they might occur, he condemned them in Jansenius, if they were really contained in that work.[1]

The question here was, if he could, without presumption, entertain a doubt that these propositions were in Jansenius, after the bishops had declared that they were.

The matter having been brought before the Sorbonne, seventy-one doctors undertook his defence, maintaining that the only reply he could possibly give to the demands made upon him in so many publications, calling on him to say if he held that these propositions were in that book, was, that he had not been able to find them, but that if they were in the book, he condemned them in the book.

Some even went a step farther, and protested that, after all the search they had made into the book, they had never stumbled upon these propositions, and that they had, on the contrary, found sentiments entirely at variance with them. They then earnestly begged that, if any doctor present had discovered them, he would have the goodness to point them out; adding, that what was so easy could not reasonably be refused, as this would be the surest way to silence the whole

posing those of the Jesuits. The disputes concerning grace which broke out about 1643 in the University of Paris, served to foment the mutual animosity between M. Arnauld and the Jesuits, who entertained a hereditary feud against the whole family, from the active part taken by their father against the Society in the close of the preceding century. In 1655 it happened that a certain duke, who was educating his grand-daughter at Port-Royal, the Jansenist monastery, and kept a Jansenist abbé in his house, on presenting himself for confession to a priest under the influence of the Jesuits, was refused absolution, unless he promised to recall his grand-daughter and discard his abbé. This produced two letters from M. Arnauld, in the second of which he exposed the calumnies and falsities with which the Jesuits had assailed him in a multitude of pamphlets. This is the letter referred to in the text.

[1] The book which occasioned these disputes was entitled *Augustinus*, and was written by Cornelius Jansenius or Jansen, bishop of Ypres, and published after his death. Five propositions, selected from this work, were condemned by the pope; and armed with these, as with a scourge, the Jesuits continued to persecute the Jansenists till they accomplished their ruin.

of them, M. Arnauld included; but this proposal has been uniformly declined. So much for the one side.

On the other side are eighty secular doctors, and some forty mendicant friars, who have condemned M. Arnauld's proposition, without choosing to examine whether he has spoken truly or falsely—who, in fact, have declared, that they have nothing to do with the veracity of his proposition, but simply with its temerity.

Besides these, there were fifteen who were not in favor of the censure, and who are called Neutrals.

Such was the issue of the question of fact, regarding which, I must say, I give myself very little concern. It does not affect my conscience in the least whether M. Arnauld is presumptuous, or the reverse ; and should I be tempted, from curiosity, to ascertain whether these propositions are contained in Jansenius, his book is neither so very rare nor so very large as to hinder me from reading it over from beginning to end, for my own satisfaction, without consulting the Sorbonne on the matter.

Were it not, however, for the dread of being presumptuous myself, I really think that I would be disposed to adopt the opinion which has been formed by the most of my acquaintances, who, though they have believed hitherto on common report that the propositions were in Jansenius, begin now to suspect the contrary, owing to this strange refusal to point them out—a refusal, the more extraordinary to me, as I have not yet met with a single individual who can say that he has discovered them in that work. I am afraid, therefore, that this censure will do more harm than good, and that the impression which it will leave on the minds of all who know its history will be just the reverse of the conclusion that has been come to. The truth is, the world has become sceptical of late, and will not believe things till it sees them. But, as I said before, this point is of very little moment, as it has no concern with religion.[1]

[1] And yet " the question of fact," which Pascal professes to treat so lightly, became the turning point of all the subsequent persecutions di-

The question of right, from its affecting the faith, appears much more important, and, accordingly, I took particular pains in examining it. You will be relieved, however, to find that it is of as little consequence as the former.

The point of dispute here, was an assertion of M. Arnauld's in the same letter, to the effect, "that the grace without which we can do nothing, was wanting to St. Peter at his fall." You and I supposed that the controversy here would turn upon the great principles of grace ; such as, whether grace is given to all men? or, if it is efficacious of itself? But we were quite mistaken. You must know I have become a great theologian within this short time ; and now for the proofs of it !

To ascertain the matter with certainty, I repaired to my neighbor, M. N——, doctor of Navarre, who, as you are aware, is one of the keenest opponents of the Jansenists, and my curiosity having made me almost as keen as himself, I asked him if they would not formally decide at once that "grace is given to all men," and thus set the question at rest. But he gave me a sore rebuff, and told me that that was not the point; that there were some of his party who held that grace was not given to all ; that the examiners themselves had declared, in a full assembly of the Sorbonne, that that opinion was *problematical ;* and that he himself held the same sentiment, which he confirmed by quoting to me what he called that celebrated passage of St. Augustine : " We know that grace is not given to all men."

I apologized for having misapprehended his sentiment, and requested him to say if they would not at least condemn that other opinion of the Jansenists which is making so much noise, "That grace is efficacious of itself, and invincibly de-

rected against the unhappy Port-Royalists ! Those who have read the sad tale of the demolition of Port-Royal, will recollect, with a sigh, the sufferings inflicted on the poor scholars and pious nuns of that establishment, solely on the ground that, from respect to Jansenius and to a good conscience, they would not subscribe a formulary acknowledging the five propositions to be contained in his book.—(See Narrative of the Demolition of the Monastery of Port-Royal, by Mary Anne Schimmelpenninck p. 170, &c.)

termines our will to what is good." But in this second query
I was equally unfortunate. "You know nothing about the
matter," he said; "that is not a heresy—it is an orthodox
opinion; all the Thomists[1] maintain it; and I myself have
defended it in my Sorbonic thesis."[2]

I did not venture again to propose my doubts, and yet I
was as far as ever from understanding where the difficulty
lay; so, at last, in order to get at it, I begged him to tell
me where, then, lay the heresy of M. Arnauld's proposition?
"It lies here," said he, "that he does not acknowledge that
the righteous have the power of obeying the commandments
of God, in the manner in which we understand it."

On receiving this piece of information, I took my leave of
him; and, quite proud at having discovered the knot of the
question, I sought M. N——, who is gradually getting better, and was sufficiently recovered to conduct me to the house
of his brother-in-law, who is a Jansenist, if ever there was
one, but a very good man notwithstanding. Thinking to insure myself a better reception, I pretended to be very high
on what I took to be his side, and said: "Is it possible that
the Sorbonne has introduced into the Church such an error
as this, 'that all the righteous have always the power of
obeying the commandments of God?'"

"What say you?" replied the doctor. "Call you that an
error—a sentiment so Catholic that none but Lutherans and
Calvinists impugn it?"

"Indeed!" said I, surprised in my turn; "so you are not
of their opinion?"

---

[1] The Thomists were so called after Thomas Aquinas, the celebrated
"Angelic Doctor" of the schools. He flourished in the thirteenth century, and was opposed, in the following century, by Duns Scotus, a
British, some say a Scottish, monk of the order of St. Francis. This
gave rise to a fierce and protracted controversy, in the course of which
the Franciscans took the side of Duns Scotus, and were called Scotists;
while the Dominicans espoused the cause of Thomas Aquinas, and
were sometimes called Thomists.

[2] *Sorbonique*—an act or thesis of divinity, delivered in the hall of the
college of the Sorbonne by candidates for the degree of doctor.

"No," he replied; "we anathematize it as heretical and impious."

Confounded by this reply, I soon discovered that I had overacted the Jansenist, as I had formerly overdone the Molinist.[2] But not being sure if I had rightly understood him, I requested him to tell me frankly if he held "that the righteous have always a real power to observe the divine precepts?" Upon this the good man got warm (but it was with a holy zeal), and protested that he would not disguise his sentiments on any consideration—that such was, indeed, his belief, and that he and all his party would defend it to the death, as the pure doctrine of St. Thomas, and of St. Augustine their master.

This was spoken so seriously as to leave me no room for doubt ; and under this impression I returned to my first doctor, and said to him, with an air of great satisfaction, that I was sure there would be peace in the Sorbonne very soon ; that the Jansenists were quite at one with them in reference to the power of the righteous to obey the commandments of God ; that I could pledge my word for them, and could make them seal it with their blood.

"Hold there !" said he. "One must be a theologian to see the point of this question. The difference between us is so subtle, that it is with some difficulty we can discern it ourselves—you will find it rather too much for your powers of comprehension. Content yourself, then, with knowing that it is very true the Jansenists will tell you that all the righteous have always the power of obeying the commandments ; that is not the point in dispute between us ; but mark you,

---

[1] The Jansenists, in their dread of being classed with Lutherans and Calvinists, condescended to quibble on this question. In reality, as we shall see, they agreed with the Reformers. for they denied that any could actually obey the commandments without efficacious grace.

[2] *Molinist.* The Jesuits were so called, in this dispute, after Lewis Molina. a famous Jesuit of Spain. who published a work, entitled *Concordia Gratiæ et Liberi Arbitrii*, in which he professed to have found out a new way of reconciling the freedom of the human will with the divine prescience. This new invention was termed *Scientia Media*, or middle knowledge, All who adopted the sentiments of Molina, whether Jesuits or not, were termed Molinists.

they will not tell you that that power is *proximate*. That is the point."

This was a new and unknown word to me. Up to this moment I had managed to understand matters, but that term involved me in obscurity; and I verily believe that it has been invented for no other purpose than to mystify. I requested him to give me an explanation of it, but he made a mystery of it, and sent me back, without any further satisfaction, to demand of the Jansenists if they would admit this *proximate power*. Having charged my memory with the phrase (as to my understanding, that was out of the question), I hastened with all possible expedition, fearing that I might forget it, to my Jansenist friend, and accosted him, immediately after our first salutations, with : "Tell me, pray, if you admit *the proximate power ?*" He smiled, and replied, coldly: "Tell me yourself in what sense you understand it, and I may then inform you what I think of it." As my knowledge did not extend quite so far, I was at a loss what reply to make ; and yet, rather than lose the object of my visit, I said at random : "Why, I understand it in the sense of the Molinists." "To which of the Molinists do you refer me ?" replied he, with the utmost coolness. I referred him to the whole of them together, as forming one body, and animated by one spirit.

"You know very little about the matter," returned he. "So far are they from being united in sentiment, that some of them are diametrically opposed to each other. But, being all united in the design to ruin M. Arnauld, they have resolved to agree on this term *proximate*, which both parties might use indiscriminately, though they understand it diversely, that thus, by a similarity of language, and an apparent conformity, they may form a large body, and get up a majority to crush him with the greater certainty."

This reply filled me with amazement ; but without imbibing these impressions of the malicious designs of the Molinists, which I am unwilling to believe on his word, and with which I have no concern, I set myself simply to ascertain the various senses which they give to that mysterious word *prox-imate*. " I would enlighten you on the subject with all my heart," he said; " but you would discover in it such a mass of contrariety and contradiction, that you would hardly believe me. You would suspect me. To make sure of the matter, you had better learn it from some of themselves ; and I shall give you some of their addresses. You have only to make a separate visit to one called M. le Moine,¹ and to Father Nicolai."²

" I have no acquaintance with any of these persons," said I.

"Let me see, then," he replied, " if you know any of those whom I shall name to you; they all agree in sentiment with M. le Moine."

I happened, in fact, to know some of them.

" Well, let us see if you are acquainted with any of the Dominicans whom they call the 'New Thomists,'³ for they are all the same with Father Nicolai."

I knew some of them also whom he named ; and, resolved to profit by this counsel, and to investigate the matter, I took my leave of him, and went immediately to one of the

---

¹ *Pierre le Moine* was a doctor of the Sorboone, whom Cardinal Richelieu employed to write against Jansenius. This Jesuit was the author of several works, which display considerable talent, though little principle. His book on Grace was forcibly answered, and himself somewhat severely handled, in a work entitled " An Apology for the Holy Fathers," which he suspected to be written by Arnauld. It was Le Moine who, according to Nicole, had the chief share in raising the storm against Arnauld, of whom he was the bitter and avowed enemy.

² *Father Nicolai* was a Dominican—an order of friars who professed to be followers of St. Thomas. He is here mentioned as a representative of his class; but Nicole informs us that he abandoned the principles of his order, and became a Molinist, or an abettor of Pelagianism.

³ *New Thomists.* It is more difficult to trace or remember the various sects into which the Roman Church is divided, than those of the Protestant Church. The New Thomists were the disciples of Diego Alvarez, a theologian of the order of St. Dominic. who flourished in the sixteenth and seventeenth centuries. He was sent from Spain to Rome in 1596, to defend the doctrine of grace against Molina, and distinguished himself in the Congregation *De Auxiliis*. The New Thomists contended for *efficacious grace*, but admitted, at the same time, a *sufficient grace*, which was given to all, and yet not sufficient for any actual performance without the efficacious. The ridiculous incongruity of this doctrine is admirably exposed by Pascal in his second letter.

disciples of M. le Moine. I begged him to inform me what it was to have the *proximate power* of doing a thing.

" It is easy to tell you that," he replied ; " it is merely to have all that is necessary for doing it in such a manner that nothing is wanting to performance."

" And so," said I, " to have the proximate power of crossing a river, for example, is to have a boat, boatmen, oars, and all the rest, so that nothing is wanting ?"

" Exactly so," said the monk.

" And to have the proximate power of *seeing*," continued I, " must be to have good eyes and the light of day; for a person with good sight in the dark would not have the proximate power of seeing, according to you, as he would want the light, without which one cannot see ?"

" Precisely," said he.

" And consequently," returned I, " when you say that all the righteous have the proximate power of observing the commandments of God, you mean that they have always all the grace necessary for observing them, so that nothing is wanting to them on the part of God."

" Stay there," he replied ; " they have always all that is necessary for observing the commandments, or at least for asking it of God."

" I understand you," said I ; " they have all that is necessary for praying to God to assist them, without requiring any new grace from God to enable them to pray."

" You have it now," he rejoined.

" But is it not necessary that they have an efficacious grace, in order to pray to God ?"

" No," said he ; " not according to M. le Moine."

To lose no time, I went to the Jacobins,[1] and requested

---

[1] *Jacobins*, another name for the Dominicans in France, where they were so called from the street in Paris, Rue de St. Jacques where their first convent was erected, in the year 1218. In England they were called Black Friars. Their founder was Dominick, a Spaniard. His mother, it is said, dreamt, before his birth, that she was to be delivered of a wolf with a torch in his mouth. The augury was realized in the barbarous humor of Dominick, and the massacres which he occasioned in various parts of the world, by preaching up crusades against the

an interview with some whom I knew to be New Thomists, and I begged them to tell me what "proximate power" was. "Is it not," said I, "that power to which nothing is wanting in order to act ?"

"No," said they.

"Indeed ! fathers," said I; "if anything is wanting to that power, do you call it proximate ? Would you say, for instance, that a man in the night time, and without any light, had the proximate power of seeing ?"

"Yes, indeed, he would have it, in our opinion, if he is not blind."

"I grant that," said I ; "but M. le Moine understands it in a different manner."

"Very true," they replied; "but so it is that we understand it."

"I have no objections to that," I said ; "for I never quarrel about a name, provided I am apprized of the sense in which it is understood. But I perceive from this, that when you speak of the righteous having always the proximate power of praying to God, you understand that they require another supply for praying, without which they will never pray."

"Most excellent !" exclaimed the good fathers, embracing me ; "exactly the thing; for they must have, besides, an efficacious grace bestowed upon all, and which determines their wills to pray ; and it is heresy to deny the necessity of that efficacious grace in order to pray."

"Most excellent !" cried I, in return ; "but, according to you, the Jansenists are Catholics, and M. le Moine a heretic ; for the Jansenists maintain that, while the righteous have power to pray, they require nevertheless an efficacious grace; and this is what you approve. M. le Moine, again, maintains that the righteous may pray without efficacious grace; and this is what you condemn."

heretics. He was the founder of the Inquisition, and his order was, before the Reformation, what the Jesuits were after it—the soul of the Romish hierarchy, and the bitterest enemies of the truth.

"Ay," said they; "but M. le Moine calls that power *proximate power.*"

"How now! fathers," I exclaimed; "this is merely playing with words, to say that you are agreed as to the common terms which you employ, while you differ with them as to the sense of these terms."

The fathers made no reply; and at this juncture, who should come in but my old friend the disciple of M. le Moine! I regarded this at the time as an extraordinary piece of good fortune; but I have discovered since then that such meetings are not rare—that, in fact, they are constantly mixing in each other's society.[1]

"I know a man," said I, addressing myself to M. le Moine's disciple, "who holds that all the righteous have always the power of praying to God, but that, notwithstanding this, they will never pray without an efficacious grace which determines them, and which God does not always give to all the righteous. Is he a heretic?"

"Stay," said the doctor; "you might take me by surprise. Let us go cautiously to work. *Distinguo.*[2] If he call that power *proximate power,* he will be a Thomist, and therefore a Catholic; if not, he will be a Jansenist, and therefore a heretic."

"He calls it neither proximate nor non-proximate," said I.

"Then he is a heretic," quoth he; "I refer you to these good fathers if he is not."

I did not appeal to them as judges, for they had already nodded assent; but I said to them: "He refuses to admit that word *proximate,* because he can meet with nobody who will explain it to him."

[1] This is a *sly* hit at the Dominicans for combining with their natural enemies the Jesuits, in order to accomplish the ruin of M. Arnauld.

[2] *Distinguo.* "I draw a distinction"—a humorous allusion to the endless distinctions of the Aristotelian school, in which the writings of the Casuists abounded, and by means of which they may be said to have more frequently eluded than elucidated the truth. M. le Moine was particularly famous for these *distinguos,* frequently introducing three or four of them in succession on one head; and the disciple in the text is made to echo the favorite phrase of his master.

Upon this one of the fathers was on the point of offering his definition of the term, when he was interrupted by M. le Moine's disciple, who said to him : " Do you mean, then, to renew our broils ? Have we not agreed not to explain that word *proximate*, but to use it on both sides without saying what it signifies ?" To this the Jacobin gave his assent.

I was thus let into the whole secret of their plot ; and rising to take my leave of them, I remarked : " Indeed, fathers, I am much afraid this is nothing better than pure chicanery ; and whatever may be the result of your convocations, I venture to predict that, though the censure should pass, peace will not be established. For though it should be decided that the syllables of that word *proximate* should be pronounced, who does not see that, the meaning not being explained, each of you will be disposed to claim the victory ? The Jacobins will contend that the word is to be understood in their sense ; M. le Moine will insist that it must be taken in his ; and thus there will be more wrangling about the explanation of the word than about its introduction. For, after all, there would be no great danger in adopting it without any sense, seeing it is through the sense only that it can do any harm. But it would be unworthy of the Sorbonne and of theology to employ equivocal and captious terms without giving any explanation of them. In short, fathers, tell me, I entreat you, for the last time, what is necessary to be believed in order to be a good Catholic ?"

" You must say," they all vociferated simultaneously, " that all the righteous have the *proximate power*, abstracting from it all sense—from the sense of the Thomists and the sense of other divines."

" That is to say," I replied, in taking leave of them, " that I must pronounce that word to avoid being the heretic of a name. For, pray, is this a Scripture word ?" " No," said they. " Is it a word of the Fathers, the Councils, or the Popes ?" " No." " Is the word, then, used by St. Thomas ?" " No." " What necessity, therefore, is there for using it, since it has neither the authority of others nor any sense of

itself?"   " You are an opinionative fellow," said they; " but
you shall say it, or you shall be a heretic, and M. Arnauld
into the bargain; for we are the majority, and should it be
necessary, we can bring a sufficient number of Cordeliers[1]
into the field to carry the day."

On hearing this solid argument, I took my leave of them,
to write you the foregoing account of my interview, from
which you will perceive that the following points remain un-
disputed and uncondemned by either party. *First,* That grace
is not given to all men. *Second,* That all the righteous have always the power of obeying the divine commandments. *Third,*
That they require, nevertheless, in order to obey them, and
even to pray, an efficacious grace, which invincibly determines
their will. *Fourth,* That this efficacious grace is not always
granted to all the righteous, and that it depends on the pure
mercy of God. So that, after all, the truth is safe, and nothing runs any risk but that word without the sense, *proximate.*

Happy the people who are ignorant of its existence!—
happy those who lived before it was born!—for I see no
help for it, unless the gentlemen of the Academy,[2] by an act .
of absolute authority, banish that barbarous term, which
causes so many divisions, from beyond the precincts of the
Sorbonne. Unless this be done, the censure appears certain;
but I can easily see that it will do no other harm than di-
minish the credit[3] of the Sorbonne, and deprive it of that
authority which is so necessary to it on other occasions.

Meanwhile, I leave you at perfect liberty to hold by the
word *proximate* or not, just as you please; for I love you
too much to persecute you under that pretext. If this account is not displeasing to you, I shall continue to apprize
you of all that happens.—I am, &c.

[1] *Cordeliers,* a designation of the Franciscans, or monks of the order
of St. Francis.
[2] The Royal Academy, which compiled the celebrated dictionary of
the French language, and was held at that time to be the great umpire
in literature.
[3] The edition of 1657 had it, *Rendre la Sorbonne meprisable*—" Render the Sorbonne contemptible"—an expression much more just, but
which the editors durst not allow to remain in the subsequent editions
7*

LETTER II.

PARIS, *January* 29, 1656.

SIR,—Just as I had sealed up my last•letter, I received a visit from our old friend M. N——. Nothing could have happened more luckily for my curiosity ; for he is thoroughly informed in the questions of the day, and is completely in the secret of the Jesuits, at whose houses, including those of their leading men, he is a constant visitor. After having talked over the business which brought him to my house, I asked him to state, in a few words, what were the points in dispute between the two parties.

He immediately complied, and informed me that the principal points were two—the *first* about the *proximate power*, and the *second* about *sufficient grace*. I have enlightened you on the first of these points in my former letter, and shall now speak of the second.

In one word, then, I found that their difference about sufficient grace may be defined thus : The Jesuits maintain that there is a grace given generally to all men, subject in such a way to free-will that the will renders it efficacious or inefficacious at its pleasure, without any additional aid from God, and without wanting anything on his part in order to acting effectively ; and hence they term this grace *sufficient*, because it suffices of itself for action. The Jansenists, on the other hand, will not allow that any grace is actually sufficient which is not also efficacious ; that is, that all those kinds of grace which do not determine the will to act effectively are insufficient for action ; for they hold that a man can never act without *efficacious grace*.

Such are the points in debate between the Jesuits and the

Jansenists ; and my next object was to ascertain the doctrine of the New Thomists.[1] "It is rather an odd one," he said: "they agree with the Jesuits in admitting a *sufficient grace* given to all men; but they maintain, at the same time, that no man can act with this grace alone, but that, in order to this, he must receive from God an efficacious grace which really determines his will to the action, and which God does not grant to all men." "So that, according to this doctrine," said I, "this grace is *sufficient* without being sufficient." "Exactly so," he replied; "for if it suffices, there is no need of anything more for acting; and if it does not suffice, why—it is not sufficient."

"But," asked I, "where, then, is the difference between them and the Jansenists?" "They differ in this," he replied, "that the Dominicans have this good qualification, that they do not refuse to say that all men have the *sufficient grace*." "I understand you," returned I; "but they say it without thinking it; for they add that, in order to action, we must have an *efficacious grace which is not given to all;* consequently, if they agree with the Jesuits in the use of a term which has no sense, they differ from them, and coincide with the Jansenists in the substance of the thing." "That is very true," said he. "How, then," said I, "are the Jesuits united with them? and why do they not combat them as well as the Jansenists, since they will always find powerful antagonists in these men, who, by maintaining the necessity of the efficacious grace which determines the will, will prevent them from establishing that grace which they hold to be of itself sufficient?"

"The Dominicans are too powerful," he replied, "and the Jesuits are too politic, to come to an open rupture with them. The Society is content with having prevailed on them so far as to admit the name of *sufficient grace,* though they understand it in another sense; by which manœuvre they gain this advantage, that they will make their opinion appear untenable, as soon as they judge it proper to do so. And

this will be no difficult matter; for, let it be once granted
that all men have the sufficient graces, nothing can be more
natural than to conclude, that the efficacious grace is not ne-.
cessary to action—the sufficiency of the general grace pre-
cluding the necessity of all others. By saying *sufficient* we
express all that is necessary for action; and it will serve little
purpose for the Dominicans to exclaim that they attach another sense to the expression; the people, accustomed to the
common acceptation of that term, would not even listen to
their explanation. Thus the Society gains a sufficient advantage from the expression which has been adopted by the
Dominicans, without pressing them any further; and were
you but acquainted with what passed under Popes Clement
VIII. and Paul V., and knew how the Society was thwarted
by the Dominicans in the establishment of the sufficient
grace, you would not be surprised to find that it avoids embroiling itself in quarrels with them, and allows them to hold
their own opinion, provided that of the Society is left un-
touched; and more especially, when the Dominicans countenance its doctrine, by agreeing to employ, on all public occasions, the term *sufficient grace.*

"The Society," he continued, "is quite satisfied with their
complaisance. It does not insist on their denying the necessity of efficacious grace; this would be urging them too far.
People should not tyrannize over their friends; and the Jesuits have gained quite enough. The world is content with
words; few think of searching into the nature of things; and
thus the name of *sufficient grace* being adopted on both sides,
though in different senses, there is nobody, except the most
subtle theologians, who ever dreams of doubting that the
thing signified by that word is held by the Jacobins as well
as by the Jesuits; and the result will show that these last are
not the greatest dupes."[1]

I acknowledged that they were a shrewd class of people,

---

[1] *Et la suite fera voir que ces derniers ne sont pas les plus dupes.*
This clause, which appears in the last Paris edition, is wanting in the
ordinary editions. The following sentence seems to require it.

these Jesuits; and, availing myself of his advice, I went
straight to the Jacobins, at whose gate I found one of my
good friends, a staunch Jansenist (for you must know I have
got friends among all parties), who was calling for another
monk, different from him whom I was in search of. I prevailed on him, however, after much entreaty, to accompany
me, and asked for one of my New Thomists. He was delighted to see me again. "How now! my dear father," I
began, "it seems it is not enough that all men have a *proximate power*, with which they can never act with effect; they
must have besides this a *sufficient grace*, with which they
can act as little. Is not that the doctrine of your school?"
"It is," said the worthy monk; "and I was upholding it
this very morning in the Sorbonne. I spoke on the point
during my whole half-hour; and but for the *sand-glass*, I
bade fair to have reversed that wicked proverb, now so current in Paris: 'He votes without speaking, like a monk in the
Sorbonne.'"[1] "What do you mean by your half-hour and
your sand-glass?" I asked; "do they cut your speeches by
a certain measure?" "Yes," said he, "they have done so
for some days past." "And do they oblige you to speak
for half an hour?" "No; we may speak as little as we
please." "But not as much as you please," said I. "O
what a capital regulation for the boobies! what a blessed
excuse for those who have nothing worth the saying! But,
to return to the point, father; this grace given to all men is
sufficient, is it not?" "Yes," said he. "And yet it has no
effect without *efficacious grace?*" "None whatever," he replied. "And all men have the sufficient," continued I, "and
all have not the efficacious?" "Exactly," said he. "That
is," returned I, "all have enough of grace, and all have not

[1] *Il opine du bonnet comme un moine en Sorbonne*—literally. "He
votes with his cap like a monk in the Sorbonne"—alluding to the custom in that place of taking off the cap when a member was not disposed
to speak, or in token of agreement with the rest. The half-hour sand-
glass was a trick of the Jesuits, or Molinist party, to prevent their opponents from entering closely into the merits of the controversy, which
required frequent references to the fathers. (Nicole, i. 184.)

enough of it—tha: is, this grace suffices, though it does not suffice—that is, it is sufficient in name, and insufficient in effect! In good sooth, father, this is particularly subtle doctrine! Have you forgotten, since you retired to the cloister, the meaning attached, in the world you have quitted, to the word *sufficient?*—don't you remember that it includes all that is necessary for acting? But no, you cannot have lost all recollection of it; for, to avail myself of an illustration which will come home more vividly to your feelings, let us suppose that you were supplied with no more than two ounces of bread and a glass of water daily, would you be quite pleased with your prior were he to tell you that this would be sufficient to support you, under the pretext that, along with something else, which, however, he would not give you, you would have all that would be necessary to support you? How, then, can you allow yourselves to say that all men have sufficient grace for acting, while you admit that there is another grace absolutely necessary to acting which all men have not? Is it because this is an unimportant article of belief, and you leave all men at liberty to believe that efficacious grace is necessary or not, as they choose? Is it a matter of indifference to say, that with sufficient grace a man may really act?" " How!" cried the good man; " indifference!—it is heresy—formal heresy. The necessity of *efficacious grace* for acting effectively, is a point of *faith*— it is heresy to deny it."

" Where are we now?" I exclaimed; " and which side am I to take here? If I deny the sufficient grace, I am a Jansenist. If I admit it, as the Jesuits do, in the way of denying that efficacious grace is necessary, I shall be a heretic, say you. And if I admit it, as you do, in the way of maintaining the necessity of efficacious grace, I sin against common sense, and am a blockhead, say the Jesuits. What must I do, thus reduced to the inevitable necessity of being a blockhead, a heretic, or a Jansenist? And what a sad pass are matters come to, if there are none but the Jansenists who avoid coming into collision either with the faith or with reason, and who save themselves at once from absurdity and from error!"

My Jansenist friend took this speech as a good omen, and already looked upon me as a convert. He said nothing to me, however; but, addressing the monk: "Pray, father," inquired he, "what is the point on which you agree with the Jesuits?" "We agree in this," he replied, "that the Jesuits and we acknowledge the sufficient grace given to all." "But," said the Jansenist, "there are two things in this expression *sufficient grace*—there is the sound, which is only so much breath; and there is the thing which it signifies, which is real and effectual. And, therefore, as you are agreed with the Jesuits in regard to the word *sufficient*, and opposed to them as to the sense, it is apparent that you are opposed to them in regard to the substance of that term, and that you only agree with them as to the sound. Is this what you call acting sincerely and cordially?"

"But," said the good man, "what cause have you to complain, since we deceive nobody by this mode of speaking? In our schools we openly teach that we understand it in a manner different from the Jesuits."

"What I complain of," returned my friend, "is, that you do not proclaim it everywhere, that by sufficient grace you understand the grace which is *not* sufficient. You are bound in conscience, by thus altering the sense of the ordinary terms of theology, to tell that, when you admit a sufficient grace in all men, you understand that they have not sufficient grace in effect. All classes of persons in the world understand the word sufficient in one and the same sense; the New Thomists alone understand it in another sense. All the women, who form one-half of the world, all courtiers, all military men, all magistrates, all lawyers, merchants, artisans, the whole populace—in short, all sorts of men, except the Dominicans, understand the word *sufficient* to express all that is necessary. Scarcely any one is aware of this singular exception. It is reported over the whole earth, simply that the Dominicans hold that all men have the *sufficient graces*.

What other conclusion can be drawn from this, than that they hold that all men have all the graces necessary for action; especially when they are seen joined in interest and intrigue with the Jesuits, who understand the thing in that sense? Is not the uniformity of your expressions, viewed in connection with this union of party, a 'manifest indication and confirmation of the uniformity of your sentiments?

"The multitude of the faithful inquire of theologians: What is the real condition of human nature since its corruption? St. Augustine and his disciples reply, that it has no sufficient grace until God is pleased to bestow it. Next come the Jesuits, and they say that all have the effectually sufficient graces. The Dominicans are consulted on this contrariety of opinion; and what course do they pursue? They unite with the Jesuits; by this coalition they make up a majority; they secede from those who deny these sufficient graces; they declare that all men possess them. Who, on hearing this, would imagine anything else than that they gave their sanction to the opinion of the Jesuits? And then they add that, nevertheless, these said sufficient graces are perfectly useless without the efficacious, which are not given to all!

"Shall I present you with a picture of the Church amidst these conflicting sentiments? I consider her very like a man who, leaving his native country on a journey, is encountered by robbers, who inflict many wounds on him, and leave him half dead. He sends for three physicians resident in the neighboring towns. The first, on probing his wounds, pronounces them mortal, and assures him that none but God can restore to him his lost powers. The second, coming after the other, chooses to flatter the man—tells him that he has still sufficient strength to reach his home; and, abusing the first physician who opposed his advice, determines upon his ruin. In this dilemma, the poor patient, observing the third medical gentleman at a distance, stretches out his hands to him as the person who should determine the controversy. This practitioner, on examining his wounds, and ascertaining the opinions of the first two doctors, embraces that of the second, and uniting with him, the two combine against the first, and being the stronger party in number, drive him from the field in disgrace. From this proceeding, the patient naturally concludes that the last comer is of the same opinion with the second; and, on putting the question to him, he assures him most positively that his strength is sufficient for prosecuting his journey. The wounded man, however, sensible of his own weakness, begs him to explain to him how he considered him sufficient for the journey. 'Because,' replies his adviser, 'you are still in possession of your legs, and legs are the organs which naturally suffice for walking.' 'But,' says the patient, 'have I all the strength necessary to make use of my legs? for, in my present weak condition, it humbly appears to me that they are wholly useless.' 'Certainly you have not,' replies the doctor; 'you will never walk *effectively*, unless God vouchsafes some extraordinary assistance to sustain and conduct you.' 'What!' exclaims the poor man, 'do you not mean to say that I have sufficient strength in me, so as to want for nothing to walk effectively?' 'Very far from it,' returns the physician. 'You must, then,' says the patient, 'be of a different opinion from your companion there about my real condition.' 'I must admit that I am,' replies the other.

"What do you suppose the patient said to this? Why, he complained of the strange conduct and ambiguous terms of this third physician. He censured him for taking part with the second, to whom he was opposed in sentiment, and with whom he had only the semblance of agreement, and for having driven away the first doctor, with whom he in reality agreed; and, after making a trial of his strength, and finding by experience his actual weakness, he sent them both about their business, recalled his first adviser, put himself under his care, and having, by his advice, implored from God the strength of which he confessed his need, obtained the mercy he sought, and, through divine help, reached his house in peace."

The worthy monk was so confounded with this parable that

he could not find words to reply. To cheer him up a little, I said to him, in a mild tone : " But, after all, my dear father, what made you think of giving the name of *sufficient* to a grace which you say it is a point of faith to believe is, in fact, insufficient ?" " It is very easy for you to talk about it," said he. " You are an independent and private man ; I am a monk, and in a community—cannot you estimate the difference between the two cases ? We depend on superiors ; they depend on others. They have promised our votes—what would you have to become of me ?" We understood the hint ; and this brought to our recollection the case of his brother monk, who, for a similar piece of indiscretion, has been exiled to Abbeville.

" But," I resumed, " how comes it about that your community is bound to admit this grace ?" " That is another question," he replied. " All that I can tell you is, in one word, that our order has defended, to the utmost of its ability, the doctrine of St. Thomas on efficacious grace. With what ardor did it oppose, from the very commencement, the doctrine of Molina ? How did it labor to establish the necessity of the efficacious grace of Jesus Christ ? Don't you know what happened under Clement VIII. and Paul V., and how the former having been prevented by death, and the latter hindered by some Italian affairs from publishing his bull, our arms still sleep in the Vatican ? But the Jesuits, availing themselves, since the introduction of the heresy of Luther and Calvin, of the scanty light which the people possess for discriminating between the error of these men and the truth of the doctrine of St. Thomas, disseminated their principles with such rapidity and success, that they became, ere long, masters of the popular belief ; while we, on our part, found ourselves in the predicament of being denounced as Calvinists, and treated as the Jansenists are at present, unless we qualified the efficacious grace with, at least, the apparent avowal of a *sufficient*.[1] In this extremity, what bet-

---

[1] " It is certain," says Bayle, " that the obligation which the Romish Church is under to respect the doctrine of St. Augustine on the subject

ter course could we have taken for saving the truth, without losing our own credit, than by admitting the name of sufficient grace, while we denied that it was such in effect? Such is the real history of the case."

This was spoken in such a melancholy tone, that I really began to pity the man; not so, however, my companion. " Flatter not yourselves," said he to the monk, " with having saved the truth; had she not found other defenders, in your feeble hands she must have perished. By admitting into the Church the name of her enemy, you have admitted the enemy himself. Names are inseparable from things. If the term sufficient grace be once established, it will be vain for you to protest that you understand by it a grace which is *not* sufficient. Your protest will be held inadmissible. Your explanation would be scouted as odious in the world, where men speak more ingenuously about matters of infinitely less moment. The Jesuits will gain a triumph—it will be their grace, which is sufficient, in fact, and not yours, which is only so in name, that will pass as established; and the converse of your creed will become an article of faith."

" We will all suffer martyrdom first," cried the father, " rather than consent to the establishment of *sufficient grace in the sense of the Jesuits.* St. Thomas, whom we have

of grace, in consequence of its having received the sanction of Popes and Councils at various times, placed it in a very awkward and ridiculous situation. It is so obvious to every man who examines the matter without prejudice, and with the necessary means of information, that the doctrine of Augustine and that of Jansenius are one and the same, that it is impossible to see, without feelings of indignation, the Court of Rome boasting of having condemned Jansenius, and nevertheless preserving to St. Augustine all his glory. The two things are utterly irreconcilable. What is 'more, the Council of Trent, by condemning the doctrine of Calvin on free-will, has, by necessity, condemned that of St. Augustine; for there is no Calvinist who has denied, or who can deny, the concourse of the human will and the liberty of the soul, in the sense which St. Augustine gives to the words concourse, co-operation, and liberty There is no Calvinist who does not acknowledge the freedom of the will, and its use in conversion, if that word is understood according to the ideas of St. Augustine. Those whom the Council of Trent condemns do not reject free-will, except as signifying the liberty of indifference. The Thomists, also, reject it under this notion, and yet they pass for very good Catholics." (Bayle's Dict., art. *Augustine.*)

sworn to follow even to the death, is diametrically opposed to such doctrine."[1]

To this my friend, who took up the matter more seriously than I did, replied: "Come now, father, your fraternity has received an honor which it sadly abuses. It abandons that grace which was confided to its care, and which has never been abandoned since the creation of the world. That victorious grace, which was waited for by the patriarchs, predicted by the prophets, introduced by Jesus Christ, preached by St. Paul, explained by St. Augustine, the greatest of the fathers, embraced by his followers, confirmed by St. Bernard, the last of the fathers,[2] supported by St. Thomas, the angel of the schools,[3] transmitted by him to your order, maintained by so many of your fathers, and so nobly defended by your monks under popes Clement and Paul—that efficacious grace, which had been committed as a sacred deposit into your hands, that it might find, in a sacred and everlasting order, a succession of preachers, who might proclaim it to the end of time— is discarded and deserted for interests the most contemptible. It is high time for other hands to arm in its quarrel. It is time for God to raise up intrepid disciples of the Doctor of grace,[4] who, strangers to the entanglements of the world, will serve God for God's sake. Grace may not, indeed, number the Dominicans among her champions, but champions she shall never want; for, by her own almighty energy, she creates them for herself. She demands hearts pure and disen-

---

[1] It is a singular fact that the Roman Church, which boasts so much of her unity, and is ever charging the Reformed with being Calvinists, Lutherans, &c., is, in reality, divided into numerous conflicting sects, each *sworn* to uphold the peculiar sentiments of its founder. If there is one principle more essential than another to the Reformation, it is that of entire independence of all masters in the faith: "Nullius addictus jurare in verba magistri."

[2] "The famous St. Bernard, abbot of Clairval, whose influence throughout all Europe was incredible—whose word was a law, and whose counsels were regarded by kings and princes as so many orders to which the most respectful obedience was due; this eminent ecclesiastic was the person who contributed most to enrich and aggrandize the Cistercian order." (Mosh. Eccl. Hist., cent. xii.)

[3] Thomas Aquinas, a scholastic divine of the thirteenth century, who was termed the *Angelic Doctor*

[4] Augustine.

gaged ; nay, she herself purifies and disengages them from worldly interests, incompatible with the truths of the Gospel. Reflect seriously on this, father; and take care that God does not remove this candlestick from its place, leaving you in darkness, and without the crown, as a punishment for the coldness which you manifest to a cause so important to his Church."[1]

He might have gone on in this strain much longer, for he was kindling as he advanced, but I interrupted him by rising to take my leave, and said : " Indeed, my dear father, had I any influence in France, I should have it proclaimed, by sound of trumpet : ' BE IT KNOWN TO ALL MEN, *that when the Jacobins* SAY *that sufficient grace is given to all, they* MEAN *that all have not the grace which actually suffices !*' After which, you might say it as often as you please, but not otherwise." And thus ended our visit.

You will perceive, therefore, that we have here a *politic sufficiency* somewhat similar to *proximate power.* Meanwhile I may tell you, that it appears to me that both the proximate power and this same sufficient grace may be safely doubted by anybody, provided he is not a Jacobin.[2]

I have just come to learn, when closing my letter, that the censure[3] has passed. But as I do not yet know in what terms it is worded, and as it will not be published till the 15th of February, I shall delay writing you about it till the next post.—I am, &c.

[1] Who can help regretting that sentiments so evangelical, so truly noble, and so eloquently expressed, should have been held by Pascai in connection with a Church which denounced him as a heretic for upholding them !
[2] An ironical reflection on the cowardly compromise of the Jacobins, or Dominicans, for having pledged themselves to the use of the term "sufficient," in order to please the Jesuits.
[3] The censure of the Theological Faculty of the Sorbonne passed against M. Arnauld, and which is fully discussed in Letter iii.

REPLY OF THE "PROVINCIAL" TO THE FIRST TWO LETTERS OF HIS FRIEND.

February 2, 1656.

SIR,—Your two letters have not been confined to me. Everybody has seen them, everybody understands them, and everybody believes them. They are not only in high repute among theologians—they have proved agreeable to men of the world, and intelligible even to the ladies.

In a communication which I lately received from one of the gentlemen of the Academy—one of the most illustrious names in a society of men who are all illustrious—who had seen only your first letter, he writes me as follows: "I only wish that the Sorbonne, which owes so much to the memory of the late cardinal,[1] would acknowledge the jurisdiction of his French Academy. The author of the letter would be satisfied; for, in the capacity of an academician, I would authoritatively condemn, I would banish, I would proscribe —I had almost said exterminate—to the extent of my power, this *proximate power*, which makes so much noise about nothing, and without knowing what it would have. The misfortune is, that our academic 'power' is a very limited and *remote* power. I am sorry for it; and still more sorry that my small power cannot discharge me from my obligations to you," &c.

My next extract is from the pen of a lady, whom I shall not indicate in any way whatever. She writes thus to a female friend who had transmitted to her the first of your letters: "You can have no idea how much I am obliged to you for the letter you sent me—it is so very ingenious, and so nicely written. It narrates, and yet it is not a narrative; it clears up the most intricate and involved of all possible

[1] The Cardinal de Richelieu, the celebrated founder of the French Academy. The Sorbonne owed its magnificence to the liberality of this eminent statesman, who rebuilt its house, enlarged its revenues, enriched its library, and took it under his special patronage.

matters ; its raillery is exquisite ; it enlightens those who
know little about the subject, and imparts double delight to
those who understand it.   It is an admirable apology ; and,
if they would so take it, a delicate and innocent censure.
In short, that letter displays so much art, so much spirit,
and so much judgment, that I burn with curiosity to know
who wrote it," &c.

You too, perhaps, would like to know who the lady is that
writes in this style ; but you must be content to esteem
without knowing her ; when you come to know her, your
esteem will be greatly enhanced.[1]

Take my word for it, then, and continue your letters ; and
let the censure come when it may, we are quite prepared for
receiving it.   These words, "proximate power," and "sufficient grace," with which we are threatened, will frighten us
no longer.   We have learned from the Jesuits, the Jacobins,
and M. le Moine, in how many different ways they may be
turned, and how little solidity there is in these new-fangled
terms, to give ourselves any trouble about them.—Meanwhile, I remain, &c.

[1] This person, if wo may believe Racine, was Mademoiselle de Scudéry.   He says in his first letter, addressed to Nicole, who condemned
all authors of romances, "You have forgotten that Mademoiselle de
Scudéry made a favorable picture of Port-Royal in her *Clélie*," etc. (See
Lefèvre's edition of the *Provincials*, p. 49.)—ED.

LETTER III.

INJUSTICE, ABSURDITY, AND NULLITY OF THE CENSURE ON

M. ARNAULD.

PARIS, *February* 9, 1656.

SIR,—I have just received your letter; and, at the same time, there was brought me a copy of the ˙ censure in manuscript. I find that I am as well treated in the former, as M. Arnauld is ill-treated in the latter. I am afraid there is some extravagance in both cases, and that neither of us is sufficiently well known by our judges. Sure I am, that were we better known, M. Arnauld would merit the approval of the Sorbonne, and I the censure of the Academy. Thus our interests are quite at variance with each other. It is his interest to make himself known, to vindicate his innocence ; whereas it is mine to remain in the dark, for fear of forfeiting my reputation. Prevented, therefore, from showing my face, I must devolve on you the task of making my acknowledgments to my illustrious admirers, while I undertake that of furnishing you with the news of the censure.

I assure you, sir, it has filled me with astonishment. I expected to find it condemning the most shocking heresy in the world, but your wonder will equal mine, when informed that these alarming preparations, when on the point of producing the grand effect anticipated, have all ended in smoke.

To understand the whole affair in a pleasant way, only recollect, I beseech you, the strange impressions which, for a long time past, we have been taught to form of the Jansenists. Recall to mind the cabals, the factions, the errors, the schisms, the outrages, with which they have been so long charged ; the manner in which they have been denounced

and vilified from the pulpit and the press; and the degree
to which this torrent of abuse, so remarkable for its violence
and duration, has swollen of late years, when they have been
openly and publicly accused of being not only heretics and
schismatics, but apostates and infidels—with "denying the
mystery of transubstantiation, and renouncing Jesus Christ
and the Gospel."[1]

After having published these startling[2] accusations, it was
resolved to examine their writings, in order to pronounce
judgment on them. For this purpose the second letter of
M. Arnauld, which was reported to be full of the greatest
errors,[3] is selected. The examiners appointed are his most
open and avowed enemies. They employ all their learning·
to discover something that they might lay hold upon, and at
length they produce one proposition of a doctrinal character,
which they exhibit for censure.

What else could any one infer from such proceedings, than
that this proposition, selected under such remarkable circumstances, would contain the essence of the blackest heresies
imaginable. And yet the proposition so entirely agrees with
what is clearly and formally expressed in the passages from
the fathers quoted by M. Arnauld, that I have not met
with a single individual who could comprehend the difference
between them. Still, however, it might be imagined that
there was a very great difference; for the passages from the
fathers being unquestionably catholic, the proposition of M.
Arnauld, if heretical, must be widely opposed[4] to them.

[1] The charge of "denying the mystery of transubstantiation,"' certainly did not justly apply to the Jansenists as such; these religious
devotees denied nothing. Their system, so far as the dogmas of the
Church were concerned, was one of implicit faith; but though Arnauld,
Nicole, and the other learned men among them, stiffly maintained the
leading tenets of the Romish Church, in opposition to those of the Reformers, the Jansenist creed, as held by their pious followers, was
practically at variance with transubstantiation, and many other errors
of the Church to which they nominally belonged. (Mad. Schimmelpenninck's Demolition of Port-Royal, pp. 77-80, &c.)
[2] *Atroces*—"atrocious." (Edit. 1657.)
[3] *Des plus detestables erreurs*—"the most detestable errors." (Edit.
1657.) *Erreurs*—"errors." (Nicole's Edit., 1767.)
[4] *Horriblement contraire*—"horribly contrary." (Edit. 1657.)

VOL. I.—8

Such was the difficulty which the Sorbonne was expected to clear up. All Christendom waited, with wide-opened eyes, to discover, in the censure of these learned doctors, the point of difference which had proved imperceptible to ordinary mortals. Meanwhile M. Arnauld gave in his defences, placing his own proposition and the passages of the fathers from which he had drawn it in parallel columns, so as to make the agreement between them apparent to the most obtuse understandings.

He shows, for example, that St. Augustine says in one passage, that "Jesus Christ points out to us, in the person of St. Peter, a righteous man warning us by his fall to avoid presumption." He cites another passage from the same father, in which he says, "that God, in order to show us that without grace we can do nothing, left St. Peter without grace." He produces a third, from St. Chrysostom, who says, "that the fall of St. Peter happened, not through any coldness towards Jesus Christ, but because grace failed him ; and that he fell, not so much through his own negligence as through the withdrawment of God, as a lesson to the whole Church, that without God we can do nothing." He then gives his own accused proposition, which is as follows : "The fathers point out to us, in the person of St. Peter, a righteous man to whom that grace without which we can do nothing, was wanting."

In vain did people attempt to discover how it could possibly be, that M. Arnauld's expression differed from those of the fathers as much as truth from error, and faith from heresy. For where was the difference to be found ? Could it be in these words, "that the fathers point out to us, in the person of St. Peter, a righteous man ?" St. Augustine has said the same thing in so many words. Is it because he says "that grace had failed him ?" The same St. Augustine, who had said that "St. Peter was a righteous man," says "that he had not had grace on that occasion." Is it, then, for his having said, "that without grace we can do nothing ?" Why, is not this just what St. Augustine says in the same

171

plaoe, and what St. Chrysostom had said before him, with
this difference only, that he expresses it in much stronger
language, as when he says "that his fall did not happen
through his own coldness or negligence, but through the failure of grace, and the withdrawment of God?"[1]

Such considerations as these kept everybody in a state of
breathless suspense, to learn in what this diversity could
consist, when at length, after a great many meetings, this
famous and long-looked for censure made its appearance.
But, alas! it has sadly baulked our expectation. Whether
it be that the Molinist doctors would not condescend so far
as to enlighten us on the point, or for some other mysterious
reason, the fact is, they have done nothing more than pronounce these words : "This proposition is rash, impious, blasphemous, accursed, and heretical!"

Would you believe it, sir, that most people, finding themselves deceived in their expectations, have got into bad humor, and begin to fall foul upon the censors themselves?
They are drawing strange inferences from their conduct in
favor of M. Arnauld's innocence. " What !" they are saying,
" is this all that could be achieved, during all this time, by
so many doctors joining in a furious attack on one individual?
Can they find nothing in all his works worthy of reprehension, but three lines, and these extracted, word for word,
from the greatest doctors of the Greek and Latin Churches?
Is there any author whatever whose writings, were it intended
to ruin him, would not furnish a more specious pretext for
the purpose? And what higher proof could be furnished
of the orthodoxy of this illustrious accused?

" How comes it to pass," they add, " that so many denun-
ciations are launched in this censure, into which they have

[1] The meaning of Chrysostom is good, but the expressions of these
ancient fathers are often more remarkable for their strength than their
precision. The Protestant reader hardly needs to be reminded, that if
divine grace can be said to have failed the Apostle Peter at his fall, it
can only be in the sense of a temporary suspension of its influences;
and that this withdrawment of grace must be regarded as the punishment, and not as the cause, of his own negligence.

crowded such terms as 'poison, pestilence, horror, rashness, impiety, blasphemy, abomination, execration, anathema, heresy'—the most dreadful epithets that could be used against Arius, or Antichrist himself; and all to combat an imperceptible heresy, and that, moreover, without telling us what it is? If it be against the words of the fathers that they inveigh in this style, where is the faith and tradition? If against M. Arnauld's proposition, let them point out the difference between the two; for we can see nothing but the most perfect harmony between them. As soon as we have discovered the evil of the proposition, we shall hold it in abhorrence; but so long as we do not see it, or rather see nothing in the statement but the sentiments of the holy fathers, conceived and expressed in their own terms, how can we possibly regard it with any other feelings than those of holy veneration?"

Such is a specimen of the way in which they are giving vent to their feelings. But these are by far too deep-thinking people. You and I, who make no pretensions to such extraordinary penetration, may keep ourselves quite easy about the whole affair. What! would we be wiser than our masters? No: let us take example from them, and not undertake what they have not ventured upon. We would be sure to get boggled in such an attempt. Why it would be the easiest thing imaginable, to render this censure itself heretical. Truth, we know, is so delicate, that if we make the slightest deviation from it, we fall into error; but this alleged error is so extremely fine-spun, that, if we diverge from it in the slightest degree, we fall back upon the truth. There is positively nothing between this obnoxious proposition and the truth but an imperceptible point. The distance between them is so impalpable, that I was in terror lest, from pure inability to perceive it, I might, in my over-anxiety to agree with the doctors of the Sorbonne, place myself in opposition to the doctors of the Church. Under this apprehension, I judged it expedient to consult one of those who, through policy, was neutral on the first question, that from him I might learn the real state of the matter. I have accordingly had an interview with one of the most intelligent of that party, whom I requested to point out to me the difference between the two things, at the same time frankly owning to him that I could see none.

He appeared to be amused at my simplicity, and replied, with a smile : " How simple it is in you to believe that there is any difference ! Why, where could it be ? Do you imagine that, if they could have found out any discrepancy between M. Arnauld and the fathers, they would not have boldly pointed it out, and been delighted with the opportunity of exposing it before the public, in whose eyes they are so anxious to depreciate that gentleman ?"

I could easily perceive, from these few words, that those who had been neutral on the first question, would not all prove so on the second ; but anxious to hear his reasons, I asked : " Why, then, have they attacked this unfortunate proposition ?"

" Is it possible," he replied, " you can be ignorant of these two things, which I thought had been known to the veriest tyro in these matters ?—that, on the one hand, M. Arnauld has uniformly avoided advancing a single tenet which is not powerfully supported by the tradition of the Church ; and that, on the other hand, his enemies have determined, cost what it may, to cut that ground from under him ; and, accordingly, that as the writings of the former afforded no handle to the designs of the latter, they have been obliged, in order to satiate their revenge, to seize on some proposition, it mattered not what, and to condemn it without telling why or wherefore. Do not you know how the Jansenists keep them in check, and annoy them so desperately, that they cannot drop the slightest word against the principles of the fathers without being incontinently overwhelmed with whole volumes, under the pressure of which they are forced to succumb ? So that, after a great many proofs of their weakness, they have judged it more to the purpose, and much less troublesome, to censure than to reply—it being a much easier matter with them to find monks than reasons."[1]

"Why then," said I, "if this be the case, their censure is not worth a straw; for who will pay any regard to it, when they see it to be without foundation, and refuted, as it no doubt will be, by the answers given to it?"

"If you knew the temper of people," replied my friend the doctor, "you would talk in another sort of way. Their censure, censurable as it is, will produce nearly all its designed effect for a time; and although, by the force of demonstration, it is certain that, in course of time, its invalidity will be made apparent, it is equally true that, at first, it will tell as effectually on the minds of most people as if it had been the most righteous sentence in the world. Let it only be cried about the streets: 'Here you have the censure of M. Arnauld!—here you have the condemnation of the Jansenists!' and the Jesuits will find their account in it. How few will ever read it! How few of them who do read, will understand it! How few will observe that it answers no objections! How few will take the matter to heart, or attempt to sift it to the bottom?—Mark then, how much advantage this gives to the enemies of the Jansenists. They are sure to make a triumph of it, though a vain one, as usual, for some months at least—and that is a great matter for them— they will look out afterwards for some new means of subsistence. They live from hand to mouth, sir. It is in this way they have contrived to maintain themselves down to the present day. Sometimes it is by a catechism in which a child is made to condemn their opponents; then it is by a procession, in which sufficient grace leads the efficacious in triumph; again it is by a comedy, in which Jansenius is represented as carried off by devils; at another time it is by an almanac; and now it is by this censure."[2]

[1] That is, they could more readily procure monks to vote against M. Arnauld, than arguments to answer him.

[2] The allusions in the text afford curious illustrations of the mode of warfare pursued by the Jesuits of the seventeenth century. The first refers to a comic catechism, in which the simple language of childhood

"In good sooth," said I, "I was on the point of finding fault with the conduct of the Molinists; but after what you have told me, I must say I admire their prudence and their policy. I see perfectly well that they could not have followed a safer or more judicious course."

"You are right," returned he; "their safest policy has always been to keep silent; and this led a certain learned divine to remark, 'that the cleverest among them are those who intrigue much, speak little, and write nothing.'

"It is on this principle that, from the commencement of the meetings, they prudently ordained that, if M. Arnauld came into the Sorbonne, it must be simply to explain what he believed, and not to enter the lists of controversy with any one. The examiners having ventured to depart a little from this prudent arrangement, suffered for their temerity. They found themselves rather too vigorously[1] refuted by his second apology.

"On the same principle, they had recourse to that rare and very novel device of the half-hour and the sand-glass.[2] By this means they rid themselves of the importunity of those troublesome doctors,[3] who might undertake to refute all their arguments, to produce books which might convict them of forgery, to insist on a reply, and reduce them to the predicament of having none to give.

was employed as a vehicle for the most calumnious charges against the opponents of the Society. Pascal refers again to this catechism in Letter xvii. The second device was a sort of school-boy masquerade. A handsome youth, disguised as a female, in splendid attire, and bearing the inscription of *sufficient grace*, dragged behind him another dressed as a bishop (representing Jansenius, bishop of Ypres), who followed with a rueful visage, amidst the hootings of the other boys. The comedy referred to was acted in the Jesuits' college of Clermont. The almanacs published in France at that period being usually embellished with rude cuts for the amusement of the vulgar, the Jesuits procured the insertion of a caricature of the Jansenists, who were represented as pursued by the pope, and taking refuge among the Calvinists. This, however, called forth a retaliation, in the shape of a poem, entitled "The Prints of the Famous Jesuitical Almanac," in which the Jesuits were so successfully held up to ridicule, that they could hardly show face for some time in the streets of Paris. Nicole, i. p. 208.

[1] *Vertement*—"smartly." (Edit. 1657.)
[2] See Letter ii.
[3] *Ces docteurs*—"those doctors." (Edit. 1767.)

"It is not that they were so blind as not to see that this encroachment on liberty, which has induced' so many doctors to withdraw from the meetings, would do no good to their censure; and that the protest of nullity, taken on this ground by M. Arnauld before it was concluded, would be a bad pre-amble for securing it a favorable reception. They know very well that unprejudiced persons place fully as much weight' on the judgment of seventy doctors, who had nothing to gain by defending M. Arnauld, as on that of a hundred others who had nothing to lose by condemning him. But, upon the whole, they considered that it would be of vast importance to have a censure, although it should be the act of a party only in the Sorbonne, and not of the whole body; although it should be carried with little or no freedom of debate, and obtained by a great many small manœuvres not exactly ac-cording to order; although it should give no explanation of the matter in dispute; although it should not point out in what this heresy consists, and should say as little as possible about it, for fear of committing a mistake. This very silence is a mystery in the eyes of the simple; and the censure will reap this singular advantage from it, that they may defy the most critical and subtle theologians to find in it a single weak argument.

"Keep yourself easy, then, and do not be afraid of being set down as a heretic, though you should make use of the condemned proposition. It is bad, I assure you, only as oc-curring in the second letter of M. Arnauld. If you will not believe this statement on my word, I refer you to M. le Moine, the most zealous of the examiners, who, in the course of con-versation with a doctor of my acquaintance this very morn-ing, on being asked by him where lay the point of difference' in dispute, and if one would no longer be allowed to say what the fathers had said before him, made the following ex-quisite reply : 'This proposition would be orthodox in the mouth of any other—it is only as coming from M. Arnauld that the Sorbonne have condemned it !' You must now be prepared to admire the machinery of Molinism, which can produce such prodigious overturnings in the Church—that what is catholic in the fathers becomes heretical in M. Arnauld—that what is heretical in the Semi-Pelagians becomes orthodox in the writings of the Jesuits; the ancient doctrine of St. Augustine becomes an intolerable innovation, and new inventions, daily fabricated before our eyes, pass for the ancient faith of the Church." So saying, he took his leave of me.

This information has satisfied my purpose. I gather from it that this same heresy is one of an entirely new species. It is not the sentiments of M. Arnauld that are heretical; it is only his person. This is a personal heresy. He is not a heretic for anything he has said or written, but simply because he is M. Arnauld. This is all they have to say against him. Do what he may, unless he cease to be, he will never be a good Catholic. The grace of St. Augustine will never be the true grace, so long as he continues to defend it. It would become so at once, were he to take it into his head to impugn it. That would be a sure stroke, and almost the only plan for establishing the truth and demolishing Molinism; such is the fatality attending all the opinions which he embraces.

Let us leave them, then, to settle their own differences. These are the disputes of theologians, not of theology. We, who are no doctors, have nothing to do with their quarrels. Tell our friends the news of the censure, and love me while I am, &c.[1]

[1] In Nicole's edition, this letter is signed with the initials[2] " E. A. A. B. P. A. F. D. E. P." which seem merely a chance medley of letters, to quiz those who were so anxious to discover the author. There may have been an allusion to the absurd story of a Jansenist conference held, it was said, at Bourg Fontaine, in 1621, to deliberate on ways and means for abolishing Christianity ; among the persons present at which, indicated by initials, Anthony Arnauld was ridiculously accused of having been one under the initials A. A. (See Bayle's Dict., art. Ant. Arnauld.
[2] Et ancien ami, Blaise Pascal, Auvergnat, fils de Etienne Pascal. (M. l'abbé Maynard.)—ED.

8*

LETTER IV.

ON ACTUAL GRACE AND SINS OF IGNORANCE.

PARIS, *February* 25, 1656.

SIR,—Nothing can come up to the Jesuits. I have seen Jacobins, doctors, and all sorts of people in my day, but such an interview as I have just had was wanting to complete my knowledge of mankind. Other men are merely copies of them. As things are always found best at the fountain-head, I paid a visit to one of the ablest among them, in company with my trusty Jansenist—the same who accompanied me to the Dominicans. Being particularly anxious to learn something of a dispute which they have with the Jansenists about what they call *actual grace*, I said to the worthy father that I would be much obliged to him if he would instruct me on this point—that I did not even know what the term meant, and would thank him to explain it. "With all my heart," the Jesuit replied ; "for I dearly love inquisitive people. Actual grace, according to our definition, 'is an inspiration of God, whereby he makes us to know his will, and excites within us a desire to perform it.' "

"And where," said I, "lies your difference with the Jansenists on this subject ?"

"The difference lies here," he replied ; " we hold that God bestows actual grace on *all men in every case of temptation ;* for we maintain, that unless a person have, whenever tempted, actual grace to keep him from sinning, his sin, whatever it may be, can never be imputed to him. The Jansenists, on the other hand, affirm that sins, though committed without actual grace, are, nevertheless, imputed ; but they are a pack of fools." I got a glimpse of his meaning ; but, to obtain from him a fuller explanation, I observed : "My dear father, it is that phrase *actual grace* that puzzles me; I am quite a stranger to it, and if you would have the goodness to tell me the same thing over again, without employing that term, you would infinitely oblige me."

"Very good," returned the father; "that is to say, you want me to substitute the definition in place of the thing defined; that makes no alteration of the sense; I have no objections. We maintain it, then, as an undeniable principle, *that an action cannot be imputed as a sin, unless God bestow on us, before committing it, the knowledge of the evil that is in the action, and an inspiration inciting us to avoid it.* Do you understand me now ?"

Astonished at such a declaration, according to which, no sins of surprise, nor any of those committed in entire forgetfulness of God, could be imputed, I turned round to my friend the Jansenist, and easily discovered from his looks that he was of a different way of thinking. But as he did not utter a word, I said to the monk, "I would fain wish, my dear father, to think that what you have now said is true, and that you have good proofs for it."

"Proofs, say you !" he instantly exclaimed : "I shall furnish you with these very soon, and the very best sort too ; let me alone for that."

So saying, he went in search of his books, and I took this opportunity of asking my friend if there was any other person who talked in this manner ? "Is this so strange to you ?" he replied. "You may depend upon it that neither the fathers, nor the popes, nor councils, nor Scripture, nor any book of devotion, employ such language ; but if you wish casuists and modern schoolmen, he will bring you a goodly number of them on his side." "O ! but I care not a fig about these authors, if they are contrary to tradition," I said. "You are right," he replied.

As he spoke, the good father entered the room, laden with books ; and presenting to me the first that came to hand, "Read that," "he said : "this is 'The Summary of Sins,' by

Father Bauny[1]—the fifth edition too, you see, which shows that it is a good book."

"It is a pity, however," whispered the Jansenist in my ear, " that this same book has been condemned at Rome, and by the bishops of France."

"Look at page 906," said the father. I did so, and read as follows : "In order to sin and become culpable in the sight of God, it is necessary to know that the thing we wish to do is not good, or at least to doubt that it is—to fear or to judge that God takes no pleasure in the action which we contemplate, but forbids it ; and in spite of this, to commit the deed, leap the fence, and transgress."

"This is a good commencement," I remarked. "And yet," said he, "mark how far envy will carry some people. It was on that very passage that M. Hallier, before he became one of our friends, bantered Father Bauny, by applying to him these words : *Ecce qui tollit peccata mundi*—'Behold the man that taketh away the sins of the world!' "

"Certainly," said I, "according to Father Bauny, we may be said to behold a redemption of an entirely new description."

"Would you have a more authentic witness on the point ?" added he. "Here is the book of Father Annat.[2] It is the

---

[1] Etienne Bauni, or Stephen Bauny, was a French Jesuit. His "Summary," which Pascal has immortalized by his frequent references to it, was published in 1633. It is a large volume, stuffed with the most detestable doctrines. In 1642, the General Assembly of the French clergy censured his books on moral theology, as containing propositions " leading to licentiousness, and the corruption of good manners, violating natural equity, and excusing blasphemy, usury, simony, and other heinous sins, as trivial matters." (Nicole, i. 164.) And yet this abominable work was formally defended in the " Apology for the Casuists," written in 1657, by Father Pirot, and acknowledged by the Jesuits as having been written under their direction ! (Nicole, Hist. des Provinciales, p. 30.

[2] Francis Annat was born in the year 1590. He was made rector of the College of Toulouse, and appointed by the Jesuits their French provincial; and, while in that situation, was chosen by Louis XIV. as his confessor. His friends have highly extolled his virtues as a man ; and the reader may judge of the value of these eulogiums from the fact, that he retained his post as the favorite confessor of that licentious monarch, without interruption, till deafness prevented him from listening any longer to the confessions of his royal penitent. (Bayle, art.

last that he wrote against M. Arnauld. Turn up to page 34, where there is a dog's ear, and read the lines which I have marked with pencil—they ought to be written in letters of gold. I then read these words: "He that has no thought of God, nor of his sins, nor any apprehension (that is, as he explained it, any knowledge) of his obligation to exercise the acts of love to God or contrition, has no actual grace for exercising those acts; but it is equally true that he is guilty of no sin in omitting them, and that, if he is damned, it will not be as a punishment for that omission." And a few lines below, he adds: "The same thing may be said of a culpable commission."

"You see," said the monk, "how he speaks of sins of *omission* and of *commission*. Nothing escapes him. What say you to that?"

"Say!" I exclaimed. "I am delighted! What a charming train of consequences do I discover flowing from this doctrine! I can see the whole results already; and such mysteries present themselves before me! Why, I see more people, beyond all comparison, justified by this ignorance and forgetfulness of God, than by grace and the sacraments![1] But, my dear father, are you not inspiring me with a delusive joy? Are you sure there is nothing here like that *suf-*

Annat.) They have also extolled his answer to the Provincial Letters, in his "Bonne Foy des Jansenistes," in which he professed to expose the falsity of the quotations made from the Casuists, with what success, appears from the Notes of Nicole, who has completely vindicated Pascal from the unfounded charges which the Jesuits have reiterated on this point. (Notes Preliminaires, vol. i. p. 256, &c.; Entretiens de Cleandre et Eudoxe, p. 79.)

[1] When Madame du Valois, a lady of birth and high accomplishments, one of the nuns of Port-Royal, among other trials by which she was harassed and tormented for not signing the formulary condemning Jansenius, was threatened with being deprived of the benefit of the sacraments at the hour of death, she replied: "If, at the awful hour of death, I should be deprived of those assistances which the Church grants to all her children, then God himself will, by his grace, immediately and abundantly supply their instrumentality. I know, indeed, that it is most painful to approach the awful hour of death without an outward participation in the sacraments; but it is better dying, to enter into heaven, though without the sacraments, for the cause of truth, than, receiving the sacraments, to be cited to irrevocable judgment for committing perjury." (Narrative of Dem. of Port-Royal, ɪ 176.)

ficiency which suffices not? I am terribly afraid of the *Distinguo*;—I was taken in with that once already! Are you quite in earnest?"

"How now!" cried the monk, beginning to get angry; "here is no matter for jesting. I assure you there is no such thing as equivocation here."

"I am not making a jest of it," said I; "but that is what I really dread, from pure anxiety to find it true."[1]

"Well then," he said, "to assure yourself still more of it, here are the writings of M. le Moine,[2] who taught the doctrine in a full meeting of the Sorbonne. He learned it from us, to be sure; but he has the merit of having cleared it up most admirably. O how circumstantially he goes to work! He shows that, in order to make out an action to be *a sin*, all these things must have passed through the mind. Read, and weigh every word."—I then read what I now give you in a translation from the original Latin: "1. On the one hand, God sheds abroad on the soul some measure of love, which gives it a bias toward the thing commanded; and on the other, a rebellious concupiscence solicits it in the opposite direction. 2. God inspires the soul with a knowledge of its own weakness. 3. God reveals the knowledge of the physician who can heal it. 4. God inspires it with a desire to be healed. 5. God inspires a desire to pray and solicit his assistance."

"And unless all these things occur and pass through the soul," added the monk, "the action is not properly a sin, and cannot be imputed, as M. le Moine shows in the same place and in what follows. Would you wish to have other authorities for this? Here they are."

"All modern ones, however," whispered my Jansenist friend.

"So I perceive," said I to him aside; and then, turning to

[1] Will it be believed that the Jesuits actually had the consummate hypocrisy to pretend that Pascal meant to throw ridicule on the grace of God, while he was merely exposing to merited contempt their own perversions of the doctrine?

[2] See before, page 148.

the monk: "O my dear sir," cried I, "what a blessing this
will be to some persons of my acquaintance! I must positively introduce them to you. You have never, perhaps, met
with people who had fewer sins to account for all your life.
For, in the first place, they never think of God at all; their
vices have got the better of their reason; they have never
known either their weakness or the physician who can cure
it; they have never thought of 'desiring the health of their
soul,' and still less of 'praying to God to bestow it;' so that,
according to M. le Moine, they are still in the state of baptismal innocence. They have 'never had a thought of loving
God or of being contrite for their sins;' so that, according to
Father Annat, they have never committed sin through the
want of charity and penitence. Their life is spent in a perpetual round of all sorts of pleasures, in the course of which
they have not been interrupted by the slightest remorse.
These excesses had led me to imagine that their perdition
was inevitable; but you, father, inform me that these same
excesses secure their salvation. Blessings on you, my good
father, for this way of justifying people! Others prescribe
painful austerities for healing the soul; but you show that
souls which may be thought desperately distempered are in
quite good health. What an excellent device for being happy
both in this world and in the next! I had always supposed
that the less a man thought of God, the more he sinned;
but, from what I see now, if one could only succeed in bringing himself not to think upon God at all, everything would
be pure with him in all time coming. Away with your half-
and-half sinners, who retain some sneaking affection for virtue! They will be damned every one of them, these semi-
sinners. But commend me to your arrant sinners—hardened,
unalloyed, out-and-out, thorough-bred sinners Hell is no
place for them; they have cheated the devil, purely by virtue
of their devotion to his service!"

The good father, who saw very well the connection between these consequences and his principle, dexterously
evaded them; and maintaining his temper, either from good

nature or policy, he merely replied : " To let you understand
how we avoid these inconveniences, you must know that,
while we affirm that these reprobates to whom you refer
would be without sin if they had no thoughts of conversion
and no desires to devote themselves to God, we maintain
that they all actually *have* such thoughts and desires, and
that God never permitted a man to sin without giving him
previously a view of the evil which he contemplated, and a
desire, either to avoid the offence, or at all events to implore
his aid to enable him to avoid it ; and none but Jansenists
will assert the contrary."

" Strange ! father," returned I ; "is this, then, the heresy
of the Jansenists, to deny that every time a man commits a
sin, he is troubled with a remorse of conscience, in spite of
which, he 'leaps the fence and transgresses,' as Father
Bauny has it ?   It is rather too good a joke to be made a
heretic for that.   I can easily believe that a man may be
damned for not having good thoughts ; but it never would
have entered my head to imagine that any man could be
subjected to that doom for not believing that all mankind
must have good thoughts !   But, father, I hold myself bound
in conscience to disabuse you, and to inform you that there
are thousands of people who have no such desires—who sin
without regret—who sin with delight—who make a boast of
sinning.   And who ought to know better about these things
than yourself ?   You cannot have failed to have confessed
some of those to whom I allude ; for it is among persons of
high rank that they are most generally to be met with.[1]

---

[1] The Jesuits were notorious for the assiduity with which they sought
admission into the families, and courted the confidence of the great, with
whom, from the laxness of their discipline and morality, as well as from
their superior manners and accomplishments, they were, as they still
are, the favorite confessors.   They have a maxim among their secret
instructions, that in dealing with the consciences of the great, the confessor must be guided by the looser sort of opinions.   The author of the
Theatre Jesuitique illustrates this by an anecdote.   A rich gentleman
falling sick, confessed himself to a Jesuit, and among other sins acknowledged an illicit intercourse with a lady, whose portrait, thinking
himself dying, he gave with many expressions of remorse, to his confessor.   The gentleman, however, recovered, and with returning health

But mark, father, the dangerous consequences of your maxim. Do you not perceive what effect it may have on those libertines who like nothing better than to find out matter of doubt in religion? What a handle do you give them, when you assure them, as an article of faith, that on every occasion when they commit a sin, they feel an inward presentiment of the evil, and a desire to avoid it? Is it not obvious that, feeling convinced by their own experience of the falsity of your doctrine on this point, which you say is a matter of faith, they will extend the inference drawn from this to all the other points? They will argue that, since you are not trust-worthy in one article, you are to be suspected in them all; and thus you shut them up to conclude, either that religion is false, or that you must know very little about it."

Here my friend the Jansenist, following up my remarks, said to him: "You would do well, father, if you wish to preserve your doctrine, not to explain so precisely as you have done to us, what you mean by *actual grace*. For, how could you, without forfeiting all credit in the estimation of men, openly declare that *nobody sins without having previously the knowledge of his weakness, and of a physician, or the desire of a cure, and of asking it of God?* Will it be believed, on your word, that those who are immersed in avarice, impurity, blasphemy, duelling, revenge, robbery and sacrilege, have really a desire to embrace chastity, humility, and the other Christian virtues? Can it be conceived that those philosophers who boasted so loudly of the powers of nature, knew its infirmity and its physician? Will you maintain that those who held it as a settled maxim that 'it is not God that bestows virtue, and that no one ever asked it from him,' would think of asking it for themselves? Who can believe that the Epicureans, who denied a divine providence, ever felt any inclination to pray to God?—men who

a salutary change was effected on his character. The Jesuit, finding himself forgotten, paid a visit to his former penitent, and gave him back the portrait, which renewed all his former passion, and soon brought him again to the feet of his confessor!

said that 'it would be an insult to invoke the Deity in our necessities, as if he were capable of wasting a thought on beings like us?' In a word, how can it be imagined that idolaters and Atheists, every time they are tempted to the commission of sin, in other words, infinitely often during their lives, have a desire to pray to the true God, of whom they are ignorant, that he would bestow on them virtues of which they have no conception?"

"Yes," said the worthy monk, in a resolute tone, "we will affirm it: and sooner than allow that any one sins without having the consciousness that he is doing evil, and the desire of the opposite virtue, we will maintain that the whole world, reprobates and infidels included, have these inspirations and desires in every case of temptation. You cannot show me, from the Scripture at least, that this is not the truth."

On this remark I struck in, by exclaiming: "What! father, must we have recourse to the Scripture to demonstrate a thing so clear as this? This is not a point of faith, nor even of reason. It is a matter of fact: we see it—we know it—we feel it."

But the Jansenist, keeping the monk to his own terms, addressed him as follows: "If you are willing, father, to stand or fall by Scripture, I am ready to meet you there; only you must promise to yield to its authority; and since it is written that 'God has not revealed his judgments to the Heathen, but left them to wander in their own ways,' you must not say that God has enlightened those whom the Sacred Writings assure us 'he has left in darkness and in the shadow of death.' Is it not enough to show the erroneousness of your principle, to find that St. Paul calls himself 'the chief of sinners,' for a sin which he committed 'ignorantly, and with zeal?' Is it not enough to find, from the Gospel, that those who crucified Jesus Christ had need of the pardon which he asked for them, although they knew not the malice of their action, and would never have committed it, according to St. Paul, if they had known it? Is it not enough that

Jesus Christ apprizes us that there will be persecutors of the Church, who, while making every effort to ruin her, will 'think that they are doing God service;' teaching us that this sin, which in the judgment of the apostle, is the greatest of all sins, may be committed by persons who, so far from knowing that they were sinning, would think that they sinned by not committing it? In fine, is it not enough that Jesus Christ himself has taught us that there are two kinds of sinners, the one of whom sin with 'knowledge of their Master's will,' and the other without knowledge; and that both of them will be 'chastised,' although, indeed, in a different manner?"

Sorely pressed by so many testimonies from Scripture, to which he had appealed, the worthy monk began to give way; and, leaving the wicked to sin without inspiration, he said: "You will not deny that *good men*, at least, never sin unless God give them"——"You are flinching," said I, interrupting him; "you are flinching now, my good father; you abandon the general principle, and finding that it will not hold good in regard to the wicked, you would compound the matter, by making it apply at least to the righteous. But in this point of view the application of it is, I conceive, so circumscribed, that it will hardly apply to anybody, and it is scarcely worth while to dispute the point."

My friend, however, who was so ready on the whole question, that I am inclined to think he had studied it all that very morning, replied: "This, father, is the last entrenchment to which those of your party who are willing to reason at all are sure to retreat; but you are far from being safe even here. The example of the saints is not a whit more in your favor. Who doubts that they often fall into sins of surprise, without being conscious of them? Do we not learn from the saints themselves how often concupiscence lays hid den snares for them; and how generally it happens, as St. Augustine complains of himself in his Confessions, that, with all their discretion, they 'give to pleasure what they mean only to give to necessity?'

"How usual is it to see the more zealous friends of truth betrayed by the heat of controversy into sallies of bitter passion for their personal interests, while their consciences, at the time, bear them no other testimony than that they are acting in this manner purely for the interests of truth, and they do not discover their mistake till long afterwards!

"What, again, shall we say of those who, as we learn from examples in ecclesiastical history, eagerly involve themselves in affairs which are really bad, because they believe them to be really good ; and yet this does not hinder the fathers from condemning such persons as having sinned on these occasions ?

"And were this not the case, how could the saints have their secret faults ? How could it be true that God alone knows the magnitude and the number of our offences ; that no one knows whether he is worthy of hatred or love; and that the best of saints, though unconscious of any culpability, ought always, as St. Paul says of himself, to remain in 'fear and trembling?' [1]

"You perceive, then, father, that this knowledge of the evil, and love of the opposite virtue, which you imagine to be essential to constitute sin, are equally disproved by the examples of the righteous and of the wicked. In the case of the wicked, their passion for vice sufficiently testifies that they have no desire for virtue ; and in regard to the righteous, the love which they bear to virtue plainly shows that they are not always conscious of those sins which, as the Scripture teaches, they are daily committing.

"So true is it, indeed, that the righteous often sin through

---

[1] "The doubtsome faith of the pope," as it was styled by our Reformers, is here lamentably apparent. The " fear and trembling" of the apostle were those of anxious care and diligence, not of doubt or apprehension. The Church of Rome, with all her pretensions to be regarded as the only safe and infallible guide to salvation, keeps her children in darkness and doubt on this point to the last moment of life ; they are never permitted to reach the peaceful assurance of God's love and the humble hope of eternal life which the Gospel warrants the believer to cherish ; and this, while it serves to keep the superstitious multitude under the sway of priestly domination, accounts for the *gloom* which has characterized, in all ages, the devotion of the best and most intelligent Romanists.

ignorance, that the greatest saints rarely sin otherwise   For
how can it be supposed that souls so pure, who avoid with
so much care and zeal the least things that can be displeasing
to God as soon as they discover them, and who yet sin many
times every day, could possibly have, every time before they
fell into sin, 'the knowledge of their infirmity on that occasion, and of their physician, and the desire of their souls'
health, and of praying to God for assistance,' and that, in
spite of these inspirations, these devoted souls 'nevertheless
transgress,' and commit the sin?

"You must conclude then, father, that neither sinners nor
yet saints have always that knowledge, or those desires and
inspirations every time they offend; that is, to use your own
terms, they have not always actual grace. Say no longer,
with your modern authors, that it is impossible for those to
sin who do not know righteousness; but rather join with St.
Augustine and the ancient fathers in saying that it is impossible *not* to sin, when we do not know righteousness: *Necesse est ut peccet, a quo ignoratur justitia.*"

The good father, though thus driven from both of his positions, did not lose courage, but after ruminating a little,
"Ha!" he exclaimed, "I shall convince you immediately."
And again taking up Father Bauny, he pointed to the same
place he had before quoted, exclaiming, "Look now—see the
ground on which he establishes his opinion! I was sure he
would not be deficient in good proofs. Read what he quotes
from Aristotle, and you will see that after so express an authority, you must either burn the books of this prince of philosophers or adopt our opinion. Hear, then, the principles which
support Father Bauny: Aristotle states first, '*that an action
cannot be imputed as blameworthy, if it be involuntary.*'"

"I grant that," said my friend.

"This is the first time you have agreed together," said I.
"Take my advice, father, and proceed no further."

"That would be doing nothing," he replied; "we must
know what are the conditions necessary to constitute an action voluntary."

"I am much afraid," returned I, "that you will get at loggerheads on that point."

"No fear of that," said he; "this is sure ground—Aristotle is on my side. Hear, now, what Father Bauny says: 'In order that an action be voluntary, it must proceed from a man who perceives, knows, and comprehends what is good and what is evil in it. *Voluntarium est*—that is a voluntary action, as we commonly say with the philosopher' (that is Aristotle, you know, said the monk, squeezing my hand;) '*quod fit a principio cognoscente singula in quibus est actio*—which is done by a person knowing the particulars of the action; so that when the will is led inconsiderately, and without mature reflection, to embrace or reject, to do or omit to do anything, before the understanding has been able to see whether it would be right or wrong, such an action is neither good nor evil; because previous to this mental inquisition, view, and reflection on the good or bad qualities of the matter in question, the act by which it is done is not voluntary.' Are you satisfied now?" said the father.

"It appears," returned I, "that Aristotle agrees with Father Bauny; but that does not prevent me from feeling surprised at this statement. What, sir! is it not enough to make an action voluntary that the man knows what he is doing, and does it just because he chooses to do it? Must we suppose, besides this, that he 'perceives, knows, and comprehends what is good and evil in the action?' Why, on this supposition there would be hardly such a thing in nature as voluntary actions, for no one scarcely thinks about all this. How many oaths in gambling—how many excesses in debauchery—how many riotous extravagances in the carnival, must, on this principle, be excluded from the list of voluntary actions, and consequently neither good nor bad, because not accompanied by those 'mental reflections on the good and evil qualities' of the action? But is it possible, father, that Aristotle held such a sentiment? I have always understood that he was a sensible man."

"I shall soon convince you of that," said the Jansenist;

and requesting a sight of Aristotle's Ethics, he opened it at
the beginning of the third book, from which Father Bauny
had taken the passage quoted, and said to the monk: "I excuse you, my dear sir, for having believed, on the word of
Father Bauny, that Aristotle held such a sentiment; but you
would have changed your mind had you read him for yourself.   It is true that he teaches, that 'in order to make an
action voluntary, we must know the particulars of that action'—*singula in quibus est actio.*   But what else does he
mean by that, than the *particular circumstances* of the action?   The examples which he adduces clearly show this to
be his meaning, for they are exclusively confined to cases in
which the persons were ignorant of some of the circumstances; such as that of 'a person who, wishing to exhibit a machine, discharges a dart which wounds a bystander; and that
of Merope, who killed her own son instead of her enemy,'
and such like.

"Thus you see what is the kind of ignorance that renders
actions involuntary; namely, that of the particular circumstances, which is termed by divines, as you must know, *ignorance of the fact.*   But with respect to *ignorance of the right*
—ignorance of the good or evil in an action—which is the
only point in question, let us see if Aristotle agrees with Father Bauny.   Here are the words of the philosopher: 'All
wicked men are ignorant of what they ought to do, and what
they ought to avoid; and it is this very ignorance which
makes them wicked and vicious.   Accordingly, a man cannot
be said to act involuntarily merely because he is ignorant of
what it is proper for him to do in order to fulfil his duty.
This ignorance in the choice of good and evil does not make
the action involuntary; it only makes it vicious.   The same
thing may be affirmed of the man who is ignorant generally
of the rules of his duty; such ignorance is worthy of blame,
not of excuse.   And consequently, the ignorance which renders actions involuntary and excusable is simply that which
relates to the fact and its particular circumstances.   In this

case the person is excused and forgiven, being considered as
having acted contrary to his inclination.'

" After this, father, will you maintain that Aristotle is of
your opinion ?   And who can help being astonished to find
that a Pagan philosopher had more enlightened views than
your doctors, in a matter so deeply affecting morals, and the
direction of conscience, too, as the knowledge of those conditions which render actions voluntary or involuntary, and
which, accordingly, charge or discharge them as sinful ?
Look for no more support, then, father, from the prince of
philosophers, and no longer oppose yourselves to the prince
of theologians,[1] who has thus decided the point in the first
book of his Retractations, chapter xv.: 'Those who sin
through ignorance, though they sin without meaning to sin,
commit the deed only because they *will* commit it.   And,
therefore, even this sin of ignorance cannot be committed
except by the will of him who commits it, though by a will
which incites him to the action merely, and not to the sin;
and yet the action itself is nevertheless sinful, for it is enough
to constitute it such that he has done what he was bound
not to do.' "

The Jesuit seemed to be confounded more with the passage from Aristotle, I thought, than that from St Augustine ;
hut while he was thinking on what he could reply, a messen-
ger came to inform him that Madame la Mareschale of ——,
and Madame the Marchioness of ——, requested his attend-
ance.   So taking a hasty leave of us, he said : " I shall speak `—
about it to our fathers.   They will find an answer to it, I
warrant you; we have got some long heads among us."

We understood him perfectly well ; and on our being left
alone, I expressed to my friend my astonishment at the subversion which this doctrine threatened to the whole system
of morals.   To this he replied that he was quite astonished at my astonishment.   "Are you not yet aware," he
said, " that they have gone to far greater excess in morals

[1] Augustine.

than in any other matter?" He gave me some strange illustrations of this, promising me more at some future time. The information which I may receive on this point, will, I hope, furnish the topic of my next communication. —I am, &c.

LETTER V.

DESIGN OF THE JESUITS IN ESTABLISHING A NEW SYSTEM OF MOR-
ALS—TWO SORTS OF CASUISTS AMONG THEM, A GREAT MANY
LAX, AND SOME SEVERE ONES—REASON OF THIS DIFFERENCE—
EXPLANATION OF THE DOCTRINE OF PROBABILITY—A MULTITUDE
OF MODERN AND UNKNOWN AUTHORS SUBSTITUTED IN THE PLACE
OF THE HOLY FATHERS.

PARIS, *March* 20, 1656.

SIR,—According to my promise, I now send you the first
outlines of the morals taught by those good fathers the Jesuits—" those men distinguished for learning and sagacity,
who are all under the guidance of divine wisdom—a surer
guide. than all philosophy." You imagine, perhaps, that I
am in jest, but I am perfectly serious; or rather, they are so
when they speak thus of themselves in their book entitled
"The Image of the First Century."[1] I am only copying
their own words, and may now give you the rest of the eulogy : "They are a society of men, or rather let us call them
angels, predicted by Isaiah in these words, ' Go, ye swift and
ready angels.' "[2] The prediction is as clear as day, is it not ?
"They have the spirit of eagles; they are a flock of phœ-
nixes (a late author having demonstrated that there are a
great many of these birds); they have changed the face of
Christendom !" Of course, we must believe all this, since

[1] *Imago Primi Seculi.*—The work to which Pascal here refers was
printed by the Jesuits in Flanders in the year 1640, under the title of
" L'Image du Premier Siècle de la Société de Jesus," being a history
of the Society of the Jesuits from the period of its establishment in 1540
—a century before the publication. The work itself is very rare. and
would probably have fallen into oblivion, had not the substance of it
been embodied in a little treatise, itself also scarce, entitled " La Morale
Pratique des Jésuites." The small specimen which Pascal has given
conveys but an imperfect idea of the mingled blasphemy and absurdity
of this Jesuitical production.
[2] Isa. xviii. 2.

they have said it; and in one sense you will find the account amply verified by the sequel of this communication, in which I propose to treat of their maxims.

Determined to obtain the best possible information, I did not trust to the representations of our friend the Jansenist, but sought an interview with some of themselves. I found, however, that he told me nothing but the bare truth, and I am persuaded he is an honest man. Of this you may judge from the following account of these conferences.

In the conversation I had with the Jansenist, he told me so many strange things about these fathers, that I could with difficulty believe them, till he pointed them out to me in their writings; after which he left me nothing more to say in their defence, than that these might be the sentiments of some individuals only, which it was not fair to impute to the whole fraternity.[1] And, indeed, I assured him that I knew some of them who were as severe as those whom he quoted to me were lax. This led him to explain to me the spirit of the Society, which is not known to every one; and you will perhaps have no objections to learn something about it.

" You imagine," he began, " that it would tell considerably in their favor to show that some of their fathers are as friendly to Evangelical maxims as others are opposed to them; and you would conclude from that circumstance, that these loose opinions do not belong to the whole Society. That I grant you; for had such been the case, they would not have suffered persons among them holding sentiments so diametrically opposed to licentiousness. But as it is equally true that there are among them those who hold these licentious doctrines, you are bound also to conclude that the Spirit of the Society is not that of Christian severity; for had such been the case, they would not have suffered persons among them holding sentiments so diametrically opposed to that severity."

" And what, then," I asked, " can be the design of the

[1] The reader is requested to notice how completely the charge brought against the Provincial Letters by Voltaire and others is here anticipated and refuted. (See Hist. Introduction.)

whole as a body? Perhaps they have no fixed principle, and every one is left to speak out at random whatever he thinks."

"That cannot be," returned my friend; "such an immense body could not subsist in such a hap-hazard sort of way, or without a soul to govern and regulate its movements; besides, it is one of their express regulations, that none shall print a page without the approval of their superiors."

"But," said I, "how can these same superiors give their consent to maxims so contradictory?"

"That is what you have yet to learn," he replied. "Know, then, that their object is not the corruption of manners— that is not their design. But as little is it their sole aim to reform them—that would be bad policy. Their idea is briefly this: They have such a good opinion of themselves as to believe that it is useful, and in some sort essentially necessary to the good of religion, that their influence should extend everywhere, and that they should govern all consciences. And the Evangelical or severe maxims being best fitted for managing some sorts of people, they avail themselves of these when they find them favorable to their purpose. But as these maxims do not suit the views of the great bulk of people, they wave them in the case of such persons, in order to keep on good terms with all the world. Accordingly, having to deal with persons of all classes and of all different nations, they find it necessary to have casuists assorted to match this diversity.

"On this principle, you will easily see that if they had none but the looser sort of casuists, they would· defeat their main design, which is to embrace all; for those that are truly pious are fond of a stricter discipline. But as there are not many of that stamp, they do not require many severe directors to guide them. They have a few for the select few; while whole multitudes of lax casuists are provided for the multitudes that prefer laxity.[1]

[1] "It must be observed that most of those Jesuits who were so severe

"It is in virtue of this 'obliging and accommodating, conduct, as Father Petau[1] calls it, that they may be said to stretch out a helping hand to all mankind. Should any person present himself before them, for example, fully resolved to make restitution of some ill-gotten gains, do not suppose that they would dissuade him from it. By no means ; on the contrary, they will applaud and confirm him in such a holy resolution. But suppose another should come who wishes to be absolved without restitution, and it will be a particularly hard case indeed, if they cannot furnish him with means of evading the duty, of one kind or another, the lawfulness of which they will be ready to guarantee.

"By this policy they keep all their friends, and defend themselves against all their foes ; for, when charged with extreme laxity, they have nothing more to do than produce their austere directors, with some books which they have written on the severity of the Christian code of morals ; and simple people, or those who never look below the surface of things, are quite satisfied with these proofs of the falsity of the accusation.

"Thus are they prepared for all sorts of persons, and so ready are they to suit the supply to the demand, that when they happen to be in any part of the world where the doctrine of a crucified God is accounted foolishness, they suppress the offence of the cross, and preach only a glorious and not a suffering Jesus Christ. This plan they followed in the Indies and in China, where they permitted Christians to practise idolatry itself, with the aid of the following ingenious contrivance :—they made their converts conceal under their clothes an image of Jesus Christ, to which they taught them

in their writings, were less so towards their penitents. It has been said of Bourdaloue himself that if he required too much in the pulpit, he abated it in the confessional chair: a new stroke of policy well understood on the part of the Jesuits, inasmuch as speculative severity suits persons of rigid morals, and practical condescension attracts the multitude." (D'Alembert, Account of Dest. of Jesuits, p. 44.)

[1] Petau was one of the obscure writers who were employed by the Jesuits to publish defamatory libels against M. Arnauld and the bishops who approved of his book on Frequent Communion. (Coudrette, ii. 426.)

to transfer mentally those adorations which they rendered ostensibly to the idol Cachinchoam and Keum-fucum. This charge is brought against them by Gravina, a Dominican, and is fully established by the Spanish memorial presented to Philip IV., king of Spain, by the Cordeliers of the Philippine Islands, quoted by Thomas Hurtado, in his ' Martyrdom of the Faith,' page 427. To such a length did this practice go, that the Congregation *De Propaganda* were obliged expressly to forbid the Jesuits, on pain of excommunication, to permit the worship of idols on any pretext whatever, or to conceal the mystery of the cross from their catechumens; strictly enjoining them to admit none to baptism who were not thus instructed, and ordering them to expose the image of the crucifix in their churches :—all which is amply detailed in the decree of that Congregation, dated the 9th of July, 1646, and signed by Cardinal Capponi.[1]

[1] The policy to which Pascal refers was introduced by Matthew Ricci, an Italian Jesuit, who succeeded the famous Francis Xavier in attempting to convert the Chinese. Ricci declared that, after consulting the writings of the Chinese literati, he was persuaded that the Xamti and Cachinchoam of the mandarins were merely other names for the King of Heaven, and that the idolatries of the natives were harmless civil ceremonies. He therefore allowed his converts to practise them, on the condition mentioned in the text. In 1631, some new paladins of the orders of Dominic and Francis, who came from the Philippine Islands to share in the spiritual conquest of that vast empire, were grievously scandalized at the monstrous compromise between Christianity and idolatry tolerated by the followers of Loyola, and carried their complaints to Rome. The result is illustrative of the papal policy. Pope Innocent X. condemned the Jesuitical policy; Pope Alexander VII., in 1656 (when this letter was written) sanctioned it; and in 1669, Pope Clement IX. ordained that the decrees of *both* of his predecessors should continue in full force. The Jesuits, availing themselves of this suspense, paid no regard either to the popes or their rival orders, the Dominicans and Franciscans, who, in the persecutions which ensued, always came off with the worst. (Coudrette, iv. 281; Hist. of D. Ign. Loyola, pp. 97–112.)
The prescription given to the Jesuits by the cardinals, to expose the image of the crucifix in their churches. appears to us a sort of homœopathic cure, very little better than the disease. Bossuet, and others who have tried to soften down the doctrines of Rome, would represent the worship ostensibly paid to the crucifix as really paid to Christ, who is represented by it. But even this does not accord with the determination of the Council of Trent, which declared of images *Eisque venerationem impertiendam ;* or with Bellarmine, who devotes a chapter expressly to prove that true and proper worship is to be given to images (Stillingfleet on Popery, by Dr. Cunningham, p. 77.)

" Such is the manner in which they have spread themselves over the whole earth, aided · by *the doctrine of probable opinions*, which is at once the source and the basis of all this licentiousness. You must get some of themselves to explain this doctrine to you. They make no secret of it, any more than of what you have already learned ; with this difference only, that they conceal their carnal and worldly policy under the garb of divine and Christian prudence; as if the faith, and tradition its ally, were not always one and the same at all times and in all places ; as if it were the part of the rule to bend in conformity to the subject which it was meant to regulate ; and as if souls, to be purified from their pollutions, had only to corrupt the law of the Lord, in place of ' the law of the Lord, which is clean and pure, converting the soul which lieth in sin,' and bringing it into conformity with its salutary lessons !

" Go and see some of these worthy fathers, I beseech you, and I am confident that you will soon discover, in the laxity of their moral system, the explanation of their doctrine about grace. You will then see the Christian virtues exhibited in such a strange aspect, so completely stripped of the charity which is the life and soul of them—you will see so many crimes palliated and irregularities tolerated, that you will no longer be surprised at their maintaining that ' all men have always enough of grace' to lead a pious life, in the sense in which they understand piety. Their morality being entirely Pagan, nature is quite competent to its observance. When we maintain the necessity of efficacious grace, we assign it another sort of virtue for its object. Its office is not to cure one vice by means of another ; it is not merely to induce men to practise the external duties of religion : it aims at a virtue higher than that propounded by Pharisees, or the greatest sages of Heathenism. The law and reason are ' sufficient graces' for these purposes. But to disenthral the soul from the love of the world—to tear it from what it holds most dear—to make it die to itself—to lift it up and bind it wholly, only, and forever, to God—can be the work of none but an all-powerful hand. And it would be as absurd to affirm that we have the full power of achieving such objects, as it would be to allege that those virtues, devoid of the love of God, which these fathers confound with the virtues of Christianity, are beyond our power."

Such was the strain of my friend's discourse, which was delivered with much feeling; for he takes these sad disorders very much to heart. For my own part, I began to entertain a high admiration of these fathers, simply on account of the ingenuity of their policy; and following his advice, I waited on a good casuist of the Society, one of my old acquaintances, with whom I now resolved purposely to renew my former intimacy. Having my instructions how to manage them, I had no great difficulty in getting him afloat. Retaining his old attachment, he received me immediately with a profusion of kindness; and after talking over some indifferent matters, I took occasion from the present season,[1] to learn something from him about fasting, and thus slip insensibly into the main subject. I told him, therefore, that I had difficulty in supporting the fast. He exhorted me to do violence to my inclinations; but as I continued to murmur, he took pity on me, and began to search out some ground for a dispensation. In fact he suggested a number of excuses for me, none of which happened to suit my case, till at length he bethought himself of asking me, whether I did not find it difficult to sleep without taking supper? " Yes, my good father," said I; "and for that reason I am obliged often to take a refreshment at mid-day, and supper at night."[2]

"I am extremely happy," he replied, "to have found out a way of relieving you without sin: go in peace—you are under no obligation to fast. However, I would not have you depend on my word: step this way to the library."

[1] Lent.
[2] " According to the rules of the Roman Catholic fast, one meal alone is allowed on a fast-day. Many, however, fall off before the end of Lent, and take to their breakfast and suppers, under the sanction of some good-natured doctor, who declares fasting injurious to their health." (Blanco White, Letters from Spain, p. 272.)

On going thither with him he took up a book, exclaiming, with great rapture, "Here is the authority for you : and, by my conscience, such an authority ! It is ESCOBAR !"[1]
"Who is Escobar ?" I inquired.
"What ! not know Escobar ?" cried the monk ; "the member of our Society who compiled this Moral Theology from twenty-four of our fathers, and on this founds an analogy, in his preface, between his book and 'that in the Apocalypse which was sealed with seven seals,' and states that 'Jesus presents it thus sealed to the four living creatures, Suarez, Vasquez, Molina, and Valencia,[2] in presence of the four-and-twenty Jesuits who represent the four-and-twenty elders ?' "
He read me, in fact, the whole of that allegory, which he pronounced to be admirably appropriate, and which conveyed to my mind a sublime idea of the excellence of the work. At length, having sought out the passage on fasting, " O here it is !" he said ; "treatise 1, example 13, no. 67 : 'If a

---

[1] Father Antoine Escobar of Mendoza was a Jesuit of Spain, and born at Valladolid in 1589, where he died in 1669. His principal work is his "Exposition of Uncontroverted Opinions in Moral Theology," in six volumes. It abounds with the most licentious doctrines, and being a compilation from numerous Jesuitical writers, afforded a rich field for the satire of Pascal. The characteristic absurdity of this author is, that his questions uniformly exhibit two faces—an affirmative and a negative ;—so that *escobarderie* became a synonym in France for *duplicity*. (Biographie Pittoresque des Jesuites, par M. C. de Plancy, Paris, 1826, p. 38.) Nicole tells us that he had in his possession a portrait of the casuist which gave him a "resolute and decisive cast of countenance"—not exactly what might have been expected from his double-faced questions. His friends describe Escobar as a good man, a laborious student, and very devout in his way. It is said that, when he heard that his name and writings were so frequently noticed in the Provincial Letters, he was quite overjoyed to think that his fame would extend as far as the *little letters* had done. Boileau has celebrated him in the following couplet:—

Si Bourdaloue un peu sévère,
Nous dit, craignez la volupté :
Escobar, lui dit-on, mon père,
Nour la permet pour la santé.

" If Bourdaloue, a little too severe,
Cries, Fly from pleasure's fatal fascination !
Dear Father, cries another, Escobar
Permits it as a healthy relaxation."

[2] Four celebrated casuists.

9*

man cannot sleep without taking supper, is he bound to fast?
Answer : *By no means !*'   Will that not satisfy you ?"

" Not exactly," replied I ; "for I might sustain the fast
by taking my refreshment in the morning, and supping at
night."

" Listen, then, to what follows ; they have provided for
all that : ' And what is to be said, if the person might make
a shift with a refreshment in the morning and supping at
night ?' "

" That's my case exactly."

" ' Answer : Still he is not obligea to fast ; because no
person is obliged to change the order of his meals.' "

" A most excellent reason !" I exclaimed.

" But tell me, pray," continued the monk, " do you take
much wine ?"

" No, my dear father," I answered ; " I cannot endure it."

" I merely put the question," returned he, " to apprize
you that you might, without breaking the fast, take a glass
or so in the morning, or whenever you felt inclined for a
drop ; and that is always something in the way of supporting nature.   Here is the decision at the same place, no. 57 :
' May one, without breaking the fast, drink wine at any hour
he pleases, and even in a large quantity?   Yes, he may :
and a dram of hippocrass too.'[1]   I had no recollection of
the hippocrass," said the monk ; " I must take a note of that
in my memorandum-book."

" He must be a nice man, this Escobar," observed I.

" Oh ! everybody likes him," rejoined the father ; " he has
such delightful questions !   Only observe this one in the
same place, no. 38 : ' If a man doubt whether he is twenty-
one years old, is he obliged to fast ?[2]   No.   But suppose I
were to be twenty-one to-night an hour after midnight, and
to-morrow were the fast, would I be obliged to fast to-mor-

---

[1] *Hippocrass*—a medicated wine.
[2] All persons above the age of one-and-twenty are bound to observe
the rules of the Roman Catholic fast during Lent.   The obligation of
fasting begins at midnight, just when the leading clock of every town
strikes twelve.   (Letters from Spain, p. 270.)

row?   No; for you were at liberty to eat as much as you pleased for an hour after midnight, not being till then fully twenty-one; and therefore having a right to break the fast-day, you are not obliged to keep it.' "

" Well, that is vastly entertaining !" cried I.

" Oh," rejoined the father, " it is impossible to tear one's self away from the book: I spend whole days and nights in reading it ; in fact, I do nothing else."

The worthy monk, perceiving that I was interested, was quite delighted, and went on with his quotations. " Now," said he, " for a taste of Filiutius, one of the four-and-twenty Jesuits : ' Is a man who has exhausted himself any way— by profligacy, for example[1] —obliged to fast ? By no means. But if he has exhausted himself expressly to procure a dis-pensation from fasting, will he be held obliged ? He will not, even though he should have had that design.'   There now ! would you have believed that ?"

"Indeed, good father, I do not believe it yet," said I. " What ! is it no sin for a man not to fast when he has it in his power ? And is it allowable to court occasions of com-mitting sin, or rather, are we not bound to shun them ? That would be easy enough, surely."

" Not always so," he replied ; " that is just as it may happen."

" Happen, how ?" cried I.

" Oho !" rejoined the monk, " so you think that if a person experience some inconvenience in avoiding the occasions of sin, he is still bound to do so ? Not so thinks Father Bauny. ' Absolution,' says he, ' is not to be refused to such as con-tinue in the proximate occasions of sin,[2] if they are so situ-ated that they cannot give them up without becoming the

---

[1] Ad insequendam amicam. (Tom. II. tr. 27, part 2, c. 6, n. 143.) The accuracy with which the references are made to the writings of these casuists shows anything but a design to garble or misrepresent them.

[2] In the technical language of theology, an " occasion of sin" is any situation or course of conduct which has a tendency to induce the com-mission of sin. " Proximate occasions" are those which have a direct and immediate tendency of this kind.

common talk of the world, or subjecting themselves to personal inconvenience.' "

"I am glad to hear it, father," I remarked; "and now that we are not obliged to avoid the occasions of sin, nothing more remains but to say that we may deliberately court them."

"Even that is occasionally permitted," added he; "the celebrated casuist Basil Ponce has said so, and Father Bauny quotes his sentiment with approbation, in his Treatise on Penance, as follows: 'We may seek an occasion of sin directly and designedly—*primo et per se*—when our own or our neighbor's spiritual or temporal advantage induces us to do so.' "

"Truly," said I, "it appears to be all a dream to me, when I hear grave divines talking in this manner! Come now, my dear father, tell me conscientiously, do *you* hold such a sentiment as that?"

"No, indeed," said he, "I do not."

"You are speaking, then, against your conscience," continued I.

"Not at all," he replied; "I was speaking on that point not according to my own conscience, but according to that of Ponce and Father Bauny, and them you may follow with the utmost safety, for I assure you that they are able men."

"What, father! because they have put down these three lines in their books, will it therefore become allowable to court the occasions of sin? I always thought that we were bound to take the Scripture and the tradition of the Church as our only rule, and not your casuists."

"Goodness!" cried the monk, "I declare you put me in mind of these Jansenists. Think you that Father Bauny and Basil Ponce are not able to render their opinion *probable*?"

"Probable won't do for me," said I; "I must have certainty."

"I can easily see," replied the good father, "that you know nothing about our doctrine of *probable opinions*. If you did, you would speak in another strain. Ah! my dear sir, I must really give you some instructions on this point; without knowing this, positively you can understand nothing at all. It is the foundation—the very A, B, C, of our whole moral philosophy."

Glad to see him come to the point to which I had been drawing him on, I expressed my satisfaction, and requested him to explain what was meant by a probable opinion ?[1]

"That," he replied, "our authors will answer better than I can do. The generality of them, and, among others, our four-and-twenty elders, describe it thus: 'An opinion is called probable, when it is founded upon reasons of some consideration. Hence it may sometimes happen that a single *very grave doctor* may render an opinion probable.' The reason is added: 'For a man particularly given to study would not adhere to an opinion unless he was drawn to it by a good and sufficient reason.' "

"So it would appear," I observed, with a smile, "that a single doctor may turn consciences round about and upside down as he pleases, and yet always land them in a safe position."

"You must not laugh at it, sir," returned the monk; "nor need you attempt to combat the doctrine. The Jansenists tried this; but they might have saved themselves the trouble—it is too firmly established. Hear Sanchez, one of the most famous of our fathers: 'You may doubt, perhaps, whether the authority of a single good and learned doctor renders an opinion probable. I answer, that it does; and this is confirmed by Angelus, Sylvester, Navarre, Emanuel Sa, &c. It is proved thus: A probable opinion is one that

---

[1] " The casuists are divided into *Probabilistæ* and *Probabilioristæ*. The first, among whom were the Jesuits, maintain that a certain degree of probability as to the lawfulness of an action is enough to secure against sin. The second, supported by the Dominicans and the Jansenists (a kind of Catholic Calvinists condemned by the Church), insist on always taking the *safest* or most probable side. The French proverb, *Le mieux est l'ennemi du bien*, is perfectly applicable to the practical effects of these two systems in Spain." (Letters from Spain. p. 277.) Nicole has a long dissertation on the subject in his Notes on this Letter.

has a considerable foundation. Now the authority of a learned and pious man is entitled to very great consideration; because (mark the reason), if the testimony of such a man has great influence in convincing us that such and such an event occurred, say at Rome, for example, why should it not have the same weight in the case of a question in morals ?' "

" An odd comparison this," interrupted I, " between the concerns of the world and those of conscience !"

" Have a little patience," rejoined the monk; " Sanchez answers that in the very next sentence : ' Nor can I assent to the qualification made here by some writers, namely, that the authority of such a doctor, though sufficient in matters of human right, is not so in those of divine right. It is of vast weight in both cases.' "

" Well, father," said I, frankly, " I really cannot admire that rule. Who can assure me, considering the freedom your doctors claim to examine everything by reason, that what appears safe to one may seem so to all the rest ? The diversity of judgments is so great"—

" You don't understand it," said he, interrupting me ; " no doubt they are often of different sentiments, but what signifies that ?—each renders his own opinion probable and safe. We all know well enough that they are far from being of the same mind ; what is more, there is hardly an instance in which they ever agree. There are very few questions, indeed, in which you do not find the one saying Yés, and the other saying No. Still, in all these cases, each of the contrary opinions is probable. And hence Diana says on a certain subject : ' Ponce and Sanchez hold opposite views of it ; but, as they are both learned men, each renders his own opinion probable.' "

" But, father," I remarked, " a person must be sadly embarrassed in choosing between them !"—" Not at all," he rejoined ; " he has only to follow the opinion which suits him best."—" What ! if the other is more probable ?" " It does not signify."—" And if the other is the safer ?" " It does not signify," repeated the monk ; " this is made quite plain by Emanuel Sa, of our Society, in his Aphorisms : ' A person may do what he considers allowable according to a probable opinion, though the contrary may be the safer one. The opinion of a single grave doctor is all that is requisite.' "

" And if an opinion be at once the less probable and the less safe, is it allowable to follow it," I asked, " even in the way of rejecting one which we believe to be more probable and safe ?"

" Once more, I say Yes," replied the monk. " Hear what Filiutius, that great Jesuit of Rome, says: ' It is allowable to follow the less probable opinion, even though it be the less safe one. That is the common judgment of modern authors.' Is not that quite clear ?"

" Well, reverend father," said I, " you have given us elbow-room, at all events ! Thanks to your probable opinions, we have got liberty of conscience with a witness ! And are you casuists allowed the same latitude in giving your responses ?"

" O yes," said he, " we answer just as we please ; or rather, I should say, just as it may please those who ask our advice. Here are our rules, taken from Fathers Layman, Vasquez, Sanchez, and the four-and-twenty worthies, in the words of Layman : ' A doctor, on being consulted, may give an advice, not only probable according to his own opinion, but contrary to his opinion, provided this judgment happens to be more favorable or more agreeable to the person that consults him—*si forte hæc favorabilior seu exoptatior sit.* Nay, I go further, and say, that there would be nothing unreasonable in his giving those who consult him a judgment held to be probable by some learned person, even though he should be satisfied in his own mind that it is absolutely false.' "

" Well, seriously, father," I said, " your doctrine is a most uncommonly comfortable one ! Only think of being allowed to answer Yes or No, just as you please ! It is impossible to prize such a privilege too highly. I see now the advantage of the contrary opinions of your doctors. One of them always serves your turn, and the other never gives you any annoyance. If you do not find your account on the one side, you fall back on the other, and always land in perfect safety."

" That is quite true," he replied; " and accordingly, we may always say with Diana, on his finding that Father Bauny was on his side, while Father Lugo was against him : *Sǽpe premente deo, fert deus alter opem.*"[1]

" I understand you," resumed I; " but a practical difficulty has just occurred to me, which is this, that supposing a person to have consulted one of your doctors, and obtained from him a pretty liberal opinion, there is some danger of his getting into a scrape by meeting a confessor who takes a different view of the matter, and refuses him absolution unless he recant the sentiment of the casuist. Have you not provided for such a case as that, father?"

" Can you doubt it?" he replied. " We have bound them, sir, to absolve their penitents who act according to probable opinions, under the pain of mortal sin, to secure their compliance. 'When the penitent,' says Father Bauny, 'follows a probable opinion, the confessor is bound to absolve him, though his opinion should differ from that of his penitent.' "

" But he does not say it would be a mortal sin not to absolve him," said I.

" How hasty you are!" rejoined the monk; " listen to what follows; he has expressly decided that, 'to refuse absolution to a penitent who acts according to a probable opinion, is a sin which is in its nature mortal.' And to settle that point, he cites the most illustrious of our fathers—Suarez, Vasquez, and Sanchez."

" My dear sir," said I, " that is a most prudent regulation. I see nothing to fear now. No confessor can dare to be refractory after this. Indeed, I was not aware that you had the power of issuing your orders on pain of damnation. I

---

[1] " When one god presses hard, another brings relief."

thought that your skill had been confined to the taking away of sins ; I had no idea that it extended to the introduction of new ones. But from what I now see, you are omnipotent."

"That is not a correct way of speaking," rejoined the father. "We do not introduce sins ; we only pay attention to them. I have had occasion to remark, two or three times during our conversation, that you are no great scholastic."

"Be that as it may, father, you have at least answered my difficulty. But I have another to suggest. How do you manage when the Fathers of the Church happen to differ from any of your casuists ?"

"You really know very little of the subject," he replied. "The Fathers were good enough for the morality of their own times ; but they lived too far back for that of the present age, which is no longer regulated by them, but by the modern casuists. On this Father Cellot, following the famous Reginald, remarks : ' In questions of morals, the modern casuists are to be preferred to the ancient fathers, though those lived nearer to the times of the apostles.' And following out this maxim, Diana thus decides : 'Are beneficiaries bound to restore their revenue when guilty of mal-appropriation of it ? The ancients would say Yes, but the moderns say No ; let us, therefore, adhere to the latter opinion, which relieves from the obligation of restitution.' "

"Delightful words these, and most comfortable they must be to a great many people !" I observed.

"We leave the fathers," resumed the monk, "to those who deal with positive divinity.[1] As for us, who are the

[1] In the twelfth century, in consequence of the writings of Peter Lombard, commonly called the "Master of the Sentences," the Christian doctors were divided into two classes—the *Positive* or dogmatic, and the *Scholastic* divines. The *Positive* divines, who were the teachers of systematic divinity, expounded, though in a wretched manner, the Sacred Writings, and confirmed their sentiments by Scripture and tradition. The scholastics, instead of the Bible, explained the book of Sentences, indulging in the most idle and ridiculous speculations.—"The practice of choosing a certain priest, not only to be the occasional confessor, but *the director of the conscience*, was greatly encouraged by the Jesuits." (Letters from Spain, p. 89.)

directors of conscience, we read very little of them, and quote
only the modern casuists. There is Diana, for instance, a
most voluminous writer; he has prefixed to his works a list
of his authorities, which amount to two hundred and ninety-
six, and the most ancient of them is only about eighty years
old."

" It would appear, then," I remarked, " that all these have
come into the world since the date of your Society ?"   ·

" Thereabouts," he replied.

" That is to say, dear father, on your advent, St. Augustine, St. Chrysostom, St. Ambrose, St. Jerome, and all the
rest, in so far as morals are concerned, disappeared from the
stage. Would you be so kind as let me know the names, at
least, of those modern authors who have succeeded them ?"

" A most able and renowned class of men they are," re-
plied the monk. " Their names are, Villalobos, Conink, Lla-
mas, Achokier, Dealkozer, Dellacruz, Veracruz, Ugolin, Tam-
bourin, Fernandez, Martinez, Suarez, Henriquez, Vasquez, Lo-
pez, Gomez, Sanchez, De Vechis, De Grassis, De Grassalis,
De Pitigianis, De Graphæis, Squilanti, Bizozeri, Barcola, De
Bobadilla, Simancha, Perez de Lara, Aldretta, Lorca, De
Scarcia, Quaranta, Scophra, Pedrezza, Cabrezza, Bisbe, Dias,
De Clavasio, Villagut, Adam à Manden, Iribarne, Binsfeld,
Volfangi à Vorberg, Vosthery, Strevesdorf."[1]

" O my dear father !" cried I, quite alarmed, " were all
these people Christians ?"

" How ! Christians !" returned the casuist ; " did I not tell.

---

[1] In this extraordinary list of obscure and now forgotten casuistical
writers, most of them belonging to Spain, Portugal, and Flanders, the
art of the author lies in stringing together the most outlandish names he
conld collect, ranging them mostly according to their terminations, and
placing them in contrast with the venerable and well-known names of
the ancient fathers. To a French ear these names must have sounded
as uncouth and barbarous as those of the Scotch which Milton has
satirized to the ear of an Englishman :—

> " Cries the stall-reader, ' Bless us ! what a word on
> A title-page is this !' Why, is it harder, sirs, than Gordon,
> Colkitto, or Macdonnel, or Galasp ?
> Those rugged names to our like mouths grow sleek,
> That would have made Quintilian stare and gasp."
> (Milton's Minor Poems.)

you that these are the only writers by whom we now govern Christendom ?"

Deeply affected as I was by this announcement, I concealed my emotion from the monk, and only asked him if all these authors were Jesuits ?

" No," said he ; " but that is of little consequence ; they have said a number of good things for all that. It is true the greater part of these same good things are extracted or copied from our authors, but we do not stand on ceremony with them on that score, more especially as they are in the constant habit of quoting our authors with applause. When Diana, for example, who does not belong to our Society, speaks of Vasquez, he calls him 'that phœnix of genius ;' and he declares more than once, ' that Vasquez alone is to him worth all the rest of men put together'—*instar omnium.* Accordingly, our fathers often make use of this good Diana; and if you understand our doctrine of probability, you will see that this is no small help in its way. In fact, we are anxious that others besides the Jesuits would render their opinions probable, to prevent people from ascribing them all to us ; for you will observe, that when any author, whoever he may be, advances a probable opinion, we are entitled, by the doctrine of probability, to adopt it if we please ; and yet, if the author do not belong to our fraternity, we are not responsible for its soundness."

" I understand all that," said I. " It is easy to see that all are welcome that come your way, except the ancient fathers ; you are masters of the field, and have only to walk the course. But I foresee three or four serious difficulties and powerful barriers which will oppose your career."

" And what are these ?" cried the monk, looking quite alarmed.

" They are, the Holy Scriptures," I replied, " the popes, and the councils, whom you cannot gainsay, and who are all in the way of the Gospel."[1]

---

[1] That is, they were all, in Pascal's opinion, favorable to the Gospel scheme of morality.

"Is that all!" he exclaimed; "I declare you put me in a fright. Do you imagine that we would overlook such an obvious scruple as that, or that we have not provided against it? A good idea, forsooth, to suppose that we would contradict Scripture, popes, and councils! I must convince you of your mistake; for I should be sorry you should go away with an impression that we are deficient in our respect to these authorities. You have doubtless taken up this notion from some of the opinions of our fathers, which are apparently at variance with their decisions, though in reality they are not. But to illustrate the harmony between them would require more leisure than we have at present; and as I would not like you to retain a bad impression of us, if you agree to meet with me to-morrow, I shall clear it all up then."

Thus ended our interview, and thus shall end my present communication, which has been long enough, besides, for one letter. I am sure you will be satisfied with it, in the prospect of what is forthcoming.—I am, &c.

LETTER VI.

VARIOUS ARTIFIJES OF THE JESUITS TO ELUDE THE AUTHORITY
OF THE GOSPEL, OF COUNCILS, AND OF THE POPES—SOME CON-
SEQUENCES WHICH RESULT FROM THEIR DOCTRINE OF PROBA-
BILITY—THEIR RELAXATION IN FAVOR OF BENEFICIARIES, PRIESTS,
MONKS, AND DOMESTICS—STORY OF JOHN D'ALBA.

PARIS, *April* 10, 1656.

SIR,—I mentioned, at the close of my last letter, that my
good friend the Jesuit had promised to show me how the
casuists reconcile the contrarieties between their opinions
and the decisions of the popes, the councils, and the Scripture.
This promise he fulfilled at our last interview, of which I
shall now give you an account.

"One of the methods," resumed the monk, " in which we
reconcile these apparent contradictions, is by the interpretation of some phrase. Thus, Pope Gregory XIV. decided
that assassins are not worthy to enjoy the benefit of sanctuary in churches, and ought to be dragged out of them; and
yet our four-and-twenty elders affirm that 'the penalty of
this bull is not incurred by all those that kill in treachery.'
This may appear to you a contradiction; but we get over
this by interpreting the word *assassin* as follows: 'Are assassins unworthy of sanctuary in churches? Yes, by the
bull of Gregory XIV. they are. But by the word *assassins*
we understand those that have received money to murder
one; and accordingly, such as kill without taking any reward for the deed, but merely *to oblige their friends*, do not
come under the category of assassins.' "

"Take another instance: It is said in the Gospel, 'Give
alms of your superfluity.'[1] Several Casuists, however, have

---

[1] Luke xi. 41.—*Quod superest, date eleemosynam* (Vulgate); τα ἐνόντα

contrived to discharge the wealthiest from the obligation of
alms-giving. This may appear another paradox, but the
matter is easily put to rights by giving such an interpretation
to the word *superfluity* that it will seldom or never happen
that any one is troubled with such an article. This feat has
been accomplished by the learned Vasquez, in his Treatise
on Alms, c. 4 : 'What men of the world lay up to improve
their circumstances, or those of their relatives, cannot be
termed superfluity ; and accordingly, such a thing as superfluity is seldom to he found among men of the world, not even
excepting kings.' Diana, too, who generally founds on our
fathers, having quoted these words of Vasquez, justly concludes, ' that as to the question whether the rich are bound
to give alms of their superfluity, even though the affirmative
were true, it will seldom or never happen to be obligatory in
practice.' "

"I see very well how that follows from the doctrine of
Vasquez," said I. "But how would you answer this objection, that, in working out one's salvation, it would he as safe,
according to Vasquez, to give no alms, provided one can
muster as much ambition as to have no superfluity ; as it
is safe, according to the Gospel, to have no ambition at all,
in order to have some superfluity for the purpose of alms-
giving ?"[1]

"Why," returned he, "the answer would he, that both

<hr />

ὅτι (Gr.); *Ea quæ penes vos sunt date* (Beza); "Give alms of such
things as ye have." (Eng. Ver.)
  [1] When Pascal speaks of alms-giving "working out our salvation,"
it is evident that he regarded it only as the evidence of our being in
a state of salvation. Judging by the history of his life, and by his
"Thoughts on Religion," no man was more free from spiritual pride, or
that poor species of it which boasts of or rests in its eleemosynary sacrifices. His charity flowed from love and gratitude to God. Such was
his regard for the poor that he could not refuse to give alms. even
though compelled to take from the supply necessary to relieve his own
infirmities ; and on his death-bed he entreated that a poor person should
be brought into the house and treated with the same attention as himself. declaring that when he thought of his own comforts and of the
multitudes who were destitute of the merest necessaries, he felt a distress which he could not endure. "One thing I have observed," he
says in his Thoughts—"that let a man be ever so poor, he has always
something to leave on his death-bed."

of these ways are safe according to the Gospel ; the one according to the Gospel in its more literal and obvious sense, and the other according to the same Gospel as interpreted by Vasquez. There you see the utility of interpretations. When the terms are so clear, however," he continued, "as not to admit of an interpretation, we have recourse to the observation of favorable circumstances. A single example will illustrate this. The popes have denounced excommunication on monks who lay aside their canonicals ; our casuists, notwithstanding, put it as a question, ' On what occasions may a monk lay aside his religious habit without incurring excommunication ?' They mention a number of cases in which they may, and among others the following : ' If he has laid it aside for an infamous purpose, such as to pick pockets or to go *incognito* into haunts of profligacy, meaning shortly after to resume it.' It is evident the bulls have no reference to cases of that description."

I could hardly believe that, and begged the father to show me the passage in the original. He did so, and under the chapter headed " Practice according to the School of the Society of Jesus"—*Praxis ex Societatis Jesu Schola*—I read these very words : *Si habitum dimittat ut furetur occulte, vel fornicetur.* He showed me the same thing in Diana, in these terms : *Ut eat incognitus ad lupanar.* " And why, father," I asked, " are they discharged from excommunication on such occasions ?"

" Don't you understand it ?" he replied. " Only think what a scandal it would be, were a monk surprised in such a predicament with his canonicals on ! And have you never heard," he continued, " how they answer the first bull *contra sollicitantes?* and how our four-and-twenty, in another chapter of the Practice according to the School of our Society, explain the bull of Pius V *contra clericos*, &c. ?"[1]

" I know nothing about all that," said I.

---

[1] These bulls were directed against gross and unnatural crimes prevailing among the clergy. (Nicolo, ii. pp. 372-376.)

"Then it is a sign you have not read much of Escobar," returned the monk.

"I got him only yesterday, father," said I; "and I had no small difficulty, too, in procuring a copy. I don't know how it is, but everybody of late has been in search of him."[1]

"The passage to which I referred," returned the monk, "may be found in treatise 1, example 8, no. 102. Consult it at your leisure when you go home."

I did so that very night; but it is so shockingly bad, that I dare not transcribe it.

The good father then went on to say : "You now understand what use we make of favorable circumstances. Sometimes, however, obstinate cases will occur, which will not admit of this mode of adjustment; so much so, indeed, that you would almost suppose they involved flat contradictions. For example, three popes have decided that monks who are bound by a particular vow to a Lenten life,[2] cannot be absolved from it even though they should become bishops. And yet Diana avers that notwithstanding this decision they *are* absolved."

"And how does he reconcile that ?" said I.

"By the most subtle of all the modern methods, and by the nicest possible application of probability," replied the monk. "You may recollect you were told the other day, that the affirmative and negative of most opinions have each, according to our doctors, some probability—enough, at least, to be followed with a safe conscience. Not that the *pro* and *con* are both true in the same sense—that is impossible—but only they are both probable, and therefore safe, as a matter of course. On this principle our worthy friend Diana remarks : 'To the decision of these three popes, which is contrary to my opinion, I answer, that they spoke in this way by adhering to the affirmative side—which, in fact, even in my judgment, is probable; but it does not follow from this

---

[1] An allusion to the popularity of the Letters, which induced many to inquire after the casuistical writings so often quoted in them.
[2] *Lenten life*—an abstemious life, or life of fasting.

that the negative may not have its probability too.' And in the same treatise, speaking of another subject on which he again differs from a pope, he says : ' The pope, I grant, has said it as the head of the Church ; but his decision does not extend beyond the sphere of the probability of his own opinion.' Now you perceive this is not doing any harm to the opinions of the popes ; such a thing would never be tolerated at Rome, where Diana is in high repute. For he does not say that what the popes have decided is not probable; but leaving their opinion within the sphere of probability, he merely says that the contrary is also probable."

" That is very respectful," said I.

" Yes," added the monk, " and rather more ingenious than the reply made by Father Bauny, when his books were censured at Rome ; for when pushed very hard on this point by M. Hallier, he made bold to write : ' What has the censure of Rome to do with that of France ?' You now see how, either by the interpretation of terms, by the observation of favorable circumstances, or by the aid of the double probability of *pro* and *con*, we always contrive to reconcile those seeming contradictions which occasioned you so much surprise, without ever touching on the decisions of Scripture, councils, or popes."

" Reverend father," said I, " how happy the world is in having such men as you for its masters ! And what blessings are these probabilities ! I never knew the reason why you took such pains to establish that a single doctor, *if a grave one*, might render an opinion probable, and that the contrary might be so too, and that one may choose any side one pleases, even though he does not believe it to be the right side, and all with such a safe conscience, that the confessor who should refuse him absolution on the faith of the casuists would be in a state of damnation. But I see now that a single casuist may make new rules of morality at his discretion, and dispose, according to his fancy, of everything pertaining to the regulation of manners."

" What you have now said," rejoined the father, " would

require to be modified a little. Pay attention now, while I
explain our method, and you will observe the progress of a
new opinion, from its birth to its maturity. First, the grave
doctor who invented it exhibits it to the world, casting it
abroad like seed, that it may take root. In this state it is
very feeble; it requires time gradually to ripen. This accounts for Diana, who has introduced a great many of these
opinions, saying: ' I advance this opinion ; but as it is new,
I give it time to come to maturity—*relinquo tempori matu-
randum.*' Thus in a few years it becomes insensibly consoli-
dated ; and after a considerable time it is sanctioned by the
tacit approbation of the Church, according to the grand maxim of Father Bauny, ' that if an opinion has been advanced
by some casuist, and has not been impugned by the Church,
it is a sign that she approves of it.' And, in fact, on this
principle he authenticates one of his own principles in his
sixth treatise, p. 312."

"Indeed, father!" cried I, "why, on this principle the
Church would approve of all the abuses which she tolerates,
and all the errors in all the books which she does not censure !"

"Dispute the point with Father Bauny," he replied. "I
am merely quoting his words, and you begin to quarrel with
me. There is no disputing with facts, sir. Well, as I was
saying, when time has thus matured an opinion, it thenceforth becomes completely probable and safe. Hence the
learned Caramuel, in dedicating his Fundamental Theology
to Diana, declares that this great Diana has rendered many
opinions probable which were not so before—*quæ antea non
erant ;* and that, therefore, in following them, persons do not
sin now, though they would have sinned formerly—*jam non
peccant, licet ante peccaverint.*"

"Truly, father," I observed, "it must be worth one's
while living in the neighborhood of your doctors. Why, of
two individuals who do the same actions, he that knows nothing about their doctrine sins, while he that knows it does no
sin. It seems, then, that their doctrine possesses at once an

edifying and a justifying virtue! The law of God, according to St. Paul, made transgressors;[1] but this law of yours makes nearly all of us innocent. I beseech you, my dear sir, let me know all about it. I will not leave you till you have told me all the maxims which your casuists have established."

"Alas!" the monk exclaimed, "our main object, no doubt, should have been to establish no other maxims than those of the Gospel in all their strictness: and it is easy to see, from the Rules for the regulation of our manners,[2] that if we tolerate some degree of relaxation in others, it is rather out of complaisance than through design. The truth is, sir, we are forced to it. Men have arrived at such a pitch of corruption now-a-days, that unable to make them come to us, we must e'en go to them, otherwise they would cast us off altogether; and what is worse, they would become perfect castaways. It is to retain such characters as these that our casuists have taken under consideration the vices to which people of various conditions are most addicted, with the view

---

[1] *Prevaricateurs.*—Alluding probably to such texts as Rom. iv. 15: "The law worketh wrath; for where no law is, there is no transgression." *Ubi enim non est lex, nec prevaricatio* (Vulg.); or Rom. v. 13, &c.

[2] The Rules (*Regulæ Communes*) of the Society of Jesus, it must be admitted, are rigid enough in the enforcement of moral decency and discipline on the members; and the perfect candor of Pascal appears in the admission. This, however, only adds weight to the real charge which he substantiates against them, of teaching maxims which tend to the subversion of morality. With regard to their personal conduct, different opinions prevail. 'Whatever we may think of the political delinquencies of their leaders" says Blanco White "their bitterest enemies have never ventured to charge the order of Jesuits with moral irregularities. The internal policy of that body," he adds, "precluded the possibility of gross misconduct" (Letters from Spain p. 89.) We are far from being sure of this. The remark seems to apply to only one species of vice, too common in monastic life, and may be true of the conventual establishments of the Jesuits, where outward decency forms part of the deep policy of the order; but what dependence can be placed on the moral purity of men whose consciences must be debauched by such maxims? Jarrige informs us that they boasted at one time in Spain of possessing an herb which preserved their chastity; and on being questioned by the king to tell what it was, they replied: "It was the fear of God." "But," says the author, "whatever they might be then, it is plain that they have since lost the seed of that herb, for it no longer grows in their garden." (Jesuites sur l'Echanfaud, ch. 6.)

of laying down maxims which, while they cannot be said to
violate the truth, are so gentle that he must be a very impracticable subject indeed who is not pleased with them.
The grand project of our Society, for the good of religion, is
never to repulse any one, let him be what he may, and so
avoid driving people to despair.[1]

"They have got maxims, therefore, for all sorts of persons ; for beneficiaries, for priests, for monks ; for gentlemen,
for servants ; for rich men, for commercial men ; for people
in embarrassed or indigent circumstances ; for devout women,
and women that are not devout; for married people, and
irregular people. In short, nothing has escaped their foresight."

" In other words," said I, " they have got maxims for the
clergy, the nobility, and the commons.[2] Well, I am quite
impatient to hear them."

"Let us commence," resumed the father, " with the beneficiaries. You are aware of the traffic with benefices that is
now carried on, and that were the matter referred to St.
Thomas and the ancients who have written on it, there might
chance to be some simoniacs in the Church. This rendered
it highly necessary for our fathers to exercise their prudence
in finding out a palliative. With what success they have
done so will appear from the following words of Valencia,
who is one of Escobar's 'four living creatures.' At the end
of a long discourse, in which he suggests various expedients,
he propounds the following at page 2039, vol. iii., which, to
my mind, is the best : 'If a person gives a temporal in exchange for a spiritual good'—that is, if he gives money for a
benefice—' and gives the money as the price of the benefice,
it is manifest simony. But if he gives it merely as the mo-

---

[1] It has been observed, with great truth, by Sir James Macintosh,
that " casuistry, the inevitable growth of the practices of confession and
absolution, has generally vibrated betwixt the extremes of impracticable severity and contemptible indulgence." (Hist. of England, vol. ii.
p. 359.)
[2] *Tiers etat.*—These were the three orders into which the people of
France were divided ; the *tiers etat* or third estate, corresponding to our
commons.

tive which inclines the will ôf the patron to confer on him the living, it is not simony, even though the person who confers it considers and expects the money as the principal object.' Tanner, who is also a member of our Society, affirms the same thing, vol. iii., p. 1519, although he 'grants that St. Thomas is opposed to it; for he expressly teaches that it is always simony to give a spiritual for a temporal good, if the temporal is the end in view.' By this means we prevent an immense number of simoniacal transactions; for who would be so desperately wicked as to refuse, when giving money for a benefice, to take the simple precaution of so directing his intentions as to give it as *a motive* to induce the benefic- iary to part with it, instead of giving it as *the price* of the benefice? No man, surely, can be so far left to himself as that would come to."

"I agree with you there," I replied; "all men, I should think, have *sufficient grace* to make a bargain of that sort."

"There can be no doubt of it," returned the monk. "Such, then, is the way in which we soften matters in re- gard to the beneficiaries. And now for the priests—we have maxims pretty favorable to them also. Take the following, for example, from our four-and-twenty elders : 'Can a priest, who has received money to say a mass, take an additional sum upon the same mass? Yes, says Filiutius, he may, by applying that part of the sacrifice which belongs to himself as a priest to the person who paid him last; provided he does not take a sum equivalent to a whole mass, but only a part, such as the third of a mass.'"

"Surely, father," said I, "this must be one of those cases in which the *pro* and the *con* have both their share of proba- bility. What you have now stated cannot fail, of course, to be probable, having the authority of such men as Filiutius and Escobar; and yet, leaving that within the sphere of probability, it strikes me that the contrary opinion might be made out to be probable too, and might be supported by such reasons as the following : That, while the Church allows priests who are in poor circumstances to take money for their

masses, seeing it is but right that those who serve at the
altar should live by the a.tar, she never intended that they
should barter the sacrifice for money,[1] and still less, that
they should deprive themselves of those benefits which they
ought themselves, in the first place, to draw from it; to which
I might add, that, according to St. Paul, the priests are to
offer sacrifice first for themselves, and then for the people ;[2]
and that accordingly, while permitted to participate with
others in the benefit of the sacrifice, they are not at liberty
to forego their share, by transferring it to another for a third

---

[1] With all respect for Pascal and his good intention, it is plain that
there is a wide difference between the duty, illustrated by the apostle
from the ancient law, of supporting those who minister in holy things
in and for their ministrations, and the practice introduced by the Church
of Rome, of putting a price on the holy things themselves. In the one
case, it was simply a recognition of the general principle that " the la-
borer is worthy of his hire." In the other, it was converting the minister into a shopman who was allowed to " barter" his sacred wares at
the market price, or any price he pleased. To this mercenary principle
most of the superstitions of Rome may be traced. The popish doctrine
of the mass is founded on transubstantiation, or the superstition broached
in the ninth century, that the bread and wine are converted by the
priest into the rea¹ body and blood of Christ. It was never settled in
the Romish Church to be a proper propitiatory sacrifice for the living
and the dead till the Council of Trent. in the sixteenth century; so that
it is comparatively a modern invention. The mass proceeds on the absurd assumption that our blessed Lord offered up his body and blood in
the institution of the supper, before offering them on the cross, and partook of them himself; and it involves the blasphemy of supposing that
a sinful mortal may, whenever he pleases, offer up the great sacrifice
of that body and blood, which could only be offered by the Son of God
and offered by him only once. This, however, is the great Diana of
the popish priests—by this craft they have their wealth—and the whole
of its history proves that it was invented for no other purposes than imposture and extortion.

[2] Heb. vii. 27.—It is astonishing to see an acute mind like that of
Pascal so warped by superstition as not to perceive that in this, and
other allusions to the Levitical priesthood, the object of the apostle was
avowedly to prove that the great sacrifice for sin. of which the ancient
sacrifices were the types, had been ¨ once offered in the end of the
world," and that ¨ there remaineth no more sacrifice for sins;" and
that the very text to which he refers, teaches that, in the person of
Jesus Christ, our high priest, all the functions of the sacrificing priesthood were fulfilled and terminated · " Who needeth not daily *as those
high priests*, to offer up sacrifice, first for his own sins. and then for
the people's : for this he did *once*, when he offered up himself." The
ministers of the New Testament are never in Scripture called priests,
though this name has been applied to the Christian people who offer up
the " spiritual sacrifices" of praise and good works. (Heb. xiii. 15, 16 ;.
1 Pet. ii. 5.)

of a mass, or, in other words, for the matter of fourpence or fivepence. Verily, father, little as I pretend to be a *grave* man, I might contrive to make this opinion probable."

"It would cost you no great pains to do that," replied the monk; "it is visibly probable already. The difficulty lies in discovering probability in the converse of opinions manifestly good; and this is a feat which none but great men can achieve. Father Bauny shines in this department. It is really delightful to see that learned casuist examining with characteristic ingenuity and subtlety, the negative and affirmative of the same question, and proving both of them to be right! Thus in the matter of priests, he says in one place: 'No law can be made to oblige the curates to say mass every day; for such a law would unquestionably (*haud dubie*) expose them to the danger of saying it sometimes in mortal sin.' And yet in another part of the same treatise, he says, 'that priests who have received money for saying mass every day ought to say it every day, and that they cannot excuse themselves on the ground that they are not always in a fit state for the service; because it is in their power at all times to do penance, and if they neglect this they have themselves to blame for it, and not the person who made them say mass.' And to relieve their minds from all scruples on the subject, he thus resolves the question: 'May a priest say mass on the same day in which he has committed a mortal sin of the worst kind, in the way of confessing himself beforehand?' Villalobos says No, because of his impurity; but Sancius says, He may without any sin; and I hold his opinion to be safe, and one which may be followed in practice— *et tuta et sequenda in praxi.*"[1]

"Follow this opinion in practice!" cried I. "Will any priest who has fallen into such irregularities, have the assurance on the same day to approach the altar, on the mere word of Father Bauny? Is he not bound to submit to the ancient laws of the Church, which debarred from the sacrifice

[1] Treatise 10, p. 474; ib., p. 441; Quest. 32, p. 457.

forever, or at least for a long time, priests who had commit·
ted sins of that description—instead of following the modern
opinions of casuists, who would admit him to it on the very
day that witnessed his fall ?"

"You have a very short memory," returned the monk.
"Did I not inform you a little ago that, according to our fathers Cellot and Reginald, 'in matters of morality we are to
follow, not the ancient fathers, but the modern casuists ?' "

"I remember it perfectly," said I ; "but we have something more here : we have the laws of the Church."

"True," he replied ; "but this shows you do not know another capital maxim of our fathers, 'that the laws of the
Church lose their authority when they have gone into desue-
tude—*cum jam desuetudine abierunt*—as Filiutus says.[1] We
know the present exigencies of the Church much better than
the ancients could do. Were we to be so strict in excluding
priests from the altar, you can understand there would not be
such a great number of masses. Now a multitude of masses
brings such a revenue of glory to God and of good to souls,
that I may venture to say, with Father Cellot, that there
would not be too many priests, 'though not only all men
and women, were that possible, but even inanimate bodies,
and even brute beasts—*bruta animalia*—were transformed
into priests to celebrate mass.' "[2]

I was so astounded at the extravagance of this imagination, that I could not utter a word, and allowed him to go on
with his discourse. "Enough, however, about priests ; I am
afraid of getting tedious : let us come to the *monks*. The
grand difficulty with them is the obedience they owe to their
superiors ; now observe the palliative which our fathers apply
in this case. Castro Palao[3] of our Society has said : 'Beyond
all dispute, a monk who has a probable opinion of his own, is

[1] Tom. ii. tr. 25. n. 33. And yet they will pretend to hold that their
Church is infallible !
[2] Book of the Hierarchy, p. 611, Rouen edition.
[3] Op. Mor. p. 1, disp. 2, p. 6. *Ferdinand de Castro Palao* was a
Jesuit of Spain, and author of a work on Virtues and Vices, published
in 1631.

not bound to obey his superior, though the opinion of the latter is the more probable. For the monk is at liberty to adopt the opinion which is more agreeable to himself—*quæ sibi gratior fuerit*—as Sanchez says. And though the order of his superior be just, that does not oblige you to obey him, for it is not just at all points or in every respect—*non unde-quaquè justè præcepit*—but only probably so; and consequently, you are only probably bound to obey him, and probably not bound—*probabiliter obligatus, et probabiliter deobligatus.*' "

"Certainly, father," said I, "it is impossible too highly to estimate this precious fruit of the double probability."

"It is of great use indeed," he replied; "but we must be brief. Let me only give you the following specimen of our famous Molina in favor of monks who are expelled from their convents for irregularities. Escobar quotes him thus: 'Molina asserts that a monk expelled from his monastery is not obliged to reform in order to get back again, and that he is no longer bound by his vow of obedience.' "

"Well, father," cried I, "this is all very comfortable for the clergy. Your casuists, I perceive, have been very indul-gent to them, and no wonder—they were legislating, so to speak, for themselves. I am afraid people of other conditions are not so liberally treated. Every one for himself in this world."

"There you do us wrong," returned the monk; "they could not have been kinder to themselves than we have been to them. We treat all, from the highest to the lowest, with an even-handed charity, sir. And to prove this, you tempt me to tell you our maxims for servants. In reference to this class, we have taken into consideration the difficulty they must experience, when they are men of conscience, in serving profligate masters. For if they refuse to perform all the er-rands in which they are employed, they lose their places; and if they yield obedience, they have their scruples. To relieve them from these, our four-and-twenty fathers have specified the services which they may render with a safe conscience;

10*

such as, 'carrying letters and presents, opening doors and
windows, helping their master to reach the window, holding
the ladder which he is mounting. All this,' say they, 'is allowable and indifferent; it is true that, as to holding the ladder, they must be threatened, more than usually, with being
punished for refusing; for it is doing an injury to the master
of a house to enter it by the window.' You perceive the
judiciousness of that observation, of course?"

"I expected nothing less," said I, "from a book edited by
four-and-twenty Jesuits."

"But," added the monk, "Father Bauny has gone beyond
this; he has taught valets how to perform these sorts of
offices for their masters quite innocently, by making them
direct their intention, not to the sins to which they are accessary, but to the gain which is to accrue from them. In his
Summary of Sins, p. 710, first edition, he thus states the
matter: 'Let confessors observe,' says he, 'that they cannot
absolve valets who perform base errands, if they consent to
the sins of their masters; but the reverse holds true, if they
have done the thing merely from a regard to their temporal
emolument.' And that, I should conceive, is no difficult matter to do; for why should they insist on consenting to sins of
which they taste nothing but the trouble? The same Father
Bauny has established a prime maxim in favor of those who
are not content with their wages: 'May servants who are dissatisfied with their wages, use means to raise them by laying
their hands on as much of the property of their masters as
they may consider necessary to make the said wages equivalent to their trouble? They may, in certain circumstances;
as when they are so poor that, in looking for a situation, they
have been obliged to accept the offer made to them, and when
other servants of the same class are gaining more than they,
elsewhere.' "

"Ha, father!" cried I, "that is John d'Alba's passage, I
declare."

"What John d'Alba?" inquired the father: "what do you
mean?"

"Strange, father!" returned I: "do you not remember
what happened in this city in the year 1647? Where in the
world were you living at that time?"

"I was teaching cases of conscience in one of our colleges
far from Paris," he replied.

"I see you don't know the story, father: I must tell it
you. I heard it related the other day by a man of honor,
whom I met in company. He told us that this John d'Alba,
who was in the service of your fathers in the College of Clermont, in the Rue St. Jacques, being dissatisfied with his wages, had purloined something to make himself amends; and
that your fathers, on discovering the theft, had thrown him
into prison on the charge of larceny. The case was reported
to the court, if I recollect right, on the 16th of April, 1647;
for he was very minute in his statements, and indeed they
would hardly have been credible otherwise. The poor fellow, on being questioned, confessed to having taken some
pewter plates, but maintained that for all that he had not
stolen them; pleading in his defence this very doctrine of Father Bauny, which he produced before the judges, along with
a pamphlet by one of your fathers, under whom he had studied cases of conscience, and who had taught him the same
thing. Whereupon M. De Montrouge, one of the most respected members of the court, said, in giving his opinion,
'that he did not see how, on the ground of the writings of
these fathers—writings containing a doctrine so illegal, pernicious, and contrary to all laws, natural, divine, and human,
and calculated to ruin all families, and sanction all sorts of
household robbery—they could discharge the accused. But
his opinion was, that this too faithful disciple should be
whipped before the college gate, by the hand of the common
hangman; and that, at the same time, this functionary should
burn the writings of these fathers which treated of larceny,
with certification that they were prohibited from teaching
such doctrine in future, upon pain of death.'

"The result of this judgment, which was heartily approved
of, was waited for with much curiosity when some incident

occurred which made them delay procedure. But in the mean time the prisoner disappeared, nobody knew how, and nothing more was heard about the affair; so that John d'Alba got off, pewter plates and all. Such was the account he gave us, to which he added, that the judgment of M. De Montrouge was entered on the records of the court, where any one may consult it. We were highly amused at the story."

"What are you trifling about now?" cried the monk. "What does all that signify? I was explaining the maxims of our casuists, and was just going to speak of those relating to gentlemen, when you interrupt me with impertinent stories."

"It was only something put in by the way, father," I observed; "and besides, I was anxious to apprize you of an important circumstance, which I find you have overlooked in establishing your doctrine of probability."

"Ay, indeed!" exclaimed the monk, "what defect can this be, that has escaped the notice of so many ingenious men?"

"You have certainly," continued I, "contrived to place your disciples in perfect safety so far as God and the conscience are concerned; for they are quite safe in that quarter, according to you, by following in the wake of a grave doctor. You have also secured them on the part of the confessors, by obliging priests, on the pain of mortal sin, to absolve all who follow a probable opinion. But you have neglected to secure them on the part of the judges; so that, in following your probabilities, they are in danger of coming into contact with the whip and the gallows. This is a sad oversight."

"You are right," said the monk; "I am glad you mentioned it. But the reason is, we have no such power over magistrates as over the confessors, who are obliged to refer to us in cases of conscience, in which we are the sovereign judges."

"So I understand," returned I; "but if, on the one hand, you are the judges of the confessors, are you not, on the other hand, the confessors of the judges? Your power is very extensive. Oblige them, on pain of being debarred from the sacraments, to acquit all criminals who act on a probable opinion; otherwise it may happen, to the great contempt and scandal of probability, that those whom you render innocent in theory may be whipped or hanged in practice. Without something of this kind, how can you expect to get disciples?"

"The matter deserves consideration," said he; "it will never do to neglect it. I shall suggest it to our father Provincial. You might, however, have reserved this advice to some other time, without interrupting the account I was about to give you of the maxims which we have established in favor of gentlemen; and I shall not give you any more information, except on condition that you do not tell me any more stories."

This is all you shall have from me at present; for it would require more than the limits of one letter to acquaint you with all that I learned in a single conversation.—Meanwhile I am, &c.

LETTER VII.[1]

PARIS, *April* 25, 1656.

SIR,—Having succeeded in pacifying the good father, who had been rather disconcerted by the story of John d'Alba, he resumed the conversation, on my assuring him that I would avoid all such interruptions in future, and spoke of the maxims of his casuists with regard to gentlemen, nearly in the following terms :—

" You know," he said, " that the ruling passion of persons in that rank of life is 'the point of honor,' which is perpetually driving them into acts of violence apparently quite at variance with Christian piety ; so that, in fact, they would be almost all of them excluded from our confessionals, had not our fathers relaxed a little from the strictness of religion, to accommodate themselves to the weakness of humanity. Anxious to keep on good terms both with the Gospel, by doing their duty to God, and with the men of the world, by showing charity to their neighbor, they needed all the wisdom they possessed to devise expedients for so nicely adjusting matters as to permit these gentlemen to adopt the methods usually resorted to for vindicating their honor, without wounding their consciences, and thus reconcile two things apparently so opposite to each other as piety and the point of honor. But, sir, in proportion to the utility of the design was the difficulty of the execution. You cannot fail, I should

[1] This Letter was revised by M. Nicole.

think, to realize the magnitude and arduousness of such an enterprize?"

"It astonishes me, certainly," said I, rather coldly.

"It astonishes you, forsooth!" cried the monk. "I can well believe that; many besides you might be astonished at it. Why, don't you know that, on the one hand, the Gospel commands us 'not to render evil for evil, but to leave vengeance to God;' and that, on the other hand, the laws of the world forbid our enduring an affront without demanding satisfaction from the offender, and that often at the expense of his life? You have never, I am sure, met with anything, to all appearance, more diametrically opposed than these two codes of morals; and yet, when told that our fathers have reconciled them, you have nothing more to say than simply that this astonishes you!"

"I did not sufficiently explain myself, father. I should certainly have considered the thing perfectly impracticable, if I had not known, from what I have seen of your fathers, that they are capable of doing with ease what is impossible to other men. This led me to anticipate that they must have discovered some method for meeting the difficulty—a method which I admire even before knowing it, and which I pray you to explain to me."

"Since that is your view of the matter," replied the monk, "I cannot refuse you. Know, then, that this marvellous principle is our grand method of *directing the intention*—the importance of which, in our moral system, is such, that I might almost venture to compare it with the doctrine of probability. You have had some glimpses of it in passing, from certain maxims which I mentioned to you. For example, when I was showing you how servants might execute certain troublesome jobs with a safe conscience, did you not remark that it was simply by diverting their intention from the evil to which they were accessary, to the profit which they might reap from the transaction? Now that is what we call *directing the intention*. You saw, too, that were it not for a similar divergence of the mind, those who give

money for benefices might be downright simoniacs. But I
will now show you this grand method in all its glory, as it
applies to the subject of homicide—a crime which it justifies in
a thousand instances ; in order that, from this startling result, you may form an idea of all that it is calculated to
effect."

"I foresee already," said I, "that, according to this mode,
everything will be permitted ; it will stick at nothing."

"You always fly from the one extreme to the other," replied the monk: "prithee avoid that habit. For just to show
you that we are far from permitting everything, let me tell
you that we never suffer such a thing as a formal intention
to sin, with the sole design of sinning ; and if any person
whatever should persist in having no other end but evil in
the evil that he does, we break with him at once : such conduct is diabolical. This holds true, without exception of age,
sex, or rank. But when the person is not of such a wretched
disposition as this, we try to put in practice our method of
directing the intention, which simply consists in his proposing
to himself, as the end of his actions, some allowable object.
Not that we do not endeavor, as far as we can, to dissuade
men from doing things forbidden ; but when we cannot prevent the action, we at least purify the motive, and thus correct the viciousness of the mean by the goodness of the end.
Such is the way in which our fathers have contrived to permit those acts of violence to which men usually resort in
vindication of their honor. They have no more to do than
to turn off their intention from the desire of vengeance,
which is criminal, and direct it to a desire to defend their
honor, which, according to us, is quite warrantable. And in
this way our doctors discharge all their duty towards God
and towards man. By permitting the action, they gratify
the world ; and by purifying the intention, they give satisfaction to the Gospel. This is a secret, sir, which was entirely
unknown to the ancients ; the world is indebted for the discovery entirely to our doctors. You understand it now, I
hope ?"

"Perfectly well," was my reply. "To men you grant the outward material effect of the action; and to God you give the inward and spiritual movement of the intention; and by this equitable partition, you form an alliance between the laws of God and the laws of men. But, my dear sir, to be frank with you, I can hardly trust your premises, and I suspect that your authors will tell another tale."

"You do me injustice," rejoined the monk; "I advance nothing but what I am ready to prove, and that by such a rich array of passages, that altogether their number, their authority, and their reasonings, will fill you with admiration. To show you, for example, the alliance which our fathers have formed between the maxims of the Gospel and those of the world, by thus regulating the intention, let me refer you to Reginald:[1] 'Private persons are forbidden to avenge themselves; for St. Paul says to the Romans (ch. 12th), 'Recompense to no man evil for evil;' and Ecclesiasticus says (ch. 28th), 'He that taketh vengeance shall draw on himself the vengeance of God, and his sins will not be forgotten.' Besides all that is said in the Gospel about forgiving offences, as in the 6th and 18th chapters of St. Matthew.'"

"Well, father, if after that he says anything contrary to the Scripture, it will not be from lack of scriptural knowledge, at any rate. Pray, how does he conclude?"

"You shall hear," he said. "From all this it appears that a military man may demand satisfaction on the spot from the person who has injured him—not, indeed, with the intention of rendering evil for evil, but with that of preserving his honor—'non ut malum pro malo reddat, sed ut conservet honorem.' See you how carefully they guard against the intention of rendering evil for evil, because the Scripture condemns it? This is what they will tolerate on no account. Thus Lessius[2] observes, that 'if a man has received a blow on the face, he must on no account have an intention to avenge himself; but he may lawfully have an intention to

[1] In praxi: liv. xxi., num. 62, p. 260.
[2] De Just., liv. ii., c. 9, d. 12, n. 79.

avert infamy, and may, with that view, repel the insult immediately, even at the point of the sword—*etiam cum gladio!*' So far are we from permitting any one to cherish the design of taking vengeance on his enemies, that our fathers will not allow any even to *wish their death*—by a movement of hatred. 'If your enemy is disposed to injure you,' says Escobar, 'you have no right to wish his death, by a movement of hatred; though you may, with a view to save yourself from harm.' So legitimate, indeed, is this wish, with such an intention, that our great Hurtado de Mendoza says, that 'we may *pray God* to visit with speedy death those who are bent on persecuting us, if there is no other way of escaping from it.'"[1]

"May it please your reverence," said I, "the Church has forgotten to insert a petition to that effect among her prayers."

"They have not put in everything into the prayers that one may lawfully ask of God," answered the monk. "Besides, in the present case the thing was impossible, for this same opinion is of more recent standing than the Breviary. You are not a good chronologist, friend. But, not to wander from the point, let me request your attention to the following passage, cited by Diana from Gaspar Hurtado,[2] one of Escobar's four-and-twenty fathers: 'An incumbent may, without any mortal sin, desire the decease of a life-renter on his benefice, and a son that of his father, and rejoice when it happens; provided always it is for the sake of the profit that is to accrue from the event, and not from personal aversion.'"

"Good!" cried I. "That is certainly a very happy hit; and I can easily see that the doctrine admits of a wide application. But yet there are certain cases, the solution of which, though of great importance for gentlemen, might present still greater difficulties."

"Propose them, if you please, that we may see," said the monk.

---

[1] In his book, De Spe, vol. ii., d. 15, sec. 4, 48.
[2] De Sub. Pecc., diff. 9; Diana, p. 5; tr. 14, r. 99.

" Show me, with all your directing of the intention," returned I, " that it is allowable to fight a duel."

" Our great Hurtado de Mendoza," said the father, " will
satisfy you on that point in a twinkling. ' If a gentleman,'
says he, in a passage cited by Diana, ' who is challenged to
fight a duel, is well known to have no religion, and if the
vices to which he is openly and unscrupulously addicted are
such as would lead people to conclude, in the event of his
refusing to fight, that he is actuated, not by the fear of God,
but by cowardice, and induce them to say of him that he
was a *hen*, and not a man—*gallina, et non vir ;* in that case
he may, to save his honor, appear at the appointed spot—
not, indeed, with the express intention of fighting a duel,
but merely with that of defending himself, should the person who challenged him come there unjustly to attack him.
His action in this case, viewed by itself, will be perfectly
indifferent ; for what moral evil is there in one stepping
into a field, taking a stroll in expectation of meeting a person, and defending one's self in the event of being attacked ?
And thus the gentleman is guilty of no sin whatever ; for
in fact it cannot be called accepting a challenge at all, his
intention being directed to other circumstances, and the
acceptance of a challenge consisting in an express intention
to fight, which we are supposing the gentleman never had.' "

" You have not kept your word with me, sir," said I.
" This is not, properly speaking, to permit duelling ; on the
contrary, the casuist is so persuaded that this practice is forbidden, that, in licensing the action in question, he carefully
avoids calling it a duel."

" Ah !" cried the monk, " you begin to get knowing on
my hand, I am glad to see. I might reply, that the author
I have quoted grants all that duellists are disposed to ask.
But since you must have a categorical answer, I shall allow
our Father Layman to give it for me. He permits duelling
in so many words, provided that, in accepting the challenge,
the person directs his intention solely to the preservation
of his honor or his property : ' If a soldier or a courtier is

in such a predicament that he must lose either his honor or
his fortune unless he accepts a challenge, I see nothing to
hinder him from doing so in self-defence.' The same thing
is said by Peter Hurtado, as quoted by our famous Escobar ;
his words are : ' One may fight a duel even to defend one's
property, should that be necessary ; because every man has
a right to defend his property, though at the expense of his
enemy's life !' "

I was struck, on hearing these passages, with the reflection that while the piety of the king appears in his exerting
all his power to prohibit and abolish the practice of duelling
in the State,[1] the piety of the Jesuits is shown in their employing all their ingenuity to tolerate and sanction it in the
Church. But the good father was in such an excellent key
for talking, that it would have been cruel to have interrupted
him ; so he went on with his discourse.

"In short," said he, "Sanchez (mark, now, what great
names I am quoting to you !) Sanchez, sir, goes a step further ;
for he shows how, simply by managing the intention rightly,
a person may not only receive a challenge, but give one.
And our Escobar follows him."

"Prove that, father," said I, "and I shall give up the
point : but I will not believe that he has written it, unless I
see it in print."

"Read it yourself, then," he replied : and, to be sure, I
read the following extract from the Moral Theology of
Sanchez : "It is perfectly reasonable to hold that a man may
fight a duel to save his life, his honor, or any considerable

---

[1] Before the age of Louis XIV. the practice of duelling prevailed in
France to such a frightful extent that a writer, who is not given to ex-
aggerate in such matters, says, that "It had done as much to depopulate the country as the civil and foreign wars, and that in the course of
twenty years, ten of which had been disturbed by war, more Frenchmen perished by the hands of Frenchmen than by those of their enemies.
(Voltaire, Siècle de Louis XIV., p. 42.) The abolition of this barbarous custom was one of the greatest services which Louis XIV. rendered
to his country. This was not fully accomplished till 1663, when a
bloody combat of four against four determined him to put an end to the
practice, by making it death, without benefit of clergy, to send or accept
a challenge.

portion of his property, when it is apparent that there is a design to deprive him of these unjustly, by law-suits and chicanery, and when there is no other way of preserving them. Navarre justly observes, that in such cases, it is lawful either to accept or to send a challenge—*licet acceptare et offerre duellum.* The same author adds, that there is nothing to prevent one from despatching one's adversary in a private way. Indeed, in the circumstances referred to, it is advisable to avoid employing the method of the duel, if it is possible to settle the affair by privately killing our enemy; for, by this means, we escape at once from exposing our life in the combat, and from participating in the sin which our opponent would have committed by fighting the duel !"[1]

" A most pious assassination !" said I. " Still, however, pious though it be, it is assassination, if a man is permitted to kill his enemy in a treacherous manner."

" Did I say that he might kill him treacherously ?" cried the monk. " God forbid ! I said he might kill him *privately,* and you conclude that he may kill him *treacherously,* as if that were the same thing ! Attend, sir, to Escobar's definition before allowing yourself to speak again on this subject ' We call it killing in treachery, when the person who is slain had no reason to suspect such a fate. He, therefore, that slays his *enemy* cannot be said to kill him in treachery, even although the blow should be given insidiously and behind his back—*licet per insidias aut a tergo percutiat.'* And again : ' He that kills his enemy, with whom he was reconciled under a promise of never again attempting his life, cannot be *absolutely* said to kill in treachery, unless there was between them all the stricter friendship—*arctior amicitia.'*[2] You see now, you do not even understand what the terms signify, and yet you pretend to talk like a doctor."

" I grant you this is something quite new to me," I replied ; " and I should gather from that definition that few, if any, were ever killed in treachery ; for people seldom take

---

[1] Sanchez, Theol. Mor., liv. ii. c. 39, n. 7.
[2] Escobar, tr. 6, ex. 4, n. 26, 56.

it into their heads to assassinate any but their enemies. Be this as it may, however, it seems that, according to Sanchez, a man may freely slay (I do not say *treacherously*, but only insidiously, and behind his back) a calumniator, for example, who prosecutes us at law ?"

" Certainly he may," returned the monk, " always, however, in the way of giving a right direction to the intention : you constantly forget the main point. Molina supports the same doctrine ; and what is more, our learned brother Reginald maintains that we may despatch the false witnesses whom he summons against us. And, to crown the whole, according to our great and famous fathers Tanner and Emanuel Sa, it is lawful to kill both the false witnesses and *the judge himself,* if he has had any collusion with them. Here are Tanner's very words : ' Sotus and Lessius think that it is not lawful to kill the false witnesses and the magistrate who conspire together to put an innocent person to death ; but Emanuel Sa and other authors with good reason impugn that sentiment, at least so far as the conscience is concerned.' And he goes on to show that it is quite lawful to kill both the witnesses and the judge."

" Well, father," said I, "I think I now understand pretty well your principle regarding the direction of the intention; but I should like to know something of its consequences, and all the cases in which this method of yours arms a man with the power of life and death. Let us go over them again, for fear of mistake, for equivocation here might be attended with dangerous results. Killing is a matter which requires to be well-timed, and to be backed with a good probable opinion. You have assured me, then, that by giving a proper turn to the intention, it is lawful, according to your fathers, for the preservation of one's honor, or even property, to accept a challenge to a duel, to give one sometimes, to kill in a private way a false accuser, and his witnesses along with him, and even the judge who has been bribed to favor them ; and you have also told me that he who has got a blow, may, without

avenging himself, retaliate with the sword. But you have
not told me, father, to what length he may go."

"He can hardly mistake there," replied the father, "for
he may go all the length of killing his man. This is satis-
factorily proved by the learned Henriquez, and others of our
fathers quoted by Escobar, as follows : ' It is perfectly right
to kill a person who has given us a box on the ear, although
he should run away, provided it is not done through hatred
or revenge, and there is no danger of giving occasion thereby
to murders of a gross kind and hurtful to society. And the
reason is, that it is as lawful to pursue the thief that has
stolen our honor, as him that has run away with our property. For, although your honor cannot be said to be in the
hands of your enemy in the same sense as your goods and
chattels are in the hands of the thief, still it may be recovered in the same way—by showing proofs of greatness and
authority, and thus acquiring the esteem of men. And, in
point of fact, is it not certain that the man who has received
a buffet on the ear is held to be under disgrace, until he has
wiped off the insult with the blood of his enemy ?' "

I was so shocked on hearing this, that it was with great
difficulty I could contain myself; but, in my anxiety to hear
the rest, I allowed him to proceed.

" Nay," he continued, "it is allowable to prevent a buffet,
by killing him that meant to give it, if there be no other way
to escape the insult. This opinion is quite common with our
fathers. For example, Azor, one of the four-and-twenty elders, proposing the question, ' Is it lawful for a man of honor
to kill another who threatens to give him a slap on the face,
or strike him with a stick ?' replies, ' Some say he may not ;
alleging that the life of our neighbor is more precious than
our honor, and that it would be an act of cruelty to kill a
man merely to avoid a blow. Others, however, think that
it is allowable ; and I certainly consider it probable, when
there is no other way of warding off the insult ; for, otherwise, the honor of the innocent would be constantly exposed
to the malice of the insolent.' The same opinion is given by

our great Filiutius; by Father Hereau, in his Treatise on
Homicide; by Hurtado de Mendoza, in his Disputations; by
Becan, in his Summary; by our Fathers Flahaut and Le-
court, in those writings which the university, in their third
petition, quoted at length, in order to bring them into disgrace (though in this they failed); and by Escobar. In
short, this opinion is so general, that Lessius lays it down as
a point which no casuist has contested; he quotes a great
many that uphold, and none that deny it; and particularly
Peter Navarre, who, speaking of affronts in general (and
there is none more provoking than a box on the ear), declares
that 'by the universal consent of the casuists, it is lawful to
kill the calumniator, if there be no other way of averting the
affront—*ex sententia omnium, licet contumeliosum occidere, si
aliter ea injuria arceri nequit.*' Do you wish any more
authorities ?" asked the monk.

I declared I was much obliged to him; I had heard rather
more than enough of them already. But just to see how far
this damnable doctrine would go, I said, "But, father, may
not one be allowed to kill for something still less ? Might
not a person so direct his intention as lawfully to kill another
for telling a lie, for example ?"

"He may," returned the monk; "and according to Father
Baldelle, quoted by Escobar, 'you may lawfully take the life
of another for saying, You have told a lie; if there is no
other way of shutting his mouth.' The same thing may be
done in the case of slanders. Our Fathers Lessius and Hereau
agree in the following sentiments: 'If you attempt to ruin
my character by telling stories against me in the presence of
men of honor, and I have no other way of preventing this
than by putting you to death, may I be permitted to do so ?
According to the modern authors, I may, and that even
though I have been really guilty of the crime which you
divulge, provided it is a secret one, which you could not
establish by legal evidence. And I prove it thus : If you
mean to rob me of my honor by giving me a box on the ear,
I may prevent it by force of arms; and the same mode of

defence is lawful when you would do me the same injury with the tongue. Besides, we may lawfully obviate affronts, and therefore slanders. In .fine, honor is dearer than life; and as it is lawful to kill in defence of life, it must be so to kill in defence of honor.' There, you see, are arguments in due form; this is demonstration, sir—not mere discussion. And, to conclude, this great man Lessius shows, in the same place, that it is lawful to kill even for a simple gesture, or a sign of contempt. 'A man's honor,' he remarks, 'may be attacked or filched away in various ways—in all which vindication appears very reasonable; as, for instance, when one offers to strike us with a stick, or give us a slap on the face, or affront us either by words or signs—*sive per signa.'* "

" Well, father," said I, " it must be owned that you have made every possible provision to secure the safety of reputation; but it strikes me that human life is greatly in danger, if any one may be conscientiously put to death simply for a defamatory speech or a saucy gesture."

" That is true," he replied; " but as our fathers are very circumspect, they have thought it proper to forbid putting this doctrine into practice on such trifling occasions. They say, at least, ' that it ought *hardly* to be reduced to practice —*practicè vix probari potest.'* And they have a good reason for that, as you shall see."

" Oh! I know what it will be," interrupted I; " because the law of God forbids us to kill, of course."

" They do not exactly take that ground," said· the father; " as a matter of conscience, and viewing the thing abstractly, they hold it allowable."

" And why, then, do they forbid it ?"

" I shall tell you that, sir. It is because, were we to kill all the defamers among us, we should very shortly depopulate the country. ' Although,' says Reginald, ' the opinion that we may kill a man for calumny is not without its probability in theory, the contrary one ought to be followed in practice; for, in our mode of defending ourselves, we should always avoid doing injury to the commonwealth; and it is evident that by killing people in this way there would be too many murders.' 'We should be on our guard,' says Lessius, 'lest the practice of this maxim prove hurtful to the State; for in this case it ought not to be permitted—*tunc enim non est permittendus.*' "

" What, father! is it forbidden only as a point of policy, and not of religion? Few people, I am afraid, will pay any regard to such a prohibition, particularly when in a passion. Very probably they might think they were doing no harm to the State, by ridding it of an unworthy member."

" And accordingly," replied the monk, " our Filiutius has fortified that argument with another, which is of no slender importance, namely, ' that for killing people after this manner, one might be punished in a court of justice.' "

" There now, father ; I told you before, that you will never be able to do anything worth the while, unless you get the magistrates to go along with you."

" The magistrates," said the father, " as they do not penetrate into the conscience, judge merely of the outside of the action, while we look principally to the intention ; and hence it occasionally happens that our maxims are a little different from theirs."

" Be that as it may, father ; from yours, at least, one thing may be fairly inferred—that, by taking care not to injure the commonwealth, we may kill defamers with a safe conscience, provided we can do it with a sound skin. But, sir, after having seen so well to the protection of honor, have you done nothing for property? I am aware it is of inferior importance, but that does not signify ; I should think one might direct one's intention to kill for its preservation also."

" Yes," replied the monk; " and I gave you a hint to that effect already, which may have suggested the idea to you. All our casuists agree in that opinion; and they even extend the permission to those cases ' where no further violence is apprehended from those that steal our property ; as, for example, where the thief runs away.' Azor, one of our Society, proves that point."

"But, sir, how much must the article be worth, to justify our proceeding to that extremity?"

"According to Reginald and Tanner, 'the article must be of great value in the estimation of a judicious man.' And so think Layman and Filiutius."

"But, father, that is saying nothing to the purpose; where am I to find 'a judicious man' (a rare person to meet with at any time), in order to make this estimation? Why do they not settle upon an exact sum at once?"

"Ay, indeed!" retorted the monk; "and was it so easy, think you, to adjust the comparative value between the life of a man, and a Christian man, too, and money? It is here I would have you feel the need of our casuists. Show me any of your ancient fathers who will tell for how much money we may be allowed to kill a man. What will they say, but 'Non occides—Thou shalt not kill?'"

"And who, then, has ventured to fix that sum?" I inquired.

"Our great and incomparable Molina," he replied—"the glory of our Society—who has, in his inimitable wisdom, estimated the life of a man 'at six or seven ducats; for which sum he assures us it is warrantable to kill a thief, even though he should run off;' and he adds, 'that he would not venture to condemn that man as guilty of any sin who should kill another for taking away an article worth a crown, or even less—unius aurei, vel minoris adhuc valoris;' which has led Escobar to lay it down as a general rule, 'that a man may be killed quite regularly, according to Molina, for the value of a crown-piece.'"

"O father!" cried I, "where can Molina have got all this wisdom to enable him to determine a matter of such importance, without any aid from Scripture, the councils, or the fathers? It is quite evident that he has obtained an illumination peculiar to himself, and is far beyond St. Augustine in the matter of homicide, as well as of grace. Well, now, I suppose I may consider myself master of this chapter of morals; and I see perfectly that, with the exception of ecclesiastics, nobody need refrain from killing those who injure them in their property or reputation."

"What say you?" exclaimed the monk. "Do you then suppose that it would be reasonable that those who ought of all men to be most respected, should alone be exposed to the insolence of the wicked? Our fathers have provided against that disorder; for Tanner declares that ' Churchmen, and even monks, are permitted to kill, for the purpose of defending not only their lives, but their property, and that of their community.' Molina, Escobar, Becan, Reginald, Layman, Lessius, and others, hold the same language. Nay, according to our celebrated Father Lamy,[1] priests and monks may lawfully prevent those who would injure them by calumnies from carrying their ill designs into effect, by putting them to death. Care, however, must be always taken to direct the intention properly. His words are: ' An ecclesiastic or a monk may warrantably kill a defamer who threatens to publish the scandalous crimes of his community, or his own crimes, when there is no other way of stopping him ; if, for instance, he is prepared to circulate his defamations unless promptly despatched. For, in these circumstances, as the monk would be allowed to kill one who threatened to take his life, he is also warranted to kill him who would deprive him of his reputation or his property, in the same way as the men of the world.' "

" I was not aware of that," said I; "in fact, I have been accustomed simply enough to believe the very reverse, without reflecting on the matter, in consequence of having heard that the Church had such an abhorrence of bloodshed as not even to permit ecclesiastical judges to attend in criminal cases."[2]

[1] Francois Amicus, or L'Amy, was chancellor of the University of Gratz. In his *Cours Theologique*, published in 1642, he advances the most dangerous tenets, particularly on the subject of murder.

[2] This is true; but in the case of heretics, at least, they found out a convenient mode of compromising the matter. Having condemned their victim as worthy of death, he was delivered over to the secular court, with the disgusting farce of a recommendation to mercy, couched in these terms: " My lord judge, we beg of you with all possible af-

"Never mind that," he replied; "our Father Lamy has completely proved the doctrine I have laid down, although, with a humility which sits uncommonly well on so great a man, he submits it to the judgment of his judicious readers. Caramuel, too, our famous champion, quoting it in his Fundamental Theology, p. 543, thinks it so certain, that he declares the contrary opinion to be destitute of probability, and draws some admirable conclusions from it, such as the following, which he calls 'the conclusion of conclusions—*conclusionum conclusio :*' 'That a priest not only may kill a slanderer, but there are certain circumstances in which it may be his *duty* to do so—*etiam aliquando debet occiﬁere.*' He examines a great many new questions on this principle, such as the following, for instance : '*May the Jesuits kill the Jansenists ?*' "

"A curious point of divinity that, father!" cried I. "I hold the Jansenists to be as good as dead men, according to Father Lamy's doctrine."

"There now, you are in the wrong," said the monk: "Caramuel infers the very reverse from the same principles."

"And how so, father ?"

"Because," he replied, "it is not in the power of the Jansenists to injure our reputation. 'The Jansenists,' says he, 'call the Jesuits Pelagians; may they not be killed for that? No; inasmuch as the Jansenists can no more obscure the glory of the Society than an owl can eclipse that of the sun; on the contrary, they have, though against their intention, enhanced it—*occidi non possunt, quia nocere non potuerunt.*' "

"Ha, father! do the lives of the Jansenists, then, depend on the contingency of their injuring your reputation ? If so, I reckon them far from being in a safe position; for suppos-

fection, for the love of God, and as you would expect the gifts of mercy and compassion, and the benefit of our prayers, not to do anything injurious to this miserable man, tending to death or the mutilation of his body !" (Crespin, Hist. des Martyres, p. 185.)

ing it should be thought in the slightest degree *probable* that they might do you some mischief, why, they are *killable* at once! You have only to draw up a sylllogism in due form, and, with a direction of the intention, you may despatch your man at once with a safe conscience. Thrice happy must those hot spirits be who cannot bear with injuries, to be instructed in this doctrine! But woe to the poor people who have offended them! Indeed, father, it would be better to have to do with persons who have no religion at all, than with those who have been taught on this system. For, after all, the intention of the wounder conveys no comfort to the wounded. The poor man sees nothing of that secret direction of which you speak; he is only sensible of the direction of the blow that is dealt him. And I am by no means sure but a person would feel much less sorry to see himself brutally killed by an infuriated villain, than to find himself conscientiously stilettoed by a devotee. To be plain with you, father, I am somewhat staggered at all this; and these questions of Father Lamy and Caramuel do not please me at all."

"How so?" cried the monk. "Are you a Jansenist?"

"I have another reason for it," I replied. "You must know I am in the habit of writing from time to time, to a friend of mine in the country, all that I can learn of the maxims of your doctors. Now, although I do no more than simply report and faithfully quote their own words, yet I am apprehensive lest my letter should fall into the hands of some stray genius, who may take into his head that I have done you injury, and may draw some mischievous conclusion from your premises."

"Away!" cried the monk; "no fear of danger from that quarter, I'll give you my word for it. Know that what our fathers have themselves printed, with the approbation of our superiors, it cannot be wrong to read nor dangerous to publish."

I write you, therefore, on the faith of this worthy father's word of honor. But, in the mean time, I must stop for want of paper—not of passages; for I have got as many more in reserve, and good ones too, as would require volumes to contain them.—I am, &c.[1]

[1] It may be noticed here, that Father Daniel has attempted to evade the main charge against the Jesuits in this letter by adroitly altering the state of the question. He argues that the *intention* is the soul of an action, and that which often makes it good or evil; thus cunningly insinuating that his casuists refer only to *indifferent* actions, in regard to which nobody denies that it is the intention that makes them good or bad. (Entretiens de Cleandre et d'Eudoxe, p. 334.) It is unnecessary to do more than refer the reader back to the instances cited in the letter, to convince him that what these casuists really maintain is, that actions in themselves *evil*, may be allowed, provided the *intentions* are good; and, moreover, that in order to make these intentions good, it is not necessary that they have any reference to God, but sufficient if they refer to our own convenience, cupidity or vanity. (Apologie des Lettres Provinciales, pp. 212-221.)

LETTER VIII.[1]

CORRUPT MAXIMS OF THE CASUISTS RELATING TO JUDGES—USU-
RERS—THE CONTRACT MOHATRA—BANKRUPTS—RESTITUTION—
DIVERS RIDICULOUS NOTIONS OF THESE SAME CASUISTS.

PARIS, *May* 28, 1656.

SIR,—You did not suppose that anybody would have the
curiosity to know who we were ; but it seems there are people who are trying to make it out, though they are not very
happy in their conjectures. Some take me for a doctor of
the Sorbonne ; others ascribe my letters to four or five persons, who, like me, are neither priests nor Churchmen. All
these false surmises convince me that I have succeeded pretty
well in my object, which was to conceal myself from all but
yourself and the worthy monk, who still continnes to bear
with my visits, while I still contrive, though with considerable
difficulty, to bear with his conversations. I am obliged, however, to restrain myself ; for were he to discover how much I
am shocked at his communications, he would discontinue
them, and thus put it out of my power to fulfil the promise
I gave you, of making you acquainted with their morality.
You ought to think a great deal of the violence which I thus
do to my own feelings. It is no easy matter, I can assure
you, to stand still and see the whole system of Christian ethics undermined by such a set of monstrous principles, without daring to put in a word of flat contradiction against them.
But after having borne so much for your satisfaction, I am
resolved I shall burst out for my own satisfaction in the end,
when his stock of information has been exhausted. Meanwhile, I shall repress my feelings as much as I possibly can ;

[1] This Letter also was revised by M. Nicole.

for I find that the more I hold my tongue, he is the more communicative. The last time I saw him, he told me so many things, that I shall have some difficulty in repeating them all. On the point of restitution you will find they have some most convenient principles. For, however the good monk palliates his maxims, those which I am about to lay before you really go to sanction corrupt judges, usurers, bankrupts, thieves, prostitutes and sorcerers—all of whom are most liberally absolved from the obligation of restoring their ill-gotten gains. It was thus the monk resumed the conversation :—

" At the commencement of our interviews, I engaged to explain to you the maxims of our authors for all ranks and classes ; and you have already seen those that relate to beneficiaries, to priests, to monks, to domestics, and to gentlemen. Let us now take a cursory glance of the remaining, and begin with the judges.

" Now I am going to tell you one of the most important and advantageous maxims which our fathers have laid down in their favor. Its author is the learned Castro Palao, one of our four-and-twenty elders. His words are: ' May a judge, in a question of right and wrong, pronounce according to a probable opinion, in preference to the more probable opinion ? He may, even though it should be contrary to his own judgment—*imo contra propriam opinionem.*' "

" Well, father," cried I, " that is a very fair commencement ! The judges, surely, are greatly obliged to you ; and I am surprised that they should be so hostile, as we have sometimes observed, to your probabilities, seeing these are so favorable to them. For it would appear from this, that you give them the same power over men's fortunes, as you have given to yourselves over their consciences."

" You perceive we are far from being actuated by self-interest," returned he ; " we have had no other end in view than the repose of their consciences ; and to the same useful purpose has our great Molina devoted his attention, in regard to the presents which may be made them. To remove

11*

any scruples which they might entertain in accepting of these on certain occasions, he has been at the pains to draw out a list of all those cases in which bribes may be taken with a good conscience, provided, at least, there be no special law forbidding them. He says : 'Judges may receive presents from parties, when they are given them either for friendship's sake, or in gratitude for some former act of justice, or to induce them to give justice in future, or to oblige them to pay particular attention to their case, or to engage them to despatch it promptly.' The learned Escobar delivers himself to the same effect : 'If there be a number of persons, none of whom have more right than another to have their causes disposed of, will the judge who accepts of something from one of them on condition—*ex pacto*—of taking up his cause first, be guilty of sin ? Certainly not, according to Layman ; for, in common equity, he does no injury to the rest, by granting to one, in consideration of his present, what he was at liberty to grant to any of them he pleased ; and besides, being under an equal obligation to them all in respect of their right, he becomes more obliged to the individual who furnished the donation, who thereby acquired for himself a preference above the rest—a preference which seems capable of a pecuniary valuation—*quæ obligatio videtur pretio æstimabilis.'* "

" May it please your reverence," said I, " after such a permission, I am surprised that the first magistrates of the kingdom should know no better. For the first president[1] has actually carried an order in Parliament to prevent certain clerks of court from taking money for that very sort of preference—a sign that he is far from thinking it allowable in judges ; and everybody has applauded this as a reform of great benefit to all parties."

The worthy monk was surprised at this piece of intelligence, and replied : " Are you sure of that ? I heard noth-

---

[1] The president referred to was Pompone de Bellievre, on whom M. Pelisson pronounced a beautiful eulogy.

ing about it. Our opinion, recollect, is only probable; the contrary is probable also."

"To tell you the truth, father," said I, "people think that the first president has acted more than probably well, and that he has thus put a stop to a course of public corruption which has been too long winked at."

"I am not far from being of the same mind," returned he; "but let us waive that point, and say no more about the judges."

"You are quite right, sir," said I; "indeed, they are not half thankful enough for all you have done for them."

"That is not my reason," said the father; "but there is so much to be said on all the different classes, that we must study brevity on each of them. Let us now say a word or two about men of business. You are aware that our great difficulty with these gentlemen is to keep them from usury— an object to accomplish which our fathers have been at particular pains; for they hold this vice in such abhorrence, that Escobar declares 'it is heresy to say that usury is no sin;' and Father Bauny has filled several pages of his Summary of Sins with the pains and penalties due to usurers. He declares them 'infamous during their life, and unworthy of sepulture after their death.'"

"O dear!" cried I, "I had no idea he was so severe."

"He can be severe enough when there is occasion for it," said the monk; "but then this learned casuist, having observed that some are allured into usury merely from the love of gain, remarks in the same place, that 'he would confer no small obligation on society, who, while he guarded it against the evil effects of usury, and of the sin which gives birth to it, would suggest a method by which one's money might secure as large, if not a larger profit, in some honest and lawful employment, than he could derive from usurious dealings.'"

"Undoubtedly, father, there would be no more usurers after that."

"Accordingly," continued he, "our casuist has suggested

'a general method for all sorts of persons—gentlemen, presidents, councillors,' &c.; and a very simple process it is, consisting only in the use of certain words which must be pronounced by the person in the act of lending his money; after which he may take his interest for it without fear of being a usurer, which he certainly would be on any other plan."

"And pray what may those mysterious words be, father?"

"I will give you them exactly in his own words," said the father; "for he has written his Summary in French, you know, 'that it may be understood by everybody,' as he says' in the preface: 'The person from whom the loan is asked, must answer, then, in this manner: I have got no money to *lend;* I have got a little, however, to lay out for an honest and lawful profit. If you are anxious to have the sum you mention in order to make something of it by your industry, dividing the profit and loss between us, I may perhaps be able to accommodate you. But now I think of it, as it may be a matter of difficulty to agree about the profit, if you will secure me a certain portion of it, and give me so much for my principal, so that it incur no risk, we may come to terms much sooner, and you shall touch the cash immediately.' Is not that an easy plan for gaining money without sin? And has not Father Bauny good reason for concluding with these words: 'Such, in my opinion, is an excellent plan by which a great many people, who now provoke the just indignation of God by their usuries, extortions, and illicit bargains, might save themselves, in the way of making good, honest, and legitimate profits?'"

"O sir!" I exclaimed, "what potent words these must be! Doubtless they must possess some latent virtue to chase away the demon of usury which I know nothing of, for, in my poor judgment, I always thought that that vice consisted in recovering more money than what was lent."

"You know little about it indeed," he replied. "Usury, according to our fathers, consists in little more than the intention of taking the interest as usurious. Escobar, accordingly, shows you how you may avoid usury by a simple shift of the intention. 'It would be downright usury,' says he, 'to take interest from the borrower, if we should exact it as due in point of justice; but if only exacted as due in point of gratitude, it is not usury. Again, it is not lawful to have directly the intention of profiting by the money lent; but to claim it through the medium of the benevolence of the borrower—*media benevolentia*—is not usury.' These are subtle methods; but, to my mind, the best of them all (for we have a great choice of them) is that of the Mohatra bargain."

"The Mohatra, father!"

"You are not acquainted with it, I see," returned he. "The name is the only strange thing about it. Escobar will explain it to you: 'The Mohatra bargain is effected by the needy person purchasing some goods at a high price and on credit, in order to sell them over again, at the same time and to the same merchant, for ready money and at a cheap rate.' This is what we call the Mohatra—a sort of bargain, you perceive, by which a person receives a certain sum of ready money, by becoming bound to pay more."

"But, sir, I really think nobody but Escobar has employed such a term as that; is it to be found in any other book?"

"How little you do know of what is going on, to be sure!" cried the father. "Why, the last work on theological morality, printed at Paris this very year, speaks of the Mohatra, and learnedly, too. It is called *Epilogus Summarum*, and is an abridgment of all the summaries of divinity—extracted from Suarez, Sanchez, Lessius, Fagundez, Hurtado, and other celebrated casuists, as the title bears. There you will find it said, at p. 54, that 'the Mohatra bargain takes place when a man who has occasion for twenty pistoles purchases from merchant goods to the amount of thirty pistoles, payable within a year, and sells them back to him on the spot for twenty pistoles ready money.' This shows you that the Mohatra is not such an unheard-of term as you supposed."

"But, father, is that sort of bargain lawful?"

"Escobar," replied he, "tells us in the same place, that there are laws which prohibit it under very severe penalties."

" It is useless, then, I suppose ?"

" Not at all; Escobar, in the same passage, suggests expedients for making it lawful : ' It is so, even though the
principal intention both of the buyer and seller is to make
money by the transaction, provided the seller, in disposing
of the goods, does not exceed their highest price, and in re-
purchasing them does not go below their lowest price, and
that no previous bargain has been made, expressly or otherwise.' Lessius, however, maintains, that ' even though the
merchant has sold his goods, with the intention of re-purchas-
ing them at the lowest price, he is not bound to make restitution of the profit thus acquired, unless, perhaps, as an act
of charity, in the case of the person from whom it has been
exacted being in poor circumstances, and not even then, if
he cannot do it without inconvenience—*si commode non
potest.*' This is the utmost length to which they could go."

" Indeed, sir," said I, " any further indulgence would, I
should think, be rather too much."

" Oh, our fathers know very well when it is time for them
to stop !" cried the monk. " So much, then, for the utility
of the Mohatra. I might have mentioned several other
methods, but these may suffice ; and I have now to say a
little in regard to those who are in embarrassed circumstances.
Our casuists have sought to relieve them, according to their
condition of life. For, if they have not enough of property
for a decent maintenance, and at the same time for paying
their debts, they permit them to secure a portion by making
a bankruptcy with their creditors.[1]   This has been decided

---

[1] The Jesuits exemplified their own maxim in this case by the famous
oankruptcy of their College of St. Hermenigilde at Seville.   We have
a full account of this in the memorial presented to the King of Spain by
the luckless creditors.   The simple pathos and sincere earnestness of
this document preclude all suspicion of the accuracy of its statements.
By the advice of their Father Provincial, the Jesuits, in March, 1645,
stopped payments, after having borrowed upwards of 450,000 ducats,
mostly from poor widows and friendless girls.   This shameful affair
was exposed before the courts of justice, during a long litigation, in the
course of which it was discovered that the Jesuit fathers had been carry=
ing on extensive mercantile transactions, and that instead of spending
the money left them for *pious uses*—such as ransoming captives, and

by Lessius, and confirmed by Escobar, as follows : 'May a person who turns bankrupt, with a good conscience keep back as much of his personal estate as may be necessary to maintain his family in a respectable way—*ne indecorè vivat?* I hold, with Lessius, that he may, even though he may have acquired his wealth unjustly and by notorious crimes—*ex injustitia et notorio delicto;* only, in this case, he is not at liberty to retain so large an amount as he otherwise might.' "

"Indeed, father! what a strange sort of charity is this, to allow property to remain in the hands of the man who has acquired it by rapine, to support him in his extravagance rather than go into the hands of his creditors, to whom it legitimately belongs!"

" It is impossible to please everybody," replied the father; "and we have made it our particular study to relieve these unfortunate people. This partiality to the poor has induced our great Vasquez, cited by Castro Palao, to say, that 'if one saw a thief going to rob a poor man, it would be lawful to divert him from his purpose by pointing out to him some rich individual, whom he might rob in place of the other.' If you have not access to Vasquez or Castro Palao, you will find the same thing in your copy of Escobar; for, as you are aware, his work is little more than a compilation from twenty-four of the most celebrated of our fathers. You will find it in his treatise, entitled ' The Practice of our Society, in the matter of Charity towards our Neighbors.' "

"A very singular kind of charity this," I observed, "to save one man from suffering loss, by inflicting it upon another! But I suppose that, to complete the charity, the charitable adviser would be bound in conscience to restore to the rich man the sum which he had made him lose ?"

" Not at all, sir," returned the monk; " for he did not rob the man—he only advised the other to do it. But only attend to this notable decision of Father Bauny, on a case which will still more astonish you, and in which you would

almsgiving—they had devoted it to the purposes of what they termed " our poor little house of profession." (Theatre Jesuitique, p. 200, &c.)

suppose there was a much stronger obligation to make restitution. Here are his identical words : 'A person asks a
soldier to beat his neighbor, or to set fire to the barn of a
man that has injured him. The question is, Whether, in the
absence of the soldier, the person who employed him to commit these outrages is bound to make reparation out of his
own pocket for the damage that has followed ? My opinion
is, that he is not. For none can be held bound to restitution,
where there has been no violation of justice ; and is justice
violated by asking another to do us a favor ? As to the
nature of the request which he made, he is at liberty either
to acknowledge or deny it ; to whatever side he may incline,
it is a matter of mere choice ; nothing obliges him to it, unless it may be the goodness, gentleness, and easiness of his
disposition. If the soldier, therefore, makes no reparation
for the mischief he has done, it ought not to be exacted from
him at whose request he injured the innocent.' "

This sentence had very nearly broken up the whole conversation, for I was on the point of bursting into a laugh at
the idea of the *goodness and gentleness* of a burner of barns,
and at these strange sophisms which would exempt from the
duty of restitution the principal and real incendiary, whom
the civil magistrate would not exempt from the halter. But
had I not restrained myself, the worthy monk, who was perfectly serious, would have been displeased ; he proceeded,
therefore, without any alteration of countenance, in his observations.

"From such a mass of evidence, you ought to be satisfied
now of the futility of your objections ; but we are losing
sight of our subject. To revert, then, to the succor which
our fathers apply to persons in straitened circumstances,
Lessius, among others, maintains that 'it is lawful to steal,
not only in a case of extreme necessity, but even where the
necessity is *grave*, though not extreme.' "

"This is somewhat startling, father," said I. "There are
very few people in this world who do not consider their cases
of necessity to be *grave* ones, and to whom, accordingly, you

would not give the right of stealing with a good conscience. And though you should restrict the permission to those only who are really and truly in that condition, you open the door to an infinite number of petty larcenies which the magistrates would punish in spite of your 'grave necessity,' and which you ought to repress on a higher principle—you who are bound by your office to be the conservators, not of justice only, but of charity between man and man, a grace which this permission would destroy. For after all, now, is it not a violation of the law of charity, and of our duty to our neighbor, to deprive a man of his property in order to turn it to our own advantage? Such, at least, is the way I have been taught to think hitherto."

"That will not always hold true," replied the monk; "for our great Molina has taught us that 'the rule of charity does not bind us to deprive ourselves of a profit, in order thereby to save our neighbor from a corresponding loss.' He advances this in corroboration of what he had undertaken to prove—'that one is not bound in conscience to restore the goods which another had put into his hands in order to cheat his creditors.' Lessius holds the same opinion, on the same ground.[1] Allow me to say, sir, that you have too little compassion for people in distress. Our fathers have had more charity than that comes to : they render ample justice to the poor, as well as the rich ; and, I may add, to sinners as well as saints. For, though far from having any predilection for criminals, they do not scruple to teach that the property gained by crime may be lawfully retained. 'No person,' says Lessius, speaking generally, 'is bound, either by the law of nature or by positive laws (that is, *by any law*), to make restitution of what has been gained by committing a criminal action, such as adultery, even though that action is contrary to justice.' For, as Escobar comments on this writer, 'though the property which a woman acquires by adultery is certainly gained in an illicit way, yet once ac-

[1] Molina, t. ii., tr. 2, disp. 338, n. 8; Lessius, liv. ii., ch. 20, dist. 19, n. 168.

quired, the possession of it is lawful—*quamvis mulier illicitè acquisat, licitè tamen retinet acquisita.*' It is on this principle that the most celebrated of our writers have formally decided that the bribe received by a judge from one of the parties who has a bad case, in order to procure an unjust decision in his favor, the money got by a soldier for killing a man, or the emoluments gained by infamous crimes, may be legitimately retained. Escobar, who has collected this from a number of our authors, lays down this general rule on the point, that 'the means acquired by infamous courses, such as murder, unjust decisions, profligacy, &c., are legitimately possessed, and none are obliged to restore them.' And further, 'they may dispose of what they have received for homicide, profligacy, &c., as they please; for the possession is just, and they have acquired a propriety in the fruits of their iniquity.' "[1]

"My dear father," cried I, "this is a mode of acquisition which I never heard of before; and I question much if the law will hold it good, or if it will consider assassination, injustice, and adultery, as giving valid titles to property."

"I do not know what your law-books may say on the point," returned the monk; "but I know well that our books, which are the genuine rules for conscience, bear me out in what I say. It is true they make one exception, in which restitution is positively enjoined; that is, in the case of any receiving money from those who have no right to dispose of their property, such as *minors and monks.* 'Unless,' says the great Molina, 'a woman has received money from one who cannot dispose of it, such as a monk or a minor—*nisi mulier accepisset ab eo qui alienare non potest, ut a religioso et filio familias.* In this case she must give back the money.' And so says Escobar."[2]

" May it please your reverence," said I, "the monks,

---

[1] Escobar, tr. 3, ex. 1, n. 23, tr. 5, ex. 5, n. 53.
[2] Molina, l. tom. i.; De Just., tr. 2, disp. 94; Escobar, tr. 1, ex 8, n. 59, tr. 3, ex. 1, n. 23.

I see, are more highly favored in this way than other people."

" By no means," he replied ; " have they not done as much generally for all minors, in which class monks may be viewed as continuing all their lives ? It is barely an act of justice to make them an exception ; but with regard to all other people, there is no obligation whatever to refund to them the money received from them for a criminal action. For, as has been amply shown by Lessius, ' a. wicked action may have its price fixed in money, by calculating the advantage received by the person who orders it to be done, and the trouble taken by him who carries it into execution ; on which account the latter is not bound to restore the money he got for the deed, whatever that may have been—homicide, injustice, or a foul act' (for such are the illustrations which he uniformly employs in this question); ' unless he obtained the money from those having no right to dispose of their property. You may object, perhaps, that he who has obtained money for a piece of wickedness is sinning, and therefore ought neither to receive nor retain it. But I reply, that after the thing is done, there can be no sin either in giving or in receiving payment for it.' The great Filiutius enters still more minutely into details, remarking, ' that a man is *bound in conscience*, to vary his payments for actions of this sort, according to the different conditions of the individuals who commit them, and some may bring a higher price than others.' This he confirms by very solid arguments."[1]

He then pointed out to me, in his authors, some things of this nature so indelicate that I should be ashamed to repeat them ; and indeed the monk himself, who is a good man, would have been horrified at them himself, were it not for

---

[1] Tr. 31, c. 9, n. 231.—" Occultæ fornicariæ debetur pretium in conscientia, et multo majore ratione, quam publicæ. Copia enim quam occulta facit mulier sui corporis, multo plus valet quam ea quam publica facit meretrix ; nec ulla est lex positiva quæ reddit eam incapacem pretii. Idem dicendum de pretio promisso virgini, conjugatæ, moniali, et cuicumque alii. Est enim omnium eadem ratio."

the profound respect which he entertains for his fathers, and which makes him receive with veneration everything that proceeds from them. Meanwhile, I held my tongue, not so much with the view of allowing him to enlarge on this matter, as from pure astonishment at finding the books of men in holy orders stuffed with sentiments at once so horrible, so iniquitous, and so silly. He went on, therefore, without interruption in his discourse, concluding as follows:—

"From these premises, our illustrious Molina decides the following question (and after this, I think you will have got enough): 'If one has received money to perpetrate a wicked action, is he obliged to restore it? We must distinguish here,' says this great man; 'if he has not done the deed, he must give back the cash; if he has, he is under no such obligation!'[1] Such are some of our principles touching restitution. You have got a great deal of instruction to-day; and I should like, now, to see what proficiency you have made. Come, then, answer me this question: 'Is a judge, who has received a sum of money from one of the parties before him, in order to pronounce a judgment in his favor, obliged to make restitution?'"

"You were just telling me a little ago, father, that he was not."

"I told you no such thing," replied the father; "did I express myself so generally? I told you he was not bound to make restitution, provided he succeeded in gaining the cause for the party who had the wrong side of the question. But if a man has justice on his side, would you have him to purchase the success of his cause, which is his legitimate right? You are very unconscionable. Justice, look you, is a debt which the judge owes, and therefore he cannot sell it; but he cannot be said to owe injustice, and therefore he may lawfully receive money for it. All our leading authors, accordingly, agree in teaching 'that though a judge is bound to restore the money he had received for doing an act of justice, unless it was given him out of mere generosity, he is not

---

[1] Quoted by Escobar, tr. 3, ex. 2, n. 138.

obliged to restore what he has received from a man in whose favor he has pronounced an unjust decision.' "[1]

This preposterous decision fairly dumbfounded me, and while I was musing on its pernicious tendencies, the monk had prepared another question for me. " Answer me again," said he, " with a little more circumspection. Tell me now, ' if a man who deals in divination is obliged to make restitution of the money he has acquired in the exercise of his art ?' "

"Just as you please, your reverence," said I.

" Eh ! what !—just as I please ! Indeed, but you are a pretty scholar ! It would seem, according to your way of talking, that the truth depended on our will and pleasure. I see that, in the present case, you would never find it out yourself : so I must send you to Sanchez for a solution of the problem—no less a man than Sanchez. In the first place, he makes a distinction between ' the case of the diviner who has recourse to astrology and other natural means, and that of another who employs the diabolical art. In the one case, he says, the diviner is bound to make restitution ; in the other he is not.' Now, guess which of them is the party bound ?"

" It is not difficult to find out that," said I.

" I see what you mean to say," he replied. " You think that he ought to make restitution in the case of his having employed the agency of demons. But you know nothing about it ; it is just the reverse. ' If,' says Sanchez, ' the sorcerer has not taken care and pains to discover, by means of the devil, what he could not have known otherwise, he must make restitution—*si nullam operam apposuit ut arte diaboli id sciret ;* but if he has been at that trouble, he is not obliged.' "

" And why so, father?"

" Don't you see ?" returned he. " It is because men may

[1] Molina, 94, 99; Reginald. 1. 10, 184 ; Filiutius, tr. 31 ; Escobar, tr 3; Lessius, l. 2, 14.

truly divine by the aid of the devil, whereas astrology is a mere sham."

"But, sir, should the devil happen not to tell the truth (and he is not much more to be trusted than astrology), the magician must, I should think, for the same reason, be obliged to make restitution?"

"Not always," replied the monk : " *Distinguo*, as Sanchez says, here. ' If the magician be ignorant of the diabolic art— *si sit artis diabolicæ ignarus*—he is bound to restore : but if he is an expert sorcerer, and has done all in his power to arrive at the truth, the obligation ceases ; for the industry of such a magician may be estimated at a certain sum of money.' "

"There is some sense in that," I said ; "for this is an excellent plan to induce sorcerers to aim at proficiency in their art, in the hope of making an honest livelihood, as you would say, by faithfully serving the public."

"You are making a jest of it, I suspect," said the father : "that is very wrong. If you were to talk in that way in places where you were not known, some people might take it amiss, and charge you with turning sacred subjects into ridicule."

"That, father, is a charge from which I could very easily vindicate myself ; for certain I am that whoever will be at the trouble to examine the true meaning of my words will find my object to be precisely the reverse ; and perhaps, sir, before our conversations are ended, I may find an opportunity of making this very amply apparent."

"Ho, ho," cried the monk, "there is no laughing in your head now."

"I confess," said I, "that the suspicion that I intended to laugh at things sacred, would be as painful for me to incur, as it would be unjust in any to entertain it."

"I did not say it in earnest," returned the father ; "but let us speak more seriously."

"I am quite disposed to do so, if you prefer it ; that depends upon you, father. But I must say, that I have been astonished to see your friends carrying their attentions to all sorts and conditions of men so far as even to regulate the legitimat: gains of sorcerers."

"One cannot write for too many people," said the monk, "nor be too minute in particularizing cases, nor repeat the same things too often in different books. You may be convinced of this by the following anecdote, which is related by one of the gravest of our fathers, as you may well suppose, seeing he is our present Provincial—the reverend Father Cellot : 'We know a person,' says he, 'who was carrying a large sum of money in his pocket to restore it, in obedience to the orders of his confessor, and who, stepping into a bookseller's shop by the way, inquired if there was anything new ?—*numquid novi ?*—when the bookseller showed him a book on moral theology, recently published ; and turning over the leaves carelessly, and without reflection, he lighted upon a passage describing his own case, and saw that he was under no obligation to make restitution : upon which, relieved from the burden of his scruples, he returned home with a purse no less heavy, and a heart much lighter, than when he left it :—*abjecta scrupuli sarcina, retento auri pondere, levior domum repetiit.*'[1]

"Say, after hearing that, if it is useful or not to know our maxims ? Will you laugh at them now ? or rather, are you not prepared to join with Father Cellot in the pious reflection which he makes on the blessedness of that incident? 'Accidents of that kind,' he remarks, 'are, with God, the effect of his providence ; with the guardian angel, the effect of his good guidance ; with the individuals to whom they happen, the effect of their predestination. From all eternity, God decided that the golden chain of their salvation should depend on such and such an author, and not upon a hundred others who say the same thing, because they never happen to meet with them. Had that man not written, this man would not have been saved. All, therefore, who find fault with the multitude of our authors, we would beseech, in the bowels of Jesus Christ, to beware of envying others those

[1] Cellot liv. viii., de la Hierarch, c. 16, 2.

books which the eternal election of God and the blood of Jesus Christ has purchased for them!' Such are the eloquent terms in which this learned man proves so successfully the proposition which he had advanced, namely, 'How useful it must be to have a great many writers on moral theology—*quàm utile sit de theologia morali multos scribere!*' "

" Father," said I, " I shall defer giving you my opinion of that passage to another opportunity ; in the mean time, I shall only say that as your maxims are so useful, and as it is so important to publish them, you ought to continue to give me further instruction in them. For I can assure you that the person to whom I send them shows my letters to a great many people. Not that we intend to avail ourselves of them in our own case ; but indeed we think it will be useful for the world to be informed about them."

" Very well," rejoined the monk, " you see I do not conceal them ; and, in continuation, I am ready to furnish you, at our next interview, with an account of the comforts and indulgences which our fathers allow, with the view of rendering salvation easy, and devotion agreeable ; so that in addition to what you have hitherto learned as to particular conditions of men, you may learn what applies in general to all classes, and thus you will have gone through a complete course of instruction."—So saying, the monk took his leave of me.—I am, &c.

P. S.—I have always forgot to tell you that there are different editions of Escobar. Should you think of purchasing him, I would advise you to choose the Lyons edition, having on the title-page the device of a lamb lying on a book sealed with seven seals ; or the Brussels edition of 1651. Both of these are better and larger than the previous editions published at Lyons in the years 1644 and 1646.[1]

---

[1] " Since all this, a new edition has been printed at Paris, by Piget, more correct than any of the rest. But the sentiments of Escobar may be still better ascertained from the great work on moral theology, printed at Lyons." (Note in Nicole's edition of the Letters.)

I may avail myself of this space to remark, that not one of the charges brought against the Jesuits in this letter has been met by Father Daniel in his celebrated reply. Indeed, after some vain efforts to contradict about a dozen passages in the letters, ho leaves avowedly more than a hundred without daring to answer them. The pretext for thus failing to perform what he professed to do, and what he so loudly boasts, at the commencement, of his being able to do, is ingenious enough. "You will easily comprehend," says one of his characters, "that this confronting of texts and quotations is not a great treat for a man of my taste. I could not stand this *disagreeable labor* much longer."—(Entretiens de Cleandre et d'Eudoxe, p. 277.) We reserve our remarks on the pretended falsifications charged against Pascal, till we come to his own masterly defence of himself in the subsequent letters.

"Escobar," says M. Saint-Beuve (*Port-Royal*, t. iii., p. 52), "was printed forty-one times previous to 1656, and forty-two times during that year."—ED.

VOL. I.—12

LETTER IX.

Paris, *July* 3, 1656.

Sir,—I shall use as little ceremony with you as the
worthy monk did with me, when I saw him last. The moment he perceived me, he came forward with his eyes fixed
on a book which he held in his hand, and accosted me thus:
"'Would you not be infinitely obliged to any one who should
open to you the gates of paradise? Would you not give
millions of gold to have a key by which you might gain ad-
mittance whenever you thought proper? You need not be
at such expense; here is one—here are a hundred for much
less money.'"

At first I was at a loss to know whether the good father
was reading, or talking to me, but he soon put the matter
beyond doubt by adding:

"These, sir, are the opening words of a fine book, written
by Father Barry of our Society; for I never give you anything of my own."

"What book is it?" asked I.

"Here is its title," he replied: "'*Paradise opened to
Philagio, in a Hundred Devotions to the Mother of God, easily practised.*'"

"Indeed, father! and is each of these easy devotions a
sufficient passport to heaven?"

"It is," returned he. "Listen to what follows: 'The devotions to the Mother of God, which you will find in this
book, are so many celestial keys, which will open wide to

you the gates of paradise, provided you practise them ;' and accordingly, he says at the conclusion, 'that he is satisfied if you practise only one of them.' "

"Pray, then, father, do teach me one of the easiest of them."

"They are all easy," he replied ; "for example—'Saluting the Holy Virgin when you happen to meet her image —saying the little chaplet of the pleasures of the Virgin— fervently pronouncing the name of Mary—commissioning the angels to bow to her for us—wishing to build her as many churches as all the monarchs on earth have done—bidding her good morrow every morning, and good night in the evening— saying the *Ave Maria* every day, in honor of the heart of Mary'—which last devotion, he says, possesses the additional virtue of securing us the heart of the Virgin."[1]

"But, father," said I, "only provided we give her our own in return, I presume ?"

"That," he replied, "is not absolutely necessary, when a person is too much attached to the world. Hear Father Barry : 'Heart for heart would, no doubt, be highly proper ; but yours is rather too much attached to the world, too much bound up in the creature, so that I dare not advise you to offer, at present, that *poor little slave* which you call your heart.' And so he contents himself with the *Ave Maria* which he had prescribed."[2]

"Why, this is extremely easy work," said I, "and I should really think that nobody will be damned after that."

"Alas!" said the monk, "I see you have no idea of the hardness of some people's hearts. There are some, sir, who

---

[1] "Towards the conclusion of the tenth century, new accessions were made to the worship of the Virgin. In this age, (the tenth century) there are to be found manifest indications of the institution of the *rosary* and *crown* (or chaplet) of the Virgin, by which her worshippers were to reckon the number of prayers they were to offer to this new divinity. The rosary consists of fifteen repetitions of the Lord's Prayer, and a hundred and fifty salutations of the blessed Virgin ; while the crown consists in six or seven repetitions of the Lord's Prayer, and seven times ten salutations, or *Ave Marias*." (Mosheim, cent. x.)

[2] These are the devotions presented at pp. 33, 59, 145, 156, 172, 258, 420 of the first edition.

would never engage to repeat, every day, even these simple
words, *Good day, Good evening,* just because such a practice would require some exertion of memory.   And, accordingly, it became necessary for Father Barry to furnish them
with expedients still easier, such as wearing a chaplet night
and day on the arm, in the form of a bracelet, or carrying
about one's person a rosary, or an image of the Virgin.[1]
' And, tell me now,' as Father Barry says, 'if I have not provided you with easy devotions to obtain the good graces of
Mary ?' "

" Extremely easy indeed, father," I observed.

" Yes," he said, " it is as much as could possibly be done,
and I think should be quite satisfactory.   For he must be a
wretched creature indeed, who would not spare a single moment in all his lifetime to put a chaplet on his arm, or a rosary in his pocket, and thus secure his salvation ; and that,
too, with so much certainty that none who have tried the
experiment have ever found it to fail, in whatever way they
may have lived ; though, let me add, we exhort people not
to omit holy living.   Let me refer you to the example of this,
given at p. 34 ; it is that of a female who, while she practised daily the devotion of saluting the images of the Virgin,
spent all her days in mortal sin, and yet was saved after all,
by the merit of that single devotion."

" And how so ?" cried I.

" Our Saviour," he replied, " raised her up again, for the
very purpose of showing it.   So certain it is, that none can
perish who practise any one of these devotions."

" My dear sir," I observed, " I am fully aware that the
devotions to the Virgin are a powerful mean of salvation, and
that the least of them, if flowing from the exercise of faith
and charity, as in the case of the saints who have practised
them, are of great merit ; but to make persons believe that,
by practising these without reforming their wicked lives, they
will be converted by them at the hour of death, or that God
will raise them up again, does appear calculated rather to

[1] See the devotions, at pp. 14, 326, 447.

keep sinners going on in their evil courses, by deluding them with false peace and fool-hardy confidence, than to draw them off from sin by that genuine conversion which grace alone can effect."[1]

"What does it matter," replied the monk, "by what road we enter paradise, provided we do enter it? as our famous Father Binet, formerly our provincial, remarks on a similar subject, in his excellent book On the Mark of Predestination, 'Be it by hook or by crook,' as he says, 'what need we care, if we reach at last the celestial city.' "

"Granted," said I; "but the great question is, if we will get there at all?"

"The Virgin will be answerable for that," returned he; "so says Father Barry in the concluding lines of his book: 'If, at the hour of death, the enemy should happen to put in some claim upon you, and occasion disturbance in the little commonwealth of your thoughts, you have only to say that Mary will answer for you, and that he must make his application to her.' "

"But, father, it might be possible to puzzle you, were one disposed to push the question a little further. Who, for example, has assured us that the Virgin will be answerable in this case?"

"Father Barry will be answerable for her," he replied. "'As for the profit and happiness to be derived from these devotions,' he says, 'I will be answerable for that; I will stand bail for the good Mother.' "

"But, father, who is to be answerable for Father Barry?"

"How!" cried the monk; "for Father Barry? is he not a member of our Society? and do you need to be told that

[1] The Jesuits raised a great outcry against Pascal for having, in this letter, as they alleged, turned the worship of the Virgin into ridicule. Nicole seriously undertakes his defense, and draws several distinctions between true and false devotion to the Virgin. The Mariolatry. or Mary-worship,·of Pascal and the Port-Royalists, was certainly a different sort of thing from that practised in the Church of Rome; but it is sad to see the straits to which these sincere devotees were reduced, in their attempts to reconcile this practice with the honor due to God and his Son.

our Society is answerable for all the books of its members? It is highly necessary and important for you to know about this. There is an order in our Society, by which all booksellers are prohibited from printing any work of our fathers without the approbation of our divines and the permission of our superiors. This regulation was passed by Henry III., 10th May 1583, and confirmed by Henry IV., 20th December 1603, and by Louis XIII., 14th February 1612; so that the whole of our body stands responsible for the publications of each of the brethren. This is a feature quite peculiar to our community. And, in consequence of this, not a single work emanates from us which does not breathe the spirit of the Society. That, sir, is a piece of information quite *apropos*."[1]

"My good father," said I, "you oblige me very much, and I only regret that I did not know this sooner, as it will induce me to pay considerably more attention to your authors."

"I would have told you sooner," he replied, "had an opportunity offered; I hope, however, you will profit by the information in future, and, in the mean time, let us prosecute our subject. The methods of securing salvation which I have mentioned are, in my opinion, very easy, very sure, and sufficiently numerous; but it was the anxious wish of our doctors that people should not stop short at this first step, where they only do what is absolutely necessary for salvation, and nothing more. Aspiring, as they do without ceasing, after the greater glory of God,[2] they sought to elevate

[1] Father Daniel makes an ingenious attempt to take off the force of this statement, by representing it as no more than what is done by other societies, universities, &c. (Entretiens, p. 32.) But while these bodies acted in good faith on this rule, the Jesuits (as Pascal afterwards shows, Letter xiii.) made it subservient to their double policy. Pascal's point was gained by establishing the fact, that the books published by the Jesuits had the imprimatur of the Society; and, in answer to all that Daniel has said on the point, it may be sufficient to ask, Why not try the simple plan of denouncing the error and censuring the author? (See Letter v., p. 117.)
[2] There is an allusion here to the phrase which is perpetually occurring in the *Constitutions* of the Jesuits, "*Ad majorem Dei gloriam*—To

men to a higher pitch of piety; and as men of the world are generally deterred from devotion by the strange ideas they have been led to form of it by some people, we have deemed it of the highest importance to remove this obstacle which meets us at the threshold. In this department Father Le Moine has acquired much fame, by his work entitled DEVOTION MADE EASY, composed for this very purpose. The picture which he draws of devotion in this work is perfectly charming. None ever understood the subject before him. Only hear what he says in the beginning of his work: 'Virtue has never as yet been seen aright; no portrait of her, hitherto produced, has borne the least verisimilitude. It is by no means surprising that so few have attempted to scale her rocky eminence. She has been held up as a cross-tempered dame, whose only delight is in solitude ; she has been associated with toil and sorrow ; and, in short, represented as the foe of sports and diversions, which are, in fact, the flowers of joy and the seasoning of life.' "

" But, father, I am sure, I have heard at least, that there have been great saints who led extremely austere lives."

" No doubt of that," he replied ; " but still, to use the language of the doctor, 'there have always been a number of genteel saints, and well-bred devotees;' and this difference in their manners, mark you, arises entirely from a difference of humors. ' I am far from denying,' says my author, ' that there are devout persons to be met with, pale and melancholy in their temperament, fond of silence and retirement, with phlegm instead of blood in their veins, and with faces of clay; but there are many others of a happier complexion, and who possess that sweet and warm humor, that genial and rectified blood, which is the true stuff that joy is made of.'

" You see," resumed the monk, " that the love of silence and retirement is not common to all devout people ; and that, as I was saying, this is the effect rather of their complexion than their piety. Those austere manners to which you refer,

the greater glory of God," which is the reason ostentatiously paraded for almost all their laws and customs.

are, in fact, properly the character of a savage and barbarian, and, accordingly, you will find them ranked by Father Le Moine among the ridiculous and brutal manners of a moping idiot. The following is the description he has drawn of one of these in the seventh book of his Moral Pictures: 'He has no eyes for the beauties of art or nature. Were he to indulge in anything that gave him pleasure, he would consider himself oppressed with a grievous load. On festival days, he retires to hold fellowship with the dead. He delights in a grotto rather than a palace, and prefers the stump of a tree to a throne. As to injuries and affronts, he is as insensible to them as if he had the eyes and ears of a statue. Honor and glory are idols with whom he has no acquaintance, and to whom he has no incense to offer. To him a beautiful woman is no better than a spectre ; and those imperial and commanding looks—those charming tyrants who hold so many slaves in willing and chainless servitude—have no more influence over his optics than the sun over those of owls,' &c."

"Reverend sir," said I, "had you not told me that Father Le Moine was the author of that description, I declare I would have guessed it to be the production of some profane fellow, who had drawn it expressly with the view of turning the saints into ridicule. For if that is not the picture of a man entirely denied to those feelings which the Gospel obliges us to renounce, I confess that I know nothing of the matter."[1]

"You may now perceive, then, the extent of your ignorance," he replied; "for these are the features of a feeble, uncultivated mind, 'destitute of those virtuous and natural affections which it ought to possess,' as Father Le Moine says at the close of that description. Such is his way of teaching 'Christian virtue and philosophy,' as he announces in his advertisement ; and, in truth, it cannot be denied that this method of treating devotion is much more agreeable to

---

[1] If Rome be in the right, Pascal's notion is correct. The religion of the monastery is the only sort of piety or seriousness known to, or sanctioned by, the Romish Church.

the taste of the world than the old way in which they went
to work before our times."

"There can be no comparison between them," was my reply, "and I now begin to hope that you will be as good as
your word."

"You will see that better by-and-by," returned the monk.
"Hitherto I have only spoken of piety in general, but, just
to show you more in detail how our fathers have disencum-
bered it of its toils and troubles, would it not be most consoling to the ambitious to learn that they may maintain genuine devotion along with an inordinate love of greatness?"

"What, father! even though they should run to the utmost excess of ambition?"

"Yes," he replied; "for this would be only a venial sin,
unless they sought after greatness in order to offend God and
injure the State more effectually. Now venial sins do not
preclude a man from being devout, as the greatest saints are
not exempt from them.[1] 'Ambition,' says Escobar, 'which
consists in an inordinate appetite for place and power, is of
itself a venial sin; but when such dignities are coveted for
the purpose of hurting the commonwealth, or having more
opportunity to offend God, these adventitious circumstances
render it mortal.'"

"Very savory doctrine, indeed, father."

"And is it not still more savory," continued the monk,
"for misers to be told, by the same authority, 'that the rich
are not guilty of mortal sin by refusing to give alms out of
their superfluity to the poor in the hour of their greatest
need?—*scio in gravi pauperum necessitate divites non dando
superflua, non peccare mortaliter.*'"

"Why truly," said I, "if that be the case, I give up all
pretension to skill in the science of sins."

"To make you still more sensible of this," returned he,
"you have been accustomed to think, I suppose, that a good

---

[1] The Romish distinction of sins into *venial* and *mortal*, afforded too
fair a pretext for such sophistical conclusions to be overlooked by Jesuitical casuists.

opinion of one's self, and a complacency in one's own works, is a most dangerous sin ? Now, will you not be surprised if I can show you that such a good opinion, even though there should be no foundation for it, is so far from being a sin, that it is, on the contrary, *the gift of God ?*"

" Is it possible, father ?"

" That it is," said the monk ; " and our good Father Garasse[1] shows it in his French work, entitled Summary of the Capital Truths of Religion: ' It is a result of commutative justice that all honest labor should find its recompense either in praise or in self-satisfaction. When men of good talents publish some excellent work, they are justly remunerated by public applause. But when a man of weak parts has wrought hard at some worthless production, and fails to obtain the praise of the public, in order that his labor may not go without its reward, God imparts to him a personal satisfaction, which it would be worse than barbarous injustice to envy him. It is thus that God, who is infinitely just, has given even to frogs a certain complacency in their own croaking.' "

" Very fine decisions in favor of vanity, ambition, and avarice !" cried I ; " and envy, father, will it be more difficult to find an excuse for it ?"

" That is a delicate point," he replied. " We require to make use here of Father Bauny's distinction, which he lays down in his Summary of Sins : ' Envy of the spiritual good of our neighbor is mortal, but envy of his temporal good is only venial.' "

" And why so, father ?"

" You shall hear," said he. " ' For the good that consists in temporal things is so slender, and so insignificant in rela-

[1] Francois Garasse was a Jesuit of Angouleme; he died in 1631. He was much followed as a preacher, his sermons being copiously interlarded with buffoonery. His controversial works are full of fire and fury; and his theological Summary, to which Pascal here refers, abounds with eccentricities. It deserves to be mentioned. as some offset to the folly of this writer, that Father Garasse lost his life in consequence of his attentions to his countrymen who were infected with the plague.

tion to heaven, that it is of no consideration in the eyes of
God and his saints.' "

" But, father, if temporal good is so *slender*, and of so little
consideration, how do you come to permit men's lives to be
taken away in order to preserve it ?"[1]

" You mistake the matter entirely," returned the monk ;
" you were told that temporal good was of no consideration
in the eyes of God, but not in the eyes of men."

"That idea never occurred to me," I replied ; "and now,
it is to be hoped that, in virtue of these same distinctions,
the world will get rid of mortal sins altogether."

" Do not flatter yourself with that," said the father ;
"there are still such things as mortal sins—there is sloth,
for example."

" Nay, then, father dear !" I exclaimed, " after that, fare-
well to all ' the joys of life !' "

" Stay," said the monk, " when you have heard Escobar's
definition of that vice, you will perhaps change your tone :
' Sloth,' he observes, ' lies in grieving that spiritual things are
spiritual, as if one should lament that the sacraments are the
sources of grace ; which would be a mortal sin.' "

" O my dear sir !" cried I, " I don't think that anybody
ever took it into his head to be slothful in that way."

" And accordingly," he replied, " Escobar afterwards remarks : ' I must confess that it is very rarely that a person
falls into the sin of sloth.' You see now how important it is
to *define* things properly ?"

" Yes, father, and this brings to my mind your other definitions about assassinations, ambuscades, and superfluities.
But why have you not extended your method to all cases,
and given definitions of all vices in your way, so that people
may no longer sin in gratifying themselves ?"

" It is not always essential," he replied, " to accomplish
that purpose by changing the definitions of things. I may
illustrate this by referring to the subject of good cheer, which
is accounted one of the greatest pleasures of life, and which

[1] See before, Letter vii., p. 159.

Escobar thus sanctions in his 'Practice according to our Society:' 'Is it allowable for a person to eat and drink to repletion, unnecessarily, and solely for pleasure? Certainly he may, according to Sanchez, provided he does not thereby injure his health; because the natural appetite may be permitted to enjoy its proper functions.' "[1]

"Well, father, that is certainly the most complete passage, and the most finished maxim in the whole of your moral system! What comfortable inferences may be drawn from it! Why, and is gluttony, then, not even a venial sin?"

"Not in the shape I have just referred to," he replied; "but, according to the same author, it would be a venial sin 'were a person to gorge himself, unnecessarily, with eating and drinking, to such a degree as to produce vomiting.'[2] So much for that point. I would now say a little about the facilities we have invented for avoiding sin in worldly conversations and intrigues. One of the most embarrassing of these cases is how to avoid telling lies, particularly when one is anxious to induce a belief in what is false. In such cases, our doctrine of equivocations has been found of admirable service, according to which, as Sanchez has it, 'it is permitted to use ambiguous terms, leading people to understand them in another sense from that in which we understand them ourselves.' "[3]

"I know that already, father," said I.

"We have published it so often," continued he, "that at length, it seems, everybody knows of it. But do you know what is to be done when no equivocal words can be got?"

"No, father."

"I thought as much," said the Jesuit; "this is something new, sir: I mean the doctrine of mental reservations. 'A

---

[1] " An comedere et bibere usque ad satietatem absque necessitate ob solam voluptatem, sit peccatum?   Cum Sanctio negative respondeo, modo non obsit valetudini, quia licite potest appetitus naturalis suis actibus frui." (N. 102.)

[2] " Si quis se usque ad vomitum ingurgitet."   (Esc., u. 56.)

[3] Op. mor., p. 2, l. 3, c. 6, u. 13.

man may swear,' as Sanchez says in the same place, 'that he never did such a thing (though he actually did it), meaning within himself that he did not do so on a certain day, or before he was born, or understanding any other such circumstance, while the words which he employs have no such sense as would discover his meaning. And this is very convenient in many cases, and quite innocent, when necessary or conducive to one's health, honor, or advantage.' "

"Indeed, father! is that not a lie, and perjury to boot?"

"No," said the father; "Sanchez and Filiutius prove that it is not; for, says the latter, 'it is the intention that determines the quality of the action.'[1] And he suggests a still surer method for avoiding falsehood, which is this: After saying aloud, *I swear that I have not done that,* to add, in a low voice, *to-day;* or after saying aloud, *I swear,* to interpose in a whisper, *that I say,* and then continue aloud, *that I have done that.* This, you perceive, is telling the truth."[2]

"I grant it," said I; "it might possibly, however, be found to be telling the truth in a low key, and falsehood in a loud one; besides, I should be afraid that many people might not have sufficient presence of mind to avail themselves of these methods."

"Our doctors," replied the Jesuit, "have taught, in the same passage, for the benefit of such as might not be expert in the use of these reservations, that no more is required of

[1] Tr. 25, chap. 11, n. 331, 328.

[2] The method by which Father Daniel evades this charge is truly Jesuitical. First, he attempts to involve the question in a cloud of difficulties, by supposing extreme cases, in which equivocation may be allowed to preserve life, &c. He has then the assurance to quote Scripture in defence of the practice, referring to the equivocations of Abraham. which he vindicates; to those of Tobit and the angel Raphael, which he applauds; and even to the sayings of our blessed Lord, which he charges with equivocation! (Entretiens, pp. 378, 382.) Even Bossuet was ashamed of this abominable maxim. "I know nothing," he says, speaking of Sanchez, "more pernicious in morality, than the opinion of that Jesuit in regard to an oath; he maintains that the intention is necessary to an oath, without which, in giving a false answer to a judge, when questioned at the bar, one is not capable of perjury." (Journal de l'Abbé le Dieu. apud Dissertation sur la foi qui est due au temoignage de Pascal, &c., p. 50.)

them, to avoid lying, than simply to say that *they have not done* what they have done, provided 'they have, in general, the intention of giving to their language the sense which an *able man* would give to it.' Be candid, now, and confess if you have not often felt yourself embarrassed, in consequence of not knowing this?"

"Sometimes," said I.

"And will you not also acknowledge," continued he, "that it would often prove very convenient to be absolved in conscience from keeping certain engagements one may have made?"

"The most convenient thing in the world!" I replied.

"Listen, then, to the general rule laid down by Escobar: 'Promises are not binding, when the person in making them had no intention to bind himself. Now, it seldom happens that any have such an intention, unless when they confirm their promises by an oath or contract; so that when one simply says, *I will do it*, he means that he will do it if he does not change his mind; for he does not wish, by saying that, to deprive himself of his liberty.' He gives other rules in the same strain, which you may consult for yourself, and tells us, in conclusion, 'that all this is taken from Molina and our other authors, and is therefore settled beyond all doubt.'"

"My dear father," I observed, "I had no idea that the direction of the intention possessed the power of rendering promises null and void."

"You must perceive," returned he, "what facility this affords for prosecuting the business of life. But what has given us the most trouble has been to regulate the commerce between the sexes; our fathers being more chary in the matter of chastity. Not but that they have discussed questions of a very curious and very indulgent character, particularly in reference to married and betrothed persons."

At this stage of the conversation I was made acquainted with the most extraordinary questions you can well imagine. He gave me enough of them to fill many letters; but as you

show my communications to all sorts of persons, and as I do
not choose to be the vehicle of such reading to those who
would make it the subject of diversion, I must decline even
giving the quotations.

The only thing to which I can venture to allude, out of all
the books which he showed me, and these in French, too, is
a passage which you will find in Father Bauny's Summary, p.
165, relating to certain little familiarities, which, provided
the intention is well directed, he explains *"as passing for
gallant ;"* and you will be surprised to find, at p. 148, a principle of morals, as to the power which daughters have to dispose of their persons without the leave of their relatives,
couched in these terms : " When that is done with the consent of the daughter, although the father may have reason
to complain, it does not follow that she, or the person to
whom she has sacrificed her honor, has done him any wrong,
or violated the rules of justice in regard to him ; for the
daughter has possession of her honor, as well as of her body,
and can do what she pleases with them, bating death or mutilation of her members." Judge, from that specimen, of the
rest. It brings to my recollection a passage from a Heathen
poet, a much better casuist, it would appear, than these reverend doctors ; for he says, " that the person of a daughter
does not belong wholly to herself, but partly to her father
and partly to her mother, without whom she cannot dispose
of it, even in marriage." And I am much mistaken if there
is a single judge in the land who would not lay down as law
the very reverse of this maxim of Father Bauny.

This is all I dare tell you of this part of our conversation,
which lasted so long that I was obliged to beseech the monk
to change the subject. He did so, and proceeded to entertain me with their regulations about female attire.

" We shall not speak," he said, " of those who are actuated by impure intentions ; but as to others, Escobar remarks,
that ' if the woman adorn herself without any evil intention,
but merely to gratify a natural inclination to vanity—*ob na-
turalem fastus inclinationem*—this is only a venial sin, or

rather no sin at all.' And Father Bauny maintains, that
'even though the woman knows the bad effect which her care
in adorning her person may have upon the virtue of those
who may behold her, all decked out in rich and precious
attire, she would not sin in so dressing.'¹   And among others, he cites our Father Sanchez as being of the same mind."

"But, father, what do your authors say to those passages of
Scripture which so strongly denounce everything of that sort ?"

"Lessius has well met that objection," said the monk, "by
observing, 'that these passages of Scripture have the force
of precepts only in regard to the women of that period, who
were expected to exhibit, by their modest demeanor, an example of edification to the Pagans.' "

"And where did he find that, father·?"

"It does not matter where he found it," replied he ; "it is
enough to know that the sentiments of these great men are
always probable of themselves.   It deserves to be noticed,
however, that Father Le Moine has qualified this general permission ; for he will on no account allow it to be extended to
the old ladies. 'Youth,' he observes, ' is naturally entitled
to adorn itself, nor can the use of ornament be condemned at
an age which is the flower and verdure of life. But there it
should be allowed to remain: it would be strangely out of
season to seek for roses on the snow. The stars alone have
a right to be always dancing, for they have the gift of perpetual youth. The wisest course in this matter, therefore,
for old women, would be to consult good sense and a good
mirror, to yield to decency and necessity, and to retire at the
first approach of the shades of night.' "²

"A most judicious advice," I observed.

----

¹ Esc. tr. 1, ex. 8 ; Summary of Sins, c. 46, p. 1094.
   "They had their Father Le Moine," said Cleandre, "and I am surprised they did not oppose him to Pascal. That father had a lively
imagination and a *florid*, *brilliant* style ; he stood high among polished
society, and his Apology written against the book entitled ' The Moral
Theology of the Jesuits,' was hardly less popular than his *Currycomb
for the Jansenist Pegasus*."   "The Society thought, perhaps," replied
Eudoxus, "that he could not easily catch the delicate and at the same
time easy style of Pascal. It was Father Le Moine's failing, to embel-

"But," continued the monk, "just to show you how care-
ful our fathers are about everything you can think of, I may
mention that, after granting the ladies permission to gamble,
and foreseeing that, in many cases, this license would be of
little avail unless they had something to gamble with, they
have established another maxim in their favor, which will be
found in Escobar's chapter on larceny, n. 13 : 'A wife,' says
he, 'may gamble, and for this purpose may pilfer money
from her husband.'"

"Well, father, that is capital!"

"There are many other good things besides that," said the
father; "but we must waive them, and say a little about
those more important maxims, which facilitate the practice of
holy things—the manner of attending mass, for example.
On this subject our great divines, Gaspard Hurtado, and
Coninck, have taught 'that it is quite sufficient to be present
at mass in body, though we may be absent in spirit, provided
we maintain an outwardly respectful deportment.' Vasquez
goes a step further, maintaining 'that one fulfils the precept
of hearing mass, even though one should go with no such
intention at all.' All this is repeatedly laid down by Escobar, who, in one passage, illustrates the point by the example of those who are dragged to mass by force, and who put
on a fixed resolution not to listen to it."

"Truly, sir," said I, "had any other person told me that,
I would not have believed it."

"In good sooth," he replied, "it requires all the support
which the authority of these great names can lend it; and
so does the following maxim by the same Escobar, 'that
even a wicked intention, such as that of ogling the women,
joined to that of hearing mass rightly, does not hinder a man
from fulfilling the service.'[1] But another very convenient

lish all he said, to be always aiming at something witty, and never to
speak simply. Perhaps, too, he did not feel himself equal for the combat, and did not like to commit himself." (Entretiens de Cleandre et
d'Eudoxe, p. 78.)
[1] " *Nec obest alia prava intentio, ut aspiciendi libidinose fœminas.*"
(Esc. tr. 1, ex. 11, n. 31.)

device, suggested by our learned brother Turrian,[1] is, that 'one may hear the half of a mass from one priest, and the other half from another; and that it makes no difference though he should hear first the conclusion of the one, and then the commencement of the other.' I might also mention that it has been decided by several of our doctors, to be lawful 'to hear the two halves of a mass at the same time, from the lips of two different priests, one of whom is commencing the mass, while the other is at the elevation; it being quite possible to attend to both parties at once, and two halves of a mass making a whole—*duæ medietates unam missam constituunt.*'[2] 'From all which,' says Escobar, 'I conclude, that you may hear mass in a very short period of time; if, for example, you should happen to hear four masses going on at the same time, so arranged that when the first is at the commencement, the second is at the gospel, the third at the consecration, and the last at the communion.' "

"Certainly, father, according to that plan, one may hear mass any day at Notre Dame in a twinkling."

"Well," replied he, "that just shows how admirably we have succeeded in facilitating the hearing of mass. But I am anxious now to show you how we have softened the use of the sacraments, and particularly that of penance. It is here that the benignity of our fathers shines in its truest splendor; and you will be really astonished to find that devotion, a thing which the world is so much afraid of, should have been treated by our doctors with such consummate skill, that, to use the words of Father Le Moine, in his Devotion made Easy, 'demolishing the bughear which the devil had placed at its threshold, they have rendered it easier than vice, and more agreeable than pleasure; so that, in fact, simply to live is incomparably more irksome than to live well. Is that not a marvellous change, now?"

"Indeed, father, I cannot help telling you a bit of my

---

[1] Select., p. 2, d. 16, Sub. 7.
[2] Bauny, Hurtado, Azor. &c. Escobar, " Practice for Hearing Mass according to our Society," Lyons edition.

mind : I am sadly afraid that you have oversl ot the mark, and that this indulgence of yours will shock more people than it will attract. The mass, for example, is a thing so grand and so holy, that, in the eyes of a great many, it would be enough to blast the credit of your doctors forever, to show them how you have spoken of it."

"With a certain class," replied the monk, "I allow that may be the case; but do you not know that we accommodate ourselves to all sorts of persons? You seem to have lost all recollection of what I have repeatedly told you on this point. The first time you are at leisure, therefore, I propose that we make this the theme of our conversation, deferring till then the lenitives we have introduced into the confessional. I promise to make you understand it so well that you will never forget it."

With these words we parted, so that our next conversation, I presume, will turn on the policy of the Society.—I am, &c.

P. S.—Since writing the above, I have seen "Paradise Opened by a Hundred Devotions easily Practised," by Father Barry; and also the "Mark of Predestination," by Father Binet; both of them pieces well worth the seeing.

LETTER X.

PARIS, *August* 2, 1656.

SIR,—I have not come yet to the policy of the Society,
but shall first introduce you to one of its leading principles.
I refer to the palliatives which they have applied to confession, and which are unquestionably the best of all the
schemes they have fallen upon to "attract all and repel
none." It is absolutely necessary to know something of this
before going any further; and, accordingly, the monk judged
it expedient to give me some instructions on the point, nearly
as follows:—

"From what I have already stated," he observed, "you
may judge of the success with which our doctors have labored to discover, in their wisdom, that a great many things,
formerly regarded as forbidden, are innocent and allowable;
but as there are some sins for which one can find no excuse,
and for which there is no remedy but confession, it became
necessary to alleviate, by the methods I am now going to
mention, the difficulties attending that practice. Thus, having shown you, in our previous conversations, how we relieve
people from troublesome scruples of conscience, by showing
them that what they believed to be sinful was indeed quite
innocent, I proceed now to illustrate our convenient plan for
expiating what is really sinful, which is effected by making
confession as easy a process as it was formerly a painful one."

"And how do you manage that, father?"

"Why," said he, "it is by those admirable subtleties

which are peculiar to our Company, and have been styled by
our fathers in Flanders, in "The Image of the First Century,"[1] 'the pious finesse, the holy artifice of devotion—
piam et religiosam calliditatem, et pietatis solertiam.'[2] By
the aid of these inventions, as they remark in the same place,
'crimes may be expiated ' now-a-days *alacrius*—with more
zeal and alacrity than they were committed in former days,
and a great many people may be washed from their stains
almost as cleverly as they contracted them—*plurimi vix citius
maculas contrahunt quam eluunt.*' "

" Pray, then, father, do teach me some of these most salutary lessons of *finesse*."

" We have a good number of them," answered the monk;
" for there are a great many irksome things about confession,
and for each of these we have devised a palliative. The
chief difficulties connected with this ordinance are the shame
of confessing certain sins, the trouble of specifying the circumstances of others, the penance exacted for them, the
resolution against relapsing into them, the avoidance of the
proximate occasions of sins, and the regret for having committed them. I hope to convince you to-day, that it is now
possible to get over all this with hardly any trouble at all;
such is the care we have taken to allay the bitterness and
nauseousness of this very necessary medicine. For, to begin
with the difficulty of confessing certain sins, you are aware
it is of importance often to keep in the good graces of one's
confessor; now, must it not be extremely convenient to be
permitted, as you are by our doctors, particularly Escobar
and Suarez, 'to have two confessors, one for the mortal sins
and another for the venial, in order to maintain a fair character with your ordinary confessor—*uti bonam famam apud
ordinarium tueatur*—provided you do not take occasion from
thence to indulge in mortal sin?' This is followed by another ingenious contrivance for confessing a sin, even to the
ordinary confessor, without his perceiving that it was committed since the last confession, which is, 'to make a general

---

[1] See before, p. 194. [2] *Imago P-imi Seculi*, l. iii., c. 8.

confession, and huddle this last sin in a lump among the rest which we confess.'[1] And I am sure you will own that the following decision of Father Bauny goes far to alleviate the shame which one must feel in confessing his relapses, namely, 'that, except in certain cases, which rarely occur, the confessor is not entitled to ask his penitent if the sin of which he accuses himself is an habitual one, nor is the latter obliged to answer such a question; because the confessor has no right to subject his penitent to the shame of disclosing his frequent relapses.'"

"Indeed, father! I might as well say that a physician has no right to ask his patient if it is long since he had the fever. Do not sins assume quite a different aspect according to circumstances? and should it not be the object of a genuine penitent to discover the whole state of his conscience to his confessor, with the same sincerity and openheartedness as if he were speaking to Jesus Christ himself, whose place the priest occupies? If so, how far is he from realizing such a disposition, who, by concealing the frequency of his relapses, conceals the aggravations of his offence!"[2]

I saw that this puzzled the worthy monk, for he attempted to elude rather than resolve the difficulty, by turning my attention to another of their rules, which only goes to establish a fresh abuse, instead of justifying in the least the decision of Father Bauny; a decision which, in my opinion, is one of the most pernicious of their maxims, and calculated to encourage profligate men to continue in their evil habits.

---

[1] Esc. tr. 7, a. 4, n. 135; also, Princ., ex. 2, n. 73.

[2] The practice of auricular confession was about three hundred years old before the Reformation, having remained undetermined till the year 1150 after Christ. The early fathers were, beyond all question, decidedly opposed to it. Chrysostom reasons very differently from the text. "But thou art ashamed to say that thou hast sinned? Confess thy faults, then, daily in thy prayer; for do I say, 'Confess them to thy fellow-servant, who may reproach thee therewith?' No; confess them to God who healeth them." (In Ps. l., hom. 2.) And to whom did Augustine make his *Confessions?* Was it not to the same Being. to whom David in the Psalms, and the publican in the Gospel, made theirs? "What have I to do with men," says this father, "that they should hear my confessions, as if they were to heal all my diseases?" (Confes., lib. x., p. 3.)

"I grant you," replied the father, "that habit aggravates the malignity of a sin, but it does not alter its nature; and that is the reason why we do not insist on people confessing it, according to the rule laid down by our fathers, and quoted by Escobar, 'that one is only obliged to confess the circumstances that alter the species of the sin, and not those that aggravate it.' Proceeding on this rule, Father Granados says, 'that if one has eaten flesh in Lent, all he needs to do is to confess that he has broken the fast, without specifying whether it was by eating flesh, or by taking two fish meals.' And, according to Reginald, 'a sorcerer who has employed the diabolical art is not obliged to reveal that circumstance; it is enough to say that he has dealt in magic, without expressing whether it was by palmistry or by a paction with the devil.' Fagundez, again, has decided that 'rape is not a circumstance which one is bound to reveal, if the woman give her consent.' All this is quoted by Escobar,[1] with many other very curious decisions as to these circumstances, which you may consult at your leisure."

"These 'artifices of devotion' are vastly convenient in their way," I observed.

"And yet," said the father, "notwithstanding all that, they would go for nothing, sir, unless we had proceeded to mollify penance, which, more than anything else, deters people from confession. Now, however, the most squeamish have nothing to dread from it, after what we have advanced in our theses of the College of Clermont, where we hold that if the confessor imposes a suitable penance, and the penitent be unwilling to submit himself to it, the latter may go home, waiving both the penance and the absolution.' Or, as Escobar says, in giving the Practice of our Society, 'if the penitent declare his willingness to have his penance remitted to the next world, and to suffer in purgatory all the pains due to him, the confessor may, for the honor of the sacrament, impose a very light penance on him, particularly if he

[1] Princ., ex. 2. n. 39, 41, 61, 62.

has reason to believe that his penitent would object to a heavier one.'"

"I really think," said I, "that, if that is the case, we ought no longer to call confession the sacrament of penance."

"You are wrong," he replied; "for we always administer something in the way of penance, for the form's sake."

"But, father, do you suppose that a man is worthy of receiving absolution, when he will submit to nothing painful to expiate his offences? And, in these circumstances, ought you not to retain rather than remit their sins? Are you not aware of the extent of your ministry, and that you have the power of binding and loosing? Do you imagine that you are at liberty to give absolution indifferently to all who ask it, and without ascertaining beforehand if Jesus Christ looses in heaven those whom you loose on earth?"[1]

"What!" cried the father, "do you suppose that we do not know that 'the confessor (as one remarks) ought to sit in judgment on the disposition of his penitent, both because he is bound not to dispense the sacraments to the unworthy, Jesus Christ having enjoined him to be a faithful steward, and not give that which is holy unto dogs; and because he is a judge, and it is the duty of a judge to give righteous judgment, by loosing the worthy and binding the unworthy, and he ought not to absolve those whom Jesus Christ condemns.'"

"Whose words are these, father?"

"They are the words of our father Filiutius," he replied.

"You astonish me," said I; "I took them to be a quotation from one of the fathers of the Church. At all events,

---

[1] John xx. 23: "Receive ye the Holy Ghost: Whose soever sins ye remit, they are remitted unto them; and whose soever sins ye retain, they are retained." All the ancient fathers. such as Basil, Ambrose, Augustine. and Chrysostom, explain this remission of sins as the work of the Holy Ghost, and not of the apostles. except ministerially, in the use of the spiritual keys of doctrine and discipline, of intercessary prayer and of the sacraments. (Ussher's Jesuits' Challenge, p. 122. &c.) Even the schoolmen held that the power of binding and loosing committed to the ministers of the Church is not absolute, but must be limited by *clave non errante*, or when no error is committed in the use of the keys.

sir, that passage ought to make an impression on the confessors, and render them very circumspect in the dispensation of this sacrament, to ascertain whether the regret of their penitents is sufficient, and whether their promises of future amendment are worthy of credit."

"That is not such a difficult matter," replied the father; "Filiutius had more sense than to leave confessors in that dilemma, and accordingly he suggests an easy way of getting out of it, in the words immediately following: 'The confessor may easily set his mind at rest as to the disposition of his penitent; for, if he fail to give sufficient evidence of sorrow, the confessor has only to ask him if he does not detest the sin in his heart, and if he answers that he does, he is bound to believe it. The same thing may be said of resolutions as to the future, unless the case involves an obligation to restitution, or to avoid some proximate occasion of sin.'"

"As to that passage, father, I can easily believe that it is Filiutius' own."

"You are mistaken though," said the father, "for he has extracted it, word for word, from Suarez."[1]

"But, father, that last passage from Filiutius overturns what he had laid down in the former. For confessors can no longer be said to sit as judges on the disposition of their penitents, if they are bound to take it simply upon their word, in the absence of all satisfying signs of contrition. Are the professions made on such occasions so infallible, that no other sign is needed? I question much if experience has taught your fathers, that all who make fair promises are remarkable for keeping them; I am mistaken if they have not often found the reverse."

"No matter," replied the monk; "confessors are bound to believe them for all that; for Father Bauny, who has probed this question to the bottom, has concluded 'that at whatever time those who have fallen into frequent relapses, without giving evidence of amendment, present themselves before a confessor, expressing their regret for the past, and a good

[1] In 3 part, t. 4, disp. 32, sect. 2, n. 2.

purpose for the future, he is bound to believe them on their simple averment, although there may be reason to presume that such resolution only came from the teeth outwards. Nay,' says he, 'though they should indulge subsequently to greater excess than ever in the same delinquencies, still, in my opinion, they may receive absolution.'[1] There now! that, I am sure, should silence you."

"But, father," said I, "you impose a great hardship, I think, on the confessors, by thus obliging them to believe the very reverse of what they see."

"You don't understand it," returned he; "all that is meant is, that they are obliged to act and absolve *as if* they believed that their penitents would be true to their engagements, though, in point of fact, they believe no such thing. This is explained, immediately afterwards, by Suarez and Filiutius. After having said that 'the priest is bound to believe the penitent on his word,' they add, 'It is not necessary that the confessor should be convinced that the good resolution of his penitent will be carried into effect, nor even that he should judge it probable; it is enough that he thinks the person has at the time the design in general, though he may very shortly after relapse. Such is the doctrine of all our authors—*ita docent omnes autores*.' Will you presume to doubt what has been taught by our authors?"

"But, sir, what then becomes of what Father Petau[2] himself is obliged to own, in the preface to his Public Penance, 'that the holy fathers, doctors, and councils of the Church

[1] Summary of Sins, c. 46, p. 1090, 1, 2.
[2] Denis Petau (Dionysius Petavius) a learned Jesuit, was born at Orleans in 1593, and died in 1652. The catalogue of his works alone would fill a volume. He wrote in elegant Latin, on all subjects, grammar, history, chronology, &c., as well as theology. Perrault informs us that he had an incredible ardor for the conversion of heretics, and had almost succeeded in converting the celebrated Grotius—a very unlikely story. (Les Hommes Illustres, p. 19.) His book on Public Penance (Paris, 1644) was intended as a refutation of Arnauld's "Frequent Communion;" but is said to have been ill-written and unsuccessful. Though he professed the theology of his order, he is said to have had a kind of predilection for austere opinions, being naturally of a melancholy temper. When invited by the pope to visit Rome, he replied, "I am too old to *flit*"—*demenager*. (Dict. Univ., art. *Petau*.)

agree in holding it as a settled point, that the penance pre-
paratory to the eucharist must be genuine, constant, resolute,
and not languid and sluggish, or subject to after-thoughts
and relapses ?' "

"Don't you observe," replied the monk, "that Father Petau is speaking of the *ancient Church?* But all that is now
so little in season, to use a common saying of our doctors,
that, according to Father Bauny, the reverse is the only true
view of the matter. 'There are some,' says he, 'who maintain that absolution ought to be refused to those who fall frequently into the same sins, more especially if, after being oft-
en absolved, they evince no signs of amendment; and others
hold the opposite view. But the only true opinion is, that
they ought not to be refused absolution; and though they
should be nothing the better of all the advice given them,
though they should have broken all their promises to lead
new lives, and been at no trouble to purify themselves, still it
is of no consequence; whatever may be said to the contrary,
the true opinion which ought to be followed is, that even in
all these cases, they ought to be absolved.' And again:
'Absolution ought neither to be denied nor delayed in the
case of those who live in habitual sins against the law of God,
of nature, and of the Church, although there should be no
apparent prospect of future amendment—*etsi emendationis
futuræ nulla spes appareat.'* "

"But, father, this certainty of always getting absolution
may induce sinners—"

"I know what you mean," interrupted the Jesuit; "but
listen to Father Bauny, q. 15 : ' Absolution may be given even
to him who candidly avows that the hope of being absolved
induced him to sin with more freedom than he would otherwise have done.' And Father Caussin, defending this proposition, says, 'that were this not true, confession would be
interdicted to the greater part of mankind; and the only resource left for poor sinners would be a branch and a rope!' "[1]

---

[1] Reply to the Moral Theol., p. 211.

"O father, how these maxims of yours will draw people to your confessionals!"

"Yes," he replied, "you would hardly believe what numbers are in the habit of frequenting them; 'we are absolutely oppressed and overwhelmed, so to speak, under the crowd of our penitents—*penitentium numero obruimur*'—as is said in 'The Image of the First Century.'"

"I could suggest a very simple method," said I, "to escape from this inconvenient pressure. You have only to oblige sinners to avoid the proximate occasions of sin; that single expedient would afford you relief at once."

"We have no wish for such a relief," rejoined the monk; "quite the reverse; for, as is observed in the same book, 'the great end of our Society is to labor to establish the virtues, to wage war on the vices, and to save a great number of souls.' Now, as there are very few souls inclined to quit the proximate occasions of sin, we have been obliged to define what a proximate occasion is. 'That cannot be called a proximate occasion,' says Escobar, 'where one sins but rarely, or on a sudden transport—say three or four times a year;'[1] or, as Father Bauny has it, 'once or twice in a month.'[2] Again, asks this author, 'what is to be done in the case of masters and servants, or cousins, who, living under the same roof, are by this occasion tempted to sin?'"

"They ought to be separated," said I.

"That is what he says, too, 'if their relapses be very frequent: but if the parties offend rarely, and cannot be separated without trouble and loss, they may, according to Suarez and other authors, be absolved, provided they promise to sin no more, and are truly sorry for what is past.'"

This required no explanation, for he had already informed me with what sort of evidence of contrition the confessor was bound to rest satisfied.

"And Father Bauny," continued the monk, "permits those who are involved in the proximate occasions of sin, 'to remain as they are, when they cannot avoid them without

---

[1] Esc., Practice of the Society, tr. 7, ex. 4, n. 226.   [2] P. 1082, 1089

becoming the common talk of the world, or subjecting themselves to inconvenience.' 'A priest,' he remarks in another work, 'may and ought to absolve a woman who is guilty of living with a paramour, if she cannot put him away honorably, or has some reason for keeping him—*si non potest honeste ejicere, aut habeat aliquam causam retinendi*—provided she promises to act more virtuously for the future.' "[1]

"Well, father," cried I, "you have certainly succeeded in relaxing the obligation of avoiding the occasions of sin to a very comfortable extent, by dispensing with the duty as soon as it becomes inconvenient; but I should think your fathers will at least allow it to be binding when there is no difficulty in the way of its performance?"

"Yes," said the father, "though even then the rule is not without exceptions. For Father Bauny says, in the same place, 'that any one may frequent profligate houses, with the view of converting their unfortunate inmates, though the probability should be that he fall into sin, having often experienced before that he has yielded to their fascinations. Some doctors do not approve of this opinion, and hold that no man may voluntarily put his salvation in peril to succor his neighbor; yet I decidedly embrace the opinion which they controvert.' "

"A novel sort of preachers these, father! But where does Father Bauny find any ground for investing them with such a mission?"

"It is upon one of his own principles," he replied, "which he announces in the same place after Basil Ponce. I mentioned it to you before, and I presume you have not forgotten it. It is, 'that one may seek an occasion of sin, directly and expressly—*primo et per se*—to promote the temporal or spiritual good of himself or his neighbor.' "

On hearing these passages, I felt so horrified that I was on the point of breaking out; but, being resolved to hear him to an end, I restrained myself, and merely inquired : "How, father, does this doctrine comport with that of the Gospel,

---

[1] Theol. Mor., tr. 4, De Pœnit., q. 13, pp. 93, 94.

which binds us to 'pluck out the right eye,' and 'cut off the
right hand,' when they 'offend,' or prove prejudicial to salvation? And how can you suppose that the man who wilfully
indulges in the occasions of sins, sincerely hates sin? Is it
not evident, on the contrary, that he has never been properly
touched with a sense of it, and that he has not yet experienced
that genuine conversion of heart, which makes a man love
God as much as he formerly loved the creature?"

"Indeed!" cried he, "do you call that genuine contrition?
It seems you do not know that, as Father Pintereau[1] says,
'all our fathers teach, with one accord, that it is an error, and
almost a heresy, to hold that *contrition* is necessary; or that
attrition alone, induced by the *sole* motive, the fear of the
pains of hell, which excludes a disposition to offend, is not
sufficient with the sacrament?'"[2]

"What, father! do you mean to say that it is almost an
article of faith, that attrition, induced merely by fear of punishment, is sufficient with the sacrament? That idea, I think,
is peculiar to your fathers; for those other doctors who hold
that attrition is sufficient along with the sacrament, always
take care to show that it must be accompanied with some
love to God at least. It appears to me, moreover, that even
your own authors did not always consider this doctrine of
yours so certain. Your Father Suarez, for instance, speaks

---

[1] The work ascribed to Pintereau was entitled, "Les Impostures et
les Ignorances du Libelle intitulé la Theologie Morale des Jesuites: par
l'Abbè du Boisic."

[2] That is, the sacrament of penance, as it is called. "That contrition is at all times necessarily required for obtaining remission of sins
and justification, is a matter determined by the fathers of Trent. But
mark yet the mystery. They equivocate with us in the term *contrition*,
and make a distinction thereof into perfect and imperfect. The former
of these is *contrition* properly; the latter they call *attrition*, which, how-
soever in itself it be no true contrition, yet when the priest, with his
power of forgiving sins, interposes himself in the business, they tell us
that attrition, by virtue of the keys, is made contrition: that is to say,
that a sorrow arising from a servile fear of punishment, and such a fruitless repentance as the reprobate may carry with them to hell, by virtue
of the priest's absolution, is made so fruitful that it shall serve the turn
for obtaining forgiveness of sins, as if it had been that godly sorrow
which worketh repentance to salvation not to be repented of. By which
spiritual cozenage many poor souls are most miserably deluded." (Ussher's Tracts, p. 153)

of it thus : • Although it is a probable opinion that attrition is sufficient with the sacrament, yet it is not certain, and it may be false—*non est certa, et potest esse falsa.* And if it is false, attrition is not sufficient to save a man ; and he that dies knowingly in this state, wilfully exposes himself to the grave peril of eternal damnation. For this opinion is neither very ancient nor very common—*nec valde antiqua, nec multum communis.'* Sanchez was not more prepared to hold it as infallible, when he said in his Summary, that ' the sick man and his confessor, who content themselves at the hour of death with attrition and the sacrament, are both chargeable with mortal sin, on account of the great risk of damnation to which the penitent would be exposed, if the opinion that attrition is sufficient with the sacrament should not turn out to be true.' Comitolus, too, says that ' we should not be too sure that attrition suffices with the sacrament.' "[1]

Here the worthy father interrupted me. "What!" he cried, "you read our authors then, it seems ? That is all very well ; but it would be still better were you never to read them without the precaution of having one of *us* beside you. Do you not see, now, that, from having read them alone, you have concluded, in your simplicity, that these passages bear hard on those who have more lately supported our doctrine of attrition ? whereas it might be shown that nothing could set them off to greater advantage. Only think what a triumph it is for our fathers of the present day to have succeeded in disseminating their opinion in such short time, and to such an extent that, with the exception of theologians, nobody almost would ever suppose but that our modern views on this subject had been the uniform belief of the faithful in all ages ! So that, in fact, when you have shown, from our fathers themselves, that, a few years ago, ' this opinion was not certain,' you have only succeeded in giving our modern authors the whole merit of its establishment !

[1] These quotations, carefully marked in the original, afford a sufficient answer to Father Daniel's long argument, which consists chiefly of citations from Jesuit writers who hold the views above given.

"Accordingly," he continued, "our cordial friend Diana, to gratify us, no doubt, has recounted the various steps by which the opinion reached its present position.[1] 'In former days, the ancient schoolmen maintained that contrition was necessary as soon as one had committed a mortal sin; since then, however, it has been thought that it is not binding except on festival days; afterwards, only when some great calamity threatened the people: others, again, that it ought not to be long delayed at the approach of death. But our fathers, Hurtado and Vasquez, have ably refuted all these opinions, and established that one is not bound to contrition unless he cannot be absolved in any other way, or at the point of death!' But, to continue the wonderful progress of this doctrine, I might add, what our fathers, Fagundez, Granados, and Escobar, have decided, 'that contrition is not necessary even at death; because,' say they, 'if attrition with the sacrament did not suffice at death, it would follow that attrition would not be sufficient with the sacrament. And the learned Hurtado, cited by Diana and Escobar, goes still further; for he asks, 'Is that sorrow for sin which flows solely from apprehension of its temporal consequences, such as having lost health or money, sufficient? We must distinguish. If the evil is not regarded as sent by the hand of God, such a sorrow does not suffice; but if the evil is viewed as sent by God, as, in fact, all evil, says Diana, except sin, comes from him, that kind of sorrow is sufficient.'[2] Our Father Lamy holds the same doctrine."[3]

"You surprise me, father; for I see nothing in all that attrition of which you speak but what is natural; and in this way a sinner may render himself worthy of absolution without

---

[1] It may be remembered that Diana, though not a Jesuit, was claimed by the Society as a favorer of their casuists. This writer was once held in such high repute, that he was consulted by people from all parts of the world as a perfect oracle in cases of conscience. He is now forgotten. His style, like that of most of these scholastics, is described as "insipid, stingy, and crawling." (Biogr. Univ., Anc. et Mod.)
[2] Esc. Pratique de notre Société, tr. 7, ex. 4, n. 91.
[3] Tr. 8, disp. 3, n. 13.

supernatural grace at all. Now everybody knows that this is a heresy condemned by the Council."[1]

"I should have thought with you," he replied; "and yet it seems this must not be the case, for the fathers of our College of Clermont have maintained (in their Theses of the 23rd May and 6th June 1644) 'that attrition may be holy and sufficient for the sacrament, although it may not be supernatural:' and (in that of August 1643) 'that attrition, though merely natural, is sufficient for the sacrament, provided it is honest.' I do not see what more could be said on the subject, unless we choose to subjoin an inference, which may be easily drawn from these principles, namely, that contrition, so far from being necessary to the sacrament, is rather prejudicial to it, inasmuch as, by washing away sins of itself, it would leave nothing for the sacrament to do at all. That is, indeed, exactly what the celebrated Jesuit Father Valencia remarks. (Tom. iv., disp. 7, q. 8, p. 4.) 'Contrition,' says he, 'is by no means necessary in order to obtain the principal benefit of the sacrament; on the contrary, it is rather an obstacle in the way of it—*imo obstat potius quominus effectus sequatur.*' Nobody could well desire more to be said in commendation of attrition."[2]

"I believe that, father," said I; "but you must allow me to tell you my opinion, and to show you to what a dreadful length this doctrine leads. When you say that 'attrition, induced by the mere dread of punishment,' is sufficient, with the sacrament, to justify sinners, does it not follow that a person may always expiate his sins in this way, and thus be

[1] Of Trent. Nicole attempts to prove that the "imperfect contrition" of this Council includes the love of God, and that they condemned as heretical the opinion, that "any could prepare himself for grace without a movement of the Holy Spirit." He is more successful in showing that the Jesuits were heretical when judged by Augustine and the Holy Scriptures. (Note 2. sur la x. Lettre.)
[2] The Jesuits are so fond of their "attrition," or purely natural repentance, that one of their own theologians (Cardinal Francis Tolet) having condemned it, they falsified the passage in a subsequent edition, making him speak the opposite sentiment. The forgery was exposed; but the worthy fathers, according to custom, allowed it to pass without notice, *ad majorem Dei gloriam.* (Nicole, iii. 95)

13*

saved without ever having loved God all his lifetime? Would your fathers venture to hold that?"

"I perceive," replied the monk, "from the strain of your remarks, that you need some information on the doctrine of our fathers regarding the love of God. This is the last feature of their morality, and the most important of all. You must have learned something of it from the passages about contrition which I have quoted to you. But here are others still more definite on the point of love to God—Don't interrupt me, now; for it is of importance to notice the connection. Attend to Escobar, who reports the different opinions of our authors, in his 'Practice of the Love of God according to our Society.' The question is: 'When is one obliged to have an actual affection for God?' Suarez says, it is enough if one loves him before being *articulo mortis*—at the point of death—without determining the exact time. Vasquez, that it is sufficient even at the very point of death. Others, when one has received baptism. Others, again, when one is bound to exercise contrition. And others, on festival days. But our father, Castro Palao, combats all these opinions, and with good reason—*merito*. Hurtado de Mendoza insists that we are obliged to love God once a-year; and that we ought to regard it as a great favor that we are not bound to do it oftener. But our Father Coninck thinks that we are bound to it only once in three or four years; Henriquez, once in five years; and Filiutius says that it is *probable* that we are not strictly bound to it even once in five years. How often, then, do you ask? Why, he refers it to the judgment of the judicious."

I took no notice of all this badinage, in which the ingenuity of man seems to be sporting, in the height of insolence, with the love of God.

"But," pursued the monk, "our Father Antony Sirmond surpasses all on this point, in his admirable book, 'The Defence of Virtue,'[1] where, as he tells the reader, 'he speaks French in France,' as follows: 'St. Thomas says that we

---

[1] Tr. 1, ex. 2, n. 21; and tr. 5, ex. 4, n. 8.

are obliged to love God as soon as we come to the use of
reason : that is rather too soon ! Scotus says, every Sunday
pray, for what reason ?   Others say, when we are sorely
tempted: yes, if there be no other way of escaping the
temptation.   Scotus says, when we have received a benefit
from God : good, in the way of thanking him for it.   Others
say, at death : rather late !   As little do I think it binding
at the reception of any sacrament : attrition in such cases is
quite enough, along with confession, if convenient.   Suarez
says that it is binding at some time or another ; but at what
time ?—he leaves you to judge of that for yourself—he does
not know ; and what that doctor did not know I know not
who should know.'   In short, he concludes that we are not
strictly bound to more than to keep the other commandments,
without any affection for God, and without giving him our
hearts, provided that we do not hate him.   To prove this is
the sole object of his second treatise.   You will find it in
every page ; more especially where he says : ' God, in commanding us to love him, is satisfied with our obeying him in
his other commandments.   If God had said, Whatever obedience thou yieldest me, if thy heart is not given to me, I will
destroy thee !—would such a motive, think you, be well fitted to promote the end which God must, and only can, have
in view ?   Hence it is said that we shall love God by doing
his will, *as if* we loved him with affection, as if the motive in
this case was real charity.   If that is really our motive, so
much the better ; if not, still we are strictly fulfilling the
commandment of love, by having its works, so that (such is
the goodness of God!) we are commanded, not so much to
love him, as not to hate him.'

   " Such is the way in which our doctors have discharged
men from the 'painful' obligation of actually loving God.
And this doctrine is so advantageous, that our Fathers Annat, Pintereau, Le Moine, and Antony Sirmond himself,
have strenuously defended it when it has been attacked.   You
have only to consult their answers to the ' Moral Theology.'
That of Father Pintereau, in particular, will enable you to

form some idea of the value of this dispensation, from the price which he tells us that it cost, which is no less than the blood of Jesus Christ. This crowns the whole. It appears, that this dispensation from the 'painful' obligation to love God, is the privilege of the Evangelical law, in opposition to the Judaical. 'It was reasonable,' he says, 'that, under the law of grace in the New Testament, God should relieve us from that troublesome and arduous obligation which existed under the law of bondage, to exercise an act of perfect contrition, in order to be justified; and that the place of this should be supplied by the sacraments, instituted in aid of an easier disposition. Otherwise, indeed, Christians, who are the children, would have no greater facility in gaining the good graces of their Father than the Jews, who were the slaves, had in obtaining the mercy of their Lord and Master.' "[1]

"O father!" cried I; "no patience can stand this any longer. It is impossible to listen without horror to the sentiments I have just heard."

"They are not my sentiments," said the monk.

"I grant it, sir," said I; "but you feel no aversion to them; and, so far from detesting the authors of these maxims, you hold them in esteem. Are you not afraid that your consent may involve you in a participation of their guilt? and are you not aware that St. Paul judges worthy of death,

[1] Shocking as these principles are, it might be easy to show that they necessarily flow from the Romish doctrine, which substitutes the imperfect obedience of the sinner as the meritorious ground of justification in the room of the all-perfect obedience and oblation of the Son of God, which renders it necessary to lower the divine standard of duty. The attempt of Father Daniel to escape from the serious charge in the text under a cloud of metaphysical distinctions about *affective* and *effective* love, is about as lame as the argument he draws from the merciful character of the Gospel, is dishonorable to the Saviour, who "came not to destroy the law and the prophets, but to fulfil." But this "confusion worse confounded" arises from putting love to God out of its proper place, and representing it as the price of our pardon, instead of the fruit of faith in pardoning mercy. Arnauld was as far wrong on *this* point as the Jesuits; and it is astonishing that he did not discover in their system the radical error of his own creed carried out to its proper consequences. (Repoase Gen. au Livre de M. Arnauld, par Elie Merlat, p. 30.)

not only the authors of evil things, but also 'those who have pleasure in them that do them?' Was it not enough to have permitted men to indulge in so many forbidden things, under the covert of your palliations? Was it necessary to go still further, and hold out a bribe to them to commit even those crimes which you found it impossible to excuse, by offering them an easy and certain absolution; and for this purpose nullifying the power of the priests, and obliging them, more as slaves than as judges, to absolve the most inveterate sinners—without any amendment of life—without any sign of contrition except promises a hundred times broken—without penance 'unless they choose to accept of it'—and without abandoning the occasions of their vices, 'if they should thereby be put to any inconvenience?'

"But your doctors have gone even beyond this; and the license which they have assumed to tamper with the most holy rules of Christian conduct amount to a total subversion of the law of God. They violate 'the great commandment on which hang all the law and the prophets;' they strike at the very heart of piety; they rob it of the spirit that giveth life; they hold that to love God is not necessary to salvation; and go so far as to maintain that 'this dispensation from loving God is the privilege which Jesus Christ has introduced into the world!' This, sir, is the very climax of impiety. The price of the blood of Jesus Christ paid to obtain us a dispensation from loving him! Before the incarnation, it seems men were obliged to love God; but since 'God has so loved the world as to give his only-begotten Son,' the world, redeemed by him, is released from loving him! Strange divinity of our days—to dare to take off the 'anathema' which St. Paul denounces on those 'that love not the Lord Jesus!' To cancel the sentence of St. John: 'He that loveth not, abideth in death!' and that of Jesus Christ himself: 'He that loveth me not keepeth not my precepts!' and thus to render those worthy of enjoying God through eternity who never loved God all their life!" Be-

---

[1] "Nothing on this point," says Nicole in a note here, "can be fine⌐

hold the Mystery of Iniquity fulfilled ! Open your eyes at length, my dear father, and if the other aberrations of your casuists have made no impression on you, let these last, by their very extravagance, compel you to abandon them. This is what I desire from the bottom of my heart, for your own sake and for the sake of your doctors ; and my prayer to God is, that he would vouchsafe to convince them how false the light must be that has guided them to such precipices ; and that he would fill their hearts with that love of himself from which they have dared to give man a dispensation !"

After some remarks of this nature, I took my leave of the monk, and I see no great likelihood of my repeating my visits to him. This, however, need not occasion you any regret; for, should it be necessary to continue these communications on their maxims, I have studied their books sufficiently to tell you as much of their morality, and more, perhaps, of their policy, than he could have done himself.— I am, &c.

than the prosopopeia in which Despréaux (Boileau) introduces God as judging mankind." He then quotes a long passage from the Twelfth Epistle of that poet, beginning—

"Quand Dieu viendra juger les vivans et les morts," &c.

Boileau was the personal friend of Arnauld and Pascal, and satirized the Jesuit with such pleasant irony that Father la Chaise, the confessor of Louis XIV., though himself a Jesuit, is said to have taken a pleasure in repeating his verses.

LETTER XI.

TO THE REVEREND FATHERS, THE JESUITS.[1]

RIDICULE A FAIR WEAPON WHEN EMPLOYED AGAINST ABSURD OPIN-
IONS—RULES TO BE OBSERVED IN THE USE OF THIS WEAPON—
THE PROFANE BUFFOONERY OF FATHERS LE MOINE AND GARASSE.

August 18, 1656.

REVEREND FATHERS,—I have seen the letters which you
are circulating in opposition to those which I wrote to one
of my friends on your morality; and I perceive that one of
the principal points of your defence is, that I have not spoken of your maxims with sufficient seriousness. This charge
you repeat in all your productions, and carry it so far as to
allege, that I have been "guilty of turning sacred things into
ridicule."

Such a charge, fathers, is no less surprising than it is unfounded. Where do you find that I have turned sacred
things into ridicule? You specify "the Mohatra contract,
and the story of John d'Alba." But are these what you
call "sacred things?" Does it really appear to you that the
Mohatra is something so venerable that it would be blasphemy not to speak of it with respect? And the lessons of
Father Bauny on larceny, which led John d'Alba to practise
it at your expense, are they so sacred as to entitle you to
stigmatize all who laugh at them as profane people?

What, fathers! must the vagaries of your doctors pass for
the verities of the Christian faith, and no man be allowed to
ridicule Escobar, or the fantastical and unchristian dogmas

---

[1] In this and the following letters, Pascal changes his style, from that
of dialogue to that of direct address, and from that of the liveliest irony
to that of serious invective and poignant satire.

of your authors, without being stigmatized as jesting at
religion ?   Is it possible you can have ventured to reiterate
so often an idea so utterly unreasonable ?   Have you no fears
that, in blaming me for laughing at your absurdities, you
may only afford me fresh subject of merriment; that you
may make the charge recoil on yourselves, by showing that
I have really selected nothing from your writings as the matter of raillery, but what was truly ridiculous ; and that thus,
in making a jest of your morality, I have been as far from
jeering at holy things, as the doctrine of your casuists is far
from the holy doctrine of the Gospel ?

Indeed, reverend sirs, there is a vast difference between
laughing at religion, and laughing at those who profane it by
their extravagant opinions.   It were impiety to be wanting
in respect for the verities which the Spirit of God has revealed ; but it were no less impiety of another sort, to be
wanting in contempt for the falsities which the spirit of man
opposes to them.[1]

For, fathers (since you will force me into this argument),
I beseech you to consider that, just in proportion as Christian truths are worthy of love and respect, the contrary
errors must deserve hatred and contempt; there being two
things in the truths of our religion—a divine beauty that
renders them lovely, and a sacred majesty that renders them
venerable ; and two things also about errors—an impiety,
that makes them horrible, and an impertinence that renders
them ridiculous.   For these reasons, while the saints have
ever cherished towards the truth the two-fold sentiment of
love and fear—the whole of their wisdom being comprised
between fear, which is its beginning, and love, which is its
end—they have, at the same time, entertained towards error
the two-fold feeling of hatred and contempt, and their zeal
has been at once employed to repel, by force of reasoning,

[1] " Religion, they tell us, ought not to be ridiculed; and they tell us
truth : yet surely the corruptions in it may ; for we are taught by the
tritest maxim in the world, that religion being the best of things, its corruptions are likely to be the worst."   (Swift's Apology for a Tale of a
Tub.)

the malice of the wicked, and to chastise, by the aid of ridicule, their extravagance and folly.

Do not then expect, fathers, to make people believe that
it is unworthy of a Christian to treat error with derision.
Nothing is easier than to convince all who were not aware of
it before, that this practice is perfectly just—that it is common with the fathers of the Church, and that it is sanctioned
by Scripture, by the example of the best of saints, and even
by that of God himself.

Do we not find that God at once hates and despises sinners;
so that even at the hour of death, when their condition is
most sad and deplorable, Divine Wisdom adds mockery to
the vengeance which consigns them to eternal punishment?
" *In interitu vestro ridebo et subsannabo*—I will laugh at your
calamity." The saints, too, influenced by the same feeling,
will join in the derision; for, according to David, when they
witness the punishment of the wicked, "they shall feár, and
yet laugh at it—*videbunt justi et timebunt, et super eum ride-
bunt.*" And Job says: " *Innocens subsannabit eos*—The
innocent shall laugh at them."[1]

It is worthy of remark here, that the very first words
which God addressed to man after his fall, contain, in the
opinion of the fathers, " bitter irony" and mockery. After
Adam had disobeyed his Maker, in the hope, suggested by
the devil, of being like God, it appears from Scripture that
God, as a punishment, subjected him to death; and after
having reduced him to this miserable condition, which was
due to his sin, he taunted him in that state with the following terms of derision: " Behold, the man has become as one
of us!—*Ecce, Adam quasi unus ex nobis!*"—which, according to St. Jerome[2] and the interpreters, is " a grievous and
cutting piece of irony," with which God " stung him to the

[1] Prov. i. 20; Ps. iii. 6; Job xxii. 19. In the first passage, the figure
is evidently what theologians call *anthropopathic*, or speaking of God
after the manner of men, and denotes his total disregard of the wicked
in the day of their calamity.
[2] In most of the editions, it is " St. Chrysostom," but I have followed
that of Nicole.

quick." "Adam," says Rupert, "deserved to be taunted in this manner, and he would be naturally made to feel his folly more acutely by this ironical expression than by a more serious one." St. Victor, after making the same remark, adds, "that this irony was due to his sottish credulity, and that this species of raillery is an act of justice, merited by him against whom it was directed."[1]

Thus you see, fathers, that ridicule is, in some cases, a very appropriate means of reclaiming men from their errors, and that it is accordingly an act of justice, because, as Jeremiah says, "the actions of those that err are worthy of derision, because of their vanity—*vana sunt et risu digna.*" And so far from its being impious to laugh at them, St Augustine holds it to be the effect of divine wisdom : "The wise laugh at the foolish, because they are wise, not after their own wisdom, but after that divine wisdom which shall laugh at the death of the wicked."

The prophets, accordingly, filled with the Spirit of God, have availed themselves of ridicule, as we find from the examples of Daniel and Elias. In short, examples of it are not wanting in the discourses of Jesus Christ himself. St. Augustine remarks that, when he would humble Nicodemus, who deemed himself so expert in his knowledge of the law, "perceiving him to be puffed up with pride, from his rank

---

[1] We may be permitted to question the correctness of this interpretation, and the propriety of introducing it in the present connection. For the former, the fathers, not Pascal, are responsible ; as to the latter, it was certainly superfluous, and not very happy, to have recourse to such an example, to justify the use of ridicule as a weapon against religious follies. Among other writers, the Abbé D'Artigny is very severe against our author on this score, and quotes with approbation the following censure on him : "Is it possible that a man of such genius and erudition could justify the most criminal excesses by such respectable examples ? Not content with making witty old fellows of the prophets and the holy fathers, nothing will serve him but to make us believe that the Almighty himself has furnished us with precedents for the most bitter slanders and pleasantries—an evident proof that there is nothing that an author will not seek to justify when he follows his own passion." (Nouveaux Mémoires D'Artigny, ii. 185.) How solemnly and eloquently will a man write down all such satires, when the jest is pointed against himself and his party ! D'Artigny quotes, within a few pages with evident relish, a bitter satire against a Protestant minister.

as doctor of the Jews, he first beats down his presumption by the magnitude of his demands, and having reduced him so low that he was unable to answer, What! says he, you a master in Israel, and not know these things!—as if he had said, Proud ruler, confess that thou knowest nothing." St. Chrysostom and St. Cyril likewise observe upon this, that "he deserved to be ridiculed in this manner."

You may learn from this, fathers, that should it so happen, in our day, that persons who enact the part of "masters" among Christians, as Nicodemus and the Pharisees did among the Jews, show themselves so ignorant of the first principles of religion as to maintain, for example, that "a man may be saved who never loved God all his life," we only follow the example of Jesus Christ, when we laugh at such a combination of ignorance and conceit.

I am sure, fathers, these sacred examples are sufficient to convince you, that to deride the errors and extravagances of man is not inconsistent with the practice of the saints; otherwise we must blame that of the greatest doctors of the Church, who have been guilty of it—such as St. Jerome, in his letters and writings against Jovinian, Vigilantius, and the Pelagians; Tertullian, in his Apology against the follies of idolaters; St. Augustine against the monks of Africa, whom he styles "the hairy men;" St. Irenæus the Gnostics; St. Bernard and the other fathers of the Church, who, having been the imitators of the apostles, ought to be imitated by the faithful in all time coming; for, say what we will, they are the true models for Christians, even of the present day.

In following such examples, I conceived that I could not go far wrong; and, as I think I have sufficiently established this position, I shall only add, in the admirable words of Tertullian, which give the true explanation of the whole of my proceeding in this matter: "What I have now done is only a little sport before the real combat. I have rather in-dicated the wounds that might be given you, than inflicted any. If the reader has met with passages which have ex-

cited his risibility, he must ascribe this to the subjects themselves. There are many things which deserve to be held up
in this way to ridicule and mockery, lest, by a serious refutation, we should attach a weight to them which they do not
deserve. Nothing is more due to vanity than laughter; and
it is the Truth properly that has a right to laugh, because
she is cheerful, and to make sport of her enemies, because
she is sure of the victory. Care must be taken, indeed, that the
raillery is not too low, and unworthy of the truth; but, keeping this in view, when ridicule may be employed with effect,
it is a duty to avail ourselves of it." Do you not think,
fathers, that this passage is singularly applicable to our subject? The letters which I have hitherto written are " merely
a little sport before a real combat." As yet I have been
only playing with the foils, and "rather indicating the
wounds that might be given you than inflicting any." I have
merely exposed your passages to the light, without making
scarcely a reflection on them. " If the reader has met with
any that have excited his risibility, he must ascribe this to
the subjects themselves." And, indeed, what is more fitted
to raise a laugh, than to see a matter so grave as that of
Christian morality decked out with fancies so grotesque as
those in which you have exhibited it ? One is apt to form
such high anticipations of these maxims, from being told that
" Jesus Christ himself has revealed them to the fathers of
the Society," that when one discovers among them such absurdities as " that a priest receiving money to say mass, may
take additional sums from other persons by giving up to them
his own share in the sacrifice ;" " that a monk is not to be excommunicated for putting off his habit, provided it is to
dance, swindle, or go incognito into infamous houses ;" and
" that the duty of hearing mass may be fulfilled by listening
to four quarters of a mass at once from different priests"—
when, I say, one listens to such decisions as these, the surprise is such that it is impossible to refrain from laughing;
for nothing is more calculated to produce that emotion than
a startling contrast between the thing looked for and the

thing looked at. And why should the greater part of these maxims be treated in any other way? As Tertullian says, "To treat them seriously would be to sanction them." What! is it necessary to bring up all the forces of Scripture and tradition, in order to prove that running a sword through a man's body, covertly and behind his back, is to murder him in treachery? or, that to give one money as a motive to resign a benefice, is to purchase the benefice? Yes, there are things which it is duty to despise, and which "deserve only to be laughed at." In short, the remark of that ancient author, "that nothing is more due to vanity than derision," with what follows, applies to the case before us so justly and so convincingly, as to put it beyond all question that we may laugh at errors without violating propriety.

And let me add, fathers, that this may be done without any breach of charity either, though this is another of the charges you bring against me in your publications. For, according to St. Augustine, "charity may sometimes oblige us to ridicule the errors of men, that they may be induced to laugh at them in their turn, and renounce them—*Hæc tu misericorditer irride, ut eis ridenda ac fugienda commendes.*" And the same charity may also, at other times, bind us to repel them with indignation, according to that other saying of St. Gregory of Nazianzen: "The spirit of meekness and charity hath its emotions and its heats." Indeed, as St. Augustine observes, "who would venture to say that truth ought to stand disarmed against falsehood, or that the enemies of the faith shall be at liberty to frighten the faithful with hard words, and jeer at them with lively sallies of wit; while the Catholics ought never to write except with a coldness of style enough to set the reader asleep?"

Is it not obvious that, by following such a course, a wide door would be opened for the introduction of the most extravagant and pernicious dogmas into the Church; while none would be allowed to treat them with contempt, through fear of being charged with violating propriety, or to confute

them with indignation, from the dread of being taxed with
want of charity?

Indeed, fathers! shall you be allowed to maintain, "that
it is lawful to kill a man to avoid a box on the ear or an
affront," and must nobody be permitted publicly to expose
a public error of such consequence? Shall you be at liberty
to say, "that a judge may in conscience retain a fee received
for an act of injustice," and shall no one be at liberty to
contradict you? Shall you print, with the privilege and approbation of your doctors, "that a man may be saved without ever having loved God;" and will you shut the mouth
of those who defend the true faith, by telling them that they
would violate brotherly love by attacking you, and Christian
modesty by laughing at your maxims? I doubt, fathers, if
there be any persons whom you could make believe this; if,
however, there be any such, who are really persuaded that,
by denouncing your morality, I have been deficient in the
charity which I owe to you, I would have them examine,
with great jealousy, whence this feeling takes its rise within
them. They may imagine that it proceeds from a holy zeal,
which will not allow them to see their neighbor impeached
without being scandalized at it; but I would entreat them
to consider, that it is not impossible that it may flow from
another source, and that it is even extremely likely that it
may spring from that secret, and often self-concealed dissatisfaction, which the unhappy corruption within us seldom
fails to stir up against those who oppose the relaxation of
morals. And to furnish them with a rule which may enable
them to ascertain the real principle from which it proceeds,
I will ask them, if, while they lament the way in which the
religious[1] have been treated, they lament still more the manner in which these religious have treated the truth. If they
are incensed, not only against the letters, but still more
against the maxims quoted in them, I shall grant it to be
barely possible that their resentment proceeds from some

---

[1] "Religious," is a general term, applied in the Romish Church to
all who are in holy orders.

zeal, though not of the most enlightened kind; and, in this case, the passages I have just cited from the fathers will serve to enlighten them. But if they are merely angry at the reprehension, and not at the things reprehended, truly, fathers, I shall never scruple to tell them that they are grossly mistaken, and that their zeal is miserably blind.

Strange zeal, indeed! which gets angry at those that censure public faults, and not at those that commit them! Novel charity this, which groans at seeing error confuted, but feels no grief at seeing morality subverted by that error! If these persons were in danger of being assassinated, pray, would they be offended at one advertising them of the stratagem that had been laid for them; and instead of turning out of their way to avoid it, would they trifle away their time in whining about the little charity manifested in discovering to them the criminal design of the assassins? Do they get waspish when one tells them not to eat such an article of food, because it is poisoned? or not to enter such a city, because it has the plague?

Whence comes it, then, that the same persons who set down a man as wanting in charity, for exposing maxims hurtful to religion, would, on the contrary, think him equally deficient in that grace were he not to disclose matters hurtful to health and life, unless it be from this, that their fondness for life induces them to take in good part every hint that contributes to its preservation, while their indifference to truth leads them, not only to take no share in its defence, but even to view with pain the efforts made for the extirpation of falsehood?

Let them seriously ponder, as in the sight of God, how shameful, and how prejudicial to the Church, is the morality which your casuists are in the habit of propagating; the scandalous and unmeasured license which they are introducing into public manners; the obstinate and violent hardihood with which you support them. And if they do not think it full time to rise against such disorders, their blindness is as much to be pitied as yours, fathers; and you and they have

equal reason to dread that saying of St. Augustine, founded
on the words of Jesus Christ, in the Gospel: "Woe to the
blind leaders! woe to the blind followers!—*Væ cæcis ducen-
tibus! væ cæcis sequentibus!*"

But to lea.re you no room in future, either to create such
impressions on the minds of others, or to harbor them in your
own, I shall tell you, fathers (and I am ashamed I should
have to teach you what I should have rather learnt from
you), the marks which the fathers of the Church have given
for judging when our animadversions flow from a principle
of piety and charity, and when from a spirit of malice and
impiety.

The first of these rules is, that the spirit of piety always
prompts us to speak with sincerity and truthfulness; whereas malice and envy make use of falsehood and calumny.
"*Splendentia et vehementia, sed rebus veris*—Splendid and
vehement in words, but true in things," as St. Augustine
says. The dealer in falsehood is an agent of the devil. No
direction of the intention can sanctify slander; and though
the conversion of the whole earth should depend on it, no
man may warrantably calumniate the innocent: because none
may do the least evil, in order to accomplish the greatest
good; and, as the Scripture says, "the truth of God stands
in no need of our lie." St. Hilary observes, that "it is the
bounden duty of the advocates of truth, to advance nothing
in its support but true things." Now, fathers, I can declare
before God, that there is nothing that I detest more than the
slightest possible deviation from the truth, and that I have ever
taken the greatest care, not only not to falsify (which would be
horrible), but not to alter or wrest, in the slightest possible
degree, the sense of a single passage. So closely have I adhered to this rule, that if I may presume to apply them to
the present case, I may safely say, in the words of the same
St. Hilary: "If we advance things that are false, let our
statements be branded with infamy; but if we can show that
they are public and notorious, it is no breach of apostolic
modesty or liberty to expose them."

It is not enough, however, to tell nothing but the truth; we must not always tell everything that is true; we should publish only those things which it is useful to disclose, and not those which can only hurt, without doing any good. And, therefore, as the first rule is to speak with truth, the second is to speak with discretion. "The wicked," says St. Augustine, "in persecuting the good, blindly follow the dictates of their passion; but the good, in their prosecution of the wicked, are guided by a wise discretion, even as the surgeon warily considers where he is cutting, while the murderer cares not where he strikes." You must be sensible, fathers, that in selecting from the maxims of your authors, I have refrained from quoting those which would have galled you most, though I might have done it, and that without sinning against discretion, as others who were both learned and catholic writers, have done before me. All who have read your authors know how far I have spared you in this respect.[1] Besides, I have taken no notice whatever of what might be brought against individual characters among you; and I would have been extremely sorry to have said a word about secret and personal failings, whatever evidence I might have of them, being persuaded that this is the distinguishing property of malice, and a practice which ought never to be resorted to, unless where it is urgently demanded for the good of the Church. It is obvious, therefore, that in what I have been compelled to advance against your moral maxims, I have been by no means wanting in due consideration : and that you have more reason to congratulate yourself on my moderation than to complain of my indiscretion.

The third rule, fathers, is: That when there is need to employ a little raillery, the spirit of piety will take care to employ it against error only, and not against things holy;

---

[1] "So far," says Nicole, "from his having told all that he might against the Jesuits, he has spared them on points so essential and important, that all who have a complete knowledge of their maxims have admired his moderation." "What would have been the case," asks another writer, "had Pascal exposed the late infamous things put out by their miserable casuists, and unfolded the chain and succession of their regicide authors?" (Dissertation sur la foi due au Pascal, &c., p. 14.)

whereas the spirit of buffoonery, impiety, and heresy, mocks at all that is most sacred. I have already vindicated myself on that score; and indeed there is no great danger of falling into that vice so long as I confine my remarks to the opinions which.I have quoted from your authors.

In short, fathers, to abridge these rules, I shall only mention another, which is the essence and the end of all the rest : That the spirit of charity prompts us to cherish in the heart a desire for the salvation of those against whom we dispute, and to address our prayers to God while we direct our accusations to men. "We ought ever," says St. Augustine, "to preserve charity in the heart, even while we are obliged to pursue a line of external conduct which to man has the appearance of harshness; we ought to smite them with a sharpness, severe but kindly, remembering that their advantage is more to be studied than their gratification." I am sure, fathers, that there is nothing in my letters, from which it can be inferred that I have not cherished such a desire towards you ; and as you can find nothing to the contrary in them, charity obliges you to believe that I have been really actuated by it. It appears, then, that you cannot prove that I have offended against this rule, or against any of the other rules which charity inculcates ; and you have no right to say, therefore, that I have violated it.

But, fathers, if you should now like to have the pleasure of seeing, within a short compass, a course of conduct directly at variance with each of these rules, and bearing the genuine stamp of the spirit of buffoonery, envy, and hatred, I shall give you a few examples of it ; and that they may be of the sort best known and most familiar to you, I shall extract them from your own writings.

To begin, then, with the unworthy manner in which your authors speak of holy things, whether in their sportive and gallant effusions, or in their more serious pieces, do you think that the parcel of ridiculous stories, which your father Binet has introduced into his "Consolation to the Sick," are exactly suitable to his professed object, which is that of im parting Christian consolation to those whom God has chastened with affliction? Will you pretend to say, that the profane, foppish style in which your Father Le Moine has talked of piety in his 'Devotion made Easy," is more fitted to inspire respect than contempt for the picture that he draws of Christian virtue? What else does his whole book of "Moral Pictures" breathe, both in its prose and poetry, but a spirit full of vanity, and the follies of this world? Take, for example, that ode in his seventh book, entitled, "Eulogy on Bashfulness, showing that all beautiful things are red, or inclined to redden." Call you that a production worthy of a priest? The ode is intended to comfort a lady, called Delphina, who was sadly addicted to blushing. Each stanza is devoted to show that certain red things are the best of things, such as roses, pomegranates, the mouth, the tongue; and it is in the midst of this badinage, so disgraceful in a clergyman, that he has the effrontery to introduce those blessed spirits that minister before God, and of whom no Christian should speak without reverence:—

> " The cherubim—those glorious choirs—
> Composed of head and plumes,
> Whom God with his own Spirit inspires,
> And with his eyes illumes.
> These splendid faces, as they fly,
> Are ever red and burning high,
> With fire angelic or divine;
> And while their mutual flames combine,
> The waving of their wings supplies
> A fan to cool their extacies!
> But redness shines with better grace,
> Delphina, on thy beauteous face,
> Where modesty sits revelling—
> Arrayed in purple, like a king," &c.

What think you of this, fathers? Does this preference of the blushes of Delphina to the ardor of those spirits, which is neither more nor less than the ardor of divine love, and this simile of the fan applied to their mysterious wings, strike you as being very Christian-like in the lips which con-

secrate the adorable body of Jesus Christ? I am quite
aware that he speaks only in the character of a gallant, and
to raise a smile; but this is precisely what is called laughing
at things holy. And is it not certain, that, were he to get
full justice, he could not save himself from incurring a censure? although, to shield himself from this, he pleads an
excuse which is hardly less censurable than the offence,
"that the Sorbonne has no jurisdiction over Parnassus, and
that the errors of that land are subject neither to censure nor
the Inquisition;"—as if one could act the blasphemer and
profane fellow only in prose! There is another passage,
however, in the preface, where even this excuse fails him,
when he says, "that the water of the river, on whose banks
he composes his verses, is so apt to make poets, that, though
it were converted into *holy water*, it would not chase away
the demon of poesy." To match this, I may add the following flight of your Father Garasse, in his "Summary of the
Capital Truths in Religion," where, speaking of the sacred
mystery of the incarnation, he mixes up blasphemy and heresy in this fashion: "The human personality was grafted, as
it were, or *set on horseback*, upon the personality of the
Word!"[1] And omitting many others, I might mention another passage from the same author, who, speaking on the
subject of the name of Jesus, ordinarily written thus, ɪ. ʜ̇. s.
observes that "some have taken away the cross from the
top of it, leaving the characters barely thus, I. H. S.—which,"
says he, "is a stripped Jesus!"

Such is the indecency with which you treat the truths of
religion, in the face of the inviolable law which binds us always to speak of them with reverence. But you have sinned
no less flagrantly against the rule which obliges us to speak
of them with truth and discretion. What is more common

---

[1] The apologists of the Jesuits attempted to justify this extraordinary
illustration, by referring to the use which Augustine and other fathers
make of the parable of the good Samaritan who " set on his own beast"
the wounded traveller. But Nicole has shown that fanciful as these
ancient interpreters often were, it is doing them injustice to *father* on
them the absurdity of Father Garasse. (Nicole's Notes iii. 340.)

in your writings than calumny?   Can those of Father Brisacier[1] be called sincere?   Does he speak with truth when
he says, that "the nuns of Port-Royal do not pray to the
saints, and have no images in their church?"   Are not these
most outrageous falsehoods, when the contrary appears before
the eyes of all Paris?   And can he be said to speak with
discretion, when he stabs the fair reputation of these virgins,
who lead a life so pure and austere, representing them as
"impenitent, unsacramentalists, uncommunicants, foolish virgins, visionaries, Calagans, desperate creatures, and anything
you please," loading them with many other slanders, which
have justly incurred the censure of the late Archbishop of
Paris?   or when he calumniates priests of the most irreproachable morals,[2] by asserting "that they practise novelties in
confession, to entrap handsome innocent females, and that he
would be horrified to tell the abominable crimes which they
commit."   Is it not a piece of intolerable assurance, to advance slanders so black and base, not merely without proof,
but without the slightest shadow, or the most distant semblance of truth?   I shall not enlarge on this topic, but defer
it to a future occasion, for I have something more to say to
you about it; but what I have now produced is enough to
show that you have sinned at once against truth and discretion.

But it may be said, perhaps, that you have not offended
against the last rule at least, which binds you to desire the
salvation of those whom you denounce, and that none can
charge you with this, except by unlocking the secrets of
your breasts, which are only known to God.   It is strange,
fathers, but true, nevertheless, that we can convict you even
of this offence; that while your hatred to your opponents
has carried you so far as to wish their eternal perdition, your

---

[1] Brisacier, who became rector of the College of Rouen, was a bitter
enemy of the Port-Royalists.   His defamatory libel against the nuns of
Port-Royal, entitled, "Le Jansenisme Confondu," published in 1651,
was censured by the Archbishop of Paris, and vigorously assailed by
M. Arnauld.
[2] The priests of Port-Royal.

infatuation has driven you to discover the abominable wish; that so far from cherishing in secret desires for their salvation, you have offered up prayers in public for their damnation; and that, after having given utterance to that hideous vow in the city of Caen, to the scandal of the whole Church, you have since then ventured, in Paris, to vindicate, in your printed books, the diabolical transaction. After such gross offences against piety, first ridiculing and speaking lightly of things the most sacred; next falsely and scandalously calumniating priests and virgins; and lastly, forming desires and prayers for their damnation, it would be difficult to add anything worse. I cannot conceive, fathers, how you can fail to be ashamed of yourselves, or how you could have thought for an instant of charging me with a want of charity, who have acted all along with so much truth and moderation, without reflecting on your own horrid violations of charity, manifested in those deplorable exhibitions, which make the charge recoil against yourselves.

In fine, fathers, to conclude with another charge which you bring against me, I see you complain that among the vast number of your maxims which I quote, there are some which have been objected to already, and that I "say over again, what others have said before me." To this I reply, that it is just because you have not profited by what has been said before, that I say it over again. Tell me now what fruit has appeared from all the castigations you have received in all the books written by learned doctors, and even the whole university? What more have your fathers Annat, Caussin, Pintereau, and Le Moine done, in the replies they have put forth, except loading with reproaches those who had given them salutary admonitions? Have you suppressed the books in which these nefarious maxims are taught?[1] Have you

---

[1] This is the real question, which brings the matter to a point, and serves to answer all the evasions of the Jesuits   They boast of their unity as a society, and their blind obedience to their head.   Have they, then, ever, *as a society,* disclaimed these maxims?—have they even, *as such,* condemned the sentiments of their fathers Becan, Mariana, and others, on the duty of dethroning and assassinating heretical kings?

restrained the authors of these maxims? Have you become
more circumspect in regard to them? On the contrary, is
it not the fact, that since that time Escobar has been repeatedly reprinted in France and in the Low Countries, and that
your fathers Cellot, Bagot, Bauny, Lamy, Le Moine, and
others, persist in publishing daily the same maxims over
again, or new ones as licentious as ever? Let us hear no
more complaints, then, fathers, either because I have charged
you with maxims*which you have not disavowed, or because
I have objected to some new ones against you, or because I
have laughed equally at them all. You have only to sit down
and look at them, to see at once your own confusion and my
defence. Who can look without laughing at the decision of
Bauny, respecting the person who employs another to set
fire to his neighbor's barn; that of Cellot on restitution; the
rule of Sanchez in favor of sorcerers; the plan of Hurtado
for avoiding the sin of duelling by taking a walk through a
field, and waiting for a man; the compliments of Bauny for
escaping usury; the way of avoiding simony by a detour of
the intention, and keeping clear of falsehood by speaking high
and low; and such other opinions of your most grave and
reverend doctors? Is there anything more necessary, fathers,
for my vindication? and as Tertullian says, " can anything
be more justly due to the vanity and weakness of these opinions than laughter?" But, fathers, the corruption of manners to which your maxims lead, deserves another sort of
consideration; and it becomes us to ask, with the same ancient writer, " Whether ought we to laugh at their folly, or
deplore their blindness?—*Rideam vanitatem, an exprobrem
cæcitatem?*" My humble opinion is, that one may either
laugh at them or weep over them, as one is in the humor.
Hæc tolerabilius vel ridentur, vel flentur, as St. Augustine
says. The Scripture tells us that "there is a time to laugh,
and a time to weep;" and my hope is, fathers, that I may
not find verified, in your case, these words in the Proverbs:

They have not; and till this is done, they must be held, *as Jesuits*, responsible for the sentiments which they refuse to disavow.

"If a wise man contendeth with a foolish man, whether he rage or laugh, there is no rest."[1]

P. S.—On finishing this letter, there was put in my hands one of your publications, in which you accuse me of falsification, in the case of six of your maxims quoted by me, and also with being in correspondence with heretics. You will shortly receive, I trust, a suitable reply ; after which, fathers, I rather think you will not feel very anxious to continue this species of warfare.[2]

[1] Prov. xxix. 9.
[2] This postscript, which appeared in the earlier editions, is dropt in that of Nicole and others.

LETTER XII.

TO THE REVEREND FATHERS, THE JESUITS.

REFUTATION OF THEIR CHICANERIES REGARDING ALMS-GIVING AND SIMONY.

September 9, 1656.

REVEREND FATHERS,—I was prepared to write you on the subject of the abuse with which you have for some time past been assailing me in your publications, in which you salute me with such epithets as " reprobate," " buffoon," " blockhead," " merry-Andrew," " impostor," " slanderer," " cheat," " heretic," " Calvinist in disguise," " disciple of Du Moulin,"[1] " possessed with a legion of devils," and everything else you can think of. As I should be sorry to have all this believed of me, I was anxious to show the public why you treated me in this manner ; and I had resolved to complain of your cal· umnies and falsifications, when I met with your Answers, in which you bring these same charges against myself. This will compel me to alter my plan ; though it will not prevent me from prosecuting it in some sort, for I hope, while defending myself, to convict you of impostures more genuine than the imaginary ones which you have ascribed to me. Indeed, fathers, the suspicion of foul play is much more sure to rest on you than on me. It is not very likely, standing

---

[1] Pierre du Moulin is termed by Bayle " one of the most celebrated ministers which the Reformed Church in France ever had to boast of." He was born in 1568, and was for some time settled in Paris; but having incurred the resentment of Louis XIII., he retired to Sedan in 1623, where he became a professor in the Protestant University, and died. in the ninetieth year of his age, in 1658, two years after the time when Pascal wrote. Of his numerous writings, few are known in this country, excepting his " Buckler of the Faith," and his " Anatomy of the Mass," which were translated into English. (Quick's Synodicon, ii., 105.)

14*

as I do, alone, without power or any human defence, against
such a large body, and having no support but truth and integrity, that I would expose myself to lose everything, by
laying myself open to be convicted of imposture. It is too
easy to discover falsifications in matters of fact such as the
present. In such a case there would have been no want of
persons to accuse me, nor would justice have been denied
them. With you, fathers, the case is very different; you
may say as much as you please against me, while I may look
in vain for any to complain to. With such a wide difference
between our positions, though there had been no other consideration to restrain me, it became me to study no little
caution. By treating me, however, as a common slanderer,
you compel me to assume the defensive, and you must be
aware that this cannot be done without entering into a fresh
exposition, and even into a fuller disclosure of the points of
your morality. In provoking this discussion, I fear you are
not acting as good politicians. The war must be waged
within your own camp, and at your own expense; and although you imagine that, by embroiling the questions with
scholastic terms, the answers will be so tedious, thorny, and
obscure, that people will lose all relish for the controversy,
this may not, perhaps, turn out to be exactly the case; I
shall use my best endeavors to tax your patience as little as
possible with that sort of writing. Your maxims have something diverting about them, which keeps up the good humor
of people to the last. At all events, remember that it is
you that oblige me to enter upon this *eclaircissement*, and let
us see which of us comes off best in self-defence.

The first of your Impostures, as you call them, is on the
opinion of Vasquez upon alms-giving. To avoid all ambiguity, then, allow me to give a simple explanation of the matter
in dispute. It is well known, fathers, that according to the
mind of the Church, there are two precepts touching alms—
1*st*, "To give out of our superfluity in the case of the ordinary necessities of the poor;" and 2*dly*, "To give even out
of our necessaries, according to our circumstances, in cases

of extreme necessity." Thus says Cajetan, after St. Thomas; so that, to get at the mind of Vasquez on this subject, we must consider the rules he lays down, both in regard to necessaries and superfluities.

With regard to superfluity, which is the most common source of relief to the poor, it is entirely set aside by that single maxim which I have quoted in my Letters : " That what the men of the world keep with the view of improving their own condition and that of their relatives, is not properly superfluity ; so that, such a thing as superfluity is rarely to be met with among men of the world, not even excepting kings." It is very easy to see, fathers, that according to this definition, none can have superfluity, provided they have ambition ; and thus, so far as the greater part of the world is concerned, alms-giving is annihilated. But even though a man should happen to have superfluity, he would be under no obligation, according to Vasquez, to give it away in the case of ordinary necessity ; for he protests against those who would thus bind the rich. Here are his own words: " Corduba," says he, " teaches, that when we have a superfluity we are bound to give out of it in cases of ordinary necessity ; but *this does not please me—sed hoc non placet—*for we have demonstrated the contrary against Cajetan and Navarre." So, fathers, the obligation to this kind of alms is wholly set aside, according to the good pleasure of Vasquez.

With regard to necessaries, out of which we are bound to give in cases of extreme and urgent necessity, it must be obvious, from the conditions by which he has limited the obligation, that the richest man in all Paris may not come within its reach once in a lifetime. I shall only refer to two of these. The first is, That " *we must know* that the poor man cannot be relieved from any other quarter—*hæc intelligo et cætera omnia, quando* scio *nullum alium opem laturum.*" What say you to this, fathers ? Is it likely to happen frequently in Paris, where there are so many charitable people, that I *must know* that there is not another soul but myself to relieve the poor wretch who begs an alms from me ? And yet, according to Vasquez, if I have not ascertained that fact, I may send him away with nothing. The second condition is, That the poor man be reduced to such straits "that he is menaced with some fatal accident, or the ruin of his character"—none of them very common occurrences. But what marks still more the rarity of the cases in which one is bound to give charity, is his remark, in another passage, that the poor man must be so ill off, "that he may conscientiously rob the rich man!" This must surely be a very extraordinary case, unless he will insist that a man may be ordinarily allowed to commit robbery. And so, after having cancelled the obligation to give alms out of our superfluities, he obliges the rich to relieve the poor only in those cases when he would allow the poor to rifle the rich! Such is the doctrine of Vasquez, to whom you refer your readers for their edification!

I now come to your pretended Impostures. You begin by enlarging on the obligation to alms-giving which Vasquez imposes on ecclesiastics. But on this point I have said nothing; and I am prepared to take it up whenever you choose. This, then, has nothing to do with the present question. As for laymen, who are the only persons with whom we have now to do, you are apparently anxious to have it understood that, in the passage which I quoted, Vasquez is giving not his own judgment, but that of Cajetan. But as nothing could be more false than this, and as you have not said it in so many terms, I am willing to believe, for the sake of your character, that you did not intend to say it.

You next loudly complain that, after quoting that maxim of Vasquez, "Such a thing as superfluity is rarely if ever to be met with among men of the world, not excepting kings," *I have inferred* from it, "that the rich are rarely, if ever, bound to give alms out of their superfluity." But what do you mean to say, fathers? If it be true that the rich have almost never superfluity, is it not obvious that they will almost never be bound to give alms out of their superfluity? I might have put it into the form of a syllogism for

you, if Diana, who has such an esteem for Vasquez that he
calls him "the phœnix of genius," had not drawn the same
conclusion from the same premises; for, after quoting the
maxim of Vasquez, he concludes, "that, with regard to the
question, whether the rich are obliged to give alms out of
their superfluity, though the affirmation were true, it would
seldom, or almost never, happen to be obligatory in practice."
I have followed this language word for word. What, then,
are we to make of this, fathers? When Diana quotes with
approbation the sentiments of Vasquez—when he finds them
probable, and "very convenient for rich people," as he says
in the same place, he is no slanderer, no falsifier, and we
hear no complaints of misrepresenting his author ; whereas,
when I cite the same sentiments of Vasquez, though without
holding him up as a phœnix, I am a slanderer, a fabricator,
a corrupter of his maxims. Truly, fathers, you have some
reason to be apprehensive, lest your very different treatment
of those who agree in their representation, and differ only in
their estimate of your doctrine, discover the real secret of
your hearts, and provoke the conclusion, that the main object you have in view is to maintain the credit and glory of
your Company. It appears that, provided your accommodating theology is treated as judicious complaisance, you
never disavow those that publish it, but laud them as con-
tributing to your design ; but let it be held forth as pernicious
laxity, and the same interest of your Society prompts you to
disclaim the maxims which would injure you in public estimation. And thus you recognize or renounce them, not
according to the truth, which never changes, but according
to the shifting exigencies of the times, acting on that motto
of one of the ancients, " *Omnia pro tempore, nihil pro veritate*—Anything for the times, nothing for the truth." Beware of this, fathers ; and that you may never have it in
your power again to say that I drew from the principle of
Vasquez a conclusion which he had disavowed, I beg to inform you that he has drawn it himself: "According to the
opinion of Cajetan, and according to MY OWN—*et secundum*

nostram—(he says, chap. i., no. 27), one is hardly obliged to give alms at all, when one is only obliged to give them out of one's superfluity." Confess then, fathers, on the testimony of Vasquez himself, that I have exactly copied his sentiment; and think how you could have the conscience to say, that "the reader, on consulting the original, would see to his astonishment, that he there teaches the very reverse!"

In fine, you insist, above all, that if Vasquez does not bind the rich to give alms out of their superfluity, he obliges them to atone for this by giving out of the necessaries of life. But you have forgotten to mention the list of conditions which he declares to be essential to constitute that obligation, which I have quoted, and which restrict it in such a way as almost entirely to annihilate it. In place of giving this honest statement of his doctrine, you tell us, in general terms, that he obliges the rich to give even what is necessary to their condition. This is proving too much, fathers; the rule of the Gospel does not go so far; and it would be an error, into which Vasquez is very far, indeed, from having fallen. To cover his laxity, you attribute to him an excess of severity which would be reprehensible; and thus you lose all credit as faithful reporters of his sentiments. But the truth is, Vasquez is quite free from any such suspicion; for he has maintained, as I have shown, that the rich are not bound, either in justice or in charity, to give of their superfluities, and still less of their necessaries, to relieve the ordinary wants of the poor; and that they are not obliged to give of the necessaries, except in cases so rare that they almost never happen.

Having disposed of your objections against me on this head, it only remains to show the falsehood of your assertion, that Vasquez is more severe than Cajetan. This will be very easily done. That cardinal teaches "that we are bound in justice to give alms out of our superfluity, even in the ordinary wants of the poor; because, according to the holy fathers, the rich are merely the dispensers of their superfluity, which they are to give to whom they please, among those who have need of it." And accordingly, unlike Diana,

who says of the maxims of Vasquez, that they will be "very
convenient and agreeable to the rich and their confessors,"
the cardinal, who has no such consolation to afford them, declares that he has nothing to say to the rich but these words
of Jesus Christ : "It is easier for a camel to go through the
eye of a needle, than for a rich man to enter into heaven ;"
and to their confessors : " If the blind lead the blind, both
shall fall into the ditch."[1]   So indispensable did he deem
this obligation !   This, too, is what the fathers and all the
saints have laid down as a certain truth.   "There are two
cases," says St. Thomas, "in which we are bound to give
alms as a matter of justice—*ex debito legali :* one, when the
poor are in danger ; the other, when we possess superfluous
property."   And again : "The three tenths which the Jews
were bound to eat with the poor, have been augmented under
the new law ; for Jesus Christ wills that we give to the poor,
not the tenth only, but the whole of our superfluity."   And
yet it does not seem good to Vasquez that we should be
obliged to give even a fragment of our superfluity ; such is
his complaisance to the rich, such his hardness to the poor,
such his opposition to those feelings of charity which teach
us to relish the truth contained in the following words of
St. Gregory, harsh as it may sound to the rich of this world :
"When we give the poor what is necessary to them, we are
not so much bestowing on them what is our property, as
rendering to them what is their own ; and it may be said to
be an act of justice, rather than a work of mercy."

It is thus that the saints recommend the rich to share with
the poor the good things of this earth, if they would expect
to possess with them the good things of heaven.   While
you make it your business to foster in the breasts of men
that ambition which leaves no superfluity to dispose of, and
that avarice which refuses to part with it, the saints have labored to induce the rich to give up their superfluity, and to
convince them that they would have abundance of it, provided they measured it, not by the standard of covetous-

[1] De Eleemosyna, c. 6.

ness, which knows no bounds to its cravings, but by that of piety, which is ingenious in retrenchments, so as to have wherewith to diffuse itself in the exercise of charity. "We will have a great deal of superfluity," says St. Augustine, "if we keep only what is necessary : but if we seek after vanities, we will never have enough. Seek, brethren, what is sufficient for the work of God"—that is, for nature—"and not for what is sufficient for your covetousness," which is the work of the devil: "and remember that the superfluities of the rich are the necessaries of the poor."

I would fondly trust, fathers, that what I have now said to you may serve, not only for my vindication—that were a small matter—but also to make you feel and detest what is corrupt in the maxims of your casuists, and thus unite us sincerely under the sacred rules of the Gospel, according to which we must all be judged.

As to the second point, which regards simony, before proceeding to answer the charges you have advanced against me, I shall begin by illustrating your doctrine on this subject. Finding yourselves placed in an awkward dilemma, between the canons of the Church, which impose dreadful penalties upon simoniacs, on the one hand, and the avarice of many who pursue this infamous traffic on the other, you have recourse to your ordinary method, which is to yield to men what they desire, and give the Almighty only words and shows. For what else does the simoniac want, but money, in return for his benefice ? And yet this is what you exempt from the charge of simony. And as the name of simony must still remain standing, and a subject to which it may be ascribed, you have substituted, in the place of this, an imaginary idea, which never yet crossed the brain of a simoniac, and would not serve him much though it did—the idea, namely, that simony lies in estimating the money considered in itself as highly as the spiritual gift or office considered in itself. Who would ever take it into his head to compare things so utterly disproportionate and heterogeneous ? And yet, provided this metaphysical comparison be not

drawn, any one may, according to your authors, give away
a benefice, and receive money in return for it, without being
guilty of simony.

Such is the way in which you sport with religion, in order
to gratify the worst passions of men; and yet only see with
what gravity your Father Valentia delivers his rhapsodies in
the passage cited in my letters. He says: " One may give
a spiritual for a temporal good in two ways—first, in the way
of prizing the temporal more than the spiritual, and that
would be simony; secondly, in the way of taking the temporal as the motive and end inducing one to give away the
spiritual, but without prizing the temporal more than the
spiritual, and then it is not simony. And the reason is, that
simony consists in receiving something temporal, as the just
price of what is spiritual. If, therefore, the temporal is
sought—*si petatur temporale*—not as the *price*, but only as
the *motive* determining us to part with the spiritual, it is by
no means simony, even although the possession of the temporal may be principally intended and expected—*minime erit
simonia, etiamsi temporale principaliter intendatur et expecte-
tur.*" Your redoubtable Sanchez has been favored with a
similar revelation; Escobar quotes him thus: " If one give a
spiritual for a temporal good, not as the *price*, but as a *motive* to induce the collator to give it, or as an *acknowledgment*
if the benefice has been actually received, is that simony?
Sanchez assures us that it is not." In your Caen Theses of
1644, you say: " It is a probable opinion, taught by many
Catholics, that it is not simony to exchange a temporal for a
spiritual good, when the former is not given as a price." And
as to Tanner, here is his doctrine, exactly the same with that
of Valentia; and I quote it again to show you how far wrong
it is in you to complain of me for saying that it does not
agree with that of St. Thomas, for he avows it himself in the
very passage which I quoted in my letter: " There is properly and truly no simony," says he, " unless when a temporal
good is taken as the price of a spiritual; but when taken
merely as the motive for giving the spiritual, or as an ac-

knowledgment for having received it, this is not simony, at least in point of conscience." And again : "The same thing may be said although the temporal should be regarded as the principal end, and even preferred to the spiritual ; although St. Thomas and others appear to hold the reverse, inasmuch as they maintain it to be downright simony to exchange a spiritual for a temporal good, when the temporal is the end of the transaction."

Such, then, being your doctrine on simony, as taught by your best authors, who follow each other very closely in this point, it only remains now to reply to your charges of misrepresentation. You have taken no notice of Valentia's opinion, so that his doctrine stands as it was before. But you fix on that of Tanner, maintaining that he has merely decided it to be no simony by divine right ; and you would have it to be believed that, in quoting the passage, I have suppressed these words, *divine right*. This, fathers, is a most unconscionable trick ; for these words, *divine right*, never existed in that passage. You add that Tanner declares it to be simony according to *positive right*. But you are mistaken ; he does not say that generally, but only of particular cases, or, as he expresses it, *in casibus a jure expressis*, by which he makes an exception to the general rule he had laid down in that passage, " that it is not simony in point of conscience," which must imply that it is not so in point of positive right, unless you would have Tanner made so impious as to maintain that simony, in point of positive right, is not simony in point of conscience. But it is easy to see your drift in mustering up such terms as "divine right, positive right, natural right, internal and external tribunal, expressed cases, outward presumption," and others equally little known ; you mean to escape under this obscurity of language, and make us lose sight of your aberrations. But, fathers, you shall not escape by these vain artifices ; for I shall put some questions to you so simple, that they will not admit of coming under your *distinguo*.[1]

---

[1] See before, page 151.

I ask you, then, without speaking of "positive rights," of "outward presumptions," or "external tribunals"—I ask if, according to your authors, a beneficiary would be simoniacal, were he to give a benefice worth four thousand livres of yearly rent, and to receive ten thousand francs ready money, not as the price of the benefice, but merely as a motive inducing him to give it? Answer me plainly, fathers: What must we make of such a case as this according to your authors? Will not Tanner tell us decidedly that "this is not simony in point of conscience, seeing that the temporal good is not the price ' of the benefice, but only the motive inducing to dispose of it?" Will not Valentia, will not your own Theses of Caen, will not Sanchez and Escobar agree in the same decision, and give the same reason for it? Is anything more necessary to exculpate that beneficiary from simony? And, whatever might be your private opinion of the case, durst you deal with that man as a simonist in your confessionals, when he would be entitled to stop your mouth by telling you that he acted according to the advice of so many grave doctors? Confess candidly, then, that, according to your views, that man would be no simonist; and, having done so, defend the doctrine as you best can.

Such, fathers, is the true mode of treating questions, in order to unravel, instead of perplexing them, either by scholastic terms, or, as you have done in your last charge against me here, by altering the state of the question. Tanner, you say, has, at any rate, declared that such an exchange is a great sin; and you blame me for having maliciously suppressed this circumstance, which, you maintain, "*completely justifies him.*" But you are wrong again, and that in more ways than one. For, first, though what you say had been true, it would be nothing to the point, the question in the passage to which I referred being, not if it was *sin,* but if it was *simony.* Now, these are two very different questions. Sin, according to your maxims, obliges only to confession— simony obliges to restitution; and there are people to whom these may appear two very different things   You have found

expedients for making confession a very easy affair ; but you
have not fallen upon ways and means to make restitution an
agreeable one.   Allow me to add, that the case which Tanner charges with sin, is not simply that in which a spiritual
good is exchanged for a temporal, the latter being the principal end in view, but that in which the party "prizes the
temporal above the spiritual," which is the imaginary case
already spoken of.   And it must be allowed he could not go
far wrong in charging such a case as that with sin, since that
man must be either very wicked or very stupid who, when
permitted to exchange the one thing for the other, would not
avoid the sin of the transaction by such a simple process as
that of abstaining from comparing the two things together.
Besides, Valentia, in the place quoted, when treating the
question, if it be sinful to give a spiritual good for a temporal, the latter being the main consideration, and after producing the reasons given for the affirmative, adds, " *Sed hoc
non videtur mihi satis certum*—But this does not appear to
my mind sufficiently certain."

Since that time, however, your father, Erade Bille, professor of cases of conscience at Caen, has decided that there
is no sin at all in the case supposed ; for probable opinions,
you know, are always in the way of advancing to maturity.[1]
This opinion he maintains in his writings of 1644, against
which M. Dupre, doctor and professor at Caen, delivered that
excellent oration, since printed and well known.   For though
this Erade Bille confesses that Valentia's doctrine, adopted
by Father Milhard, and condemned by the Sorbonne, "is
contrary to the common opinion, suspected of simony, and
punishable at law when discovered in practice," he does not
scruple to say that it is a probable opinion, and consequently
sure in point of conscience, and that there is neither simony
nor sin in it.   "It is a probable opinion," he says, "taught
by many Catholic doctors, that there is neither any simony
nor any sin in giving money, or any other temporal thing, for
a benefice, either in the way of acknowledgment, or as a mo-

[1] See before, page 218.

tive, without which it would not be given, provided it is not given as a price equal to the benefice." This is all that could possibly be desired. In fact, according to these maxims of yours, simony would be so exceedingly rare, that we might exempt from this sin even Simon Magus himself, who desired to purchase the Holy Spirit, and is the emblem of those simonists that buy spiritual things ; and Gehazi, who took money for a miracle, and may be regarded as the prototype of the simonists that sell them. There can be no doubt that when Simon, as we read in the Acts, " offered the apostles money, saying, Give me also this power ;" he said nothing about buying or selling, or fixing the price ; he did no more than offer the money as a motive to induce them to give him that spiritual gift ; which being, according to you, no simony at all, he might, had he but been instructed in your maxims, have escaped the anathema of St. Peter. The same unhappy ignorance was a great loss to Gehazi, when he was struck with leprosy by Elisha ; for, as he accepted the money from the prince who had been miraculously cured, simply as an acknowledgment, and not as a price equivalent to the divine virtue which had effected the miracle, he might have insisted on the prophet healing him again on pain of mortal sin ; seeing, on this supposition, he would have acted according to the advice of your grave doctors, who, in such cases, oblige confessors to absolve their penitents, and to wash them from that spiritual leprosy of which the bodily disease is the type.

Seriously, fathers, it would be extremely easy to hold you up to ridicule in this matter, and I am at a loss to know why you expose yourselves to such treatment. To produce this effect, I have nothing more to do than simply to quote Escobar, in his " Practice of Simony according to the Society of Jesus ;" " Is it simony when two Churchmen become mutually pledged thus: Give me your vote for my election as provincial, and I shall give you mine for your election as prior ? By no means." Or take another: " It is not simony to get possession of a benefice by promising a sum of money, when one has no intention of actually paying the money ;

for this is merely making a show of simony, and is as far from being real simony as counterfeit gold is from the genuine." By this quirk of conscience, he has contrived means, in the way of adding swindling to simony, for obtaining benefices without simony and without money.

But I have no time to dwell longer on the subject, for I must say a word or two in reply to your third accusation, which refers to the subject of bankrupts. Nothing can be more gross than the manner in which you have managed this charge. You rail at me as a libeller in reference to a sentiment of Lessius, which I did not quote myself, but took from a passage in Escobar; and therefore, though it were true that Lessius does not hold the opinion ascribed to him by Escobar, what can be more unfair than to charge me with the misrepresentation? When I quote Lessius or others of your authors myself, I am quite prepared to answer for it; but as Escobar has collected the opinions of twenty-four of your writers, I beg to ask, if I am bound to guarantee anything beyond the correctness of my citations from his book? or if I must, in addition, answer for the fidelity of all his quotations of which I may avail myself? This would be hardly reasonable; and yet this is precisely the case in the question before us. I produced in my letter the following passage from Escobar, and you do not object to the fidelity of my translation: "May the bankrupt, with a good conscience, retain as much of his property as is necessary to afford him an honorable maintenance—*ne indecore vivat?* I answer, with Lessius, that he may—*cum Lessio assero posse.*" You tell me that Lessius does not hold that opinion. But just consider for a moment the predicament in which you involve yourselves. If it turns out that he does hold that opinion, you will be set down as impostors for having asserted the contrary; and if it is proved that he does not hold it, Escobar will be the impostor; so it must now of necessity follow, that one or other of the Society will be convicted of imposture. Only think what a scandal! You cannot, it would appear, foresee the consequences of things. You seem to imagine that you have nothing more to do than to cast aspersions upon people, without considering on whom they may recoil. Why did you not acquaint Escobar with your objection before venturing to publish it? He might have given you satisfaction. It is not so very troublesome to get word from Valladolid, where he is living in perfect health, and completing his grand work on Moral Theology, in six volumes, on the first of which I mean to say a few words by-and-by. They have sent him the first ten letters; you might as easily have sent him your objection, and I am sure he would have soon returned you an answer, for he has doubtless seen in Lessius the passage from which he took the *ne indecore vivat*. Read him yourselves, fathers, and you will find it word for word, as I have done. Here it is: "The same thing is apparent from the authorities cited, particularly in regard to that property which he acquires after his failure, out of which even the delinquent debtor may retain as much as is necessary for his honorable maintenance, according to his station of life—*ut non indecore vivat*. Do you ask if this rule applies to goods which he possessed at the time of his failure? Such seems to be the judgment of the doctors."

I shall not stop here to show how Lessius, to sanction his maxim, perverts the law that allows bankrupts nothing more than a mere livelihood, and that makes no provision for "honorable maintenance." It is enough to have vindicated Escobar from such an accusation—it is more, indeed, than what I was in duty bound to do. But you, fathers, have not done your duty. It still remains for you to answer the passage of Escobar, whose decisions, by the way, have this advantage, that being entirely independent of the context, and condensed in little articles, they are not liable to your distinctions. I quoted the whole of the passage, in which "bankrupts are permitted to keep their goods, though unjustly acquired, to provide an honorable maintenance for their families"—commenting on which in my letters, I exclaim: "Indeed, father! by what strange kind of charity would you have the ill-gotten property of a bankrupt appropriated to

his own use, instead of that of his lawful creditors ?"[1]   This
is the question which must be answered ; but it is one that
involves you in a sad dilemma, and from which you in vain
seek to escape by altering the state of the question, and
quoting other passages from Lessius, which have no connection with the subject.   I ask you, then, May this maxim of
Escobar be followed by bankrupts with a safe conscience, or
no ?   And take care what you say.   If you answer, No,
what becomes of your doctor, and your doctrine of probability ?   If you say, Yes—I delate you to the Parliament.[2]

In this predicament I must now leave you, fathers ; for
my limits will not permit me to overtake your next accusation, which respects homicide.   This will serve for my next
letter, and the rest will follow.

In the mean while, I shall make no remarks on the advertisements which you have tagged to the end of each of your
charges, filled as they are with scandalous falsehoods.   I
mean to answer all these in a separate letter, in which I hope
to show the weight due to your calumnies.   I am sorry
fathers, that you should have recourse to such desperate resources.   The abusive terms which you heap on me will not
clear up our disputes, nor will your manifold threats hinder
me from defending myself.   You think you have power and
impunity on your side ; and I think that I have truth and innocence on mine.   It is a strange and tedious war, when violence attempts to vanquish truth.   All the efforts of violence
cannot weaken truth, and only serve to give it fresh vigor.
All the lights of truth cannot arrest violence, and only serve
to exasperate it.   When force meets force, the weaker must
succumb to the stronger ; when argument is opposed to argument, the solid and the convincing triumphs over the
empty and the false ; but violence and verity can make no impression on each other.   Let none suppose, however, that
the two are, therefore, equal to each other ; for there is this

---

[1] See before. p. 177.
[2] "The Parliament of Paris was originally the court of the kings of
France, to which they committed the supreme administration of justice."   (Robertson's Charles V., vol. i. 171.)

vast difference between them, that violence has only a certain course to run, limited by the appointment of Heaven, which overrules its effects to the glory of the truth which it assails; whereas verity endures forever, and eventually triumphs over its enemies, being eternal and almighty as God himself.[1]

[1] In most of the French editions, another letter is inserted after this, being a refutation of a reply which appeared at the time to Letter xii. But as this letter, though well written, was not written by Pascal, and as it does not contain anything that would now be interesting to the reader, we omit it. Suffice it to say, that the reply of the Jesuits consisted, as usual, of the most barefaced attempts to fix the charge of misrepresentation on their opponent, accusing him of omitting to quote passages from his authors which they never wrote, of not answering objections which were never brought against him, of not adverting to cases which neither he nor his authors dreamt of—in short, like all Jesuitical answers, it is anything and everything but a refutation of the charges which have been substantiated against them.

VOL. I.—15

LETTER XIII.

TO THE REVEREND FATHERS OF THE SOCIETY OF JESUS.

THE DOCTRINE OF LESSIUS ON HOMICIDE THE SAME WITH THAT OF VALENTIA—HOW EASY IT IS TO PASS FROM SPECULATION TO PRACTICE—WHY THE JESUITS HAVE RECOURSE TO THIS DIS-TINCTION, AND HOW LITTLE IT SERVES FOR THEIR VINDICATION.

September 30, 1656.

REVEREND FATHERS,—I have just seen your last produc-tion, in which you have continued your list of Impostures up to the twentieth, and intimate that you mean to conclude with this the first part of your accusations against me, and to pro-ceed to the second, in which you are to adopt a new mode of defence, by showing that there are other casuists besides those of your Society who are as lax as yourselves. I now see the precise number of charges to which I have to reply ; and as the fourth, to which we have now come, relates to homicide, it may be proper, in answering it, to include the 11th, 13th, 14th, 15th, 16th, 17th, and 18th, which refer to the same subject.

In the present letter, therefore, my object shall be to vin-dicate the correctness of my quotations from the charges of falsity which you bring against me. But as you have ven-tured, in your pamphlets, to assert that " the sentiments of your authors on murder are agreeable to the decisions of popes and ecclesiastical laws," you will compel me, in my next letter, to confute a statement at once so unfounded and so injurious to the Church. It is of some importance to show that she is innocent of your corruptions, in order that heretics may be prevented from taking advantage of your aberrations, to draw conclusions tending to her dishonor.[1] And thus, viewing on the one hand your pernicious maxims, and on the other the canons of the Church which have uniformly condemned them, people will see, at one glance, what they should shun and what they should follow.

Your fourth charge turns on a maxim relating to murder, which you say I have falsely ascribed to Lessius. It is as follows: "That if a man has received a buffet, he may immediately pursue his enemy, and even return the blow with the sword, not to avenge himself, but to retrieve his honor." This, you say, is the opinion of the casuist Victoria. But this is nothing to the point. There is no inconsistency in saying, that it is at once the opinion of Victoria and of Lessius; for Lessius himself says that it is also held by Navarre and Henriquez, who teach identically the same doctrine. The only question, then, is, if Lessius holds this view as well as his brother casuists. You maintain "that Lessius quotes this opinion solely for the purpose of refuting it, and that I therefore attribute to him a sentiment which he produces only to overthrow—the basest and most disgraceful act of which a writer can be guilty." Now I maintain, fathers, that he quotes the opinion solely for the purpose of supporting it. Here is a question of fact, which it will be very easy to settle. Let us see, then, how you prove your allegation, and you will see afterwards how I prove mine.

To show that Lessius is not of that opinion, you tell us that he condemns the practice of it; and in proof of this, you quote one passage of his (l. 2, c. 9, n. 92), in which he says, in so many words, "I condemn the practice of it." I grant that, on looking for these words, at number 92, to which you refer, they will be found there. But what will people say, fathers, when they discover, at the same time, that he is treating in that place of a question totally different

<hr/>

[1] The Church of Rome has not left those whom she terms heretics so doubtfully to "take advantage" of Jesuitical aberrations. She has done everything in her power to *give* them this advantage. By identifying herself, at various times, with the Jesuits, she has virtually stamped their doctrines with her approbation.

from that of which we are speaking, and that the opinion of
which he there says that he condemns the practice, has no
connection with that now in dispute, but is quite distinct?
And yet to be convinced that this is the fact, we have only
to open the book to which you refer, and there we find the
whole subject in its connection as follows: At number 79 he
treats the question, "If it is lawful to kill for a buffet?" and
at number 80 he finishes this matter without a single word
of condemnation. Having disposed of this question, he opens
a new one at art. 81, namely, "If it is lawful to kill for
slanders?" and it is when speaking of *this* question that he
employs the words you have quoted —"I condemn the practice of it."

Is it not shameful, fathers, that you should venture to produce these words to make it be believed that Lessius condemns
the opinion that it is lawful to kill for a buffet? and that, on
the ground of this single proof, you should chuckle over it,
as you have done, by saying: "Many persons of honor in
Paris have already discovered this notorious falsehood by
consulting Lessius, and have thus ascertained the degree of
credit due to that slanderer?" Indeed! and is it thus that
you abuse the confidence which those persons of honor repose in you? To show them that Lessius does not hold a
certain opinion, you open the book to them at a place where
he is condemning another opinion; and these persons not
having begun to mistrust your good faith, and never thinking
of examining whether the author speaks in that place of the
subject in dispute, you impose on their credulity. I make no
doubt, fathers, that to shelter yourselves from the guilt of
such a scandalous lie, you had recourse to your doctrine of
equivocations; and that, having read the passage *in a loud
voice*, you would say, *in a lower key*, that the author was
speaking there of something else. But I am not so sure
whether this saving clause, which is quite enough to satisfy
your consciences, will be a very satisfactory answer to the
just complaint of those "honorable persons," when they
shall discover that you have hoodwinked them in this style.

FIDELITY OF PASCAL'S DESCRIPTIONS. 341

Take care, then, fathers, to prevent them by all means from seeing my letters; for this is the only method now left you to preserve your credit for a short time longer. This is not the way in which I deal with your writings: I send them to all my friends : I wish everybody to see them. And I verily believe that both of us are in the right for our own interests; for after having published with such parade this fourth Imposture, were it once discovered that you have made it up by foisting in one passage for another, you would be instantly denounced. It will be easily seen, that if you could have found what you wanted in the passage where Lessius treated of this matter, you would not have searched for it elsewhere, and that you had recourse to such a trick only because you could find nothing in that passage favorable to your purpose.

You would have us believe that we may find in Lessius what you assert, " that he does *not* allow that this opinion (that a man may be lawfully killed for a buffet) is probable in theory ;" whereas Lessius distinctly declares, at number 80 : "This opinion, that a man may kill for a buffet, *is* probable in theory." Is not this, word for word, the reverse of your assertion ? And can we sufficiently admire the hardihood with which you have advanced, in set phrase, the very reverse of a matter of fact! To your conclusion, from a fabricated passage, that Lessius was *not* of that opinion, we have only to place Lessius himself, who, in the genuine passage, declares that he *is* of that opinion.

Again, you would have Lessius to say "that he condemns the practice of it ;" and, as I have just observed, there is not in the original a single word of condemnation ; all that he says is : "It appears that it ought not to be EASILY permitted in practice—*In praxi non videtur* FACILE *permittenda.*" Is that, fathers, the language of a man who condemns a maxim ? Would you say that adultery and incest ought not to be *easily permitted* in practice ? Must we not, on the contrary, conclude, that as Lessius says no more than that the practice ought not to be easily permitted, his opinion is, that

it may be permitted sometimes, though rarely? And, as if
he had been anxious to apprize everybody when it might be
permitted, and to relieve those who have received affronts
from being troubled with unreasonable scruples, from not
knowing on what occasions they might lawfully kill in practice, he has been at pains to inform them what they ought to
avoid in order to practise the doctrine with a safe conscience.
Mark his words: "It seems," says he, "that it ought not to
be easily permitted, *because* of the danger that persons may
act in this matter out of hatred or revenge, or with excess, or
that this may occasion too many murders." From this it
appears that murder is freely permitted by Lessius, if one
avoids the inconveniences referred to—in other words, if one
can act without hatred or revenge, and in circumstances that
may not open the door to a great many murders. To illustrate the matter, I may give you an example of recent occurrence—the case of the buffet of Compiègne.[1] You will grant
that the person who received the blow on that occasion has
shown by the way in which he has acted, that he was sufficiently master of the passions of hatred and revenge. It
only remained for him, therefore, to see that he did not give
occasion to too many murders; and you need hardly be told,
fathers, it is such a rare spectacle to find Jesuits bestowing
buffets on the officers of the royal household, that he had no
great reason to fear that a murder committed on this occasion would be likely to draw many others in its train. You
cannot, accordingly, deny that the Jesuit who figured on
that occasion was *killable* with a safe conscience, and that the
offended party might have converted him into a practical
illustration of the doctrine of Lessius. And very likely, fathers, this might have been the result had he been educated
in your school, and learnt from Escobar that the man who

[1] The reference here is to an affray which made a considerable noise
at the time, between Father Borin, a Jesuit, and M. Guille, one of the
officers of the royal kitchen, in the College of Compiègne. A quarrel
having taken place, the enraged Jesuit struck the royal cook in the face
while he was in the act of preparing dinner, by his majesty's order, for
Christina, queen of Sweden, in honor, perhaps, of her conversion to
the Romish faith. (Nicole, iv. 37.)

has received a buffet is held to be disgraced until he has taken the life of him who insulted him. But there is ground to believe, that the very different instructions which he re ceived from a curate, who is no great favorite of yours, have contributed not a little in this case to save the life of a Jesuit.

Tell us no more, then, of inconveniences which may, in many instances, be so easily got over, and in the absence of which, according to Lessius, murder is permissible even in practice. This is frankly avowed by your authors, as quoted by Escobar, in his " Practice of Homicide, according to your Society." " Is it allowable," asks this casuist, " to kill him who has given me a buffet ? Lessius says it is permissible in speculation, though not to be followed in practice—*non consulendum in praxi*—on account of the risk of hatred, or of murders prejudicial to the State. Others, however, have judged that, BY AVOIDING THESE INCONVENIENCES, THIS IS PERMISSIBLE AND SAFE IN PRACTICE—*in praxi probabilem et tutam judicarunt Henriquez,"* &c. See how your opinions mount up, by little and little, to the climax of probabilism ! The present one you have at last elevated to this position; by permitting murder without any distinction between speculation and practice, in the following terms : " It is lawful, when one has received a buffet, to return the blow immediately with the sword, not to avenge one's self, but to preserve one's honor." Such is the decision of your fathers of Caen in 1644, embodied in their publications produced by the university before parliament, when they presented their third remonstrance against your doctrine of homicide, as shown in the book then emitted by them, at page 339.

Mark, then, fathers, that your own authors have themselves demolished this absurd distinction between speculative and practical murder—a distinction which the university treated with ridicule, and the invention of which is a secret of your policy, which it may now be worth while to explain. The knowledge of it, besides being necessary to the right understanding of your 15th, 16th, 17th, and 18th charges, is well calculated, in general, to open up, by little and little, the principles of that mysterious policy.

In attempting, as you have done, to decide cases of conscience in the most agreeable and accommodating manner, while you met with some questions in which religion alone was concerned—such as those of contrition, penance, love to God, and others only affecting the inner court of conscience —you encountered another class of cases in which civil society was interested as well as religion—such as those relating to usury, bankruptcy, homicide, and the like. And it is truly distressing to all that love the Church, to observe that, in a vast number of instances, in which you had only Religion to contend with, you have violated her laws without reservation, without distinction, and without compunction; because you knew that it is not here that God visibly administers his justice. But in those cases in which the State is interested as well as Religion, your apprehension of man's justice has induced you to divide your decisions into two shares. To the first of these you give the name of *speculation;* under which category crimes, considered in themselves, without regard to society, but merely to the law of God, you have permitted, without the least scruple, and in the way of trampling on the divine law which condemns them. The second you rank under the denomination of *practice;* and here, considering the injury which may be done to society, and the presence of magistrates who look after the public peace, you take care, in order to keep yourselves on the safe side of the law, not to approve always in practice the murders and other crimes which you have sanctioned in speculation. Thus, for example, on the question, " If it be lawful to kill for slanders ?" your authors, Filiutius, Reginald, and others, reply : " This is permitted in speculation—*ex probabile opinione licet ;* but is not to be approved in *practice,* on account of the great number of murders which might ensue, and which might injure the State, if all slanderers were to be killed, *and also because one might be punished in a court of justice for having killed another for that matter."* Such is the style in which

your opinions begin to develop th·mselves, under the shelter of this distinction, in virtue of which, without doing any sensible injury to society, you only ruin religion. In acting thus, you consider yourselves quite safe. You suppose that, on the one hand, the influence you have in the Church will effectually shield from punishment your assaults on truth; and that, on the other, the precautions you have taken against too easily reducing your permissions to practice will save you on the part of the civil powers, who, not being judges in cases of conscience, are properly concerned only with the outward practice. Thus an opinion which would be condemned under the name of practice, comes out quite safe under the name of speculation. But this basis once established, it is not difficult to erect on it the rest of your maxims. There is an infinite distance between God's prohibition of murder, and your speculative permission of the crime ; but between that permission and the practice the distance is very small indeed. It only remains to show, that what is allowable in speculation is also so in practice ; and there can be no want of reasons for this. You have contrived to find them in far more difficult cases. Would you like to see, fathers, how this may be managed ? I refer you to the reasoning of Escobar, who has distinctly decided the point in the first of the six volumes of his grand Moral Theology, of which I have already spoken—a work in which he shows quite another spirit from that which appears in his former compilation from your four-and-twenty elders. At that time he thought that there might be opinions probable in speculation, which might not be safe in practice ; but he has now come to form an opposite judgment, and has, in this, his latest work, confirmed it. Such is the wonderful growth attained by the doctrine of probability in general, as well as by every probable opinion in particular, in the course of time. Attend, then, to what he says : "I cannot see how it can be that an action which seems allowable in speculation should not be so likewise in practice ; because what may be done in practice depends on what is found to be lawful in speculation, and the things
15*

differ from each other only as cause and effect. Speculation
is that which determines to action. WHENCE IT FOLLOWS
THAT OPINIONS PROBABLE IN SPECULATION MAY BE FOLLOWED
WITH A SAFE CONSCIENCE IN PRACTICE, and that even with
more safety than those which have not been so well examined
as matters of speculation."[1]

Verily, fathers, your friend Escobar reasons uncommonly
well sometimes ; and, in point of fact, there is such a close
connection between speculation and practice, that when the
former has once taken root, you have no difficulty in permitting the latter, without any disguise. A good illustration
of this we have in the permission " to kill for a buffet," which,
from being a point of simple speculation, was boldly raised
by Lessius into a practice " which ought not easily to be allowed ;" from that promoted by Escobar to the character of
" an easy practice ;" and from thence elevated by your fathers
of Caen, as we have seen, without any distinction between
theory and practice, into a full permission. Thus you bring
your opinions to their full growth very gradually. Were
they presented all at once in their finished extravagance,
they would beget horror ; but this slow imperceptible progress gradually habituates men to the sight of them, and
hides their offensiveness. And in this way the permission
to murder, in itself so odious both to Church and State, creeps
first into the Church, and then from the Church into the
State.

A similar success has attended the opinion of " killing for
slander," which has now reached the climax of a permission
without any distinction. I should not have stopped to quote
my authorities on this point from your writings, had it not
been necessary in order to put down the effrontery with
which you have asserted, twice over, in your fifteenth Imposture, " that there never was a Jesuit who permitted killing
for slander." Before making this statement, fathers, you
should have taken care to prevent it from coming under my
notice, seeing that it is so easy for me to answer it. For,

[1] In Prælog., n. 15.

not to mention that your fathers Reginald, Filiutius, and others, have permitted it in speculation, as I have already shown, and that the principle laid down by Escobar leads us safely on to the practice, I have to tell you that you have authors who have permitted it in so many words, and among others Father Hereau in his public lectures, on the conclusion of which the king put him under arrest in your house, for having taught, among other errors, that when a person who has slandered us in the presence of men of honor, continues to do so after being warned to desist, it is allowable to kill him, not publicly, indeed, for fear of scandal, but IN A PRIVATE WAY—*sed clam.*

I have had occasion already to mention Father Lamy, and you do not need to be informed that his doctrine on this subject was censured in 1649 by the University of Louvain.[1] And yet two months have not elapsed since your Father Des Bois maintained this very censured doctrine of Father Lamy, and taught that "it was allowable for a monk to defend the honor which he acquired by his virtue, EVEN BY KILLING the person who assails his reputation—*etiam cum morte invasoris ;*" which has raised such a scandal in that town, that the whole of the curés united to impose silence on him, and to oblige him, by a canonical process, to retract his doctrine. The case is now pending in the Episcopal court.

What say you now, fathers ? Why attempt, after that, to maintain that "no Jesuit ever held that it was lawful to kill for slander?" Is anything more necessary to convince you of this than the very opinions of your fathers which you quote, since they do not condemn murder in speculation, but only in practice, and that, too, "on account of the injury that might thereby accrue to the State ?" And here I would

[1] The doctrines advanced by Lamy are too gross for repetition. Suffice it to say, that they sanctioned the murder not only of the slanderer, but of the person who might tell tales against a religious order, of one who might stand in the way of another enjoying a legacy or a benefice, and even of one whom a priest might have robbed of her honor, if she threatened to rob him of his. These horrid maxims were condemned by civil tribunals and theological faculties ; but the Jesuits persisted in justifying them. (Nicole, Notes, iv. 41, &c.)

just beg to ask, whether the whole matter in dispute between
us is not simply and solely to ascertain if you have or have
not subverted the law of God which condemns murder?   The
point in question is, not whether you have injured the commonwealth, but whether you have injured religion.   What
purpose, then, can it serve, in a dispute of this kind, to show
that you have spared the State, when you make it apparent,
at the same time, that you have destroyed the faith?   Is
this not evident from your saying that the meaning of Reginald, on the question of killing for slanders, is, " that a private individual has a right to employ that mode of defence,
viewing it simply *in itself?*"   I desire nothing beyond this
concession to confute you.   " A private individual," you say,
" has a right to employ that mode of defence" (that is, killing for slanders), " viewing the thing in itself;" and, consequently, fathers, the law of God, which forbids us to kill, is
nullified by that decision.

It serves no purpose to add, as you have done, " that such
a mode is unlawful and criminal, even according to the law
of God, on account of the murders and disorders which
would follow in society, because the law of God obliges us
to have regard to the good of society." This is to evade
the question : for there are two laws to be observed—one
forbidding us to kill, and another forbidding us to harm society.   Reginald has not perhaps, broken the law which forbids us to do harm to society ; but he has most certainly
violated that which forbids us to kill.   Now this is the only
point with which we have to do.   I might have shown, besides, that your other writers, who have permitted these
murders in practice, have subverted the one law as well as
the other.   But, to proceed, we have seen that you *sometimes*
forbid doing harm to the State ; and you allege that your
design in that is to fulfil the law of God, which obliges us to
consult the interests of society.   That may be true, though
it is far from being certain, as you might do the same thing
purely from fear of the civil magistrate.   With your per-

mission, then, we shall scrutinize the real secret of this movement.

Is it not certain, fathers, that if you had really any regard
to God, and if the observance of his law had been the prime
and principal object in your thoughts, this respect would
have invariably predominated in all your leading decisions,
and would have engaged you at all times on the side of religion? But if it turns out, on the contrary, that you violate,
in innumerable instances, the most sacred commands that
God has laid upon men, and that, as in the instances before
us, you annihilate the law of God, which forbids these actions as criminal in themselves, and that you only scruple to
approve of them in practice, from bodily fear of the civil
magistrate, do you not afford us ground to conclude that you
have no respect to God in your apprehensions, and that if
you yield an apparent obedience to his law, in so far as regards the obligation to do no harm to the State, this is not
done out of any regard to the law itself, but to compass
your own ends, as has ever been the way with politicians of
no religion?

What, fathers! will you tell us that, looking simply to the
law of God, which says, "Thou shalt not kill," we have a
right to kill for slanders? And after having thus trampled
on the eternal law of God, do you imagine that you atone
for the scandal you have caused, and can persuade us of your
reverence for him, by adding that you prohibit the practice
for State reasons, and from dread of the civil arm? Is not
this, on the contrary, to raise a fresh scandal?—I mean not
by the respect which you testify for the magistrate; that is
not my charge against you, and it is ridiculous in you to ban-
ter, as you have done, on this matter. I blame you, not for
fearing the magistrate, but for fearing none but the magistrate. And I blame you for this, because it is making God
less the enemy of vice than man. Had you said that to kill
for slander was allowable according to men, but not according to God, that might have been something more endurable;
but when you maintain, that what is too criminal to be tol-

erated among men, may yet be innocent and right in the eyes
of that Being who is righteousness itself, what is this but to
declare before the whole world, by a subversion of principle
as shocking in itself as it is alien to the spirit of the saints,
that while you can be braggarts before God, you are cowards
before men ?

Had you really been anxious to condemn these homicides
you would have allowed the commandment of God which
forbids them to remain intact ; and had you dared at once to
permit them, you would have permitted them openly, in spite
of the laws of God and men. But your object being to permit them imperceptibly, and to cheat the magistrate, who
watches over the public safety, you have gone craftily to
work. You separate your maxims into two portions. On
the one side, you hold out "that it is lawful in speculation to
kill a man for slander ;"—and nobody thinks of hindering
you from taking a speculative view of matters. On the other
side, you come out with this detached axiom, "that what is
permitted in speculation is also permissible in practice ;"—
and what concern does society seem to have in this general
and metaphysical-looking proposition ? And thus these two
principles, so little suspected, being embraced in their separate form, the vigilance of the magistrate is eluded ; while
it is only necessary to combine the two together, to draw
from them the conclusion which you aim at—namely, that
it is lawful in practice to put a man to death for a simple
slander.

It is, indeed, fathers, one of the most subtle tricks of your
policy, to scatter through your publications the maxims
which you club together in your decisions. It is partly in
this way that you establish your doctrine of probabilities,
which I have frequently had occasion to explain. That general principle once established, you advance propositions
harmless enough when viewed apart, but which, when taken
in connection with that pernicious dogma, become positively
horrible. An example of this, which demands an answer,
may be found in the 11th page of your " Impostures," where

you allege that "several famous theologians have decided that it is lawful to kill a man for a box on the ear." Now, it is certain, that if that had been said by a person who did not hold probabilism, there would be nothing to find fault with in it; it would in this case amount to no more than a harmless statement, and nothing could be elicited from it. But you, fathers, and all who hold that dangerous tenet, "that whatever has been approved by celebrated authors is probable and safe in conscience," when *you* add to this "that several celebrated authors are of opinion that it is lawful to kill a man for a box on the ear," what is this but to put a dagger into the hand of all Christians, for the purpose of plunging it into the heart of the first person that insults them, and to assure them that, having the judgment of so many grave authors on their side, they may do so with a perfectly safe conscience ?

What monstrous species of language is this, which, in announcing that certain authors hold a detestable opinion, is at the same time giving a decision in favor of that opinion—which solemnly teaches whatever it simply tells ! We have learnt, fathers, to understand this peculiar dialect of the Jesuitical school; and it is astonishing that you have the hardihood to speak it out so freely, for it betrays your sentiments somewhat too broadly. It convicts you of permitting murder for a buffet, as often as you repeat that many celebrated authors have maintained that opinion.

This charge, fathers, you will never be able to repel; nor will you be much helped out by those passages from Vasquez and Suarez that you adduce against me, in which they condemn the murders which their associates have approved. These testimonies, disjoined from the rest of your doctrine, may hoodwink those who know little about it ; but we, who know better, put your principles and maxims together. You say, then, that Vasquez condemns murders ; but what say you on the other side of the question, my reverend fathers ? Why, "that the probability of one sentiment does not hinder the probability of the opposite sentiment; and that it is warrantable to follow the less probable and less safe opinion, giving up the more probable and more safe one." What follows from all this taken in connection, but that we have perfect freedom of conscience to adopt any one of these conflicting judgments which pleases us best? And what becomes of all the effect which you fondly anticipate from your quotations? It evaporates in smoke, for we have no more to do than to conjoin for your condemnation the maxims which you have disjoined for your exculpation. Why, then, produce those passages of your authors which I have not quoted, to qualify those which I have quoted, as if the one could excuse the other? What right does that give you to call me an "impostor?" Have I said that all your fathers are implicated in the same corruptions? Have I not, on the contrary, been at pains to show that your interest lay in having them of all different minds, in order to suit all your purposes? Do you wish to kill your man?—here is Lessius for you. Are you inclined to spare him?—here is Vasquez. Nobody need go away in ill humor—nobody without the authority of a grave doctor. Lessius will talk to you like a Heathen on homicide, and like a Christian, it may be, on charity. Vasquez, again, will descant like a Heathen on charity, and like a Christian on homicide. But by means of probabilism, which is held both by Vasquez and Lessius, and which renders all your opinions common property, they will lend their opinions to one another, and each will be held bound to absolve those who have acted according to opinions which each of them has condemned. It is this very variety, then, that confounds you. Uniformity, even in evil, would be better than this. Nothing is more contrary to the orders of St. Ignatius[1] and the first generals of your Society, than

[1] It is very sad to see Pascal reduced to the necessity of saluting the founder of the sect which he held up to the scorn of the world, as *Saint Ignatius!* Ignatius Loyola was a native of Spain, and born in 1491. At first a soldier of fortune, he was disabled from service by a wound in the leg at the siege of Pampeluna, and his brain having become heated by reading romances and legendary tales, he took it into his head to become the Don Quixote of the Virgin, and wage war against all heretics and infidels By indomitable perseverance he succeeded in estab-

this confused medley of all sorts of opinions, good and bad. I may, perhaps, enter on this topic at some future period ; and it will astonish many to see how far you have degenerated from the original spirit of your institution, and that your own generals have foreseen that the corruption of your doctrine on morals might prove fatal, not only to your Society, but to the Church universal.[1]

Meanwhile, I repeat that you can derive no advantage from the doctrine of Vasquez. It would be strange, indeed, if, out of all the Jesuits that have written on morals, one or two could not be found who may have hit upon a truth which has been confessed by all Christians. There is no glory in maintaining the truth, according to the Gospel, that it is unlawful to kill a man for smiting us on the face ; but it is foul shame to deny it. So far, indeed, from justifying you, nothing tells more fatally against you than the fact that, having doctors among you who have told you the truth, you abide not in the truth, but love the darkness rather than the light. You have been taught by Vasquez that it is a heathen, and not a Christian, opinion to hold that we may knock down a man for a blow on the cheek ; and that it is subversive both of the Gospel and of the decalogue to say that we may kill for such a matter. The most profligate of men will acknowledge as much. And yet you have allowed Lessius, Escobar, and others, to decide, in the face of these well-known truths, and in

lishing the sect calling itself "the Society of Jesus." This ignorant fanatic. who, in more enlightened times, would have been consigned to a mad-house, was beatified by one pope, and canonized, or put into the list of saints, by another! Jansenius, in his correspondence with St. Cyran, indignantly complains of pope Gregory XV. for having canonized Ignatius and Xavier. (Leydecker, Hist. Jansen. 23.)

[1] This is rather a singular fact. and applies only to one of the Society's generals, viz., Vitelleschi, who. in a circular letter, addressed, January 1617, to the Company, much to his own honor, strongly recommended a purer morality, and denounced probabilism. But, says Nicole, the Jesuits did not profit by his good advice. (Nicole, iv., p. 33.) It is true, however, that the Jesuits, during this century, had lost sight of the original design of their order. and of all the ascetic rules of their founders Ignatius and Aquaviva. "The spirit which once animated them had fallen before the temptations of the world, and their sole endeavor now was to make themselves necessary to mankind, let the means be what they might." (Ranke's Hist. of the Popes, iii. 139.)

spite of all the laws of God against manslaughter, that it is quite allowable to kill a man for a buffet!

What purpose, then, can it serve to set this passage of Vasquez over against the sentiment of Lessius, unless you mean to show that, in the opinion of Vasquez, Lessius is a "heathen" and a "profligate?" and that, fathers, is more than I durst have said myself. What else can be deduced from it than that Lessius "subverts both the Gospel and the decalogue;" that, at the last day, Vasquez will condemn Lessius on this point, as Lessius will condemn Vasquez on another; and that all your fathers will rise up in judgment one against another, mutually condemning each other for their sad outrages on the law of Jesus Christ?

To this conclusion, then, reverend fathers, must we come at length, that as your probabilism renders the good opinions of some of your authors useless to the Church, and useful only to your policy, they merely serve to betray, by their contrariety, the duplicity of your hearts. This you have completely unfolded, by telling us, on the one hand, that Vasquez and Suarez are against homicide, and on the other hand, that many celebrated authors are for homicide; thus presenting two roads to our choice, and destroying the simplicity of the Spirit of God, who denounces his anathema on the deceitful and the double-hearted: " *Væ duplici corde, et ingredienti duabus viis!*—Woe be to the double hearts, and the sinner that goeth two ways!"[1]

---

[1] Ecclesiasticus (Apocrypha), ii. 12

LETTER XIV.

TO THE REVEREND FATHERS, THE JESUITS.

IN WHICH THE MAXIMS OF THE JESUITS ON MURDER ARE REFUTED FROM THE FATHERS—SOME OF THEIR CALUMNIES ANSWERED BY THE WAY—AND THEIR DOCTRINE COMPARED WITH THE FORMS OBSERVED IN CRIMINAL TRIALS.

October 23, 1656.

REVEREND FATHERS,—If I had merely to reply to the three remaining charges on the subject of homicide, there would be no need for a long discourse, and you will see them refuted presently in a few words ; but as I think it of much more importance to inspire the public with a horror at your opinions on this subject, than to justify the fidelity of my quotations, I shall be obliged to devote the greater part of this letter to the refutation of your maxims, to show you how far you have departed from the sentiments of the Church, and even of nature itself. The permissions of murder, which you have granted in such a variety of cases, render it very apparent, that you have so far forgotten the law of God, and quenched the light of nature, as to require to be remanded to the simplest principles of religion and of common sense.

What can be a plainer dictate of nature than that "no private individual has a right to take away the life of another?" "So well are we taught this of ourselves," says St. Chrysostom, "that God, in giving the commandment not to kill, did not add as a reason that homicide was an evil; because," says that father, "the law supposes that nature has taught us that truth already." Accordingly, this commandment has been binding on men in all ages. The Gospel has confirmed the requirement of the law; and the decalogue only

renewed the command which man had received from God
before the law, in the person of Noah, from whom all men
are descended. On that renovation of the world, God said
to the patriarch: "At the hand of man, and at the hand of
every man's brother, will I require the life of man. Whoso
sheddeth man's blood, by man shall his blood be shed; for
man is made in the image of God." (Gen. ix. 5, 6.) This
general prohibition deprives man of all power over the life
of man. And so exclusively has the Almighty reserved this
prerogative in his own hand, that, in accordance with Christianity, which is at utter variance with the false maxims of
Paganism, man has no power even over his own life. But, as
it has seemed good to his providence to take human society
under his protection, and to punish the evil-doers that give it
disturbance, he has himself established laws for depriving
criminals of life; and thus those executions which, without
his sanction, would be punishable outrages, become, by virtue of his authority, which is the rule of justice, praiseworthy
penalties. St. Augustine takes an admirable view of this
subject. "God," he says, "has himself qualified this general prohibition against manslaughter, both by the laws which
he has instituted for the capital punishment of malefactors,
and by the special orders which he has sometimes issued to
put to death certain individuals. And when death is inflicted
in such cases, it is not man that kills, but God, of whom man
may be considered as only the instrument, in the same way
as a sword in the hand of him that wields it. But, these
instances excepted, whosoever kills incurs the guilt of murder."[1]

It appears, then, fathers, that the right of taking away the
life of man is the sole prerogative of God, and that having
ordained laws for executing death on criminals, he has depu-
ted kings or commonwealths as the depositaries of that power
—a truth which St. Paul teaches us, when, speaking of the
right which sovereigns possess over the lives of their subjects, he deduces it from Heaven in these words: "He bear-

[1] City of God, book i. ch. 28.

eth not the sword in vain ; for he is the minister of God to execute wrath upon .him that doeth evil." (Rom. xiii. 4.) But as it is God who has put this power into their hands, so he requires them to exercise it in the same manner as he does himself ; in other words, with perfect justice ; according to what St. Paul observes in the same passage : " Rulers are not a terror to good works, but to the evil.   Wilt thou, then, not be afraid of the power ?   Do that which is good : for he is the minister of God to thee for good."   And this restriction, so far from lowering their prerogative, exalts it, on the contrary, more than ever ; for it is thus assimilated to that of God, who has no power to do evil, but is all-powerful to do good ; and it is thus distinguished from that of devils, who are impotent in that which is good, and powerful only for evil.   There is this difference only to be observed betwixt the King of Heaven and earthly sovereigns, that God, being justice and wisdom itself, may inflict death instantaneously on whomsoever and in whatsoever manner he pleases ; for, besides his being the sovereign Lord of human life, it is certain that he never takes it away either without cause or without judgment, because he is as incapable of injustice as he is of error.   Earthly potentates, however, are not at liberty to act in this manner ; for, though the ministers of God, still they are but men, and not gods.   They may be misguided by evil counsels, irritated by false suspicions, transported by passion, and hence they find themselves obliged to have recourse, in their turn also, to human agency, and appoint magistrates in their dominions, to whom they delegate their power, that the authority which God has bestowed on them may be employed solely for the purpose for which they received it.

I hope you understand, then, fathers, that to avoid the crime of murder, we must act at once by the authority of God, and according to the justice of God ; and that when these two conditions are not united, sin is contracted ; whether it be by taking away life with his authority, but without his justice ; or by taking it away with justice, but without his authority.   From this indispensable connection it follows, according to St. Augustine, "that he who, without proper authority, kills a criminal, becomes a criminal himself, chiefly for this reason, that he usurps an authority which God has not given him ;" and on the other hand, magistrates, though they possess this authority, are nevertheless chargeable with murder, if, contrary to the laws which they are bound to follow, they inflict death on an innocent man.

Such are the principles of public safety and tranquillity which have been admitted at all times and in all places, and on the basis of which all legislators, sacred and profane, from the beginning of the world, have founded their laws. Even Heathens have never ventured to make an exception to this rule, unless in cases where there was no other way of escaping the loss of chastity or life, when they conceived, as Cicero tells us, "that the law itself seemed to put its weapons into the hands of those who were placed in such an emergency."

But with this single exception, which has nothing to do with my present purpose, that such a law was ever enacted, authorizing or tolerating, as you have done, the practice of putting a man to death, to atone for an insult, or to avoid the loss of honor or property, where life is not in danger at the same time; that, fathers, is what I deny was ever done, even by infidels. They have, on the contrary, most expressly forbidden the practice. The law of the Twelve Tables of Rome bore, "that it is unlawful to kill a robber in the day-time, when he does not defend himself with arms ;" which, indeed, had been prohibited long before in the 22d chapter of Exodus. And the law *Furem*, in the *Lex Cornelia*, which is borrowed from Ulpian, forbids the killing of robbers even by night, if they do not put us in danger of our lives.[1]

Tell us now, fathers, what authority you have to permit what all laws, human as well as divine, have forbidden ; and who gave Lessius a right to use the following language ? " The book of Exodus forbids the killing of thieves by day, when they do not employ arms in their defence ; and in a

[1] See Cujas, tit. dig. de just. et jur. ad l. 3.

court of justice, punishment is inflicted on those who kill
under these circumstances. *In conscience*, however, no blame
can be attached to this practice, when a person is not sure
of being able otherwise to recover his stolen goods, or entertains a doubt on the subject, as Sotus expresses it; for he is
not obliged to run the risk of losing any part of his property
merely to save the life of a robber. The same privilege extends even to clergymen."[1] Such extraordinary assurance!
The law of Moses punishes those who kill a thief when he
does not threaten our lives, and the law of the Gospel, according to you, will absolve them! What, fathers! has
Jesus Christ come to destroy the law, and not to fulfil it?
"The civil judge," says Lessius, " would inflict punishment
on those who should kill under such circumstances; but no
blame can be attached to the deed in conscience." Must we
conclude, then, that the morality of Jesus Christ is more
sanguinary, and less the enemy of murder, than that of
Pagans, from whom our judges have borrowed their civil
laws which condemn that crime? Do Christians make more
account of the good things of this earth, and less account of
human life, than infidels and idolaters? On what principle
do you proceed, fathers? Assuredly not upon any law that
ever was enacted either by God or man—on nothing, indeed,
but this extraordinary reasoning: " 'The laws,'" say you, " permit us to defend ourselves against robbers, and to repel force
by force; self-defence, therefore, being permitted, it follows
that murder, without which self-defence is often impracticable, may be considered as permitted also."

It is false, fathers, that because self-defence is allowed,
murder may be allowed also. This barbarous method of
self-vindication lies at the root of all your errors, and has
been justly stigmatized by the Faculty of Louvain, in their
censure of the doctrine of your friend Father Lamy, as a
murderous defence—defensio occisiva." I maintain that the
laws recognize such a wide difference between murder and
self-defence, that in those very cases in which the latter is

[1] L. 2, c. 9, n. 66, 72.

sanctioned, they have made a provision against murder, when
the person is in no danger of his life. Read the words, fathers, as they run in the same passage of Cujas : "It is lawful to repulse the person who comes to invade our property ;
but *we are not permitted to kill him.* And again : "If any
should threaten to strike us, and not to deprive us of life, it
is quite allowable to repulse him ; but *it is against all law
to put him to death."*

Who, then, has given you a right to say, as Molina, Reginald, Filiutius, Escobar, Lessius, and others among you,
have said, "that it is lawful to kill the man who offers to
strike us a blow ?" or, "that it is lawful to take the life of
one who means to insult us, by the common consent of all
the casuists," as Lessius says. By what authority do you,
who are mere private individuals, confer upon other private
individuals, not excepting clergymen, this right of killing and
slaying ? And how dare you usurp the power of life and
death, which belongs essentially to none but God, and which
is the most glorious mark of sovereign authority ? These
are the points that demand explanation ; and yet you conceive that you have furnished a triumphant reply to the
whole, by simply remarking, in your thirteenth Imposture,
"that the value for which Molina permits us to kill a thief,
who flies without having done us any violence, is not so
small as I have said, and that it must be a much larger sum
than six ducats !" How extremely silly ! Pray, fathers,
where would you have the price to be fixed ? At fifteen or
sixteen ducats ? Do not suppose that this will produce any
abatement in my accusations. At all events, you cannot
make it exceed the value of a horse ; for Lessius is clearly of
opinion, "that we may lawfully kill the thief that runs off
with our horse."[1] But I must tell you, moreover, that I
was perfectly correct when I said that Molina estimates the
value of the thief's life at six ducats ; and, if you will not
take it upon my word, we shall refer it to an umpire, to
whom you cannot object. The person whom I fix upon for

[1] L. ii., c. 9, n. 74.

this office is your own Father Reginald, who, in his explanation of the same passage of Molina (l. 28, n. 68), declares
that "Molina there DETERMINES the sum for which it is not
allowable to kill at three, or four, or five ducats." And
thus, fathers, I shall have Reginald in addition to Molina, to
bear me out.

It will be equally easy for me to refute your fourteenth
Imposture, touching Molina's permission to "kill a thief who
offers to rob us of a crown." This palpable fact is attested
by Escobar, who tells us "that Molina has regularly determined the sum for which it is lawful to take away life, at one
crown."[1] And all you have to lay to my charge in the
fourteenth imposture is, that I have suppressed the last
words of this passage, namely, "that in this matter every
one ought to study the moderation of a just self-defence."
Why do you not complain that Escobar has also omitted to
mention these words ? But how little tact you have about
you ! You imagine that nobody understands what you mean
by self-defence. Don't we know that it is to employ "a
murderous defence?" You would persuade us that Molina
meant to say, that if a person, in defending his crown, finds
himself in danger of his life, he is then at liberty to kill his
assailant, in self-preservation. If that were true, fathers,
why should Molina say in the same place, that "in this matter he was of a contrary judgment from Carrer and Bald,"
who give permission to kill in self-preservation ? I repeat,
therefore, that his plain meaning is, that provided the person
can save his crown without killing the thief, he ought not to
kill him ; but that, if he cannot secure his object without
shedding blood, even though he should run no risk of his
own life, as in the case of the robber being unarmed, he is
permitted to take up arms and kill the man, in order to save
his crown ; and in so doing, according to him, the person
does not transgress "the moderation of a just defence." To
show you that I am in the right, just allow him to explain
himself: "One does not exceed the moderation of a just de-

---

[1] Treat. i., examp. 7, n. 44.

fence," says he, " when he takes up arms against a thief who
has none, or employs weapons which give him the advantage
over his assailant. I know there are some who are of a contrary judgment ; but I do not approve of their opinion, even
in the external tribunal."¹
    Thus, fathers, it is unquestionable that your authors have
given permission to kill in defence of property and honor,
though life should be perfectly free from danger. And it is
upon the same principle that they authorize duelling, as I
have shown by a great variety of passages from their writings, to which you have made no reply. You have animad-
verted in your writings only on a single passage taken from
Father Layman, who sanctions the above practice, " when
otherwise a person would be in danger of sacrificing his
fortune or his honor ;" and here you accuse me with having
suppressed what he adds, " that such a case happens very
rarely." You astonish me, fathers : these are really curious
impostures you charge me withal. You talk as if the question were, Whether that is a rare case ? when the real question is, If, in such a case, duelling is lawful ? These are two
very different questions. Layman, in the quality of a casuist,
ought to judge whether duelling is lawful in the case supposed ; and he declares that it is. We can judge without his
assistance, whether the case be a rare one ; and we can tell
him that it is a very ordinary one. Or, if you prefer the
testimony of your good friend Diana, he will tell you that
'' the case is exceedingly common."² But be it rare or not,
and let it be granted that Layman follows in this the example of Navarre, a circumstance on which you lay so much
stress, is it not shameful that he should consent to such an
opinion as that, to preserve a false honor, it is lawful in con-

---

¹ In casuistical divinity, a distinction is drawn between the internal
and the external tribunal, or *forum*, as it is called.   The internal tribunal, or the *forum poli*, is that of conscience, or the judgment formed of
actions according to the law of God.   The external tribunal, or the
forum soli, is that of human society, or the judgment of actions in the
estimation of men, and according to civil law.   (Voet. Disp. Theol., iv.
62.)
² Part. 5, tr. 19, misc. 2, resol. 99.

science to accept of a challenge, in the face of the edicts of all Christian states, and of all the canons of the Church, while, in support of these diabolical maxims, you can produce neither laws, nor canons, nor authorities from Scripture, or from the fathers, nor the example of a single saint, nor, in short, anything but the following impious syllogism: "Honor is more than life it is allowable to kill in defence of life; therefore it is allowable to kill in defence of honor!" What, fathers! because the depravity of men disposes them to prefer that factitious honor before the life which God hath given them to be devoted to his service, must they be permitted to murder one another for its preservation? To love that honor more than life, is in itself a heinous evil; and yet this vicious passion, which, when proposed as the end of our conduct, is enough to tarnish the holiest of actions, is considered by you capable of sanctifying the most criminal of them!

What a subversion of all principle is here, fathers! And who does not see to what atrocious excesses it may lead? It is obvious, indeed, that it will ultimately lead to the commission of murder for the most trifling things imaginable, when one's honor is considered to be staked for their preservation—murder, I venture to say, even *for an apple!* You might complain of me, fathers, for drawing sanguinary inferences from your doctrine with a malicious intent, were I not fortunately supported by the authority of the grave Lessius, who makes the following observation, in number 68: "It is not allowable to take life for an article of small value, such as for a crown or *for an apple—aut pro pomo*—unless it would be deemed dishonorable to lose it. In this case, one may recover the article, and even, if necessary, *kill the aggressor;* for this is not so much defending one's property as retrieving one's honor." This is plain speaking, fathers; and, just to crown your doctrine with a maxim which includes all the rest, allow me to quote the following from Father Hereau, who has taken it from Lessius: "The right of self-defence extends to whatever is necessary to protect ourselves from all injury."

What strange consequences does this inhuman principle involve! and how imperative is the obligation laid upon all, and especially upon those in public stations, to set their face against it! Not the general good alone, but their own personal interest should engage them to see well to it; for the casuists of your school whom I have cited in my letters, extend their permissions to kill far enough to reach even them. Factious men, who dread the punishment of their outrages, which never appear to them in a criminal light, easily persuade themselves that they are the victims of violent oppression, and will be led to believe at the same time, "that the right of self-defence extends to whatever is necessary to protect themselves from all injury." And thus, relieved from contending against the checks of conscience, which stifle the greater number of crimes at their birth, their only anxiety will be to surmont external obstacles.

I shall say no more on this subject, fathers; nor shall I dwell on the other murders, still more odious and important to governments, which you sanction, and of which Lessius, in common with many others of your authors, treats in the most unreserved manner.[1] It was to be wished that these horrible maxims had never found their way out of hell; and that the devil, who is their original author, had never discovered men sufficiently devoted to his will to publish them among Christians.[2]

From all that I have hitherto said, it is easy to judge what a contrariety there is betwixt the licentiousness of your opinions and the severity of civil laws, not even excepting those

---

[1] Doubts 4th and 10th.

[2] " I am happy," says Nicole, in a note, " to state here an important fact, which confers the highest honor on M. Arnauld. A work of considerable size was sent him before going 'o press, in which there was a collection of all the authorities, from Jesuit writers, prejudicial to the life of kings and princes. That celebrated doctor prevented the impression of the work, on the ground that it was dangerous for the life of monarchs and for the honor of the Jesuits that it should ever see the light; and, in fact, the work was never printed. Some other writer, less delicate than M. Arnauld, has published something similar, in a work entitled *Recueil de Pieces concernant l' Histoire de la Compagnie de Jesus par le P. Jouvenci*."

of heathens. How much more apparent must the contrast be with ecclesiastical laws, which must be incomparably more holy than any other, since it is the Church alone that knows and possesses the true holiness! Accordingly, this chaste spouse of the Son of God, who, in imitation of her heavenly husband, can shed her own blood for others, but never the blood of others for herself, entertains a horror at the crime of murder altogether singular, and proportioned to the peculiar illumination which God has vouchsafed to bestow upon her. She views man, not simply as man, but as the image of the God whom she adores. She feels for every one of the race a holy respect, which imparts to him, in her eyes, a venerable character, as redeemed by an infinite price, to be made the temple of the living God. And therefore she considers the death of a man, slain without the authority of his Maker, not as murder only, but as sacrilege, by which she is deprived of one of her members; for whether he be a believer or an unbeliever, she uniformly looks upon him, if not as one, at least as capable of becoming one, of her own children.[1]

Such, fathers, are the holy reasons which, ever since the time that God became man for the redemption of men, have rendered their condition an object of such consequence to the Church, that she uniformly punishes the crime of homicide, not only as destructive to them, but as one of the grossest outrages that can possibly be perpetrated against God. In proof of this I shall quote some examples, not from the idea that all the severities to which I refer ought to be kept up (for I am aware that the Church may alter the arrange-

[1] Surely Pascal is here describing the Church of Christ as she ought to be, and not the Church of Rome as she existed in 1656, at the very time when she was urging, sanctioning, and exulting in the bloody barbarities perpetrated in her name on the poor Piedmontese; or the same Church as she appeared in 1572, when one of her popes ordered a medal to be struck in honor of the Bartholomew massacre, with the inscription, "*Strages Hugonotarum*—The massacre of the Hugunots!" Of what Church, if not the Romish, can it be said with truth, that, "in her was found the blood of prophets, and of saints, and of all that were slain on the earth?"

ment of such exterior discipline), but to demonstrate her immutable spirit upon this subject. The penances which she ordains for murder may differ according to the diversity of the times, but no change of time can ever effect an alteration of the horror with which she regards the crime itself.

For a long time the Church refused to be reconciled, till the very hour of death, to those who had been guilty of wilful murder, as those are to whom you give your sanction. The celebrated Council of Ancyra adjudged them to penance during their whole lifetime; and, subsequently, the Church deemed it an act of sufficient indulgence to reduce that term to a great many years. But, still more effectually to deter Christians from wilful murder, she has visited with most severe punishment even those acts which have been committed through inadvertence, as may be seen in St. Basil, in St. Gregory of Nyssen, and in the decretals of Popes Zachary and Alexander II. The canons quoted by Isaac, bishop of Langres (tr. 2. 13), "ordain seven years of penance for having killed another in self-defence." And we find St. Hildebert, bishop of Mans, replying to Yves de Chartres, "that he was right in interdicting for life a priest who had, in self-defence, killed a robber with a stone."

After this, you cannot have the assurance to persist in saying that your decisions are agreeable to the spirit or the canons of the Church. I defy you to show one of them that permits us to kill solely in defence of our property (for I speak not of cases in which one may be called upon to defend his life—*se suaqae liberando*); your own authors, and, among the rest, Father Lamy, confess that no such canon can be found. "There is no authority," he says, "human or divine, which gives an express permission to kill a robber who makes no resistance." And yet this is what you permit most expressly. I defy you to show one of them that permits us to kill in vindication of honor, for a buffet, for an affront, or for a slander. I defy you to show one of them that permits the killing of witnesses, judges, or magistrates, whatever injustice we may apprehend from them. The spirit of the church is

diametrically opposite to these seditious maxims, opening the
door to insurrections to which the mob is naturally prone
enough already. She has invariably taught her children that
they ought not to render evil for evil; that they ought to
give place unto wrath; to make no resistance to violence; to
give unto every one his due—honor, tribute, submission; to
obey magistrates and superiors, even though they should be
unjust, because we ought always to respect in them the power
of that God who has placed them over us. She forbids them,
still more strongly than is done by the civil law, to take justice into their own hands; and it is in her spirit that Christian kings decline doing so in cases of high treason, and
remit the criminals charged with this grave offence into the
hands of the judges, that they may be punished according
to the laws and the forms of justice, which in this matter
exhibit a contrast to your mode of management, so striking
and complete that it may well make you blush for shame.

As my discourse has taken this turn, I beg you to follow
the comparison which I shall now draw between the style
in which you would dispose of your enemies, and that in
which the judges of the land dispose of criminals. Everybody knows, fathers, that no private individual has a right to
demand the death of another individual; and that though a
man should have ruined us, maimed our body, burnt our
house, murdered our father, and was prepared. moreover, to
assassinate ourselves, or ruin our character, our private demand for the death of that person would not be listened to in
a court of justice. Public officers have been appointed for
that purpose, who make the demand in the name of the king,
or rather, I would say, in the name of God. Now, do you
conceive, fathers, that Christian legislators have established
this regulation out of mere show and grimace? Is it not
evident that their object was to harmonize the laws of the
state with those of the Church, and thus prevent the external
practice of justice from clashing with the sentiments which
all Christians are bound to cherish in their hearts? It is
easy to see how this, which forms the commencement of a

civil process, must stagger you; its subsequent procedure
absolutely overwhelms you.

Suppose, then, fathers, that these official persons have demanded the death of the man who has committed all the
above mentioned crimes, what is to be done next? Will
they instantly plunge a dagger in his breast? No, fathers;
the life of man is too important to be thus disposed of; they
go to work with more decency; the laws have committed it,·
not to all sorts of persons, but exclusively to the judges,
whose probity and competency have been duly tried. And
is one judge sufficient to condemn a man to death? No; it
requires seven at the very least; and of these seven there
must not be one who has been injured by the criminal, lest
his judgment should be warped or corrupted by passion.
You are aware also, fathers, that the more effectually to secure
the purity of their minds, they devote the hours of the morning to these functions. Such is the care taken to prepare
them for the solemn action of devoting a fellow-creature to
death; in performing which they occupy the place of God,
whose ministers they are, appointed to condemn such only as
have incurred his condemnation.

For the same reason, to act as faithful administrators of
the divine power of taking away human life, they are bound
to form their judgment solely according to the depositions
of the witnesses, and according to all the other forms pre·
scribed to them; after which they can pronounce conscientiously only according to law, and can judge worthy of death
those only whom the law condemns to that penalty. And
then, fathers, if the command of God obliges them to deliver
over to punishment the bodies of the unhappy culprits, the·
same divine statute binds them to look after the interests of
their guilty souls, and binds them the more to this just be
cause they are guilty; so that they are not delivered up to
execution till after they have been afforded the means of pro
viding for their consciences.[1]   All this is quite fair and in

<hr>

[1] *Providing for their consciences*—that is, for the relief of conscience,
by confessing to a priest, and receiving absolution.

nocent; and yet, such is the abhorrence of the Church to blood, that she judges those.to be incapable of ministering at her altars who have borne any share in passing or executing a sentence of death, accompanied though it be with these religious circumstances; from which we may easily conceive what idea the Church entertains of murder.

Such, then, being the manner in which human life is disposed of by the legal forms of justice, let us now see how you dispose of it. According to your modern system of legislation, there is but one judge, and that judge is no other than the offended party. He is at once the judge, the party, and the executioner. He himself demands from himself the death of his enemy; he condemns him, he executes him on the spot; and, without the least respect either for the soul or the body of his brother, he murders and damns him for whom Jesus Christ died; and all this for the sake of avoiding a blow on the cheek, or a slander, or an offensive word, or some other offence of a similar nature, for which, if a magistrate, in the exercise of legitimate authority, were condemning any to die, he would himself be impeached; for, in such cases, the laws are very far indeed from condemning any to death. In one word, to crown the whole of this extravagance, the person who kills his neighbor in this style, without authority, and in the face of all law, contracts no sin and commits no disorder, though he should be religious, and even a priest! Where are we, fathers? Are these really religious, and priests, who talk in this manner? Are they Christians? are they Turks? are they men? or are they demons? And are these "the mysteries revealed by the Lamb to his Society?" or are they not rather abominations suggested by the Dragon to those who take part with him?

To come to the point with you, fathers, whom do you wish to be taken for?—for the children of the Gospel, or for the enemies of the Gospel? You must be ranged either on the one side or on the other; for there is no medium here. "He that is not with Jesus Christ is against him." Into these two two classes all mankind are divided. There are, according to

16*

St. Augustine, two peoples and two worlds, scattered abroad
over the earth. There is the world of the children of God,
who form one body, of which Jesus Christ is the king and
the head ; and there is the world at enmity with God, of
which the devil is the king and the head. Hence Jesus
Christ is called the King and God of the world, because he
has everywhere his subjects and worshippers ; and hence the
devil is also termed in Scripture the prince of this world, and
the god of this world, because he has everywhere his agents
and his slaves. Jesus Christ has imposed upon the Church,
which is his empire, such laws as he, in his eternal wisdom,
was pleased to ordain ; and the devil has imposed on the
world, which is his kingdom, such laws as he chose to establish. Jesus Christ has associated honor with suffering ; the
devil with not suffering. Jesus Christ has told those who
are smitten on the one cheek to turn the other also ; and the
devil has told those who are threatened with a buffet to kill
the man that would do them such an injury. Jesus Christ
pronounces those happy who share in his reproach ; and the
devil declares those to be unhappy who lie under ignominy.
Jesus Christ says, Woe unto you when men shall speak well
of you ! and the devil says, Woe unto those of whom the
world does not speak with esteem !

    Judge then, fathers, to which of these kingdoms you be-
long. You have heard the language of the city of peace,
the mystical Jerusalem ; and you have heard the language of
the city of confusion, which Scripture terms " the spiritual
Sodom." Which of these two languages do you understand ?
which of them do you speak ? Those who are on the side
of Jesus Christ have, as St. Paul teaches us, the same mind
which was also in him ; and those who are the children of
the devil—ex patre diabolo—who has been a murderer from
the beginning, according to the saying of Jesus Christ, follow
the maxims of the devil. Let us hear, therefore, the language of your school. I put this question to your doctors :
When a person has given me a blow on the cheek, ought I
rather to submit to the injury than kill the offender ? or may I

not kill the man in order to escape the affront ? Kill him by all means—it is quite lawful ! exclaim, in one breath, Lessius, Molina, Escobar, Reginald, Filiutius, Baldelle, and other Jesuits. Is that the language of Jesus Christ? One question more : Would I lose my honor by tolerating a box on the ear, without killing the person that gave it ? " Can there be a doubt," cries Escobar, " that so long as a man suffers another to live who has given him a buffet, that man remains without honor ?" Yes, fathers, without that honor which the devil transfuses, from his own proud spirit into that of his proud children. This is the honor which has ever been the idol of worldly-minded men. For the preservation of this false glory, of which the god of this world is the appropriate dispenser, they sacrifice their lives by yielding to the madness of duelling; their honor, by exposing themselves to ignominious punishments ; and their salvation, by involving themselves in the peril of damnation—a peril which, according to the canons of the Church, deprives them even of Christian burial. We have reason to thank God, however, for having enlightened the mind of our monarch with ideas much purer than those of your theology. His edicts bearing so severely on this subject, have not made duelling a crime— they only punish the crime which is inseparable from duelling. He has checked, by the dread of his rigid justice, those who were not restrained by the fear of the justice of God ; and his piety has taught him that the honor of Christians consists in their observance of the mandates of Heaven and the rules of Christianity, and not in the pursuit of that phantom which, airy and unsubstantial as it is, you hold to be a legitimate apology for murder. Your murderous decisions being thus universally detested, it is highly advisable that you should now change your sentiments, if not from religious principle, at least from motives of policy. Prevent, fathers, by a spontaneous condemnation of these inhuman dogmas, the melancholy consequences which may result from them, and for which you will be responsible. And to impress your minds with a deeper horror at homicide, remember that the first crime of fallen man was a murder, committed on the person of the first holy man; that the greatest crime was a murder, perpetrated on the person of the King of saints; and that of all crimes, murder is the only one which involves in a common destruction the Church and the state, nature and religion.

I have just seen the answer of your apologist to my Thirteenth Letter; but if he has nothing better to produce in the shape of a reply to that letter, which obviates the greater part of his objections, he will not deserve a rejoinder. I am sorry to see him perpetually digressing from his subject, to indulge in rancorous abuse both of the living and the dead. But, in order to gain some credit to the stories with which you have furnished him, you should not have made him publicly disavow a fact so notorious as that of the buffet of Compiègne.[1] Certain it is, fathers, from the deposition of the injured party, that he received upon his cheek a blow from the hand of a Jesuit; and all that your friends have been able to do for you has been to raise a doubt whether he received the blow with the back or the palm of the hand, and to discuss the question whether a stroke on the cheek with the back of the hand can be properly denominated a buffet. I know not to what tribunal it belongs to decide this point; but shall content myself, in the mean time, with believing that it was, to say the very least, *a probable buffet*. This gets me off with a safe conscience.

<hr>

[1] See Letter xiii., p. 842.

LETTER XV.[1]

TO THE REVEREND FATHERS, THE JESUITS.

SHOWING THAT THE JESUITS FIRST EXCLUDE CALUMNY FROM THEIR
CATALOGUE OF CRIMES, AND THEN EMPLOY IT IN DENOUNCING
THEIR OPPONENTS.

November 25, 1656.

REVEREND FATHERS,—As your scurrilities are daily increasing, and as you are employing them in the merciless
abuse of all pious persons opposed to your errors, I feel myself obliged, for their sake and that of the Church, to bring
out that grand secret of your policy, which I promised to
disclose some time ago, in order that all may know, through
means of your own maxims, what degree of credit is due to
your calumnious accusations.

I am aware that those who are not very well acquainted
with you, are at a great loss what to think on this subject, as
they find themselves under the painful necessity, either of
believing the incredible crimes with which you charge your
opponents, or (what is equally incredible) of setting you
down as slanderers. " Indeed !" they exclaim, " were these
things not true, would clergymen publish them to the world
—would they debauch their consciences and damn themselves
by venting such libels ?" Such is their way of reasoning,
and thus it is that the palpable proof of your falsifications
coming into collision with their opinion of your honesty, their
minds hang in a state of suspense between the evidence of
truth which they cannot gainsay, and the demands of charity
which they would not violate. It follows, that since their

---

[1] Pascal was assisted by M. Arnauld in the preparation of this letter.
(Nicole, iv. 162.)

high esteem for you is the only thing that prevents them from discrediting your calumnies, if we can succeed in convincing them that you have quite a different idea of calumny from that which they suppose you to have, and that you actually believe that in blackening and defaming your adversaries you are working out your own salvation, there can be little question that the weight of truth will determine them immediately to pay no regard to your accusations.   This, fathers, will be the subject of the present letter.

My design is, not simply to show that your writings are full of calumnies: I mean to go a step beyond this.   It is quite possible for a person to say a number of false things believing them to be true; but the character of a liar implies the intention to tell lies.   Now I undertake to prove, fathers, that it is your deliberate intention to tell lies, and that it is both knowingly and purposely that you load your opponents with crimes of which you know them to be innocent, because you believe that you may do so without falling from a state of grace.   Though you doubtless know this point of your morality as well as I do, this need not prevent me from telling you about it; which I shall do, were it for no other purpose than to convince all men of its existence, by showing them that I can maintain it to your face, while you cannot have the assurance to disavow it, without confirming, by that very disavowment, the charge which I bring against you.

The doctrine to which I allude is so common in your schools, that you have maintained it not only in your books, but, such is your assurance, even in your public theses; as, for example, in those delivered at Louvain in the year 1645, where it occurs in the following terms: " What is it but a venial sin to calumniate and forge false accusations to ruin the credit of those who speak evil of us ?"[1]   So settled is this point among you, that if any one dare to oppose it, you treat him as a blockhead and a hare-brained idiot.   Such

[1] Quidni non nisi veniale sit, detrahentes autoritatem magnam, tibi noxiam, falso crimine elidere ?

was the way in which you treated Father Quiroga, the German Capuchin, when he was so unfortunate as to impugn the doctrine. The poor man was instantly attacked by Dicastille, one of your fraternity; and the following is a specimen of the manner in which he manages the dispute: " A certain rueful-visaged, bare-footed, cowled friar—*cucullatus gymnopoda*—whom I do not choose to name, had the boldness to denounce this opinion, among some women and ignorant people, and to allege that it was scandalous and pernicious against all good manners, hostile to the peace of states and societies, and, in short, contrary to the judgment not only of all Catholic doctors, but of all true Catholics. But in opposition to him I maintained, as I do still, that calumny, when employed against a calumniator, though it should be a falsehood, is not a mortal sin, either against justice or charity : and to prove the point, I referred him to the whole body of our fathers, and to whole universities, exclusively composed of them, whom I had consulted on the subject; and among others the reverend Father John Gans, confessor to the emperor; the reverend Father Daniel Bastele, confessor to the archduke Leopold ;· Father Henri, who was preceptor to these two princes ; all the public and ordinary professors of the university of Vienna" (wholly composed of Jesuits); "all the professors of the university of Gratz" (all Jesuits); "all the professors of the university of Prague" (where Jesuits are the masters) ;—"from all of whom I have in my possession approbations of my opinions, written and signed with their own hands ; besides having on my side the reverend Father Panalossa, a Jesuit, preacher to the emperor and the king of Spain ; Father Pilliceroli, a Jesuit, and many others, who had all judged this opinion to be probable, before our dispute began."[1] You perceive, fathers, that there are few of your opinions which you have been at more pains to establish than the present, as indeed there were few of them of which you stood more in need. For this reason, doubtless, you have authenticated it so well, that the casuists

[1] Dicastillus, De Just., l. 2, tr. 2, disp. 12, n. 404.

appeal to it as an indubitable principle. "There can be no
doubt," says Caramuel, "that it is a probable opinion that
we contract no mortal sin by calumniating another, in order
to preserve our own reputation. For it is maintained by
more than twenty grave doctors, by Gaspard Hurtado, and
Dicastille, Jesuits, &c.; so that, were this doctrine not probable, it would be difficult to find any one such in the whole
compass of theology."

Wretched indeed must that theology be, and rotten to
the very core, which, unless it has been decided to be safe in
conscience to defame our neighbor's character to preserve
our own, can hardly boast of a safe decision on any other
point! How natural is it, fathers, that those who hold this
principle should occasionally put it in practice! The corrupt propensity of mankind leans so strongly in that direction of itself, that the obstacle of conscience once being removed, it would be folly to suppose that it will not burst
forth with all its native impetuosity. If you desire an example of this, Caramuel will furnish you with one that occurs in the same passage: "This maxim of Father Dicastille,"
he says, "having been communicated by a German countess
to the daughters of the empress, the belief thus impressed
on their minds that calumny was only a venial sin, gave rise
in the course of a few days to such an immense number of
false and scandalous tales, that the whole court was thrown
into a flame and filled with alarm. It is easy, indeed, to
conceive what a fine use these ladies would make of the new
light they had acquired. Matters proceeded to such a length,
that it was found necessary to call in the assistance of a worthy Capuchin friar, a man of exemplary life, called Father
Quiroga" (the very man whom Dicastille rails at so bitterly),
"who assured them that the maxim was most pernicious,
especially among women, and was at the greatest pains to
prevail upon the empress to abolish the practice of it entirely." We have no reason, therefore, to be surprised at the
bad effects of this doctrine; on the contrary, the wonder
would be, if it had failed to produce them. Self-love is al-

ways ready enough to whisper in our ear, when we are attacked, that we suffer wrongfully ; and more particularly in
your case, fathers, whom vanity has blinded so egregiously
as to make you believe that to wound the honor of your Society, is to wound that of the Church.   There would have
been good ground to look on it as something miraculous, if
you had *not* reduced this maxim to practice. - Those who
do not know you are ready to say, How could these good
fathers slander their enemies, when they cannot do so but
at the expense of their own salvation ?   But if they knew
you better, the question would be, How could these good
fathers forego the advantage of decrying their enemies, when
they have it in their power to do so without hazarding their
salvation ?   Let none, therefore, henceforth be surprised to
find the Jesuits calumniators ; they can exercise this vocation
with a safe conscience ; there is no obstacle in heaven or on
earth to prevent them.   In virtue of the credit they have
acquired in the world, they can practise defamation without
dreading the justice of mortals ; and, on the strength of their
self-assumed authority in matters of conscience, they have
invented maxims for enabling them to do it without any fear
of the justice of God.

    This, fathers, is the fertile source of your base slanders.
On this principle was Father Brisacier led to scatter his calumnies about him, with such zeal as to draw down on his
head the censure of the late Archbishop of Paris.   Actuated
by the same motives, Father D'Anjou launched his invectives from the pulpit of the Church of St. Benedict in Paris,
on the 8th of March, 1655, against those honorable gentlemen who were intrusted with the charitable funds raised for
the poor of Picardy and Champagne, to which they themselves had largely contributed ; and, uttering a base falsehood,
calculated (if your slanders had been considered worthy of
any credit) to dry up the stream of that charity, he had the
assurance to say, " that he knew, from good authority, that
certain persons had diverted that money from its proper use,
to employ it against the Church and the State ;" a calumny

which obliged the curate of the parish, who is a doctor of
the Sorbonne, to mount the pulpit the very next day, in
order to give it the lie direct. To the same source must be
traced the conduct of your Father Crasset, who preached
calumny at such a furious rate in Orleans that the archbishop
of that place was under the necessity of interdicting him as
a public slanderer. In his mandate, dated the 9th of September last, his lordship declares, " That whereas he had
been informed that Brother Jean Crasset, priest of the Society of Jesus, had delivered from the pulpit a discourse filled
with falsehoods and calumnies against the ecclesiastics of this
city, falsely and maliciously charging them with maintaining
impious and heretical propositions, such as, That the commandments of God are impracticable; that internal grace is
irresistible ; that Jesus Christ did not die for all men ; and
others of a similar kind, condemned by Innocent X.: he
therefore hereby interdicts the aforesaid Crasset from preaching in his diocese, and forbids all his people to hear him, on
pain of mortal disobedience." The above, fathers, is your
ordinary accusation, and generally among the first that you
bring against all whom it is your interest to denounce. And
although you should find it as impossible to substantiate the
charge against any of them, as Father Crasset did in the
case of the clergy of Orleans, your peace of conscience will
not be in the least disturbed on that account ; for you believe that this mode of calumniating your adversaries is
permitted you with such certainty, that you have no scruple
to avow it in the most public manner, and in the face of a
whole city.

A remarkable proof of this may be seen in the dispute you
had with M. Puys, curate of St. Nisier at Lyons ; and the
story exhibits so complete an illustration of your spirit, that
I shall take the liberty of relating some of its leading circumstances. You know, fathers, that, in the year 1649, M.
Puys translated into French an excellent book, written by
another Capuchin friar, " On the duty which Christians owe
to their own parishes, against those that would lead them

away from them," without using a single invective, or pointing to any monk or any order of monks in particular. Your
fathers, however, were pleased to put the cap on their own
heads ; and without any respect to an aged pastor, a judge
in the Primacy of France, and a man who was held in the
highest esteem by the whole city, Father Alby wrote a furious tract against him, which you sold in your own church
upon Assumption-day ; in which book, among other various
charges, he accused him of having " made himself scandalous
by his gallantries," described him as suspected of having
no religion, as a heretic, excommunicated, and, in short,
worthy of the stake. To this M. Puys made a reply ; and
Father Alby, in a second publication, supported his former
allegations. Now, fathers, is it not a clear point, either that
you were calumniators, or that you believed all that you
alleged against that worthy priest to be true ; and that, on
this latter assumption, it became you to see him purified
from all these abominations before judging him worthy of
your friendship ? Let us see, then, what happened at the
accommodation of the dispute, which took place in the presence of a great number of the principal inhabitants of the
town, whose names will be found at the foot of the page,[1]
exactly as they are set down in the instrument drawn up on
the 25th of September, 1650. Before all these witnesses
M. Puys made a declaration, which was neither more nor
less than this : " That what he had written was not directed
against the fathers of the Society of Jesus ; that he had spoken in general of those who alienated the faithful from their
parishes, without meaning by that to attack the Society ;
and that so far from having such an intention, the Society

---

[1] M. De Ville, Vicar-General of M., the Cardinal of Lyons; M.
Scarron, Canon and Curate of St. Paul ; M. Margat. Chanter; MM.
Bouvand, Seve, Aubert, and Dervien, Canons of St. Nisler; M. de Cud,
President of the Treasurers of France: M. Grosficr. Provost of the Mer-
chants; M. de Flèchre. President and Lieutenant-General; MM. De
Boissart, De St. Romain, and De Bartoly. gentlemen ; M. Bourgeois,
the King's First Advocate in the Court of the Treasurers of France ; MM.
De Cotton, father and son; and M. Boniel: who have all signed the
original copy of the Declaration, along with M. Puys and Father Alby.

was the object of his esteem and affection." By virtue of these words alone, without either retractation or absolution, M. Puys recovered, all at once, from his apostasy, his scandals, and his excommunication; and Father Alby immediately thereafter addressed him in the following express terms: "Sir, it was in consequence of my believing that you meant to attack the Society to which.I have the honor to belong, that I was induced to take up the pen in its defence; and I considered that the mode of reply which I adopted was *such as I was permitted to employ*. But, on a better understanding of your intention, I am now free to declare, that *there is nothing in your work* to prevent me from regarding you as a man of genius, enlightened in judgment, profound and *orthodox* in doctrine, and *irreproachable* in manners; in one word, as a pastor worthy of your Church. It is with much pleasure that I make this declaration, and I beg these gentlemen to remember what I have now said."

They do remember it, fathers; and, allow me to add, they were more scandalized by the reconciliation than by the quarrel. For who can fail to admire this speech of Father Alby? He does not say that he retracts, in consequence of having learnt that a change had- taken place in the faith and manners of M. Puys, but solely because, *having understood that he had no intention of attacking your Society*, there was nothing further to prevent him from regarding the author as a good Catholic. He did not then believe him to be actually a heretic! And yet, after having, contrary to his conviction, accused him of this crime, he will not acknowledge he was in the wrong, but has the hardihood to say, that he considered the method he adopted to be "such as he was *permitted* to employ!"

What can you possibly mean, fathers, by so publicly avowing the fact, that you measure the faith and the virtue of men only by the sentiments they entertain towards your Society? Had you no apprehension of making yourselves pass, by your own acknowledgment, as a band of swindlers and slanderers? What, fathers! must the same individual without undergoing any personal transformation, but simply according as you judge him to have honored or assailed your community, be "pious" or "impious," "irreproachable" or "excommunicated," "a pastor worthy of the Church" or "worthy of the stake;" in short, "a Catholic" or "a heretic?" To attack your Society and to be a heretic, are, therefore, in your language, convertible terms! An odd sort of heresy this, fathers! And so it would appear, that when we see many good Catholics branded, in your writings, by the name of heretics, it means nothing more than that *you think they attack you!* It is well, fathers, that we understand this strange dialect, according to which there can be no doubt that I must be a great heretic. It is in *this* sense, then, that you so often favor me with this appellation! Your sole reason for cutting me off from the Church is, because you conceive that my letters have done you harm; and, accordingly, all that I have to do, in order to become a good Catholic, is either to approve of your extravagant morality, or to convince you that my sole aim in exposing it has been your advantage. The former I could not do without renouncing every sentiment of piety that I ever possessed; and the latter you will be slow to acknowledge till you are well cured of your errors. Thus am I involved in heresy, after a very singular fashion; for, the purity of my faith being of no avail for my exculpation, I have no means of escaping from the charge, except either by turning traitor to my own conscience, or by reforming yours. Till one or other of these events happen, I must remain a reprobate and a slanderer; and, let me be ever so faithful in my citations from your writings, you will go about crying everywhere, "What an instrument of the devil must that man be, to impute to us things of which there is not the least mark or vestige to be found in our books!" And, by doing so, you will only be acting in conformity with your fixed maxim and your ordinary practice; to such latitude does your privilege of telling lies extend! Allow me to give you an example of this, which I select on purpose: it will give me an opportunity of replying, at the same time, to your ninth Imposture : for, in truth, they only deserve to be refuted in passing.

About ten or twelve years ago, you were accused of holding that maxim of Father Bauny, " that it is permissible to seek directly (*primo et per se*) a proximate occasion of sin, for the spiritual or temporal good of ourselves or our neighbor" (tr. 4, q. 14); as an example of which, he observes, " It is allowable to visit infamous places, for the purpose of converting abandoned females, even although the practice should be very likely to lead into sin, as in the case of one who has found from experience that he has frequently yielded to their temptations." What answer did your Father Caussin give to this charge in the year 1644 ? " Just let any one look at the passage in Father Bauny," said he, " let him peruse the page, the margins, the preface, the appendix, in short, the whole book from beginning to end, and he will not discover the slightest vestige of such a sentence, which could only enter into the mind of a man totally devoid of conscience, and could hardly have been forged by any other but an instrument of Satan."[1] Father Pintereau talks in the same style : "That man must be lost to all conscience who would teach so detestable a doctrine ; but he must be worse than a devil who attributes it to Father Bauny. Reader, there is not a single trace or vestige of it in the whole of his book."[2] Who would not believe that persons talking in this tone have good reason to complain, and that Father Bauny has, in very deed, been misrepresented ? Have you ever asserted anything against me in stronger terms ? And, after such a solemn asseveration, that " there was not a single trace or vestige of it in the whole book," who would imagine that the passage is to be found, word for word, in the place referred to ?

Truly, fathers, if this be the means of securing your reputation, so long as you remain unanswered, it is also, unfortunately, the means of destroying it forever, so soon as an an-

[1] Apology for the Society of Jesus, p. 128.
[2] First Part, p. 24.

swer makes its appearance. For so certain is it that you told
a lie at the period before mentioned, that you make no scruple of acknowledging, in your apologies of the present day,
that the maxim in question is to be found in the very place
which had been quoted ; and what is most extraordinary, the
same maxim which, twelve years ago, was "detestable," has
now become so innocent, that in your ninth Imposture (p. 10)
you accuse me of "ignorance and malice, in quarrelling with
Father Bauny for an opinion which has not been rejected in
the School." What an advantage it is, fathers, to have to
do with people that deal in contradictions ! I need not the
aid of any but yourselves to confute you ; for I have only
two things to show—first, That the maxim in dispute is a
worthless one ; and, secondly, That it belongs to Father
Bauny ; and I can prove both by your own confession. In
1644, you confessed that it was "detestable ;" and, in 1656,
you avow that it is Father Bauny's. This double acknowledgment completely justifies me, fathers ; but it does more,
it discovers the spirit of your policy. For, tell me, pray,
what is the end you propose to yourselves in your writings ?
Is it to speak with honesty ? No, fathers ; that cannot be,
since your defences destroy each other. Is it to follow the
truth of the faith ? As little can this be your end ; since, according to your own showing, you authorize a "detestable"
maxim. But, be it observed, that while you said the maxim
was "detestable," you denied, at the same time, that it was
the property of Father Bauny, and so he was innocent ; and
when you now acknowledge it to be his, you maintain, at the
same time, that it is a good maxim, and so he is innocent
still. The innocence of this monk, therefore, being the only
thing common to your two answers, it is obvious that this
was the sole end which you aimed at in putting them forth ;
and that, when you say of one and the same maxim, that it
is in a certain book, and that it is not ; that it is a good
maxim, and that it is a bad one ; your sole object is to white-
wash some one or other of your fraternity ; judging in the
matter, not according to the truth, which never changes, but

according to your own interest, which is varying every hour. Can I say m)re than this? You perceive that it amounts to a demonstration; but it is far from being a singular instance; and, to omit a multitude of examples of the same thing, I believe you will be contented with my quoting only one more.

You have been charged, at different times, with another proposition of the same Father Bauny, namely, "That absolution ought to be neither denied nor deferred in the case of those who live in the habits of sin against the law of God, of nature, and of the Church, although there should be no apparent prospect of future amendment—*etsi emendationis futuræ spes nulla appareat*."[1]   Now, with regard to this maxim, I beg you to tell me, fathers, which of the apologies that have been made for it is most to your liking; whether that of Father Pintereau, or that of Father Brisacier, both of your Society, who have defended Father Bauny, in your *two different* modes—the one by condemning the proposition, but disavowing it to be Father Bauny's; the other by allowing it to be Father Bauny's, but vindicating the proposition? Listen, then, to their respective deliverances.   Here comes that of Father Pintereau (p. 8): "I know not what can be called a transgression of all the bounds of modesty, a step beyond all ordinary impudence, if the imputation to Father Bauny of so damnable a doctrine is not worthy of that designation.   Judge, reader, of the baseness of that calumny; see what sort of creatures the Jesuits have to deal with; and say, if the author of so foul a slander does not deserve to be regarded from henceforth as the interpreter of the father of lies."   Now for Father Brisacier: "It is true, Father Bauny says what you allege."   (That gives the lie direct to Father Pintereau, plain enough.)   "But," adds he, in defence of Father Bauny, "if you who find so much fault with this sentiment, wait, when a penitent lies at your feet, till his guardian angel find security for his rights in the inheritance of heaven; if you wait till God the Father, swear by himself that David

[1] Tr. 4, q. 22, p. 100

told a lie, when he said, by the Holy Ghost, that 'all men are liars,' fallible and perfidious ; if you wait till the penitent be no longer a liar, no longer frail and changeable, no longer a sinner, like other men ; if you wait, I say, till then, you will never apply the blood of Jesus Christ to a single soul."[1]

What do you really think now, fathers, of these impious and extravagant expressions ? According to them, if we would wait "till there be some hope of amendment" in sinners before granting their absolution, we must wait "till God the Father swear by himself," that they will never fall into sin any more ! What, fathers ! is no distinction to be made between *hope* and *certainty ?* How injurious is it to the grace of Jesus Christ, to maintain that it is so impossible for Christians ever to escape from crimes against the laws of God, nature, and the Church, that such a thing cannot be looked for, without supposing "that the Holy Ghost has told a lie ;" and if absolution is not granted to those who give no hope of amendment, the blood of Jesus Christ will be useless, forsooth, and "would never be applied to a single soul !" To what a sad pass have you come, fathers, by this extravagant desire of upholding the glory of your authors, when you can find only two ways of justifying them—by imposture or by impiety ; and when the most innocent mode by which you can extricate yourselves, is by the barefaced denial of facts as patent as the light of day !

This may perhaps account for your having recourse so frequently to that very convenient practice. But this does not complete the sum of your accomplishments in the art of self-defence. To render your opponents odious, you have had recourse to the forging of documents, such as that *Letter of a Minister to M. Arnauld*, which you circulated through all Paris, to induce the belief that the work on Frequent Communion, which had been approved by so many bishops and doctors, but which, to say the truth, was rather against you, had been concocted through secret intelligence with the min-

[1] Part. 4, p. 21

isters of Charenton.[1]   At other times, you attribute to your adversaries writings full of impiety, such as the *Circular Letter of the Jansenists*, the absurd style of which renders the fraud too gross to be swallowed, and palpably betrays the malice of your Father Meynier, who has the impudence to make use of it for supporting his foulest slanders. Sometimes, again, you will quote books which were never in existence, such as *The Constitution of the Holy Sacrament*, from which you extract passages, fabricated at pleasure, and calculated to make the hair on the heads of certain good simple people, who have no idea of the effrontery with which you can invent and propagate falsehoods, actually to bristle with horror. There is not, indeed, a single species of calumny which you have not put into requisition ; nor is it possible that the maxim which excuses the vice could have been lodged in better hands.

But those sorts of slander to which we have adverted are rather too easily discredited ; and, accordingly, you have others of a more subtle character, in which you abstain from specifying particulars, in order to preclude your opponents from getting any hold, or finding any means of reply ; as, for example, when Father Brisacier says that "his enemies are guilty of abominable crimes, *which he does not choose to mention*." Would you not think it were impossible to prove a charge so vague as this to be a calumny? An able man, however, has found out the secret of it ; and it is a Capuchin again, fathers.   You are unlucky in Capuchins, as times now go ; and I foresee that you may be equally so some other time in Benedictines.   The name of this Capuchin is Father

---

[1] That is, the Protestant ministers of Paris, who are called "the ministers of Charenton," from the village of that name near Paris, where they had their place of worship.   The Protestants of Paris were forbidden to hold meetings in the city, and were compelled to travel five leagues to a place of worship, till 1606, when they were *graciously* permitted to erect their temple at Charenton, about two leagues from the city !   (Benoit, Hist. de l'Edit. de Nantes, i. 435.)   Even there they were harassed by the bigoted populace, and at last "the ministers of Charenton," among whom were the famous Claude and Daillé, were driven from their homes, their chapel burnt to the ground, and their people scattered abroad.

Valerien, of the house of the Counts of Magnis. You shall hear, by this brief narrative, how he answered your calumnies. He had happily succeeded in converting Prince Ernest, the Landgrave of Hesse-Rheinsfelt.[1] Your fathers, however, seized, as it would appear, with some chagrin at seeing a sovereign prince converted without their having had any hand in it, immediately wrote a book against the friar (for good men are everywhere the objects of your persecution), in which, by falsifying one of his passages, they ascribed to him an heretical doctrine. They also circulated a letter against him, in which they said: "Ah, we have such things to disclose" (without mentioning what) "as will gall you to the quick! If you don't take care, we shall be forced to inform the pope and the cardinals about it." This manœuvre was pretty well executed ; and I doubt not, fathers, but you may speak in the same style of me ; but take warning from the manner in which the friar answered in his book, which was printed last year at Prague (p. 112, &c.) : "What shall I do," he says, "to counteract these vague and indefinite insinuations ? How shall I refute charges which have never been specified ? Here, however, is my plan. I declare, loudly and publicly, to those who have threatened me, that they are notorious slanderers, and most impudent liars, if they do not discover these crimes before the whole world. Come forth, then, mine accusers ! and publish your lies upon the house tops, in place of telling them in the ear, and keeping yourselves out of harm's way by telling them in the ear. Some may think this a scandalous way of managing the dispute. It was scandalous, I grant, to impute to me such a crime as heresy, and to fix upon me the suspicion of many others besides ; but, by asserting my innocence, I am merely applying the proper remedy to the scandal already in existence."

Truly, fathers, never were your reverences more roughly handled, and never was a poor man more completely vindi-

[1] In the first edition it was said to be the Landgrave of Darmstat, by mistake, as shown in a note by Nicole.

cated.   Since you have made no reply to such a peremptory
challenge, it must be concluded that you are unable to discover the slightest shadow of criminality against him.   You
have had very awkward scrapes to get through occasionally;
but experience has made you nothing the wiser.   For, some
time after this happened, you attacked the same individual
in a similar strain, upon another subject; and he defended
himself after the same spirited manner, as follows : " This
class of men, who have become an intolerable nuisance to the
whole of Christendom, aspire, under the pretext of good
works, to dignities and domination, by perverting to their
own ends almost all laws, human and divine, natural and
revealed.   They gain over to their side, by their doctrine,
by the force of fear, or of persuasion, the great ones of the
earth, whose authority they abuse for the purpose of accom-
plishing their detestable intrigues.   Meanwhile their enter-
prises, criminal as they are, are neither punished nor suppressed ; on the contrary, they are rewarded ; and the villains
go about them with as little fear or remorse as if they were
doing God service.   Everybody is aware of the fact I have
now stated; everybody speaks of it with execration ; but few
are found capable of opposing a despotism so powerful.   This,
however, is what I have done.   I have already curbed their
insolence ; and, by the same means, I shall curb it again.
I declare, then, that *they are most impudent liars*—MENTIRIS
IMPUDENTISSIME.   If the charges they have brought against
me be true, let them prove it ; otherwise they stand convicted
of falsehood, aggravated by the grossest effrontery.   Their
procedure in this case will show who has the right upon his
side.   I desire all men to take a particular observation of it ;
and beg to remark, in the mean time, that this precious cabal,
who will not suffer the most trifling charge which' they can
possibly repel to lie upon them, made a show of enduring,
with great patience, those from which they cannot vindicate
themselves, and conceal, under a counterfeit virtue, their real
impotency.   My object, therefore, in provoking their modesty,
by this sharp retort, is to let the plainest people understand,

that if my enemies hold their peace, their forbearance must
be ascribed, not to the meekness of their natures, but to the
power of a guilty conscience." He concludes with the following sentence : "These gentry, whose history is well known
throughout the whole world, are so glaringly iniquitous in
their measures, and have become so insolent in their impunity, that if I did not detest their conduct, and publicly
express my detestation too, not merely for my own vindication, but to guard the simple against its seducing influence, I
must have renounced my allegiance to Jesus Christ and his
Church."

Reverend fathers, there is no room for tergiversation. You
must pass for convicted slanderers, and take comfort in your
old maxim, that calumny is no crime. This honest friar has
discovered the secret of shutting your mouths ; and it must
be employed on all occasions when you accuse people without proof. We have only to reply to each slander as it appears, in the words of the Capuchin, *Mentiris impudentissime*
—"You are most impudent liars." For instance, what
better answer does Father Brisacier deserve when he says
of his opponents that they are "the gates of hell; the devil's
bishops; persons devoid of faith, hope, and charity; the
builders of Antichrist's exchequer ;" adding, "I say this of
him, not by way of insult, but from deep conviction of its
truth ?" Who would be at the pains to demonstrate that he
is not "a gate of hell," and that he has no concern with "the
building up of Antichrist's exchequer ?"

In like manner, what reply is due to all the vague speeches
of this sort which are to be found in your books and advertisements on my letters ; such as the following, for example :
"That restitutions have been converted to private uses, and
thereby creditors have been reduced to beggary ; that bags
of money have been offered to learned monks, who declined
the bribe ; that benefices are conferred for the purpose of
disseminating heresies against the faith ; that pensioners are
kept in the houses of the most eminent churchmen, and in
the courts of sovereigns ; that I also am a pensioner of Port-

Royal ; and that, before writing my letters, I had composed *romances*"—I, who never read one in my life, and who do not know so much as the names of those which your apologist has published ? What can be said in reply to all this, fathers, if you do not mention the names of all these persons you refer to, their words, the time, and the place, except— *Mentiris impudentissime ?* You should either be silent altogether, or relate and prove all the circumstances, as I did when I told you the anecdotes of Father Alby and John d'Alba. Otherwise, you will hurt none but yourselves. Your numerous fables might, perhaps, have done you some service, before your principles were known ; but now that the whole has been brought to light, when you begin to whisper as usual, " A man of honor, who desired us to conceal his name, has told us some horrible stories of these same people" —you will be cut short at once, and reminded of the Capuchin's *Mentiris impudentissime.* Too long by far have you been permitted to deceive the world, and to abuse the confidence which men were ready to place in your calumnious accusations. It is high time to redeem the reputation of the multitudes whom you have defamed. For what innocence can be so generally known, as not to suffer some injury from the daring aspersions of a body of men scattered over the face of the earth, and who, under religious habits, conceal minds so utterly irreligious, that they perpetrate crimes like calumny, not in opposition to, but in strict accordance with, their moral maxims? I cannot, therefore, be blamed for destroying the credit which might have been awarded you ; seeing it must be allowed to be a much greater act of justice to restore to the victims of your obloquy the character which they did not deserve to lose, than to leave you in the possession of a reputation for sincerity which you do not deserve to enjoy. And as the one could not be done without the other, how important was it to show you up to the world as you really are ! In this letter I have commenced the exhibition ; but it will require some time to complete it. Published it shall be, fathers, and all your policy will be inadequate to save you from the disgrace; for the efforts which you may make to avert the blow, will only serve to convince the most obtuse observers that you were terrified out of your wits, and that, your consciences anticipating the charges I had to bring against you, you have put every oar in the water to prevent the discovery.

LETTER XVI.[1]

TO THE REVEREND FATHERS, THE JESUITS.

SHAMEFUL CALUMNIES OF THE JESUITS AGAINST PIOUS CLERGYMEN AND INNOCENT NUNS.

December 4, 1656.

REVEREND FATHERS,—I now come to consider the rest of your calumnies, and shall begin with those contained in your advertisements, which remain to be noticed. As all your other writings, however, are equally well stocked with slander, they will furnish me with abundant materials for entertaining you on this topic as long as I may judge expedient. In the first place, then, with regard to the fable which you have propagated in all your writings against the Bishop of Ypres,[2] I beg leave to say, in one word, that you have maliciously wrested the meaning of some ambiguous expressions in one of his letters, which being capable of a good sense, ought, according to the spirit of the Gospel, to have been taken in good part, and could only be taken otherwise according to the spirit of your Society. For example, when he says to a friend, " Give yourself no concern about your nephew; I will furnish him with what he requires from the money that lies in my hands," what reason have you to interpret this to mean, that he would take that money without restoring it, and not that he merely advanced it with the purpose of re-placing it? And how extremely imprudent was it for you to

---

[1] The plan and materials of this letter were furnished by M. Nicole. (Nicole, iv. 243.)
[2] Jansenius, who was made Bishop of Ipres or Ypres, in 1636. The letters to which Pascal refers were printed at that time by the Jesuits themselves, who retained the originals in their possession ; these having come into their hands in consequence of the arrest of M. De St. Cyran.

furnish a refutation of your own lie, by printing the other letters of the Bishop of Ypres, which clearly show that, in point of fact, it was merely *advanced* money, which he was bound to refund. This appears, to your confusion, from the following terms in the letter, to which you give the date of July 30, 1619: " Be not uneasy about the money *advanced*, he shall want for nothing so long as he is here;" and likewise from another, dated January 6, 1620, where he says: " You are in too great haste ; when the account shall become due, I have no fear but that the little credit which I have in this place will bring me as much money as I require."

If you are convicted slanderers on this subject, you are no less so in regard to the ridiculous story about the charity-box of St. Merri. What advantage, pray, can you hope to derive from the accusation which one of your worthy friends has trumped up against that ecclesiastic ? Are we to conclude that a man is guilty, because he is accused ? No, fathers. Men of piety, like him, may expect to be perpetually accused, so long as the world contains calumniators like you. We must judge of him, therefore, not from the accusation, but from the sentence ; and the sentence pronounced on the case (February 23, 1656) justifies him completely. Moreover, the person who had the temerity to involve himself in that iniquitous process, was disavowed by his colleagues, and himself compelled to retract his charge. And as to what you allege, in the same place, about "that famous director, who pocketed at once nine hundred thousand livres," I need only refer you to Messieurs the curés of St. Roch and St. Paul, who will bear witness, before the whole city of Paris, to his perfect disinterestedness in the affair, and to your inexcusable malice in that piece of imposition.

Enough, however, for such paltry falsities. These are but the first raw attempts of your novices, and not the master-strokes of your "grand professed."[1] To these do I now come, fathers ; I come to a calumny which is certainly one

---

[1] The Jesuits must pass through a long novitiate, before they are admitted as " professed" members of the Society.

of the basest that ever issued from the spirit of your Society.
I refer to the insufferable audacity with which you have imputed to holy nuns, and to their directors, the charge of
"disbelieving the mystery of transubstantiation, and the real
presence of Jesus Christ in the eucharist." Here, fathers,
is a slander worthy of yourselves. Here is a crime which
God alone is capable of punishing, as you alone were capable of committing it. To endure it with patience, would require an humility as great as that of these calumniated ladies ; to give it credit would demand a degree of wickedness
equal to that of their wretched defamers. I propose not,
therefore, to vindicate them ; they are beyond suspicion.
Had they stood in need of defence, they might have commanded abler advocates than me. My object in what I say
here is to show, not their innocence, but your malignity. I
merely intend to make you ashamed of yourselves, and to let
the whole world understand that, after this, there is nothing
of which you are not capable.

You will not fail, I am certain, notwithstanding all this, to
say that I belong to Port-Royal; for this is the first thing
you say to every one who combats your errors : as if it were
only at Port-Royal that persons could be found possessed of
sufficient zeal to defend, against your attacks, the purity of
Christian morality. I know, fathers, the work of the pious
recluses who have retired to that monastery, and how much
the Church is indebted to their truly solid and edifying labors. I know the excellence of their piety and their learning.
For, though I have never had the honor to belong to their
establishment, as you, without knowing who or what I am,
would fain have it believed, nevertheless, I do know some of
them, and honor the virtue of them all. But God has not
confined within the precincts of that society all whom he
means to raise up in opposition to your corruptions. I hope,
with his assistance, fathers, to make you feel this ; and if he
vouchsafe to sustain me in the design he has led me to form,
of employing in his service all the resources I have received
from him, I shall speak to you in such a strain as will, per-

haps, give you reason to regret that you have *not* had to do with a man of Port-Royal. And to convince you of this, fathers, I must tell you that, while those whom you have abused with this notorious slander content themselves with lifting up their groans to Heaven to obtain your forgiveness for the outrage, I feel myself obliged, not being in the least affected by your slander, to make you blush in the face of the whole Church, and so bring you to that wholesome shame of which the Scripture speaks, and which is almost the only remedy for a hardness of heart like yours : *"Imple facies eorum ignominiâ, et quærent nomen tuum, Domine—* Fill their faces with shame, that they may seek thy name, O Lord."[1]

A stop must be put to this insolence, which does not spare the most sacred retreats. For who can be safe after a calumny of this nature ? For shame, fathers ! to publish in Paris such a scandalous book, with the name of your Father Meynier on its front, and under this infamous title, " Port-Royal and Geneva in concert against the most holy Sacrament of the Altar," in which you accuse of this apostasy, not only Monsieur the abbé of St. Cyran, and M. Arnauld, but also Mother Agnes, his sister, and all the nuns of that monastery, alleging that " their faith, in regard to the eucharist, is as suspicious as that of M. Arnauld," whom you maintain to be " a downright Calvinist."[2] I here ask the whole world if there be any class of persons within the pale of the Church, on whom you could have advanced such an abominable charge with less semblance of truth. For tell me, fathers, if these nuns and their directors, had been "in concert with Geneva against the most holy sacrament of the altar" (the very thought of which is shocking), how they should have come to select as the principal object of their piety that very sacrament which they held in abomination ? How should they have assumed the habit of the holy sacrament ? taken the name of the Daughters of the Holy Sacrament ? called their church the Church of the Holy Sacra-

[1] Ps. lxxxiii. 16. [2] Pp. 96, 4.

ment ?   How should they have requested and obtained from
Rome the confirmation of that institution, and the right of
saying every Thursday the office of the holy sacrament, in
which the faith of the Church is so perfectly expressed, if
they had conspired with Geneva to banish that faith from
the Church ?   Why would they have bound themselves, by
a particular devotion, also sanctioned by the pope, to have
some of their sisterhood, night and day without intermission,
in presence of the sacred host, to compensate, by their perpetual adorations towards that perpetual sacrifice, for the
impiety of the heresy that aims at its annihilation ?   Tell me,
fathers, if you can, why, of all the mysteries of our religion,
they should have passed by those in which they believed,
to fix upon that in which they believed not ?   and how they
should have devoted themselves, so fully and entirely, to
that mystery of our faith, if they took it, as the heretics do,
for the mystery of iniquity ?   And what answer do you give
to these clear evidences, embodied not in words only, but in
actions : and not in some particular actions, but in the whole
tenor of a life expressly dedicated to the adoration of Jesus
Christ, dwelling on our altars ?   What answer, again, do
you give to the books which you ascribe to Port-Royal, all
of which are full of the most precise terms employed by the
fathers and the councils to mark the essence of that mystery ?
It is at once ridiculous and disgusting to hear you replying
to these, as you have done throughout your libel.   M. Arnauld, say you, talks very well about transubstantiation ; but
he understands, perhaps, only " a significative transubstantiation."   True, he professes to believe in " the real presence ;" who can tell, however, but he means nothing more
than " a true and real figure ?"   How now, fathers ! whom,
pray, will you not make pass for a Calvinist whenever you
please, if you are to be allowed the liberty of perverting the
most canonical and sacred expressions by the wicked subtilties of your modern equivocations ?   Who ever thought of
using any other terms than those in question, especially in
simple discourses of devotion, where no controversies are

handled? And yet the love and the reverence in which they hold this sacred mystery, have induced them to give it such a prominence in all their writings, that I defy you, fathers, with all your cunning, to detect in them either the least appearance of ambiguity, or the slightest correspondence with the sentiments of Geneva.

Everybody knows, fathers, that the essence of the Genevan heresy consists, as it does according to your own showing, in their believing that Jesus Christ is not contained (*enfermé*), in this sacrament ; that it is impossible he can be in many places at once ; that he is, properly speaking, only in heaven, and that it is as there alone that he ought to be adored, and not on the altar ;[1] that the substance of the bread remains ; that the body of Jesus Christ does not enter into the mouth or the stomach ; that he can only be eaten by faith, and accordingly wicked men do not eat him at all; and that the mass is not a sacrifice, but an abomination.   Let us now hear, then, in what way "Port-Royal is in concert with Geneva." In the writings of the former we read, to your confusion, the following statement: That "the flesh and blood of Jesus Christ are contained under the species of bread and wine ;"[2] that "the Holy of Holies is present in the sanctuary, and that there he ought to be adored ;"[3] that "Jesus Christ dwells in the sinners who communicate, by the real and veritable presence of his body in their stomach, although not by

---

[1] It is hardly necessary to observe, that in this passage the Protestant faith on the supper is not fairly represented.   The Reformers did not deny that Christ was really present in that sacrament.   They held that he was present spiritually, though not corporeally.   Some of them expressed themselves strongly in opposition to those who spoke of the supper as a mere or bare sign.   Calvin says: "There are two things in the sacrament—corporeal symbols, by which things invisible are proposed to the senses; and a spiritual truth, which is represented and sealed by the symbols.   In the mystery of the supper, Christ is *truly* exhibited to us, and therefore his body and blood." (Inst., lib. iv.. cap. 17, 11.)   "The body of Christ," says Peter Martyr (Loc. Com., iv. 10), " is not *substantially* present anywhere but in heaven.   I do not, however, deny that his true body and true blood, which were offered for human redemption on the cross, are *spiritually* partaken of by believers in the holy supper."   This is the general sentiment of Protestant divines. (De Moor, in Marck, Compend. Theol., p. v. 679, &c.)
[2] Second letter of M. Arnauld, p. 259.   [3] Ibid., p. 243.

the presence of his Spirit in their hearts ;"[1] that " the dead
ashes of the bodies of the saints derive their principal dignity
from that seed of life which they retain from the touch of
the immortal and vivifying flesh of Jesus Christ ;"[2] that " it
is not owing to any natural power, but to the almighty
power of God, to whom nothing is impossible, that the body
of Jesus Christ is comprehended under the host, and under
the smallest portion of every host ;"[3] that " the divine virtue
is present to produce the effect which the words of consecration signify ;"[4] that " Jesus Christ, while he is lowered
(rabaissé), and hidden upon the altar, is, at the same time,
elevated in his glory ; that he subsists, of himself and by his
own ordinary power, in divers places at the same time—in
the midst of the Church triumphant, and in the midst of the
Church militant and travelling ;"[5] that " the sacramental
species remain suspended, and subsist extraordinarily, without being upheld by any subject ; and that the body of
Jesus Christ is also suspended under the species, and that it
does not depend upon these, as substances depend upon
accidents ;"[6] that " the substance of the bread is changed,
the immutable accidents remaining the same ;"[7] that " Jesus
Christ reposes in the eucharist with the same glory that he
has in heaven ;"[8] that " his glorious humanity resides in
the tabernacles of the Church, under the species of bread,
which forms its visible covering ; and that, knowing the
grossness of our natures, he conducts us to the adoration of
his divinity, which is present in all places, by the adoring of
his humanity, which is present in a particular place ;"[9] that
" we receive the body of Jesus Christ upon the tongue,
which is sanctified by its divine touch ;"[10] " that it enters
into the mouth of the priest ;"[11] that " although Jesus Christ

[1] Frequent Communion, 3d part, ch. 16.   *Poitrine*—that is, the
bodily breast or stomach, in opposition to *cœur*—the heart or soul.
[2] Ibid.. 1st part, ch. 40.
[3] Theolog. Fam., lec. 15.   [5] Ibid.
[4] De la Suspension, Rais. 21.   [8] Ibid., p. 23.
[7] Hours of the Holy Sacrament, in Prose.
[6] Letters of M. de St. Cyran, tom. i., let. 93.   [10] Ibid.
[9] Letter 32.   [11] Letter 72.

has made himself accessible in the holy sacrament, by an act
of his love and graciousness, he preserves, nevertheless, in
that ordinance, his inaccessibility, as an inseparable condition
of his divine nature; because, although the body alone and
the blood alone are there, by virtue of the words *vi verborum*,
as the schoolmen say, his whole divinity may, notwithstanding, be there also, as well as his whole humanity, by a necessary conjunction."[1]   In fine, that "the eucharist is at the
same time sacrament and sacrifice;"[2] and that "although
this sacrifice is a commemoration of that of the cross, yet
there is this difference between them, that the sacrifice of the
mass is offered for the Church only, and for the faithful in
her communion; whereas that of the cross has been offered
for all the world, as the Scripture testifies."[3]

I have quoted enough, fathers, to make it evident that
there was never, perhaps, a more imprudent thing attempted
than what you have done.   But I will go a step farther, and
make you pronounce this sentence against yourselves.   For
what do you require from a man, in order to remove all suspicion of his being in concert and correspondence with
Geneva?   "If M. Arnauld," says your Father Meynier,
p. 93, "had said that in this adorable mystery, there is no
substance of the bread under the species, but only the flesh
and the blood of Jesus Christ, I should have confessed that
he had declared himself absolutely against Geneva."   Confess it, then, ye revilers! and make him a public apology.
How often have you seen this declaration made in the passages I have just cited?   Besides this, however, the Familiar Theology of M. de St. Cyran having been approved by
M. Arnauld, it contains the sentiments of both.   Read,
then, the whole of lesson 15th, and particularly article 2d,
and you will there find the words you desiderate, even
more formally stated than you have done yourselves.   "Is
there any bread in the host, or any wine in the chalice?
No : for all the substance of the bread and the wine

[1] Defence of the Chaplet of the H. Sacrament, p. 217.
[2] Theol. Famil., lec. 15.   [3] Itid., p. 153.

is taken away, to give place to that of the body and blood of Jesus Christ, the which substance alone remains therein, covered by the qualities and species of bread and wine."

How now, fathers! will you still say that Port-Royal teaches "nothing that Geneva does not receive," and that M. Arnauld has said nothing in his second letter "which might not have been said by a minister of Charenton?" See if you can persuade Mestrezat[1] to speak as M. Arnauld does in that letter, at page 237? Make him say, that it is an infamous calumny to accuse him of denying transubstantiation; that he takes for the fundamental principle of his writings the truth of the real presence of the Son of God, in opposition to the heresy of the Calvinists; and that he accounts himself happy for living in a place where the Holy of Holies is continually adored in the sanctuary"—a sentiment which is still more opposed to the belief of the Calvinists than the real presence itself; for as Cardinal Richelieu observes in his Controversies (page 536): "The new ministers of France having agreed with the Lutherans, who believe the real presence of Jesus Christ in the eucharist; they have declared that they remain in a state of separation from the Church on the point of this mystery, only on account of the adoration which Catholics render to the eucharist."[2] Get all the passages which I have extracted from the books of Port-Royal subscribed at Geneva,

---

[1] *John Mestrezat,* Protestant minister of Paris, was born at Geneva in 1592, and died in May 1657. His Sermons on the Epistle to the Hebrews and other discourses. published after his death. are truly excellent. This learned and eloquent divine frequently engaged in controversy with the Romanists. and on one occasion managed the debate with such spirit that Cardinal Richelieu, taking hold of his shoulder, exclaimed: "This is the boldest minister in France." (Bayle, Dict., art. *Mestrezat.*)

[2] The statement of the Protestant faith, given in a preceding note, may suffice to show that it differs, *toto cœlo*, from that of Rome, as this is explained in the text. The leading fallacy of the Romish creed on this subject is the monstrous dogma of transubstantiation; the adoration of the host is merely a corollary. Calvinists and Lutherans, thougL differing in their views of the ordinance. always agreed in acknowledging the *real* presence of Christ in the eucharist, though they consider the sense in which Romanists interpret that term to be chargeable with blasphemy and absurdity.

and not the isolated passages merely, but the entire treatises regarding this mystery, such as the Book of Frequent Communion, the Explication of the Ceremonies of the Mass, the Exercise during Mass, the Reasons of the Suspension of the Holy Sacrament, the Translation of the Hymns in the Hours of Port-Royal, &c.; in one word, prevail upon them to establish at Charenton that holy institution of adoring, without intermission, Jesus Christ contained in the eucharist, as is done at Port-Royal, and it will be the most signal service which you could render to the Church; for in this case it will turn out, not that Port-Royal is in concert with Geneva, but that Geneva is in concert with Port-Royal, and with the whole Church.

Certainly, fathers, you could not have been more unfortunate than in selecting Port-Royal as the object of attack for not believing in the eucharist; but I will show what led you to fix upon it. You know I have picked up some small acquaintance with your policy; in this instance you have acted upon its maxims to admiration. If Monsieur the abbé of St. Cyran, and M. Arnauld, had only spoken of what ought to be believed with great respect to this mystery, and said nothing about what ought to be done in the way of preparation for its reception, they might have been the best Catholics alive; and no equivocations would have been discovered in their use of the terms " real presence" and " transubstantiation." But since all who combat your licentious principles must needs be heretics, and heretics too, in the very point in which they condemn your laxity, how could M. Arnauld escape falling under this charge on the subject of the eucharist, after having published a book expressly against your profanations of that sacrament? What! must he be allowed to say, with impunity, that " the body of Jesus Christ ought not to be given to those who habitually lapse into the same crimes, and who have no prospect of amendment; and that such persons ought to be excluded, for some time, from the altar, to purify themselves by sincere penitence, that they may approach it afterwards with benefit?"

Suffer no one to talk in this strain, fathers, or you will find that fewer people will come to your confessionals. Father Brisacier says, that "were you to adopt this course, you would never apply the blood of Jesus Christ to a single individual." It would be infinitely more for your interest were every one to adopt the views of your Society, as set forth by your Father Mascarenhas, in a book approved by your doc- tors, and even by your reverend Father-General, namely, "That persons of every description, and even priests, may receive the body of Jesus Christ on the very day they have polluted themselves with odious crimes; that so far from such communions implying irreverence, persons who partake of them in this manner act a 'commendable part; that con- fessors ought not to keep them back from the ordinance, but, on the contrary, ought to advise those who have recently committed such crimes to communicate immediately; be- cause, although the Church has forbidden it, this prohibition is annulled by the universal practice in all places of the earth."[1]

See what it is, fathers, to have Jesuits in all places of the earth! Behold the universal practice which you have intro- duced, and which you are anxious everywhere to maintain! It matters nothing that the tables of Jesus Christ are filled with abominations, provided that your churches are crowded with people. Be sure, therefore, cost what it may, to set down all that dare to say a word against your practice, as heretics on the holy sacrament. But how can you do this, after the irrefragable testimonies which they have given of their faith? Are you not afraid of my coming out with the four grand proofs of their heresy which you have adduced? You ought, at least, to be so, fathers, and I ought not to spare your blushing. Let us, then, proceed to examine proof the first.

"M. de St. Cyran," says Father Meynier, "consoling one of his friends upon the death of his mother (tom. i., let 14), says that the most acceptable sacrifice that can be offered up

---

[1] Mascar., tr. 4, disp. 5, n. 284.

to God on such occasions, is that of patience; therefore he is a Calvinist." This is marvellously shrewd reasoning, fathers; and I doubt if anybody will be able to discover the precise point of it. Let us learn it, then, from his own mouth. "Because," says this mighty controversialist, "it is obvious that he does not believe in the sacrifice of the mass; for this is, of all other sacrifices, the most acceptable unto God." Who will venture to say now that the Jesuits do not know how to reason? Why, they know the art to such perfection, that they will extract heresy out of anything you choose to mention, not even excepting the Holy Scripture itself! For example, might it not be heretical to say, with the wise man in Ecclesiasticus, "There is nothing worse than to love money;"[1] as if adultery, murder, or idolatry, were not far greater crimes? Where is the man who is not in the habit of using similar expressions every day? May we not say, for instance, that the most acceptable of all sacrifices in the eyes of God is that of a contrite and humbled heart; just because, in discourses of this nature, we simply mean to compare certain internal virtues with one another, and not with the sacrifice of the mass, which is of a totally different order, and infinitely more exalted? Is this not enough to make you ridiculous, fathers? And is it necessary, to complete your discomfiture, that I should quote the passages of that letter in which M. de St. Cyran speaks of the sacrifice of the mass, as "the most excellent" of all others, in the following terms? "Let there be presented to God, daily and in all places, the sacrifice of the body of his Son, who could not find *a more excellent way* than that by which he might honor his Father." And afterwards : "Jesus Christ has enjoined us to take, when we are dying, his sacrificed body, to render more acceptable to God the sacrifice of our own, and to join himself with us at the hour of dissolution, to the end that he may strengthen us for the struggle, sanctifying, by his presence, the last sacrifice which we make to God of our life and our body?" Pretend to take no notice of all this, fathers, and

[1] Ecclesiasticus (Apocrypha).

persist in maintaining, as you do in page 39, that he refused to take the communion on his death-bed, and that he did not believe in the sacrifice of the mass. Nothing can be too gross for calumniators by profession.

Your second proof furnishes an excellent illustration of this. To make a Calvinist of M. de St. Cyran, to whom you ascribe the book of *Petrus Aurelius*, you take advantage of a passage (page 80) in which Aurelius explains in what manner the Church acts towards priests, and even bishops, whom she wishes to degrade or depose. "The Church," he says, "being incapable of depriving them of the power of the order, the character of which is indelible, she does all that she can do ;—she banishes from her memory the character which she cannot banish from the souls of the individuals who have been once invested with it ; she regards them in the same light as if they were not bishops or priests ; so that, according to the ordinary language of the Church, it may be said they are no longer such, although they always remain such, in as far as the character is concerned—*ob indelebilitatem characteris.*" You perceive, fathers, that this author, who has been approved by three general assemblies of the clergy of France, plainly declares that the character of the priesthood is indelible ; and yet you make him say, on the contrary, in the very same passage, that "the character of the priesthood is *not* indelible." This is what I would call a notorious slander; in other words, according to your nomenclature, a small venial sin. And the reason is, this book has done you some harm, by refuting the heresies of your brethren in England touching the Episcopal authority. But the folly of the charge is equally remarkable; for, after having taken it for granted, without any foundation, that M. de St. Cyran holds the priestly character to be not indelible, you conclude from this that he does not believe in the real presence of Jesus Christ in the eucharist.

Do not expect me to answer this, fathers. If you have got no common sense, I am not able to furnish you with it. All who possess any share of it will enjoy a hearty laugh at your expense. Nor will they treat with greater respect your third proof, which rests upon the following words, taken from the Book of Frequent Communion : "In the eucharist God vouchsafes us *the same food* that he bestows on the saints in heaven, with this difference only, that here he withholds from us its sensible sight and taste, reserving both of these for the heavenly world."[1] These words express the sense of the Church so distinctly, that I am constantly forgetting what reason you have for picking a quarrel with them, in order to turn them to a bad use ; for I can see nothing more in them than what the Council of Trent teaches (sess. xiii., c. 8), namely, that there is no difference between Jesus Christ in the eucharist and Jesus Christ in heaven, except that here he is veiled, and there he is not. M. Arnauld does not say that there is no difference in the manner of receiving Jesus Christ, but only that there is no difference in Jesus Christ who is received. And yet you would, in the face of all reason, interpret his language in this passage to mean, that Jesus Christ is no more eaten with the mouth in this world than he is in heaven ; upon which you ground the charge of heresy against him.

You really make me sorry for you, fathers. Must we explain this further to you ? Why do you confound that divine nourishment with the manner of receiving it ? There is but one point of difference, as I have just observed, betwixt that nourishment upon earth and in heaven, which is, that here it is hidden under veils which deprive us of its sensible sight and taste ; but there are various points of dissimilarity in the manner of receiving it here and there, the principal of which is, as M. Arnauld expresses it (p. 3, ch. 16), "that here it enters into the mouth and the breast both of the good and of the wicked," which is not the case in heaven.

And if you require to be told the reason of this diversity, I may inform you, fathers, that the cause of God's ordaining these different modes of receiving the same food, is the difference that exists betwixt the state of Christians in this life

[1] Freq. Com., 3 part, ch. 11.

and that of the blessed in heaven. The state of the Christian, as Cardinal Perron observes after the fathers, holds a
middle place between the state of the blessed and the state
of the Jews. The spirits in bliss possess Jesus Christ really,
without veil or figure. The Jews possessed Jesus Christ
only in figures and veils, such as the manna and the paschal
lamb. And Christians possess Jesus Christ in the eucharist
really and truly, although still concealed under veils. " God,"
says St. Eucher, " has made three tabernacles—the syna-
gogue, which had the shadows only, without the truth ; the
Church, which has the truth and shadows together; and
heaven, where there is no shadow, but the truth alone." It
would be a departure from our present state, which is the
state of faith, opposed by St. Paul alike to the law and to
open vision, did we possess the figures only, without Jesus
Christ ; for it is the property of the law to have the mere
figure, and not the substance of things. And it would be
equally a departure from our present state if we possessed
him visibly ; because faith, according to the same apostle,
deals not with things that are seen. And thus the eucharist,
from its including Jesus Christ truly, though under a veil, is
in perfect accordance with our state of faith. It follows,
that this state would be destroyed, if, as the heretics maintain, Jesus Christ were not really under the species of bread
and wine ; and it would be equally destroyed if we received
him openly, as they do in heaven: since, on these supposi-
tions, our state would be confounded, either with the state of
Judaism or with that of glory.

Such, fathers, is the mysterious and divine reason of this
most divine mystery. This it is that fills us with abhorrence
at the Calvinists, who would reduce us to the condition of
the Jews ; and this it is that makes us aspire to the glory of
the beatified, where we shall be introduced to the full and
eternal enjoyment of Jesus Christ. From hence you must
see that there are several points of difference between the
manner in which he communicates himself to Christians and
to the blessed ; and that, amongst others, he is in this world

received by the mouth, and not so in heaven ; but that they all depend solely on the diŝtinction between our state of faith and their state of immediate vision. And this is precisely, fathers, what M. Arnauld has expressed, with great plainness, in the following terms : "There can be no other difference between the purity of those who receive Jesus Christ in the eucharist and that of the blessed, than what exists between faith and the open vision of God, upon which alone depends the different manner in which he is eaten upon earth and in heaven." You were bound in duty, fathers, to have revered in· these words the sacred truths they express, instead of wresting them for the purpose of detecting an heretical meaning which they never contained, nor could possibly contain, namely, that Jesus Christ is eaten by faith only, and not by the mouth ; the malicious perversion of your Fathers Annat and Meynier, which forms the capital count of their indictment.

Conscious, however, of the wretched deficiency of your proofs, you have had recourse to a new artifice, which is nothing less than to falsify the Council of Trent, in order to convict M. Arnauld of nonconformity with it ; so vast is your store of methods for making people heretics. This feat has been achieved by Father Meynier, in fifty different places of his book, and about eight or ten times in the space of a single page (the 54th), wherein he insists that to speak like a true Catholic, it is not enough to say, "I believe that Jesus Christ is really present in the eucharist," but we must say, "I believe, *with the council*, that he is present by a true *local presence*, or locally." And in proof of this, he cites the council, session xiii., canon 3d, canon 4th, and canon 6th. Who would not suppose, upon seeing the term *local presence* quoted from three canons of· a universal council, that the phrase was actually to be found in them ? This might have served your turn very well, before the appearance of my fifteenth letter ; but as matters now stand, fathers, the trick has become too stale for us. We go our way and consult the council, and discover only that you are falsifiers. Such

terms as *local presence, locally*, and *locality*, never existed in
the passages to which you refer; and let me tell you further,
they are not to be found in any other canon of that council,
nor in any other previous council, nor in any father of the
Church. Allow me, then, to ask you, fathers, if you mean
to cast the suspicion of Calvinism upon all that have not
made use of that peculiar phrase? If this be the case, the
Council of Trent must be suspected of heresy, and all the
holy fathers without exception. Have you no other way
of making M. Arnauld heretical, without abusing so many
other people who never did you any harm, and among the
rest, St. Thomas, who is one of the greatest champions of the
eucharist, and who, so far from employing that term, has expressly rejected it—"*Nullo modo corpus Christi est in hoc
sacramento localiter?*—By no means is the body of Christ in
this sacrament *locally?*" Who are you, then, fathers, to
pretend, on your authority, to impose new terms, and ordain
them to be used by all for rightly expressing their faith; as
if the profession of the faith, drawn up by the popes according to the plan of the council, in which this term has no
place, were defective, and left an ambiguity in the creed of
the faithful, which you had the sole merit of discovering?
Such a piece of arrogance, to prescribe these terms, even to
learned doctors! such a piece of forgery, to attribute them
to general councils! and such ignorance, not to know the objections which the most enlightened saints have made to their
reception! "Be ashamed of the error of your ignorance,"[1]
as the Scripture says of ignorant impostors like you—*De
mendacio ineruditionis tuæ confundere.*

Give up all further attempts, then, to act the masters;
you have neither character nor capacity for the part. If,
however, you would bring forward your propositions with
a little more modesty, they might obtain a hearing. For
although this phrase, *local presence*, has been rejected, as
you have seen, by St. Thomas, on the ground that the body
of Jesus Christ is not in the eucharist, in the ordinary exten-

---

[1] Eccles. iv. 25 (Apocrypha).

sion of bodies in their places, the expression has, nevertheless, been adopted by some modern controversial writers, who
understand it simply to mean that the body of Jesus Christ
is truly under the species, which being in a particular place,
the body of Jesus Christ is there also. And in this sense M.
Arnauld will make no scruple to admit the term, as M. de
St. Cyran[1] and he have repeatedly declared that Jesus Christ
in the eucharist is truly in a particular place, and miraculously
in many places at the same time. Thus all your subtleties
fall to the ground ; and you have failed to give the slightest
semblance of plausibility to an accusation, which ought not to
have been allowed to show its face, without being supported
by the most unanswerable proofs.

But what avails it, fathers, to oppose their innocence to
your calumnies ? You impute these errors to them, not in
the belief that they maintain heresy, but from the idea that
they have done you injury. That is enough, according to
your theology, to warrant you to calumniate them without
criminality ; and you can, without either penance or confession, say mass, at the very time that you charge priests, who
say it every day, with holding it to be pure idolatry ; which,
were it true, would amount to sacrilege no less revolting than
that of your own Father Jarrige, whom you yourselves ordered to be hanged in effigy, for having said mass " at the
time he was in agreement with Geneva."[2]

What surprises me, therefore, is not the little scrupulosity
with which you load them with crimes of the foulest and
falsest description, but the little prudence you display, by fixing on them charges so destitute of plausibility. You dispose

---

[1] *Jean du Verger de Hauranne, the Abbé de Saint Cyran,* was born
at Bayonne in 1581. He was the intimate friend of Jansenius, and a
man of great piety and talents, but was seized as a heretic, and thrown
by Cardinal Richelieu into the dungeon of Vincennes. After five years'
imprisonment he was released, but died shortly after, October, 11, 1643.
By his followers, M. de Saint Cyran was reverenced as a saint and a
martyr.

This Father Jarrige was a famous Jesuit, who became a Protestant, and published, after his separation from Rome, a book, entitled
"*Le Jesuite sur l'Echaffaut*—The Jesuit on the Scaffold," in which he
treats his old friends with no mercy.

of sins, it is true, at your pleasure; but do you mean to dispose of men's beliefs too? Verily, fathers, if the suspicion of Calvinism must needs fall either on them or on you, you would stand, I fear, on very ticklish ground. Their language is as Catholic as yours; but their conduct confirms their faith, and your conduct belies it. For if you believe, as well as they do, that the bread is really changed into the body of Jesus Christ, why do you not require, as they do, from those whom you advise to approach the altar, that the heart of stone and ice should be sincerely changed into a heart of flesh and of love? If you believe that Jesus Christ is in that sacrament in a state of death, teaching those that approach it to die to the world, to sin, and to themselves, why do you suffer those to profane it in whose breasts evil passions continue to reign in all their life and vigor? And how do you come to judge those worthy to eat the bread of heaven, who are not worthy to eat that of earth?

Precious votaries, truly, whose zeal is expended in persecuting those who honor this sacred mystery by so many holy communions, and in flattering those who dishonor it by so many sacrilegious desecrations! How comely is it in these champions of a sacrifice so pure and so venerable, to collect around the table of Jesus Christ a crowd of hardened profligates, reeking from their debaucheries; and to plant in the midst of them a priest, whom his own confessor has hurried from his obscenities to the altar; there, in the place of Jesus Christ, to offer up that most holy victim to the God of holiness, and convey it, with his polluted hands, into mouths as thoroughly polluted as his own! How well does it become those who pursue this course "in all parts of the world," in conformity with maxims sanctioned by their own general, to impute to the author of Frequent Communion, and to the Sisters of the Holy Sacrament, the crime of not believing in that sacrament!

Even this, however, does not satisfy them. Nothing less will satiate their rage than to accuse their opponents of having renounced Jesus Christ and their baptism. This is no air-built fable, like those of your invention; it is a fact, and

denotes a delirious frenzy, which marks the fatal consumma-
tion of your calumnies. Such a notorious falsehood as this
would not have been in hands worthy to support it, had it
remained in those of your good friend Filleau, through whom
you ushered it into the world: your Society has openly
adopted it; and your Father Meynier maintained it the other
day to be *" a certain truth,"* that Port-Royal has, for the
space of thirty-five years, been forming a secret plot, of
which M. de St. Cyran and M. D'Ypres have been the ringleaders, " to ruin the mystery of the incarnation—to make
the Gospel pass for an apocryphal fable—to exterminate the
Christian religion, and to erect Deism upon the ruins of
Christianity." Is this enough, fathers? Will you be satisfied if all this be believed of the objects of your hate? Would
your animosity be glutted at length, if you could but succeed
in making them odious, not only to all within the Church, by
the charge of *" consenting with Geneva,"* of which you accuse
them, but even to all who believe in Jesus Christ, though
beyond the pale of the Church, by the imputation of *Deism?*
But whom do you expect to convince, upon your simple
asseveration, without the slightest shadow of proof, and in
the face of every imaginable contradiction, that priests who
preach nothing but the grace of Jesus Christ, the purity of
the Gospel, and the obligations of baptism, have renounced
at once their baptism, the Gospel, and Jesus Christ? Who
will believe it, fathers? Wretched as you are,[1] do you believe it yourselves? What a sad predicament is yours, when
you must either prove that they do not believe in Jesus
Christ, or must pass for the most abandoned calumniators.
Prove it, then, fathers. Name that *" worthy clergyman,"*
who, you say, attended that assembly at Bourg-Fontaine[2]

---

[1] *Misérables que vous êtes*—one of the bitterest expressions which
Pascal has applied to his opponents, and one which they have deeply
felt, but the full force of which can hardly be rendered into English.

[2] With regard to this famous assembly at Bourg-Fontaine, in which
it was alleged a conspiracy was formed by the Jansenists against the
Christian religion, the curious reader may consult the work of M. Arnauld, entitled *Morale Pratique des Jesuites*, vol. viii., where there is a
detailed account of the whole proceedings. (Nicole, iv. 283.)

in 1621, and discovered to Brother Filleau the design there concerted of overturning the Christian religion. Name those six persons who you allege to have formed that conspiracy. Name the *individual who is designated by the letters A. A.*, who you say "*was not Antony Arnauld*" (because he convinced you that he was at that time only nine years of age), "*but another person, who you say is still in life, but too good a friend of M. Arnauld not to be known to him.*" You know him, then, fathers ; aud consequently; if you are not destitute of religion yourselves, you are bound to delate that impious wretch to the king and parliament, that he may be punished according to his deserts. You must speak out, fathers ; you must name the person, or submit to the disgrace of being henceforth regarded in no other light than as common liars, unworthy of being ever credited again. Good Father Valerien has taught us that this is the way in which such characters should be "put to the rack," and brought to their senses. Your silence upon the present challenge will furnish a full and satisfactory confirmation of this diabolical calumny. Your blindest admirers will he constrained to admit, that it will be "the result, not of your goodness, but your impotency ;" and to wonder how you could be so wicked as to extend your hatred even to the nuns of Port-Royal, and to say, as you do in page 14, that *The Secret Chaplet of the Holy Sacrament*,[1] composed by one of their number, was the first-fruit of that conspiracy against Jesus Christ; or, as in page 95, that "they have imbihed all the detestable principles of that work;" which is, according to your account, "a lesson in Deism." Your falsehoods regarding that hook have already been triumphantly refuted, in the defence of

---

[1] *The Secret Chaplet of the most Holy Sacrament.*—Such was the title of a very harmless piece of mystic devotion of three or four pages, the production of a nun of Port-Royal, called Sister Agnès de Saint Paul, which appeared in 1628. It excited the jealousy of the Archbishop of Sens—set the doctors of Paris and those of Louvain by the ears—occasioned a war of pamphlets. and was finally carried by appeal to the Court of Rome, by which it was suppressed. (Nicole, iv. 302.) Agnès de St. Paul was the younger sister of the Mère Angélique Arnauld, and both of them were sisters of the celebrated M. Arnauld.

the censure of the late Archbishop of Paris against Father Brisacier. That publication you are incapable of answering; and yet you do not scruple to abuse it in a more shameful manner than ever, for the purpose of charging women, whose piety is universally known, with the vilest blasphemy.

Cruel, cowardly persecutors! Must, then, the most retired cloisters afford no retreat from your calumnies? While these consecrated virgins are employed, night and day, according to their institution, in adoring Jesus Christ in the holy sacrament, you cease not, night nor day, to publish abroad that they do not believe that he is either in the eucharist or even at the right hand of his Father; and you are publicly excommunicating them from the Church, at the very time when they are in secret praying for the whole ·Church, and for you! You blacken with your slanders those who have neither ears to hear nor mouths to answer you! But Jesus Christ, in whom they are now hidden, not to appear till one day together with him, hears you, and answers for them. At the moment I am now writing, that holy and terrible voice is heard which confounds nature and consoles the Church.[1] And I fear, fathers, that those who

---

[1] This refers to the celebrated miracles of "the Holy Thorn," the first of which, said to have lately taken place in Port-Royal, was then creating much sensation. The facts are briefly these: A thorn, said to have belonged to the crown of thorns worn by our Saviour, having been presented, in March 1656, to the Monastery of Port-Royal, the nuns and their young pupils were permitted, each in turn, to kiss the relic. One of the latter, Margaret Perier, the niece of Pascal, a girl of about ten or eleven years of age, had been long troubled with a disease in the eye (*fistula lachrymalis*), which had baffled the skill of all the physicians of Paris. On approaching the holy thorn, she applied it to the diseased organ, and shortly thereafter exclaimed, to the surprise and delight of all the sisters, that her eye was completely cured. A certificate, signed by some of the most celebrated physicians, attested the cure as, in their opinion a miraculous one. The friends of Port-Royal, and none more than Pascal, were overjoyed at this interposition, which, being followed by other extraordinary cures, they regarded as a voice from heaven in favor of that institution. The Jesuits alone rejected it with ridicule, and published a piece, entitled "*Rabat-joie*, &c.—A Damper: or, Observations on what has lately happened at Port-Royal as to the affair of the Holy Thorn." This was answered in November 1656, in a tract supposed to have been written by M. de Pont Château, who was called "the Clerk of the Holy Thorn," assisted by Pascal. (Recueil de Pieces, &c., de Port-Royal, pp. 283–448.) It has been well observed,

PROVINCIAL LETTERS.

now harden their hearts, and refuse with obstinacy to hear him, while he speaks in the character of God, will one day be compelled to hear him with terror, when he speaks to them in the character of a Judge. What account, indeed, fathers, will you be able to render to him of the many calumnies you have uttered, seeing that he will examine them, in that day, not according to the fantasies of Fathers Dicastille, Gans, and Pennalossa, who justify them, but according to the eternal laws of truth, and the sacred ordinances of his own Church, which, so far from attempting to vindicate that crime, abhors it to such a degree that she visits it with the same penalty as wilful murder? By the first and second Councils of Arles she has decided that the communion shall be denied to slanderers as well as murderers, till the approach of death. The Council of Lateran has judged those unworthy of admission into the ecclesiastical state who have been convicted of the crime, even though they may have reformed. The popes have even threatened to deprive of the communion at death those who have calumniated bishops, priests, or deacons. And the authors of a defamatory libel, who fail to prove what they have advanced, are condemned by Pope Adrian *to be whipped ;*—yes, reverend fathers, *flagellentur* is the word. So strong has been the repugnance of the Church at all times to the errors of your Society—a Society so thoroughly depraved as to invent excuses for the grossest of crimes, such as calumny, chiefly that it may enjoy the greater freedom in perpetrating them itself. There can be no doubt, fathers, that you would be capable of producing abundance of mischief in this way, had God not permitted you to fur-

"that many laborious and voluminous discussions might have been saved, if the simple and very reasonable rule had been adopted of waiving investigation into the credibility of any narrative of supernatural or pretended supernatural events, said to have taken place *upon consecrated ground, or under sacred roofs.*" (Natural Hist. of Enthusiasm, p. 236.) "It is well known," says Mosheim. "that the Jansenists and Augustinians have long pretended to confirm their doctrine by miracles; and they even acknowledge that these miracles have saved them when their affairs have been reduced to a desperate situation." (Mosh. Eccl. Hist., cent. xvii., sect. 2.)

nish with your own hands the means of preventing the. evil, and of rendering your slanders perfectly innocuous ; for, to deprive you of all credibility, it was quite enough to publish the strange maxim, that it is no crime to calumniate. Calumny is nothing, if not associated with a high reputation for honesty. The defamer can make no impression, unless he has the character of one that abhors defamation, as a crime of which he is incapable. And thus, fathers, you are betrayed by your own principle. You established the doctrine to secure yourselves a safe conscience, that you might slander without risk of damnation, and be ranked with those "pious and holy calumniators" of whom St. Athanasius speaks. To save yourselves from hell, you have embraced a maxim which promises you this security on the faith of your doctors ; but this same maxim, while it guarantees you, according to their idea, against the evils you dread in the future world, deprives you of all the advantage you may have expected to reap from it in the present ; so that, in attempting to escape the guilt, you have lost the benefit of calumny. Such is the self-contrariety of evil, and so completely does it confound and destroy itself by its own intrinsic malignity.

You might have slandered, therefore, much more advantageously for yourselves, had you professed to hold, with St. Paul, that evil speakers are not worthy to see God ; for in this case, though you would indeed have been condemning yourselves, your slanders would at least have stood a better chance of being believed. But by maintaining, as you have done, that calumny against your enemies is no crime, your slanders will be discredited, and you yourselves damned into the bargain ; for two things are certain, fathers—first, That it will never be in the power of your grave doctors to annihilate the justice of God ; and, secondly, That you could not give more certain evidence that you are not of the Truth than by your resorting to falsehood. If the Truth were on your side, she would fight for you—she would conquer for you ; and whatever enemies you might have to encounter, " the Truth would set you free" from them, according to her promise. But you have had recourse to falsehood, for no other design than to support the errors with which you flatter the sinful children of this world, and to bolster up the calumnies with which you persecute every man of piety who sets his face against these delusions. The truth being diametrically opposed to your ends, it behooved you, to use the language of the prophet, "to put your confidence in lies." You have said, "The scourges which afflict mankind shall not come nigh unto us; for we have made lies our refuge, and under falsehood have we hid ourselves."[1] But what says the prophet in reply to such ? "Forasmuch," says he, "as ye have put your trust in calumny and tumult—*sperastis in calumnia et in tumultu*—this iniquity and your ruin shall be like that of a high wall whose breaking cometh suddenly at an instant. And he shall break it as the breaking of the potter's vessel that is shivered in pieces"—with such violence that "there shall not be found in the bursting of it a shred to take fire from the hearth, or to take water withal out of the pit."[2] "Because," as another prophet says, "ye have made the heart of the righteous sad, whom I have not made sad ; and ye have flattered and strengthened the malice of the wicked ; I will therefore deliver my people out of your hands, and ye shall know that I am their Lord and yours."[3]

Yes, fathers, it is to be hoped that if you do not repent, God will deliver out of your hands those whom you have so long deluded, either by flattering them in their evil courses with your licentious maxims, or by poisoning their minds with your slanders. He will convince the former that the false rules of your casuists will not screen them from his indignation ; and he will impress on the minds of the latter the just dread of losing their souls by listening and yielding credit to your slanders, as you lose yours by hatching these

---

[1] Isa. xxviii. 15.   [2] Isa. xxx. 12–14.
[3] Ezek. xiii. 23. Pascal does not, either here or elsewhere, when quoting from Scripture, adhere very closely to the original, nor even to the Vulgate version.

slanders and disseminating them through the world. Let
no man be deceived ; God is not mocked ; none may violate
with impunity the commandment which he has given us in
the Gospel, not to condemn our neighbor without being well
assured of his guilt. And, consequently, what profession soever of piety those may make who lend a willing ear to your
lying devices, and under what pretence soever of devotion
they may entertain them, they have reason to apprehend exclusion from the kingdom of God, solely for having imputed
crimes of such a dark complexion as heresy and schism to
Catholic priests and holy nuns, upon no better evidence than
such vile fabrications as yours. "The devil," says M. de
Geneve,[1] "is on the tongue of him that slanders, and in the
ear of him that listens to the slanderer." "And evil speaking," says St. Bernard, "is a poison that extinguishes charity
in both of the parties ; so that a single calumny may prove
mortal to an infinite number of souls, killing not only those
who publish it, but all those besides by whom it is not re-
pudiated."[2]

Reverend fathers, my letters were not wont either to be so
prolix, or to follow so closely on one another. Want of
time must plead my excuse for both of these faults. The
present letter is a very long one, simply because I had no
leisure to make it shorter. You know the reason of this
haste better than I do. You have been unlucky in your
answers. You have done well, therefore, to change your
plan ; but 1 am afraid that you will get no credit for it, and
that people will say it was done for fear of the Benedictines.

I have just come to learn that the person who was generally reported to be the author of your Apologies, disclaims
them, and is annoyed at their having been ascribed to him.
He has good reason ; and I was wrong to have suspected
him of any such thing ; for, in spite of the assurances which

[1] This was the name given to St. Francis de Sales, bishop and prince
of Geneva, previously to his canonization, which took place in 1665.
[2] Serm. 24 in Cantic.

18*

I received, I ought to have considered that he was a man of too much good sense to believe your accusations, and of too much honor to publish them if he did not believe them. There are few people in the world capable of your extravagances ; they are peculiar to yourselves, and mark your character too plainly to admit of any excuse for having failed to recognize your hand in their concoction. I was led away by the common report; but this apology, which would be too good for you, is not sufficient for me, who profess to advance nothing without certain proof. In no other instance have I been guilty of departing from this rule. I am sorry for what I said. I retract it; and I only wish that you may profit by my example."[1]

[1] These two postscripts have been often admired—the former for the author's elegant excuse for the length of his letter; the latter for the adroitness with which he turns his apology for an undesigned mistake into a stroke at the disingenuousness of his opponents.

LETTER XVII.[1]

TO THE REVEREND FATHER ANNAT, JESUIT.[2]

THE AUTHOR OF THE LETTERS VINDICATED FROM THE CHARGE OF
HERESY—AN HERETICAL PHANTOM—POPES AND GENERAL COUN-
CILS NOT INFALLIBLE IN QUESTIONS OF FACT.

January 23, 1657.

REVEREND FATHER,—Your former behavior had induced
me to believe that you were anxious for a truce in our hos-
tilities ; and I was quite disposed to agree that it should be
so. Of late, however, you have poured forth such a volley
of pamphlets, in such rapid succession, as to make it apparent that peace rests on a very precarious footing when it depends on the silence of Jesuits. I know not if this rupture
will prove very advantageous to you ; but, for my part, I am
far from regretting the opportunity which it affords me of
rebutting that stale charge of heresy with which your writings abound.

It is full time, indeed, that I should, once for all, put a
stop to the liberty you have taken to treat me as a heretic—
a piece of gratuitous impertinence which seems to increase
by indulgence, and which is exhibited in your last book in a
style of such intolerable assurance, that were I not to answer the charge as it deserves, I might lay myself open to
the suspicion of being actually guilty. So long as the insult
was confined to your associates I despised it, as I did a thousand others with which they interlarded their productions.
To these my fifteenth letter was a sufficient reply. But you

---

[1] M. Nicole furnished the materials for this letter. (Nicole, iv. 324.)
[2] *Francis Annat*, the same person formerly referred to at p. 180.
He became French provincial of the Jesuits, and confessor to Louis XIV

now repeat the charge with a different air : you make it the main point of your vindication. It is, in fact, almost the only thing in the shape of argument that you employ. You say that, "as a complete answer to my fifteen letters, it is enough to say fifteen times that I am a heretic ; and having been pronounced such, I deserve no credit." In short, you make no question of my apostasy, but assume it as a settled point, on which you may build with all confidence. You are serious then, father, it would seem, in deeming me a heretic. I shall be equally serious in replying to the charge.

You are well aware, sir, that heresy is a charge of so grave a character, that it is an act of high presumption to advance, without being prepared to substantiate it. I now demand your proofs. When was I seen at Charenton ? When did I fail in my presence at mass, or in my Christian duty to my parish church ? What act of union with heretics, or of schism with the Church, can you lay to my charge ? What council have I contradicted ? What papal constitution have I violated ? You *must* answer, father, else —— You know what I mean.[1]   And what *do* you answer ? I beseech all to observe it : First of all, you assume " that the author of the letters is a Port-Royalist ;" then you tell us " that Port-Royal is declared to be heretical ;" and, therefore, you conclude, " the author of the letters must be a heretic." It is not on me, then, father, that the weight of this indictment falls, but on Port-Royal ; and I am only involved in the crime because you suppose me to belong to that establishment ; so that it will be no difficult matter for me to exculpate myself from the charge. I have no more to say than that I am not a member of that community ; and to refer you to my letters, in which I have declared that " I am a private individual ;" and again in so many words, that " I am not of Port-Royal," as I said in my sixteenth letter, which preceded your publication.

You must fall on some other way, then, to prove me a

---

[1] A threat, evidently, of administering to him the *Mentiris impuden-tissime* of the Capuchin, mentioned at p. 388.

heretic, otherwise the whole world will be convinced that it is beyond your power to make good your accusation. Prove from my writings that I do not receive the constitution.[1] My letters are not very voluminous—there are but sixteen of them—and I defy you or anybody else to detect in them the slightest foundation for such a charge. I shall, however, with your permission, produce something out of them to prove the reverse. When, for example, I say in the fourteenth that, "by killing our brethren in mortal sin, according to your maxims, we are damning those for whom Jesus Christ died," do I not plainly acknowledge that Jesus Christ died for those who may be damned, and, consequently, declare it to be false "that he died only for the predestinated," which is the error condemned in the fifth proposition? Certain it is, father, that I have not said a word in behalf of these impious propositions, which I detest with all my heart.[2] And even though Port-Royal should hold them, I protest against your drawing any conclusion from this against me, as, thank God, I have no sort of connection with any community except the Catholic, Apostolic and Roman Church, in the bosom of which I desire to live and die, in communion with the pope, the head of the Church, and beyond the pale of which I am persuaded there is no salvation.

[1] *The constitution*—that is, the bull of Pope Alexander VII., issued in October 1656, in which he not only condemned the Five Propositions, but, in compliance with the solicitations of the Jesuits, added an express clause, to the effect that these had been faithfully extracted from Jansenius, and were heretical in the sense in which he (Jansenius) employed them. This was a more stringent constitution than the first; but the Jansenists were ready to meet him on this point; they replied that a declaration of this nature overstepped the limits of the papal authority, and that the pope's infallibility did not extend to a judgment of *facts*.

[2] *The Five Propositions.*—A brief view of these celebrated Propositions may be here given, as necessary to the understanding of the text. They were as follows:—I. That some commandments of God are impracticable even to the righteous, who desire to keep them, according to their present strength. II. That grace is irresistible. III. That moral freedom consists, not in exemption from necessity, but from constraint. IV. That to assert that the will may resist or obey the motions of converting grace as it pleased, was a heresy of the semi-Pelagians. V. That to assert that Jesus Christ died for all men, without exception, is an error of the semi-Pelagians. For a fuller explication of the controversy, the reader must be referred to the Introduction.

How are you to get at a person who talks in this way, father? On what quarter will you assail me, since neither my words nor my writings afford the slightest handle to your accusations, and the obscurity in which my person is enveloped forms my protection against your threatenings? You feel yourselves smitten by an invisible hand—a hand, however, which makes your delinquencies visible to all the earth; and in vain do you endeavor to attack me in the person of those with whom you suppose me to be associated. I fear you not, either on my own account or on that of any other, being bound by no tie either to a community or to any individual whatsoever.[1] All the influence which your Society possesses can be of no avail in my case. From this world I have nothing to hope, nothing to dread, nothing to desire. Through the goodness of God, I have no need of any man's money or any man's patronage. Thus, my father, I elude all your attempts to lay hold of me. You may touch Port-Royal if you choose, but you shall not touch me. You may turn people out of the Sorbonne, but that will not turn me out of my domicile. You may contrive plots against priests and doctors, but not against me, for I am neither the one nor the other. And thus, father, you never perhaps had to do, in the whole course of your experience, with a person so completely beyond your reach, and therefore so admirably qualified for dealing with your errors—one perfectly free— one without engagement, entanglement, relationship, or business of any kind—one, too, who is pretty well versed in your maxims, and determined, as God shall give him light, to discuss them, without permitting any earthly consideration to arrest or slacken his endeavors.

---

[1] Pascal might say this with truth, for his only relatives being nuns, the tie of earthly relationship was considered by him as no longer existing; and beyond personal friendship, he had really no connection with Port-Royal. There is as little truth as force therefore, in the taunt of a late advocate of the Jesuits, who says, in reference to this passage: "Pascal was intimately connected with Port-Royal, he was even numbered among its recluses; and yet, in the act of unmasking the presumed duplicity of the Jesuits, the sublime writer did not scruple to imitate it." (Hist. de la Comp. de Jésus, par J. Crétineau-Joly, tom. iv. p. 54. Paris, 1845.)

Since, then, you can do nothing against me, what good purpose can it serve to publish so many calumnies, as you and your brethren are doing, against a class of persons who are in no way implicated in our disputes ?   You shall not escape under these subterfuges : you shall be made to feel the force of the truth in spite of them.   How does the case stand ?   I tell you that you are ruining Christian morality by divorcing it from the love of God, and dispensing with its obligation ; and you talk about " the death of Father Mester"—a person whom I never saw in my life.   I tell you that your authors permit a man to kill another for the sake of an apple, when it would be dishonorable to lose it ; and you reply by informing me that somebody "has broken into the poor—box at St. Merri !"   Again, what can you possibly mean by mixing me up perpetually with the book "On the Holy Virginity," written by some father of the Oratory, whom I never saw, any more than his book ?"[1]   It is rather extraordinary, father, that you should thus regard all that are opposed to you as if they were one person.   Your hatred would grasp them all at once, and would hold them as a body of reprobates, every one of whom is responsible for all the rest.

There is a vast difference between Jesuits and all their opponents.   There can be no doubt that you compose one body, united under one head ; and your regulations, as I have shown, prohibit you from printing anything without the approbation of your superiors, who are responsible for all the errors of individual writers, and who "cannot excuse themselves by saying that they did not observe the errors in any publication, for they ought to have observed them."   So say your ordinances, and so say the letters of your generals,

---

[1] " This book of the *Holy Virginity* was a translation from St. Augustine. made by Father Seguenot, priest of the Oratory.   So far, all was right ; but the priest had added to the original text some odd and peculiar remarks of his own, which merited censure.   As the publication came from the Oratory, a community always attached to the doctrine of St. Augustine, an attempt was made to throw the blame on those called Jansenists."   (Note by Nicole, iv. 332.)

Aquaviva, Vitelleschi, &c.   We have good reason, therefore, for charging upon you the errors of your associates, when we find they are sanctioned by your superiors and the divines of your Society.   With me, however, father, the case stands otherwise.   I have not subscribed the book of the Holy Virginity.   All the alms-boxes in Paris may be broken into, and yet I am not the less a good Catholic for all that.   In short, I beg to inform you, in the plainest terms, that nobody is responsible for my letters but myself, and that I am responsible for nothing but my letters.

Here, father, I might fairly enough have brought our dispute to an issue, without saying a word about those other persons whom you stigmatize as heretics, in order to comprehend me under that condemnation.   But as I have been the occasion of their ill treatment, I consider myself bound in some sort to improve the occasion, and I shall take advantage of it in three particulars.   One advantage, not inconsiderable in its way, is that it will enable me to vindicate the innocence of so many calumniated individuals.   Another, not inappropriate to my subject, will be to disclose, at the same time, the artifices of your policy in this accusation.   But the advantage which I prize most of all is, that it affords me an opportunity of apprizing the world of the falsehood of that scandalous report which you have been so busily disseminating, namely, " that the Church is divided by a new heresy." And as you are deceiving multitudes into the belief that the points on which you are raising such a storm are essential to the faith, I consider it of the last importance to quash these unfounded impressions, and distinctly to explain here what these points are, so as to show that, in point of fact, there are no heretics in the Church.

I presume, then, that were the question to be asked, Wherein consists the heresy of those called Jansenists? the immediate reply would be, " These people hold that the commandments of God are impracticable to men—that grace is irresistible—that we have not free will to do either good or evil—that Jesus Christ did not die for all men, but only for the elect; in short, they maintain the five propositions condemned by the pope." Do you not give it out to all that this is the ground on which you persecute your opponents? Have you not said as much in your books, in your conversations, in your catechisms? A specimen of this you gave at the late Christmas festival at St. Louis. One of your little shepherdesses was questioned thus :—

"For whom did Jesus Christ come into the world, my dear?"

"For all men, father."

"Indeed, my child; so you are not one of those new heretics who say that he came only for the elect?"

Thus children are led to believe you, and many others beside children; for you entertain people with the same stuff in your sermons, as Father Crasset did at Orleans, before he was laid under an interdict. And I frankly own that, at one time, I believed you myself. You had given me precisely the same idea of these good people; so that when you pressed them on these propositions, I narrowly watched their answer, determined never to see them more, if they did not renounce them as palpable impieties.

This, however, they have done in the most unequivocal way. M. de Sainte-Beuve,[1] king's professor in the Sorbonne, censured these propositions in his published writings long before the pope; and other Augustinian doctors, in various publications, and, among others, in a work "On Victorious Grace,"[2] reject the same articles as both heretical and strange doctrines. In the preface to that work they say that these propositions are " heretical and Lutheran, forged and fabricated at pleasure, and are neither to be found in Jansenius, nor

[1] " M. Jacques de Sainte-Beuve, one of the ablest divines of his age, preferred to relinquish his chair in the Sorbonne rather than concur in the censure of M. Arnauld, whose orthodoxy he regarded as beyond suspicion. He died in 1677." (Note by Nicole.)
[2] This work was entitled " On the Victorious Grace of Jesus Christ; or, Molina and his followers convicted of the error of the Pelagians and Semi-Pelagians. By the Sieur de Bonlieu. Paris, 1651." The real author was the celebrated M. de l aLane, well known in that controversy. (Note by Nicole.)

426 PROVINCIAL LETTERS.

in his defenders." They complain of being charged with such
sentiments, and address you in the words of St. Prosper, the
first disciple of St. Augustine their master, to whom the
semi-Pelagians of France had ascribed similar opinions, with
the view of bringing him into disgrace: "There are persons
who denounce us, so blinded by passion that they have
adopted means for doing so which ruin their own reputation.
They have, for this purpose, fabricated propositions of the
most impious and blasphemous character, which they indus-
triously circulate, to make people believe that we maintain
them in the wicked sense which they are pleased to attach to
them. But our reply will show at once our innocence, and the
malignity of these persons who have ascribed to us a set of impious tenets, of which they are themselves the sole inventors."

Truly, father, when I found that they had spoken in this
way before the appearance of the papal constitution—when
I saw that they afterwards received that decree with all possible respect, that they offered to subscribe it, and that M.
Arnauld had declared all this in his second letter, in stronger
terms than I can report him, I should have considered it a sin
to doubt their soundness in the faith. And, in fact, those
who were formerly disposed to refuse absolution to M. Arnauld's friends, have since declared, that after his explicit dis-
claimer of the errors imputed to him, there was no reason
left for cutting off either him or them from the communion
of the Church. Your associates, however, have acted very
differently; and it was this that made me begin to suspect
that you were actuated by prejudice.

You threatened first to compel them to sign that constitution, so long as you thought they would resist it; but no
sooner did you see them quite ready of their own accord to
submit to it, than we heard no more about this. Still, however, though one might suppose this ought to have satisfied
you, you persisted in calling them heretics, "because," said
you, "their heart belies their hand; they are Catholics outwardly, but inwardly they are heretics."[1]

¹ Réponse a quelques demandes, pp. 27, 47.

This, father, struck me as very strange reasoning; for where is the person of whom as much may not be said at any time? And what endless trouble and confusion would ensue, were it allowed to go on! "If," says Pope St. Gregory, "we refuse to believe a confession of faith made in conformity to the sentiments of the Church, we cast a doubt over the faith of all Catholics whatsoever." I am afraid, father, to use the words of the same pontiff, when speaking of a similar dispute in his time, "that your object is to make these persons heretics in spite of themselves; because to refuse to credit those who testify by their confession that they are in the true faith, is not to purge heresy, but to create it—*hoc non est hæresim purgare, sed facere.* But what confirmed me in my persuasion that there was indeed no heretic in the Church, was finding that our so-called heretics had vindicated themselves so successfully, that you were unable to accuse them of a single error in the faith, and that you were reduced to the necessity of assailing them on questions of *fact* only, touching Jansenius, which could not possibly be construed into heresy. You insist, it now appears, on their being compelled to acknowledge "that these propositions are contained in Jansenius, word for word, every one of them, in so many terms," or, as you express it, *Singulares, individuæ, totidem verbis apud Jansenium contentæ.*

Thenceforth your dispute became, in my eyes, perfectly indifferent. So long as I believed that you were debating the truth or falsehood of the propositions, I was all attention, for that quarrel touched the faith ; but when I discovered that the bone of contention was whether they were to be found, word for word, in Jansenius or not, as religion ceased to be interested in the controversy, I ceased to be interested in it also. Not but that there was some presumption that you were speaking the truth ; because to say that such and such expressions are to be found, word for word, in an author, is a matter in which there can be no mistake. I do not wonder, therefore, that so many people, both in France

and at Rome, should have been led to believe, on the authority of a phrase so little liable to suspicion, that Jansenius has
actually taught these obnoxious tenets. And for the same
reason, I was not a little surprised to learn that this same
point of fact, which you had propounded as so certain and
so important, was false ; and that after being challenged to
quote the pages of Jansenius, in which you had found these
propositions " word for word," you have not been able to
point them out to this day.

I am the more particular in giving this statement, because,
in my opinion, it discovers, in a very striking light, the spirit
of your Society in the whole of this affair ; and because some
people will be astonished to find that, notwithstanding all
the facts above mentioned, you have not ceased to publish
that they are heretics still. But you have only altered the
heresy to suit the time ; for no sooner had they freed themselves from one charge than your fathers, determined that
they should never want an accusation, substituted another in
its place. Thus, in 1653, their heresy lay in the *quality* of
the propositions ; then came the *word for word* heresy ;
after that, we had the *heart* heresy. And now we hear
nothing of any of these, and they must be heretics, forsooth,
unless they sign a declaration to the effect, *" that the sense
of the doctrine of Jansenius is contained in the sense of the
five propositions."*

Such is your present dispute. It is not enough for you
that they condemn the five propositions, and everything in
Jansenius that bears any resemblance to them, or is contrary to St. Augustine ; for all that they have done already.
The point at issue is not, for example, if Jesus Christ died
for the elect only—they condemn that as much as you do ;
but, is Jansenius of that opinion, or not ? And here I declare, more strongly than ever, that your quarrel affects me
as little as it affects the Church. For although I am no
doctor, any more than you, father, I can easily see, nevertheless, that it has no connection with the faith. The only
question is, to ascertain what is the sense of Jansenius. Did

they believe that his doctrine corresponded to the proper
and literal sense of these propositions, they would condemn
it; and they refuse to do so, because they are convinced it is
quite the reverse; so that although they should misunderstand it, still they would not be heretics, seeing they understand it only in a Catholic sense.

To illustrate this by an example, I may refer to the conflicting sentiments of St. Basil and St. Athanasius, regarding
the writings of St. Denis of Alexandria, which St. Basil,
conceiving that he found in them the sense of Arius against
the equality of the Father and the Son, condemned as heretical, but which St. Athanasius, on the other hand, judging
them to contain the genuine sense of the Church, maintained
to be perfectly orthodox. Think you, then, father, that St.
Basil, who held these writings to be Arian, had a right to
brand St. Athanasius as a heretic, because he defended
them? And what ground would he have had for so doing,
seeing that it was not Arianism that his brother defended,
but the true faith which he considered these writings to contain? Had these two saints agreed about the true sense of
these writings, and had both recognized this heresy in them,
unquestionably St. Athanasius could not have approved of
them, without being guilty of heresy; but as they were at
variance respecting the sense of the passages, St. Athanasius
was orthodox in vindicating them, even though he may have
understood them wrong; because in that case it would have
been merely an error in a matter of fact, and because what
he defended was really the Catholic faith, which he supposed
to be contained in these writings.

I apply this to you, father. Suppose you were agreed
upon the sense of Jansenius, and your adversaries were ready
to admit with you that he held, for example, *that grace cannot be resisted*; those who refused to condemn him would be
heretical. But as your dispute turns upon the meaning of
that author, and they believe that, according to his doctrine,
grace may be resisted, whatever heresy you may be pleased
to attribute to him, you have no ground to brand them as

430   PROVINCIAL LETTERS.

heretics, seeing they condemn the sense which you put on
Jansenius, and you dare not condemn the sense which they
put on him. If, therefore, you mean to convict them, show
that the sense which they ascribe to Jansenius is heretical;
for then they will be heretical themselves. But how could
you accomplish this, since it is certain, according to your
own showing, that the meaning which they give to his language has never been condemned ?

To elucidate the point still further, I shall assume as a
principle, what you yourselves acknowledge—*that the doctrine of efficacious grace has never been condemned, and that
the pope has not touched it by his constitution.* And, in fact,
when he proposed to pass judgment on the five propositions,
the question of efficacious grace was protected against all
censure. This is perfectly evident from the judgments of
the consulters,[1] to whom the pope committed them for examination. These judgments I have in my possession, in common with many other persons in Paris, and, among the rest,
the Bishop of Montpelier,[2] who brought them from Rome.
It appears from this document, that they were divided in
their sentiments ; that the chief persons among them, such as
the Master of the Sacred Palace, the Commissary of the
Holy Office, the General of the Augustinians, and others,
conceiving that these propositions might be understood in the
sense of *efficacious grace,* were of opinion that they ought not
to be censured ; whereas the rest, while they agreed that the
propositions would not have merited condemnation, had they
borne that sense, judged that they ought to be censured, because, as they contended, this was very far from being their
proper and natural sense. The pope, accordingly, con-

    [1] These judgments, or *Vota Consultorum,* as they were called, have
been often printed, and particularly at the end of the *Journal de M. de
St. Amour*—a book essentially necessary to the right understanding of
all the intrigues employed in the condemnation of Jansenius. (Note
by Nicole.)
    [2] This was *Francis du Bosquet,* who, from being Bishop of Lodeve,
was made Bishop of Montpelier in 1655, and died in 1676. He was one
of the most learned bishops of his time in ecclesiastical matters. (Note
by Nicole.)

demned them; and all parties have acquiesced in his judgment.

It is certain, then, father, that efficacious grace has not been condemned. Indeed, it is so powerfully supported by St. Augustine, by St. Thomas, and all his school, by a great many popes and councils, and by all tradition, that to tax it with heresy would be an act of impiety. Now, all those whom you condemn as heretics declare that they find nothing in Jansenius, but this doctrine of efficacious grace. And this was the only point which they maintained at Rome. You have acknowledged this yourself, when you declare that, "when pleading before the pope, they did not say a single word about the propositions, but occupied the whole time in talking about efficacious grace."[1] So that whether they be right or wrong in this supposition, it is undeniable, at least, that what they suppose to be the sense is not heretical sense; and that, consequently, they are no heretics: for, to state the matter in two words, either Jansenius has merely taught the doctrine of efficacious grace, and in this case he has no errors; or he has taught some other thing, and in this case he has no defenders. The whole question turns on ascertaining whether Jansenius has actually maintained something different from efficacious grace; and should it be found that he has, you will have the honor of having better understood him, but they will not have the misfortune of having erred from the faith.

It is matter of thankfulness to God, then, father, that there is in reality no heresy in the Church. The question relates entirely to a point of fact, of which no heresy can be made; for the Church, with divine authority, decides the points of *faith*, and cuts off from her body all who refuse to receive them. But she does not act in the same manner in regard to matters of *fact*. And the reason is, that our salvation is attached to the faith which has been revealed to us, and which is preserved in the Church by tradition, but that it has no dependence on facts which have not been revealed

[1] Cavill, p. 35.

by God. Thus we are bound to believe that the commandments of God are not impracticable; but we are under no
obligation to know what Jansenius has said upon that subject. In the determination of points of faith God guides the
Church by the aid of his unerring Spirit; whereas in matters
of fact, he leaves her to the direction of reason and the
senses, which are the natural judges of such matters. None
but God was able to instruct the Church in the faith; but to
learn whether this or that proposition is contained in Jansenius, all we require to do is to read his book. And from hence
it follows, that while it is heresy to resist the decisions of the
faith, because this amounts to an opposing of our own spirit
to the Spirit of God, it is no heresy, though·it may be an act
of presumption, to disbelieve certain particular facts, because
this is no more than opposing reason—it may be enlightened
reason—to an authority which is great indeed, but in this matter not infallible.

What I have now advanced is admitted by all theologians,
as appears from the following axiom of Cardinal Bellarmine,
a member of your Society: "General and lawful councils
are incapable of error in defining the dogmas of faith; but
they may err in questions of fact." In another place he
says: "The pope, as pope, and even as the head of a universal council, may err in particular controversies of fact,
which depend principally on the information and testimony
of men." Cardinal Baronius speaks in the same manner:
"Implicit submission is due to the decisions of councils in
points of faith; but, in so far as persons and their writings
are concerned, the censures which have been pronounced
against them have not been so rigorously observed, because
there is none who may not chance to be deceived in such
matters." I may add that, to prove this point, the Archbishop of Toulouse[1] has deduced the following rule from the
letters of two great popes—St. Leon and Pelagius II. : " That

---

[1] M. de Marca, an illustrious prelate, who was Archbishop of Toulouse, before he was nominated to the see of Paris, of which he was
only prevented by death from taking possession. (Nicole.)

the proper object of councils is the faith ; and whatsoever is determined by them, independently of the faith, may be reviewed and examined anew : whereas nothing ought to be re-examined that has been decided in a matter of faith ; because, as Tertullian observes, the rule of faith alone is immovable and irrevocable."

Hence it has been seen that, while general and lawful councils have never contradicted one another in points of faith, because, as M. de Toulouse has said, "it is not allowable to examine *de novo* decisions in matters of faith ;" several instances have occurred in which these same councils have disagreed in points of fact, where the discussion turned upon the sense of an author ; because, as the same prelate observes, quoting the popes as his authorities, "everything determined in councils, not referring to the faith, may be reviewed and examined *de novo*." An example of this contrariety was furnished by the fourth and fifth councils, which differed in their interpretation of the same authors. The same thing happened in the case of two popes, about a proposition maintained by certain monks of Scythia. Pope Hormisdas, understanding it in a bad sense, had condemned it ; but Pope John II., his successor, upon re-examining the doctrine, understood it in a good sense, approved it, and pronounced it to be orthodox. Would you say that for this reason one of these popes was a heretic ? And must you not, consequently, acknowledge that, provided a person condemn the heretical sense which a pope may have ascribed to a book, he is no heretic because he declines condemning that book, while he understands it in a sense which it is certain the pope has not condemned ? If this cannot be admitted, one of these popes must have fallen into error.

I have been anxious to familiarize you with these discrepancies among Catholics regarding questions of fact, which involve the understanding of the sense of a writer, showing you father against father, pope against pope, and council against council, to lead you from these to other examples of opposition, similar in their nature, but somewhat more disproportioned in respect of the parties concerned. For, in the instances I am now to adduce, you will see councils and popes ranged on one side, and Jesuits on the other; and yet you have never charged your brethren, for this opposition, even with presumption, much less with heresy.

You are well aware, father, that the writings of Origen were condemned by a great many popes and councils, and particularly by the fifth general council, as chargeable with certain heresies, and, among others, that of *the reconciliation of the devils at the day of judgment.* Do you suppose that, after this, it became absolutely imperative, as a test of Ca-tholicism, to confess that Origen actually maintained these errors, and that it is not enough to condemn them, without attributing them to him? If this were true, what would become of your worthy Father Halloix, who has asserted the purity of Origen's faith, as well as many other Catholics, who have attempted the same thing, such as Pico Mirandola, and Genebrard, doctor of the Sorbonne? Is it not, moreover, a certain fact, that the same fifth general council condemned the writings of Theodoret against St. Cyril, describing them as impious, " contrary to the true faith, and tainted with the Nestorian heresy?"[1] And yet this has not prevented Father Sirmond,[2] a Jesuit, from defending him, or from saying, in his life of that father, that "his writings are entirely free from the heresy of Nestorius."

It is evident, therefore, that as the Church, in condemning a book, assumes that the error which she condemns is contained in that book, it is a point of faith to hold that error as

[1] *Nestorian heresy*—so called from Nestorius, Bishop of Constanti-nople, in the fifth century, who was accused of dividing Christ into *two persons;* in other words, representing his human nature a distinct per-son from his divine. There is some reason to think, however, that he was quite sound in the faith, and that his real offence was his opposi-tion to the use of the phrase, which then came into vogue, *the Mother of God* as applied to the Virgin, whom he called, in preference, *the Mother of Christ.*
[2] This was James Sirmond (the uncle of Anthony, formerly men-tioned), a learned Jesuit, and confessor to Louis XIII. He was dis-tinguished as an ecclesiastical historian. (Tableau de la Litt. Fran. iv. 202.)

condemned; but it is not a point of faith to hold that the book, in fact, contains the error which the Church supposes it does. Enough has been said, I think, to prove this; I shall, therefore, conclude my examples by referring to that of Pope Honorius, the history of which is so well known. At the commencement of the seventh century, the Church being troubled by the heresy of the Monothelites,[1] that pope, with the view of terminating the controversy, passed a decree which seemed favorable to these heretics, at which many took offence. The affair, nevertheless, passed over without making much disturbance during his pontificate; but fifty years after, the Church being assembled in the sixth general council, in which Pope Agathon presided by his legates, this decree was impeached, and, after being read and examined, was condemned as containing the heresy of the Monothelites, and under that character burnt, in open court, along with the other writings of these heretics. Such was the respect paid to this decision, and such the unanimity with which it was received throughout the whole Church, that it was afterwards ratified by two other general councils, and likewise by two popes, Leon II. and Adrian II., the latter of whom lived two hundred years after it had passed; and this universal and harmonious agreement remained undisturbed for seven or eight centuries. Of late years, however, some authors, and among the rest Cardinal Bellarmine, without seeming to dread the imputation of heresy, have stoutly maintained, against all this array of popes and councils, that the writings of Honorius are free from the error which had been ascribed to them; "because," says the cardinal, "general councils being liable to err in questions of fact, we have the best grounds for asserting that the sixth council was mistaken with regard to the fact now under consideration; and that, misconceiving the sense of the Letters of Honorius, it has placed this pope most unjustly in the ranks of heretics." Observe, then, I

[1] *The Monothelites*, who arose in the seventh century, were so called from holding that there was but *one will* in Christ, his human will being absorbed, as it were, in the divine.

pray you, father, that a man is not heretical for saying that
Pope Honorius was not a heretic ; even though a great many
popes and councils, after examining his writings, should have
declared that he was so.

I now come to the question before us, and shall allow you
to state your case as favorably as you can. What will you
then say, father, in order to stamp your opponents as heretics ?
That "Pope Innocent X. has declared that the error of the
five propositions is to be found in Jansenius ?" I grant you
that; what inference do you draw from it? That "it is
heretical to deny that the error of the five propositions is to
be found in Jansenius ?" How so, father ? have we not here
a question of fact, exactly similar to the preceding examples ?
The pope has declared that the error of the five propositions
is contained in Jansenius, in the same way as his predecessors
decided that the errors of the Nestorians and the Monothelites polluted the pages of Theodoret and Honorius. In the
latter case, your writers hesitate not to say, that while they
condemn the heresies, they do not allow that these authors
actually maintained them ; and, in like manner, your opponents now say, that they condemn the five propositions, but
cannot admit that Jansenius has taught them. Truly, the
two cases are as like as they could well be; and if there be
any disparity between them, it is easy to see how far it must
go in favor of the present question, by a comparison of many
particular circumstances, which, as they are self-evident, I do
not specify. How comes it to pass, then, that when placed
in precisely the same predicament, your friends are Catholics
and your opponents heretics? On what strange principle
of exception do you deprive the latter of a liberty which you
freely award to all the rest of the faithful ? What answer
will you make to this, father? Will you say, " The pope
has confirmed his constitution by a brief." To this I would
reply, that two general councils and two popes confirmed the
condemnation of the Letters of Honorius. But what argument do you found upon the language of that brief, in which
all that the pope says is, that "he has condemned the doc-

trine of Jansenius in these five propositions ?" What does that add to the constitution, or what more can you infer from it ? Nothing certainly, except that as the sixth council condemned the doctrine of Honorius, in the belief that it was the same with that of the Monothelites, so the pope has said that he has condemned the doctrine of Jansenius in these five propositions, because he was led to suppose it was the same with that of the five propositions. And how could he do otherwise than suppose it ? Your Society published nothing else ; and you, yourself, father, who have asserted that the said propositions were in that author "word for word," happened to be in Rome (for I know all your motions) at the time when the censure was passed. Was he to distrust the sincerity or the competence of so many grave ministers of religion ? And how could he help being convinced of the fact, after the assurance which you had given him that the propositions were in that author "word for word ?" It is evident, therefore, that in the event of its being found that Jansenius has not supported these doctrines, it would be wrong to say, as your writers have done in the cases before mentioned, that the pope has deceived himself in this point of fact, which it is painful and offensive to publish at any time ; the proper phrase is, that you have deceived the pope, which, as you are now pretty well known, will create no scandal.

Determined, however, to have a heresy made out, let it cost what it may, you have attempted, by the following manœuvre, to shift the question from the point of fact, and make it bear upon a point of faith. "The pope," say you, "declares that he has condemned the doctrine of Jansenius in these five propositions ; therefore it is essential to the faith to hold that the doctrine of Jansenius touching these five propositions is heretical, *let it be what it may.*" Here is a strange point of faith, that a doctrine is heretical *be what it may.* What ! if Jansenius should happen to maintain that *"we are capable of resisting internal grace,"* and that *"it is false to say that Jesus Christ died for the elect only,"* would this doctrine be condemned just because it is his doctrine ?

Will the proposition, that "*man has a freedom of will to do good or evil*," be true when found in the pope's constitution, and false when discovered in Jansenius? By what fatality must he be reduced to such a predicament, that truth, when admitted into his book, becomes heresy? You must confess, then, that he is only heretical on the supposition that he is friendly to the errors condemned, seeing that the constitution of the pope is the rule which we must apply to Jansenius, to judge if his character answer the description there given of him; and, accordingly, the question, *Is his doctrine heretical?* must be resolved by another question of fact, *Does it correspond to the natural sense of these propositions?* as it must necessarily be heretical if it does correspond to that sense, and must necessarily be orthodox if it be of an opposite character. For, in one word, since, according to the pope and the bishops, "the propositions are condemned *in their proper and natural sense*," they cannot possibly be condemned in the sense of Jansenius, except on the understanding that the sense of Jansenius is the same with the proper and natural sense of these propositions; and this I maintain to be purely a question of fact.

The question, then, still rests upon the point of fact, and cannot possibly be tortured into one affecting the faith. But though incapable of twisting it into a matter of heresy, you have it in your power to make it a pretext for persecution, and might, perhaps, succeed in this, were there not good reason to hope that nobody will be found so blindly devoted to your interests as to countenance such a disgraceful proceeding, or inclined to compel people, as you wish to do, to sign a declaration *that they condemn these propositions in the sense of Jansenius*, without explaining what the sense of Jansenius is. Few people are disposed to sign a blank confession of faith. Now this would really be to sign one of that description, leaving you to fill up the blank afterwards with whatsoever you pleased, as you would be at liberty to interpret according to your own taste the unexplained sense of Jansenius. Let it be explained, then, beforehand, otherwise we shall have, I fear, another version of your *proximate power*, without any sense at all—*abstrahendo ab omni sensu.*[1]   This mode of proceeding, you must be aware, does not take with the world.   Men in general detest all ambiguity, especially in the matter of religion, where it is highly reasonable that one should know at least what one is asked to condemn. And how is it possible for doctors, who are persuaded that Jansenius can bear no other sense than that of efficacious grace, to consent to declare that they condemn his doctrine without explaining it, since, with their present convictions, which no means are used to alter, this would be neither more nor less than to condemn efficacious grace, which cannot be condemned without sin ?   Would it not, therefore, be a piece of monstrous tyranny to place them in such an unhappy dilemma, that they must either bring guilt upon their souls in the sight of God, by signing that condemnation against their consciences, or be denounced as heretics for refusing to sign it ?[2]

But there is a mystery under all this.   You Jesuits cannot move a step without a stratagem.   It remains for me to explain why you do not explain the sense of Jansenius.   The sole purpose of my writing is to discover your designs, and, by discovering, to frustrate them.   I must, therefore, inform those who are not already aware of the fact, that your great concern in this dispute being to uphold the *sufficient grace* of your Molina, you could not effect this without destroying the *efficacious grace* which stands directly opposed to it.   Perceiving, however, that the latter was now sanctioned at Rome, and by all the learned in the Church, and unable to combat the doctrine on its own merits, you resolved to attack it in a clandestine way, under the name of the doctrine of Jansenius.   You were resolved, accordingly, to get Jansenius condemned without explanation ; and, to gain your purpose, gave out that his doctrine was not that of efficacious grace,

---

[1] See Letter i., p. 152.
[2] The persecution here supposed was soon lamentably realized, and exactly in the way which our author seemed to think impossible.

so that every one might think he was at liberty to condemn the one without denying the other. Hence your efforts, in the present day, to impress this idea upon the minds of such as have no acquaintance with that author; an object which you yourself, father, have attempted, by means of the following ingenious syllogism: " The pope has condemned the doctrine of Jansenius; but the pope has not condemned efficacious grace: therefore, the doctrine of efficacious grace must be different from that of Jansenius."[1] If this mode of reasoning were conclusive, it might be demonstrated in the same way that Honorius and all his defenders are heretics of the same kind. " The sixth council has condemned the doctrine of Honorius; but the council has not condemned the doctrine of the Church: therefore the doctrine of Honorius is different from that of the Church; and therefore all who defend him are heretics." It is obvious that no conclusion can be drawn from this; for the pope has done no more than condemned the doctrine of the five propositions, which was represented to him as the doctrine of Jansenius.

But it matters not; you have no intention to make use of this logic for any length of time. Poor as it is, it will last sufficiently long to serve your present turn. All that you wish to effect by it, in the mean time, is to induce those who are unwilling to condemn efficacious grace to condemn Jansenius with the less scruple. When this object has been accomplished, your argument will soon be forgotten, and their signatures remaining as an eternal testimony in condemnation of Jansenius, will furnish you with an occasion to make a direct attack upon efficacious grace, by another mode of reasoning much more solid than the former, which shall be forthcoming in proper time. " The doctrine of Jansenius," you will argue, " has been condemned by the universal subscriptions of the Church. Now this doctrine is manifestly that of efficacious grace" (and it will be easy for you to prove that); " therefore the doctrine of efficacious grace is condemned even by the confession of his defenders."

[1] Cavill, p. 23.

Behold your reason for proposing to sign the condemnation of a doctrine without giving an explanation of it! Behold the advantage you expect to gain from subscriptions thus procured! Should your opponents, however, refuse to subscribe, you have another trap laid for them. Having dexterously combined the question of faith with that of fact, and not allowing them to separate between them, nor to sign the one without the other, the consequence will be, that, because they could not subscribe the two together, you will publish it in all directions that they have refused the two together. And thus though, in point of fact, they simply decline acknowledging that Jansenius has maintained the propositions which they condemn, which cannot be called heresy, you will boldly assert that they have refused to condemn the propositions themselves, and that it is this that constitutes their heresy.

Such is the fruit which you expect to reap from their re·fusal, and which will be no less useful to you than what you might have gained from their consent. So that, in the event of these signatures being exacted, they will fall into your snares, whether they sign or not, and in both cases you will gain your point.; such is your dexterity in uniformly putting matters into a train for your own advantage, whatever bias they may happen to take in their course!

How well I know you, father! and how grieved am I to see that God has abandoned you so far as to allow you such happy success in such an unhappy course! Your good fortune deserves commiseration, and can excite envy only in the breasts of those who know not what truly good fortune is. It is an act of charity to thwart the success you aim at in the whole of this proceeding, seeing that you can only reach it by the aid of falsehood, and by procuring credit to one of two lies oithor that the Ohurch has condemned efficacious grace, or that those who defend that doctrine maintain the five condemned errors.

The world must, therefore, be apprized of two facts: First, That, by your own confession, efficacious grace has not been condemned; and secondly, That nobody supports these errors. So that it may be known that those who may refuse to sign what you are so anxious to exact from them, refuse merely in consideration of the question of *fact*; and that, being quite ready to subscribe that of *faith*, they cannot be deemed heretical on that account; because, to repeat it once more, though it be matter of faith to believe these propositions to be heretical, it will never be matter of faith to hold that they are to be found in the pages of Jansenius. They are innocent of all error; that is enough. It may be that they interpret Jansenius too favorably; but it may be also that you do not interpret him favorably enough. I do not enter upon this question. All that I know is, that, according to your maxims, you believe that you may, without sin, publish him to be a heretic contrary to your own knowledge; whereas, according to their maxims, they cannot, without sin, declare him to be a Catholic, unless they are persuaded that he is one. They are, therefore, more honest than you, father; they have examined Jansenius more faithfully than you; they are no less intelligent than you; they are, therefore, no less credible witnesses than you. But come what may of this point of fact, they are certainly Catholics; for, in order to be so, it is not necessary to declare that another man is not a Catholic; it is enough, in all conscience, if a person, without charging error upon anybody else, succeed in discharging himself.

———

Reverend father,—If you have found any difficulty in deciphering this letter, which is certainly not printed in the best possible type, blame nobody but yourself. Privileges are not so easily granted to me as they are to you. You can procure them even for the purpose of combating miracles; I cannot have them even to defend myself. The printing-houses are perpetually haunted. In such circumstances, you yourself would not advise me to write you any more letters;

for it is really a sad annoyance to be obliged to have recourse to an Osnabruck impression.[1]

[1] This postscript, which is wanting in the ordinary editions, appeared in the first edition at the close of this letter. From this it appears that, in consequence of the extreme desire of the Jesuits to discover the author, and their increasing resentment against him, he was compelled to send this letter to Osnabruck, an obscure place in Germany, where it was printed in a very small and indistinct character. The *privileges* referred to were official licenses to print books, which, at this time, when the Jesuits were in power, it was difficult for their opponents to obtain. Annat had published against the miracles of Port-Royal. Pascal was not permitted to publish in self-defence. At the same period, no Protestant books could be printed at Paris; they were generally sent to Geneva or the Low Countries for this purpose, or published furtively under fictitious names.

LETTER XVIII.

TO THE REVEREND FATHER ANNAT, JESUIT.

SHOWING STILL MORE PLAINLY, ON THE AUTHORITY OF FATHER ANNAT
HIMSELF, THAT THERE IS REALLY NO HERESY IN THE CHURCH,
AND THAT IN QUESTIONS OF FACT WE MUST BE GUIDED BY OUR
SENSES, AND NOT BY AUTHORITY EVEN OF THE POPES.

March 24, 1657.

REVEREND FATHER,—Long have you labored to discover
some error in the creed or conduct of your opponents; but I
rather think you will have to confess, in the end, that it is a
more difficult task than you imagined to make heretics of
people who are not only no heretics, but who hate nothing
in the world so much as heresy. In my last letter I succeeded in showing that you accuse them of one heresy after
another, without being able to stand by one of the charges
for any length of time; so that all that remained for you
was to fix on their refusal to condemn " the sense of Jansenius," which you insist on their doing without explanation.
You must have been sadly in want of heresies to brand them
with, when you were reduced to this. For, who ever heard
of a heresy which nobody could explain? The answer was
ready, therefore, that if Jansenius has no errors, it is wrong
to condemn him; and if he has, you were bound to point
them out, that we might know at least what we were condemning. This, however, you have never yet been pleased
to do; but you have attempted to fortify your position by
decrees,[1] which made nothing in your favor, as they gave no
sort of explanation of the sense of Jansenius, said to have

---

[1] Decrees of the pope.

been condemned in the five propositions. This was not the way to terminate the dispute. Had you mutually agreed as to the genuine sense of Jansenius, and had the only difference between you been as to whether that sense was heretical or not, in that case the decisions which might pronounce it to be heretical, would have touched the real question in dispute. But the great dispute being about the sense of Jansenius, the one party saying that they could see nothing in it inconsistent with the sense of St. Augustine and St. Thomas, and the other party asserting that they saw in it an heretical sense which they would not express. It is clear that a constitution[1] which does not say a word about this difference of opinion, and which only condemns in general and without explanation the sense of Jansenius, leaves the point in dispute quite undecided.

You have accordingly been repeatedly told, that as your discussion turns on a matter of fact, you would never be able to bring it to a conclusion without declaring what you understand by the sense of Jansenius. But, as you continued obstinate in your refusal to make this explanation, I endeavored, as a last resource, to extort it from you, by hinting, in my last letter, that there was some mystery under the efforts you were making to procure the condemnation of this sense without explaining it, and that your design was to make this indefinite censure recoil, some day or other, upon the doctrine of efficacious grace, by showing, as you could easily do, that this was exactly the doctrine of Jansenius. This has reduced you to the necessity of making a reply; for, had you pertinaciously refused, after such an insinuation, to explain your views of that sense, it would have been apparent, to persons of the smallest penetration, that you condemned it in the sense of efficacious grace—a conclusion which, considering the veneration in which the Church holds that holy doctrine, would have overwhelmed you with disgrace.

You have, therefore, been forced to speak out your mind; and we find it expressed in your reply to that part of my let-

[1] The papal constitution formerly referred to.

ter in which I remarked, that "if Jansenius was capable of
any other sense than that of efficacious grace, he had no defenders; but if his writings bore no other sense, he had no
errors to defend." You found it impossible to deny this position, father; but you have attempted to parry it by the following distinction: "It is not sufficient," say you, "for the
vindication of Jansenius, to allege that he merely holds the
doctrine of efficacious grace, for that may be held in two ways
—the one heretical, according to Calvin, which consists in
maintaining that the will, when under the influence of grace,
has not the power of resisting it; the other orthodox, according to the Thomists and the Sorbonists, which is founded on
the principles established by the councils, and which is, that
efficacious grace of itself governs the will in such a way that
it still has the power of resisting it."

All this we grant, father; but you conclude by adding:
"Jansenius would be orthodox, if he defended efficacious
grace in the sense of the Thomists; but he is heretical, because he opposes the Thomists, and joins issue with Calvin,
who denies the power of resisting grace." I do not here enter
upon the question of fact, whether Jansenius really agrees
with Calvin. It is enough for my purpose that you assert
that he does, and that you now inform me that by the sense
of Jansenius you have all along understood nothing more than
the sense of Calvin. Was this all you meant, then, father?
Was it only the error of Calvin that you were so anxious to
get condemned, under the name of "the sense of Jansenius?"
Why did you not tell us this sooner? You might have saved
yourself a world of trouble; for we were all ready, without
the aid of bulls or briefs, to join with you in condemning
that error. What urgent necessity there was for such an explanation! What a host of difficulties has it removed! We
were quite at a loss, my dear father, to know what error the
popes and bishops meant to condemn, under the name of
"the sense of Jansenius." The whole Church was in the utmost perplexity about it, and not a soul would relieve us by
an explanation. This, however, has now been done by you,

father—you whom the whole of your party regard as the chief and prime mover of all their councils, and who are acquainted with the whole secret of this proceeding. You, then, have told us that the sense of Jansenius is neither more nor less than the sense of Calvin, which has been condemned by the council.[1] Why, this explains everything. We know now that the error which they intended to condemn, under these terms—*the sense of Jansenius*—is neither more nor less than the sense of Calvin; and that, consequently, we, by joining with them in the condemnation of Calvin's doctrine, have yielded all due obedience to these decrees. We are no longer surprised at the zeal which the popes and some bishops manifested against "the sense of Jansenius." How, indeed, could they be otherwise than zealous against it, believing as they did the declarations of those who publicly affirmed that it was identically the same with that of Calvin?

I must maintain, then, father, that you have no further reason to quarrel with your adversaries; for they detest that doctrine as heartily as you do. I am only astonished to see that you are ignorant of this fact, and that you have such an imperfect acquaintance with their sentiments on this point, which they have so repeatedly expressed in their published works. I flatter myself that, were you more intimate with these writings, you would deeply regret your not having made yourself acquainted sooner, in the spirit of peace, with a doctrine which is in every respect so holy and so Christian, but which passion, in the absence of knowledge, now prompts you to oppose. You would find, father, that they not only hold that an effective resistance may be made to those feebler graces which go under the name of *exciting* or *inefficacious*, from their not terminating in the good with which they inspire us; but that they are, moreover, as firm in maintaining, in opposition to Calvin, the power which the will has to resist even efficacious and victorious grace, as they are in contending against Molina for the power of this grace over the

---

[1] The Council of Trent is meant, when Pascal speaks of *the council*, without any other specification.

will, and fully as jealous for the one of these truths as they are for the other. They know too well that man, of his own nature, has always the power of sinning and of resisting grace; and that, since he became corrupt, he unhappily carries in his breast a fount of concupiscence which infinitely augments that power; but that, notwithstanding this, when it pleases God to visit him with his mercy, he makes the soul do what he wills, and in the manner he wills it to be done, while, at the same time, the infallibility of the divine operation does not in any way destroy the natural liberty of man, in consequence of the secret and wonderful ways by which God operates this change. This has been most admirably explained by St. Augustine, in such a way as to dissipate all those imaginary inconsistencies which the opponents of efficacious grace suppose to exist between the sovereign power of grace over the free-will and the power which the free-will has to resist grace. For, according to this great saint, whom the popes and the Church have held to be a standard authority on this subject, God transforms the heart of man, by shedding abroad in it a heavenly sweetness, which, surmounting the delights of the flesh, and inducing him to feel, on the one hand, his own mortality and nothingness, and to discover, on the other hand, the majesty and eternity of God, makes him conceive a distaste for the pleasures of sin, which interpose between him and incorruptible happiness. Finding his chiefest joy in the God who charms him, his soul is drawn towards him infallibly, but of its own accord, by a motion perfectly free, spontaneous, love-impelled; so that it would be its torment and punishment to be separated from him. Not but that the person has always the power of forsaking his God, and that he may not actually forsake him, provided he choose to do it. But how *could* he choose such a course, seeing that the will always inclines to that which is most agreeable to it, and that in the case we now suppose nothing can be more agreeable than the possession of that *one good,* which comprises in itself all other good things. " *Quod enim* (says St. Augustine) *amplius nos delectat, secundum operemur necesse est*—Our actions are necessarily determined by that which affords us the greatest pleasure."

Such is the manner in which God regulates the free will of man without encroaching on its freedom, and in which the free will, which always may, but never will, resist his grace, turns to God with a movement as voluntary as it is irresistible, whensoever he is pleased to draw it to himself by the sweet constraint of his efficacious inspirations.[1]

These, father, are the divine principles of St. Augustine and St. Thomas, according to which it is equally true that *we have the power of resisting grace*, contrary to Calvin's opinion, and that, nevertheless, to employ the language of Pope Clement VIII., in his paper addressed to the Congregation *de Auxiliis*, "God forms within us the motion of our will, and effectually disposes of our hearts, by virtue of that empire which his supreme majesty has over the volitions of men, as well as over the other creatures under heaven, according to St. Augustine."

On the same principle, it follows that we act of ourselves, and thus, in opposition to another error of Calvin, that we have merits which are truly and properly *ours ;* and yet, as God is the first principle of our actions, and as, in the language of St. Paul, he "worketh in us that which is pleasing in his sight;" "our merits are the gifts of God," as the Council of Trent says.

By means of this distinction we demolish the profane sentiment of Luther, condemned by that Council, namely, that "we co-operate in no way whatever towards our salvation, any more than inanimate things ;"[2] and, by the same mode of reasoning, we overthrow the equally profane sentiment of the school of Molina, who will not allow that it is by the strength of divine grace that we are enabled to co-operate with it in the work of our salvation, and who thereby comes

---

[1] The reader may well be at a loss to see the difference between this and the Reformed doctrine. Some explanations will be found in the Historical Introduction.

[2] This sentiment was falsely ascribed to Luther by the Council. (Leydeck, De Dogm. Jan. 275.)

into hostile collision with that principle of faith established by St. Paul, "That it is God who worketh in us both to will and to do."

In fine, in this way we reconcile all those passages of Scripture which seem quite inconsistent with each other, such as the following: "Turn ye unto God"—"Turn thou us, and we shall be turned"—"Cast away iniquity from you" —"It is God who taketh away iniquity from his people"— "Bring forth works meet for repentance"—"Lord, thou hast wrought all our works in us"—"Make ye a new heart and a new spirit"—"A new spirit will I give you, and a new heart will I create within you," &c.

The only way of reconciling these apparent contrarieties, which ascribe our good actions at one time to God, and at another time to ourselves, is to keep in view the distinction, as stated by St. Augustine, that "our actions are ours in respect of the free will which produces them; but that they are also of God, in respect of his grace which enables our free will to produce them;" and that, as the same writer elsewhere remarks, "God enables us to do what is pleasing in his sight, by making us will to do even what we might have been unwilling to do."

It thus appears, father, that your opponents are perfectly at one with the modern Thomists, for the Thomists hold, with them, both the power of resisting grace, and the infallibility of the effect of grace ; of which latter doctrine they profess themselves the most strenuous advocates, if we may judge from a common maxim of their theology, which Alvarez,[1] one of the leading men among them, repeats so often in his book, and expresses in the following terms (disp. 72, n. 4): "When efficacious grace moves the free will, it infal-

---

[1] Diego (or Didacus) Alvarez was one of the most celebrated theologians of the order of St. Dominick ; he flourished in the sixteenth and seventeenth centuries, and died in 1635.   He was brought from Spain to Rome, to advocate there, along with Father Thomas Lemos, the cause of the grace of Jesus Christ, which the Jesuit Molina weakened, and indeed annihilated.   He shone greatly in the famous Congregation *de Auxiliis.*   (Nicole's Note.)

libly consents; because the effect of grace is such, that, although the will has the power of withholding its consent, it nevertheless consents in effect." He corroborates this by a quotation from his master, St. Thomas: "The will of God cannot fail to be accomplished; and, accordingly, when it is his pleasure that a man should consent to the influence of grace, he consents infallibly, and even necessarily, not by an absolute necessity, but by a necessity of infallibility." In effecting this, divine grace does not trench upon "the power which man has to resist it, if he wishes to do so;" it merely prevents him from wishing to resist it. This has been acknowledged by your Father Petau, in the following passage (tom. i. p. 602): "The grace of Jesus Christ insures infallible perseverance in piety, though not by necessity; for a person may refuse to yield his consent to grace, if he he so inclined, as the council states; but that same grace provides that he shall never be so inclined."

This, father, is the uniform doctrine of St. Augustine, of St. Prosper, of the fathers who followed them, of the councils, of St. Thomas, and of all the Thomists in general. It is likewise, whatever you may think of it, the doctrine of your opponents. And let me add, it is the doctrine which you yourself have lately sealed with your approbation. I shall quote your own words: "The doctrine of efficacious grace, which admits that we have a power of resisting it, is orthodox, founded on the councils, and supported by the Thomists and Sorbonists." Now, tell us the plain truth, father; if you had known that your opponents really held this doctrine, the interests of your Society might perhaps have made you scruple before pronouncing this public approval of it; but, acting on the supposition that they were hostile to the doctrine, the same powerful motive has induced you to authorize sentiments which you know in your heart to be contrary to those of your Society; and by this blunder, in your anxiety to ruin their principles, you have yourself completely confirmed them. So that, by a kind of prodigy, we now behold the advocates of efficacious grace vindicated

by the advocates of Molina—an admirable instance of the
wisdom of God in making all things concur to advance the
glory of the truth.

Let the whole world observe, then, that by your own admission, the truth of this efficacious grace, which is so essential to all the acts of piety, which is so dear to the Church,
and which is the purchase of her Saviour's blood, is so indis-
putably Catholic, that there is not a single Catholic, not even
among the Jesuits, who would not acknowledge its orthodoxy. And let it be noticed, at the same time, that, according to your own confession, not the slightest suspicion of
error can fall on those whom you have so often stigmatized
with it. For so long as you charged them with clandestine
heresies, without choosing to specify them by name, it was
as difficult for them to defend themselves as it was easy for
you to bring such accusations. But now, when you have
come to declare that the error which constrains you to oppose them, is the heresy of Calvin which you supposed them
to hold, it must be apparent to every one that they are innocent of all error; for so decidedly hostile are they to this,
the only error you charge upon them, that they protest, by
their discourses, by their books, by every mode, in short, in
which they can testify their sentiments, that they condemn
that heresy with their whole heart, and in the same manner
as it has been condemned by the Thomists, whom you acknowledge, without scruple, to be Catholics, and who have
never been suspected to be anything else.

What will you say against them now, father? Will you
say that they are heretics still, because, although they do
not adopt the sense of Calvin, they will not allow that the
sense of Jansenius is the same with that of Calvin? Will
you presume to say that this is matter of heresy? Is it not
a pure question of fact, with which heresy has nothing to
do? It would be heretical to say that we have not the power
of resisting efficacious grace ; but would it be so to doubt
that Jansenius held that doctrine? Is this a revealed truth ?
Is it an article of faith which must be believed, on pain of

damnation? or is it not, in spite of you, a point of fact, on
account of which it would be ridiculous to hold that there
were heretics in the Church.

Drop this epithet, then, father, and give them some other
name, more suited to the nature of your dispute. Tell them,
they are ignorant and stupid—that they misunderstand Jansenius. These would be charges in keeping with your controversy; but it is quite irrelevant to call them heretics. As
this, however, is the only charge from which I am anxious to
defend them, I shall not give myself much trouble to show
that they rightly understand Jansenius. All I shall say on
the point, father, is, that it appears to me that were he to be
judged according to your own rules, it would be difficult to
prove him not to be a good Catholic. We shall try him by
the test you have proposed. "To know," say you, "whether
Jansenius is sound or not, we must inquire whether he de-
fends efficacious grace in the manner of Calvin, who denies
that man has the power of resisting it—in which case he
would be heretical; or in the manner of the Thomists, who
admit that it may be resisted—for then he would be Catholic." Judge, then, father, whether he holds that grace•may
be resisted, when he says, "That we have always a power to
resist grace, according to the council; that free will may always act or not act, will or not will, consent or not consent,
do good or do evil; and that man, in this life, has always
these two liberties, which may be called by some contradictions."[1] Judge, likewise, if he be not opposed to the error
of Calvin, as you have described it, when he occupies a whole
chapter (21st) in showing " that the Church has condemned
that heretic who denies that efficacious grace acts on the free
will in the manner which has been so long believed in the
Church, so as to leave it in the power of free will to consent
or not to consent; whereas, according to St. Augustine and
the council, we have always the power of withholding our
consent if we choose; and according to St. Prosper, God be-

[1] His Treatise *passim*, and particularly tom. 3, l. 8, c. 20.

stows even upon his elect the will to persevere, in such a way as not to deprive them of the power to will the contrary." And, in one word, judge if he do not agree with the Thomists, from the following declaration in chapter 4th : " That all that the Thomists have written with the view of reconciling the efficaciousness of grace with the power of resisting it, so entirely coincides with his judgment, that to ascertain his sentiments on this subject, we have only to consult their writings."

Such being the language he holds on these heads, my opinion is, that he believes in the power of resisting grace ; that he differs from Calvin, and agrees with the Thomists, because he has said so ; and that he is, therefore, according to your own showing, a Catholic. If you have any means of knowing the sense of an author otherwise than by his expressions ; and if, without quoting any of his passages, you are disposed to maintain, in direct opposition to his own words, that he denies this power of resistance, and that he is for Calvin and against the Thomists, do not be afraid, father, that I will accuse you of heresy for that. I shall only say, that you do not seem properly to understand Jansenius ; but we shall not be the less on that account children of the same Church.

How comes it, then, father, that you manage this dispute in such a passionate spirit, and that you treat as your most cruel enemies, and as the most pestilent of heretics, a class of persons whom you cannot accuse of any error, nor of anything whatever, except that they do not understand Jansenius as you do ? For what else in the world do you dispute about, except the sense of that author ? You would have them to condemn it. They ask what you mean them to condemn. You reply, that you mean the error of Calvin. They rejoin that they condemn that error ; and with this acknowledgment (unless it is syllables you wish to condemn, and not the thing which they signify), you ought to rest satisfied. If they refuse to say that they condemn the sense of Jansenius, it is because they believe it to be that of St. Thomas, and thus this unhappy phrase has a very equivocal meaning betwixt you. In your mouth it signifies the sense of Calvin; in theirs the sense of St. Thomas. Your dissensions arise entirely from the different ideas which you attach to the same term. Were I made umpire in the quarrel, I would interdict the use of the word Jansenius, on both sides; and thus, by obliging you merely to express what you understand by it, it would be seen that you ask nothing more than the condemnation of Calvin, to which they willingly agree; and that they ask nothing more than the vindication of the sense of St. Augustine and St. Thomas, in which you again perfectly coincide.

I declare, then, father, that for my part I shall continue to regard them as good Catholics, whether they condemn Jansenius, on finding him erroneous, or refuse to condemn him, from finding that he maintains nothing more than what you yourself acknowledge to be orthodox; and that I shall say to them what St. Jerome said to John, bishop of Jerusalem, who was accused of holding the eight propositions of Origen: "Either condemn Origen, if you acknowledge that he has maintained these errors, or else deny that he has maintained them—*Aut nega hoc dixisse eum qui arguitur; aut si locutus est talia, eum damna qui dixerit.*"

See, father, how these persons acted, whose sole concern was with principles, and not with persons; whereas you who aim at persons more than principles, consider it a matter of no consequence to condemn errors, unless you procure the condemnation of the individuals to whom you choose to impute them.

How ridiculously violent your conduct is, father! and how ill calculated to insure success! I told you before, and I repeat it, violence and verity can make no impression on each other. Never were your accusations more outrageous, and never was the innocence of your opponents more discernible: never has efficacious grace been attacked with greater subtility, and never has it been more triumphantly established. You have made the most desperate efforts to convince peo-

ple that your disputes involved points of faith; and never
was it more apparent that the whole controversy turned upon
a mere point of fact. In fine, you have moved heaven and
earth to make it appear that this point of fact is founded on
truth; and never were people more disposed to call it in
question. And the obvious reason of this is, that you do not
take the natural course to make them believe a point of fact,
which is to convince their senses, and point out to them in a
book the words which you allege are to be found in it. The
means you have adopted are so far removed from this
straightforward course, that the most obtuse minds are un-
avoidably struck by observing it. Why did you not take
the plan which I followed in bringing to light the wicked
maxims of your authors—which was to cite faithfully the
passages of their writings from which they were extracted?
This was the mode followed by the curés of Paris, and it
never fails to produce conviction. But, when you were
charged by them with holding, for example, the proposition
of Father Lamy, that a "monk may kill a person who threatens to publish calumnies against himself or his order, when
he cannot otherwise prevent the publication,"—what would
you have thought, and what would the public have said, if
they had not quoted the place where that sentiment is literally
to be found? or if, after having been repeatedly demanded
to quote their authority, they still obstinately refused to do
it? or if, instead of acceding to this, they had gone off to
Rome, and procured a bull, ordaining all men to acknowledge the truth of their statement? Would it not be undoubtedly concluded that they had surprised the pope, and
that they would never have had recourse to this extraordinary method, but for want of the natural means of substan-
tiating the truth, which matters of fact furnish to all who
undertake to prove them? Accordingly, they had no more
to do than to tell us that Father Lamy teaches this doctrine
in tome 5, disp. 36, n. 118, *page 544, of the Douay edition;*
and by this means everybody who wished to see it found it out,
and nobody could doubt about it any longer. This appears

to be a very easy and prompt way of putting an end to controversies of fact, when one has got the right side of the question.

How comes it, then, father, that you do not follow this plan ? You said, in your book, that the five propositions are in Jansenius, word for word, in the identical terms—*iisdem verbis*. You were told they were not. What had you to do after this, but either to cite the page, if you had really found the words, or to acknowledge that you were mistaken. But you have done neither the one nor the other. In place of this, on finding that all the passages from Jansenius, which you sometimes adduce for the purpose of hoodwinking the people, are not " the condemned propositions in their individual identity," as you had engaged to show us, you present us with Constitutions from Rome, which, without specifying any particular place, declare that the propositions have been extracted from his book.

I am sensible, father, of the respect which Christians owe to the Holy See, and your antagonists give sufficient evidence of their resolution ever to abide by its decisions. Do not imagine that it implied any deficiency in this due deference on their part, that they represented to the pope, with all the submission which children owe to their father, and members to their head, that it was possible he might be deceived on this point of fact—that he had not caused it to be investigated during his pontificate ; and that his predecessor, Innocent X., had merely examined into the heretical character of the propositions, and not into the fact of their connection with Jansenius. This they stated to the commissary of the Holy Office, one of the principal examinators, stating, that they could not be censured, according to the sense of any author, because they had been presented for examination on their own merits, and without considering to what author they might belong : further, that upwards of sixty doctors, and a vast number of other persons of learning and piety, had read that book carefully over, without ever having encountered the proscribed propositions, and that they have found

some of a quite opposite description : that those who had
produced that impression on the mind of the pope, might be
reasonably presumed to have abused the confidence he repos-
ed in them, inasmuch as they had an interest in decrying
that author, who has convicted Molina of upwards of fifty
errors :[1] that what renders this supposition still more probable is, that they have a certain maxim among them, one of
the best authenticated in their whole system of theology,
which is, "that they may, without criminality, calumniate
those by whom they conceive themselves to be unjustly attacked :" and that, accordingly, their testimony being so
suspicious, and the testimony of the other party so respectable, they had some ground for supplicating his holiness, with
the most profound humility, that he would ordain an investigation to be made into this fact, in the presence of doctors
belonging to both parties, in order that a solemn and regular
decision might be formed on the point in dispute. "Let
there be a convocation of able judges (says St. Basil on a
similar occasion, Ep. 75); let each of them be left at perfect
freedom; let them examine my writings ; let them judge if
they contain errors against the faith ; let them read the objections and the replies ; that so a judgment may be given
in due form, and with proper knowledge of the case, and not
a defamatory libel without examination."

It is quite vain for you, father, to represent those who
would act in the manner I have now supposed as deficient
in proper subjection to the Holy See. The popes are very
far from being disposed to treat Christians with that impe-

---

[1] " It may be proper here to give an explanation of the hatred of
the Jesuits against Jansenius. When the *Augustinus* of that author
was printed in 1640, Libertus Fromond, the celebrated professor of
Louvain, resolved to insert in the end of the book of his friend, who had
died two years before, a parallel between the doctrine of the Jesuits on
grace, and the errors of the Marseillois or demi-Pelagians. This was
quite enough to raise the rancor of the Jesuits against Jansenius, whom
they erroneously supposed was the author of that parallel. And as
these fathers have long since erased from their code of morals the duty
of the forgiveness of injuries, they commenced their campaign against
the book of Jansenius in the Low Countries, by a large volume of Theological Theses (in folio, 1641), which are very singular productions."
(Note by Nicole.)

riousness which some would fain exercise under their name. "The Church," says Pope St. Gregory,[1] "which has been trained in the school of humility, does not command with authority, but persuades by reason, her children whom she believes to be in error, to obey what she has taught them." And so far from deeming it a disgrace to review a judgment into which they may have been surprised, we have the testimony of St. Bernard for saying that they glory in acknowledging the mistake. "The Apostolic See (he says, Ep. 180) can boast of this recommendation, that it never stands on the point of honor, but willingly revokes a decision that has been gained from it by surprise; indeed, it is highly just to prevent any from profiting by an act of injustice, and more especially before the Holy See."

Such, father, are the proper sentiments with which the popes ought to be inspired; for all divines are agreed that they may be surprised,[2] and that their supreme character, so far from warranting them against mistakes, exposes them the more readily to fall into them, on account of the vast number of cares which claim their attention. This is what the same St. Gregory says to some persons who were astonished at the circumstance of another pope having suffered himself to be deluded: "Why do you wonder," says he, "that we should be deceived, we who are but men? Have you not read that David, a king who had the spirit of prophecy, was induced, by giving credit to the falsehoods of Ziba, to pronounce an unjust judgment against the son of Jonathan? Who will think it strange, then, that we, who are not prophets, should sometimes be imposed upon by deceivers? A multiplicity of affairs presses on us, and our minds, which, by being obliged to attend to so many things at once, apply themselves less closely to each in particular, are the more easily liable to be imposed upon in individual cases."[3] Truly, father, I should suppose that the popes

[1] On the Book of Job, lib. viii., cap. 1.
[2] *Surprise* is the word used to denote the case of the pope when taken at unawares, or deceived by false accounts.
[3] Lib. i in Dial.

know better than you whether they may be deceived or not.
They themselves tell us that popes, as well as the greatest
princes, are more exposed to deception than individuals who
are less occupied with important avocations. This must be
believed on their testimony. And it is easy to imagine by
what means they come to be thus over-reached. St. Bernard,
in the letter which he wrote to Innocent II., gives us the
following description of the process: "It is no wonder, and
no novelty, that the human mind may be deceived, and is
deceived. You are surrounded by monks who come to you
in the spirit of lying and deceit. They have filled your ears
with stories against a bishop, whose life has been most exemplary, but who is the object of their hatred. These persons bite like dogs, and strive to make good appear evil.
Meanwhile, most holy father, you put yourself into a rage
against your own son. Why have you afforded matter of
joy to his enemies ? Believe not every spirit, but try the
spirits whether they be of God. I trust that, when you
have ascertained the truth, all this delusion, which rests on a
false report, will be dissipated. I pray the Spirit of truth to
grant you the grace to separate light from darkness, and to
favor the good by rejecting the evil." You see then, father,
that the eminent rank of the popes does not exempt them
from the influence of delusion ; and I may now add, that it
only serves to render their mistakes more dangerous and important than those of other men. This is the light in which
St. Bernard represents them to Pope Eugenius : "There is
another fault, so common among the great of this world, that
I never met one of them who was free from it ; and that is,
holy father, an excessive credulity, the source of numerous
disorders. From this proceed violent persecutions against
the innocent, unfounded prejudices against the absent, and
tremendous storms about nothing (*pro nihilo*). This, holy
father, is a universal evil, from the influence of which, if you
are exempt, I shall only say, you are the only individual
among all your compeers who can boast of that privilege."[1]

          [1] De Consid. lib. ii., c. ult.

I imagine, father, that the proofs I have brought are beginning to convince you that the popes are liable to be surprised. But, to complete your conversion, I shall merely
remind you of some examples, which you yourself have
quoted in your book, of popes and emperors whom heretics
have actually deceived. You will remember, then, that you
have told us that Apollinarius surprised Pope Damasius, in
the same way that Celestius surprised Zozimus. You inform
us, besides, that one called Athanasius deceived the Emperor
Heraclius, and prevailed on him to persecute the Catholics.
And lastly, that Sergius obtained from Honorius that infamous decretal which was burned at the sixth council, "by
playing the busy-body," as you say, "about the person of
that pope."

It appears, then, father, by your own confession, that those
who act this part about the persons of kings and popes, do
sometimes artfully entice them to persecute the faithful defenders of the truth, under the persuasion that they are persecuting heretics. And hence the popes, who hold nothing
in greater horror than these surprisals, have, by a letter of
Alexander III., enacted an ecclesiastical statute, which is
inserted in the canonical law, to permit the suspension of the
execution of their bulls and decretals, when there is ground
to suspect that they have been imposed upon. "If," says
that pope to the Archbishop of Ravenna, "we sometimes
send decretals to your fraternity which are opposed to your
sentiments, give yourselves no distress on that account. We
shall expect you either to carry them respectfully into execution, or to send us the reason why you conceive they ought
not to be executed ; for we deem it right that you should
not execute a decree, which may have been procured from
us by artifice and surprise." Such has been the course pursued by the popes, whose sole object is to settle the disputes
of Christians, and not to follow the passionate counsels of
those who strive to involve them in trouble and perplexity.
Following the advice of St. Peter and St. Paul, who in this
followed the commandment of Jesus Christ, they avoid dom-

ination.   The spirit which appears in their whole conduct is
that of peace and truth.¹   In this spirit they ordinarily insert in their letters this clause, which is tacitly understood
in them all—" *Si ita est—si preces veritate nitantur*—If it be
so as we have heard it—if the facts be true."   It is quite
clear, if the popes themselves give no force to their bulls,
except in so far as they are founded on genuine facts, that it
is not the bulls alone that prove the truth of the facts, but
that, on the contrary, even according to the canonists, it
is the truth of the facts which renders the bulls lawfully
admissible.

In what way, then, are we to learn the truth of facts?   It
must be by the eyes, father, which are the legitimate judges
of such matters, as reason is the proper judge of things
natural and intelligible, and faith of things supernatural and
revealed.   For, since you will force me into this discussion,
you must allow me to tell you, that, according to the sentiments of the two greatest doctors of the Church, St. Augustine and St. Thomas, these three principles of our knowledge,
the senses, reason, and faith, have each their separate objects,
and their own degrees of certainty.   And as God has been
pleased to employ the intervention of the senses to give entrance to faith (for "faith cometh by hearing"), it follows,
that so far from faith destroying the certainty of the senses,
to call in question the faithful report of the senses, would
lead to the destruction of faith.   It is on this principle that
St. Thomas explicitly states that God has been pleased that
the sensible accidents should subsist in the eucharist, in order
that the senses, which judge only of these accidents, might
not be deceived.

We conclude, therefore, from this, that whatever the proposition may be that is submitted to our examination, we
must first determine its nature, to ascertain to which of those
three principles it ought to be referred.   If it relate to a supernatural truth, we must judge of it neither by the senses nor
by reason, but by Scripture and the decisions of the Church.

¹ Alas! alas!

Should it concern an unrevealed truth, and something within the reach of natural reason, reason must be its proper judge. And if it embrace a point of fact, we must yield to the testimony of the senses, to. which it naturally belongs to take cognizance of such matters.

So general is this rule, that, according to St. Augustine and St. Thomas, when we meet with a passage even in the Scripture, the literal meaning of which, at first sight, appears contrary to what the senses or reason are certainly persuaded of, we must not attempt to reject their testimony in this case, and yield them up to the authority of that apparent sense of the Scripture, but we must interpret the Scripture, and seek out therein another sense agreeable to that sensible truth; because, the Word of God being infallible in the facts which it records, and the information of the senses and of reason, acting in their sphere, being certain also, it follows that there must be an agreement between these two sources of knowledge. And as Scripture may be interpreted in different ways, whereas the testimony of the senses is uniform, we must in these matters adopt as the true interpretation of Scripture that view which corresponds with the faithful report of the senses. "Two things," says St. Thomas, "must be observed, according to the doctrine of St. Augustine: first, That Scripture has always one true sense; and secondly, That as it may receive various senses, when we have discovered one which reason plainly teaches to be false, we must not persist in maintaining that this is the natural sense, but search out another with which reason will agree."[1]

St. Thomas explains his meaning by the example of a passage in Genesis, where it is written that " God created two great lights, the sun and the moon, and also the stars," in which the Scripture appears to say that the moon is greater than all the stars, but as it is evident, from unquestionable demonstration, that this is false, it is not our duty, says that saint, obstinately to defend the literal sense of that passage ; another meaning must be sought, consistent with

[1] I. p. q. 68, a. 1.

the truth of the fact, such as the following, " That the phrase *great light*, as applied to the moon, denotes the greatness of that luminary merely as it appears in our eyes, and not the magnitude of its body considered in itself."

An opposite mode of treatment, so far from procuring respect to the Scripture, would only expose it to the contempt of infidels; because, as St. Augustine says, " when they found that .we believed, on the authority of Scripture, in things which they assuredly knew to be false, they would laugh at our credulity with regard to its more recondite truths, such as the resurrection of the dead and eternal life." ",And by this means," adds St. Thomas, " we should render our religion contemptible in their eyes, and shut up its entrance into their minds,"

And let me add, father, that it would in the same manner be the likeliest means to shut up the entrance of Scripture into the minds of heretics, and to render the pope's authority contemptible in their eyes, to refuse all those the name of Catholics who would not believe that certain words were in a certain book, where they are not to be found, merely because a pope by mistake has declared that they are. It is only by examining a book that we can ascertain what words it contains. Matters of fact can only be proved by the senses. If the position which you maintain be true, show it, or else ask no man to believe it—that would be to no purpose. Not all the powers on earth can, by the force of authority, persuade us of a point of fact, any more than they can alter it ; for nothing can make that to be not which really is.

It was to no purpose, for example, that the monks of Ratisbon procured from Pope St. Leo IX. a solemn decree, by which he declared that the body of St. Denis, the first bishop of Paris, who is generally held to have been the Areopagite, had been transported out of France, and conveyed into the chapel of their monastery. It is not the less true, for all this, that the body of that saint always lay, and lies to this hour, in the celebrated abbey which bears his name, and within the walls of which you would find it no easy matter to obtain a cordial reception to this bull, although the pope has therein assured us that he has examined the affair " with all possible diligence (*diligentissimè*), and with the advice of many bishops and pielates; so that he strictly enjoins all the French (*districte prœcipientes*) to own and confess that these holy relics are no longer in their country." The French, however, who knew that fact to be untrue, by the evidence of their own eyes, and who, upon opening the shrine, found all those relics entire, as the historians of that period inform us, believed then, as they have always believed since, the reverse of what that holy pope had enjoined them to believe, well knowing that even saints and prophets are liable to be imposed upon.

It was to equally little purpose that you obtained against Galileo a decree from Rome, condemning his opinion respecting the motion of the earth. It will never be proved by such an argument as this that the earth remains stationary; and if it can be demonstrated by sure observation that it is the earth and not the sun that revolves, the efforts and arguments of all mankind put together will not hinder our planet from revolving, nor hinder themselves from revolving along with her.

Again, you must not imagine that the letters of Pope Zachary, excommunicating St. Virgilius for maintaining the existence of the antipodes, have annihilated the New World; nor must you suppose that, although he declared that opinion to be a most dangerous heresy, the king of Spain was wrong in giving more credence to Christopher Columbus, who came from the place, than to the judgment of the pope, who had never been there, or that the Church has not derived a vast benefit from the discovery, inasmuch as it has brought the knowledge of the Gospel to a great multitude of souls, who might otherwise have perished in their infidelity.

You see, then, father, what is the nature of matters of fact, and on what principles they are to be determined; from

all which, to recur to our subject, it is easy to conclude, that
if the five propositions are not in Jansenius, it is impossible
that they can have been extracted from him; and that the
only way to form a judgment on the matter, and to produce
universal conviction, is to examine that book in a regular
conference, as you have been desired to do long ago.   Until
that be done, you have no right to charge your opponents
with contumacy; for they are as blameless in regard to the
point of fact as they are of errors in point of faith—Catholics
in doctrine, reasonable in fact, and innocent in both.

Who can help feeling astonishment, then, father, to see on
the one side a vindication so complete, and on the other accusations so outrageous!   Who would suppose that the only
question between you relates to a single fact of no importance,
which the one party wishes the other to believe without
showing it to them!   And who would ever imagine that
such a noise should have been made in the Church for nothing (*pro nihilo*), as good St. Bernard says!   But this is just
one of the principal tricks of your policy, to make people believe that everything is at stake, when, in reality, there is
nothing at stake; and to represent to those influential persons who listen to you, that the most pernicious errors of
Calvin, and the most vital principles of the faith, are involved
in your disputes, with the view of inducing them, under this
conviction, to employ all their zeal and all their authority
against your opponents, as if the safety of the Catholic religion depended upon it; whereas, if they came to know that
the whole dispute was about this paltry point of fact, they
would give themselves no concern about it, but would, on
the contrary, regret extremely that, to gratify your private
passions, they had made such exertions in an affair of no
consequence to the Church.   For, in fine, to take the worst
view of the matter, even though it should be true that Jansenius maintained these propositions, what great misfortune
would accrue from some persons doubting of the fact, provided they detested the propositions, as they have publicly
declared that they do?   Is it not enough that they are con-

demned by everybody, without exception, and that, too, in
the sense in which you have explained that you wish them
to be condemned? Would they be more severely censured
by saying that Jansenius maintained them? What purpose,
then, would be served by exacting this acknowledgment, except that of disgracing a doctor and bishop, who died in the
communion of the Church? I cannot see how that should
be accounted so great a blessing as to deserve to be purchased at the expense of so many disturbances. What interest has the state, or the pope, or bishops, or doctors, or the
Church at large, in this conclusion? It does not affect them
in any way whatever, father; it can affect none but your
Society, which would certainly enjoy some pleasure from the
defamation of an author who has done you some little injury.
Meanwhile everything is in confusion, because you have made
people believe that everything is in danger. This is the secret spring giving impulse to all those mighty commotions,
which would cease immediately were the real state of the
controversy once known. And therefore, as the peace of the
Church depended on this explanation, it was, I conceive, of
the utmost importance that it should be given, that, by exposing all your disguises, it might be manifest to the whole
world that your accusations were without foundation, your
opponents without error, and the Church without heresy.

    Such, father, is the end which it has been my desire to
accomplish; an end which appears to me, in every point of
view, so deeply important to religion, that I am at a loss to
conceive how those to whom you furnish so much occasion
for speaking can contrive to remain in silence. Granting
that they are not affected with the personal wrongs which
you have committed against them, those which the Church
suffers ought, in my opinion, to have forced them to complain. Besides, I am not altogether sure if ecclesiastics
ought to make a sacrifice of their reputation to calumny,
especially in the matter of religion. They allow you, nevertheless, to say whatever you please; so that, had it not been
for the opportunity which, by mere accident, you afforded

me of taking their part, the scandalous impressions which you are circulating against them in all quarters would, in all probability, have gone forth without contradiction. Their patience, I confess, astonishes me ; and the more so, that I cannot suspect it of proceeding either from timidity or from incapacity, being well assured that they want neither argu ments for their own vindication, nor zeal for the truth. And yet I see them religiously bent on silence, to a degree which appears to me altogether unjustifiable. For my part, father, I do not believe that I can possibly follow their example. Leave the Church in peace, and I shall leave you as you are, with all my heart ; but so long as you make it ·your sole business to keep her in confusion, doubt not but that there shall always be found within her bosom children of peace. who will consider themselves bound to employ all their en· deavors to preserve her tranquillity.

LETTER XIX.

FRAGMENT OF A NINETEENTH PROVINCIAL LETTER, ADDRESSED TO PERE ANNAT.

REVEREND SIR,—If I have caused you some dissatisfaction, in former Letters, by my endeavors to establish the innocence of those whom you were laboring to asperse, I shall afford you pleasure in the present, by making you acquainted with the sufferings which you have inflicted upon them. Be comforted, my good father, the objects of your enmity are in distress ! And if the Reverend the Bishops should be induced to carry out, in their respective dioceses, the advice you have given them, to cause to be subscribed and sworn a certain matter of fact, which is, in itself, not credible, and which it cannot be obligatory upon any one to believe—you will indeed succeed in plunging your opponents to the depth of sorrow, at witnessing the Church brought into so abject a condition.

Yes, sir, I have seen them ; and it was with a satisfaction inexpressible ! I have seen these holy. men ; and this was the attitude in which they were found. They were not wrapt up in a philosophic magnanimity ; they did not affect to exhibit that indiscriminate firmness which urges implicit obedience to every momentary impulsive duty ; nor yet were they in a frame of weakness and timidity, which would prevent them from either discerning the truth, or following it when discerned. But I found them with minds pious, composed, and unshaken ; impressed with a meek deference for ecclesiastical authority ; with tenderness of spirit, zeal for truth, and a desire to ascertain and obey her dictates : filled with a salutary suspicion of themselves, distrusting their own infirmity, and regretting that it should be thus exposed to trial ;

yet withal, sustained by a modest hope that their Lord will deign to instruct them by his illuminations, and sustain them by his power; and believing, that that peace of their Saviour, whose sacred influences it is their endeavor to maintain, and for whose cause they are brought into suffering, will be, at once, their guide and their support! I have, in fine, seen them maintaining a character of Christian piety, whose power . . . .

I found them surrounded by their friends, who had hastened to impart those counsels which they deemed the most fitting in their present exigency. I have heard those counsels; I have observed the manner in which they were received, and the answers given : and truly, my father, had you yourself been present, I think you would have acknowledged that, in their whole procedure, there was the entire absence of a spirit of insubordination and schism; and that their only desire and aim was, to preserve inviolate two things—to them infinitely precious—peace and truth.

For, after due representations had been made to them of the penalties they would draw upon themselves by their refusal to sign the Constitution, and the scandal it might cause in the Church, their reply was . . . .

. . . .

END OF VOL. I.

www.ingramcontent.com/pod-product-compliance
Lightning Source LLC
Chambersburg PA
CBHW031820270326
41932CB00008B/483